Modernity and Culture

SPONSORED BY THE JOINT COMMITTEE ON THE NEAR AND MIDDLE EAST OF THE SOCIAL
SCIENCES RESEARCH COUNCIL AND THE AMERICAN COUNCIL OF LEARNED SOCIETIES AND
BY THE FARES CENTER FOR EASTERN MEDITERRANEAN STUDIES AT TUFTS UNIVERSITY

D1394423

FRONTISPIECE General View. Entrance to the Suez Canal, Port Said. *Courtesy of Harvard University, Fine Arts Library*

Modernity and Culture

From the Mediterranean to the Indian Ocean

Edited by Leila Tarazi Fawaz and C. A. Bayly
with the Collaboration of Robert Ilbert

COLUMBIA UNIVERSITY PRESS   NEW YORK

COLUMBIA UNIVERSITY PRESS
Publishers Since 1893
New York   Chichester, West Sussex
Copyright © 2002 Columbia University Press

Library of Congress Cataloging-in-Publication Data

Modernity and culture : from the Mediterranean to the Indian Ocean /
edited by Leila Tarazi Fawaz and C. A. Bayly with collaboration of
Robert Ilbert.
    p. cm.
  Includes bibliographical references and index.
  ISBN 0-231-11426-5 (cloth : alk. paper) — ISBN 0-231-11427-3 (pbk.
: alk. paper)
  1. Middle East—Civilization—19th century. 2. Middle
East—Civilization—20th century. 3. India—Civilization—1765–1947.
4. Cities and towns—Middle East—History—19th century. 5. Cities and
towns—Middle East—History—20th century. 6. Cities and
towns—India—History—19th century. 7. Cities and
towns—India—History—20th century. 8. East and West. I. Fawaz,
Leila Tarazi. II. Bayly, C. A. (Christopher Alan) III.
Ilbert, Robert.
  DS57.M63 2002
  956—dc21   2001047443

⊗ Casebound editions of Columbia University Press books
are printed on permanent and durable acid-free paper.
Printed in the United States of America

c 10 9 8 7 6 5 4 3 2 1
p 10 9 8 7 6 5 4 3 2 1

Contents

Acknowledgments

This volume originated in a series of meetings organized under the auspices of the Social Science Research Council (SSRC) and co-sponsored by the Maison Méditerranéenne des Sciences de l'Homme (MMSH) at the Université de Provence, St. Antony's College and St. John's College at Oxford University, and Tufts University. The meetings sought to look into a set of comparative questions on culture and society in the cities and in the regions of the Mediterranean and Indian Ocean in the late nineteenth and early twentieth century. The problems and themes to be studied were tentatively identified and discussed at a first workshop held at the Université de Provence in September 1995, attended by nine scholars. A second workshop was then held at Oxford University in October 1996 to familiarize scholars who specialize in South Asia or the Middle East with the literature on the other region and to refine the project's main questions, interdisciplinary perspectives, and comparative methodology. At a final meeting, held at Aix-en-Provence in September 1998, most of the papers in this volume were presented. Robert Ilbert helped us organize and fund the meetings at the MMSH and Robin Ostle did the same for the meeting at Oxford.

Funding for this book was provided by the SSRC, the MMSH, Tufts University's Issam M. Fares Lecture Series and the Fares Center for Eastern Mediterranean Studies, the President's Office, and the Program in Southwest Asia and Islamic Civilization at the Fletcher School of Law and Diplomacy. We are grateful to the members of the SSRC Joint Committee of the Near and Middle East for encouraging the project, particularly committee chairman Joel Migdal and past SSRC program director of the Joint Committee on the Middle and Near East Steven Heydemann, and to SSRC program director for Latin America and the Caribbean Eric Hershberg, who helped turn the project into a publication. At Tufts Andrew Hess helped fund the final meeting; and Sol Gittleman and General John R. Galvin, USA (RET), enthusiastically supported the project.

Robert Ilbert inspired the project throughout, and André Raymond encouraged us to look at the role of the Red Sea in linking the two areas and provided intellectual stimulation. An important intellectual contribution to the project also came from Engin Akarli for the Mediterranean and from Sugata Bose for the Indian Ocean. Meropi Anastassiadou, K. N. Chaudhuri, Paul Dumont, Cornell H. Fleischer, Çağlar Keyder, Hasan Kayali, Jean-Paul Pascual, and David Washbrook participated in earlier workshops and, together with Feroz Ahmad, Eugene Rogan, Thomas Philipp, Abdul-Karim Rafeq, and Wheeler M. Thackston, Jr., had many helpful suggestions. Susan Bayly and Karim Fawaz provided ideas, support, and inspiration. Elisabeth J. M. Higonnet-Dugua and Bernard T. Higonnet translated Colette Dubois and Michel Tuchscherer's articles from French to English. We are also grateful to John Esposito, Fares I. Fares, Hossein Fateh, Gerald Gill, Maha Kaddoura, Howard Malchow, George Marcopoulos, Hoda and Elie Saddi, Randa and Nakhle Tarazi, and John Voll for their help, and to the late Fouad Debbas, Evelyne Disdier, Frederic Gilly, Section Iconographique, Archives d'Outre-Mer, Jean-Paul Pascual, Nadim Shehadi, Abdul-Karim Rafeq and André Raymond for their willingness to help with photographs, maps, and sources, and to Jeffrey B. Spurr, Cataloger for Islamic Art, Aga Khan Program for Islamic Architecture at the Fine Arts Library, Harvard University, for his generosity in helping us locate and select photographs of the Middle East and South Asia. At the MMSH, Christiane Laye helped us repeatedly over the years. The staff at several libraries, including Tufts's Tisch and Ginn, Harvard University's Widener and Pusey, the Archives d'Outre-Mer, and the MMSH, provided indispensable information, as did faculty and staff at the American University of Beirut's History Department and Jafet Library, and the Deutsche Orient-Institut in Beirut. Margaret Ševčenko edited the articles and made innumerable suggestions; we thank her for her insights and friendship.

We are also indebted to a number of former and present students, including Carole Corm, Tamara Corm, Charles Davidson, Matthew Lehfeld, Peter Neisuler, and Dalia Mroue Fateh, and to former and present staff assistants at the SSRC, the Fletcher School and the rest of Tufts University, including Julia Deeks, Greg Czarnecki, Steve Guerra, Roselle Levy, Mirja Troppenhagen, and Claudia Zelada. At the Columbia University Press, we thank Peter Dimock, Anne Routon, and most of all, Kate Wittenberg, who encouraged the project from the start and supported it in every way she could, Leslie Bialler followed it to its completion with humor and efficiency, and Ed Henderson copyedited the text.

C. A. Bayly, Cambridge, England
Leila Fawaz, Cambridge, Massachusetts

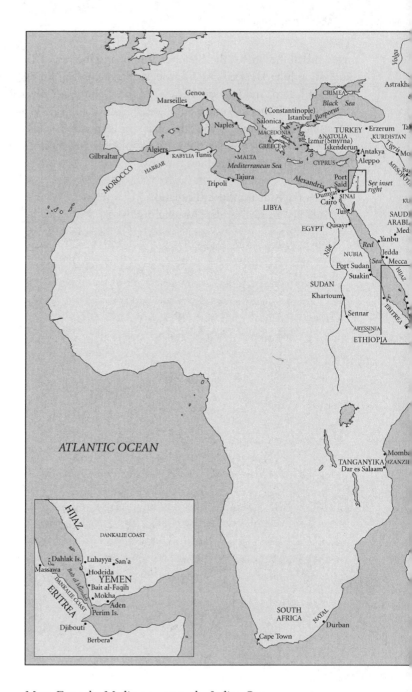

MAP From the Mediterranean to the Indian Ocean

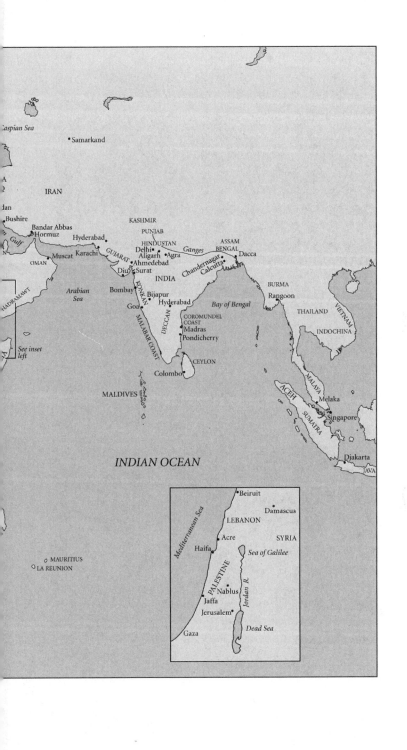

Contributors

Engin Akarlı is Joukowsky Family Professor of History at Brown University. He has taught at several universities, serves on the editorial board of *Islamic Law and Society*, and is the author of several publications including *The Long Peace: Ottoman Lebanon, 1861–1920* (1993).

C. A. Bayly is Vere Harmsworth Professor of Imperial and Naval History, University of Cambridge, and Fellow of St. Catharine's College. His publications include *Rulers, Townsmen and Bazaars: North Indian Society in the Age of British Expansion, 1770–1870* (1983); *Indian Society and the Making of the British Empire* (1988); *Imperial Meridian: The British Empire and the World 1780–1830* (1989); *Empire and Information: Intelligence Gathering and Social Communication in India, 1780–1870* (1996); and *Origins of Nationality in South Asia: Patriotism and Ethical Government in the Making of Modern India* (1998).

Susan Bayly is University Lecturer in Social Anthropology in the Department of Social Anthropology at the University of Cambridge. She is the editor of the *Journal of the Royal Anthropological Institute*. Her publications include *Saints, Goddesses and Kings: Muslims and Christians in South Indian Society, 1700–1900* (1989); and *Caste, Society and Politics in India from the 18th Century to the Modern Age* (2000).

Sugata Bose is the Gardiner Professor of Oceanic History and Affairs at Harvard University and formerly Professor at Tufts University. He was awarded a Guggenheim fellowship in 1997. His publications include *Agrarian Bengal: Economy, Social Structure and Politics, 1919–1947* (1986); *Peasant Labour and Colonial Capital: Rural Bengal since 1770* (1993); and, with Ayesha Jalal, *Modern South Asia* (1998).

Juan Cole is a Professor of Modern Middle Eastern and South Asian History at the University of Michigan. He is current editor of the *International Journal of Middle East Studies*. His publications include *Roots of North Indian Shi'ism in Iran and Iraq: Religion and State in Awadh, 1722–1859* (1988); *Colonialism and Revolution in the Middle East: Social and Cultural Origins of Egypt's Urabi Movement* (1993); and *Modernity and the Millennium: The Genesis of the Bahai Faith in the Nineteenth-Century Middle East* (1998).

Colette Dubois is a Professor of History and African Studies at the Université de Provence at Aix-en-Provence, and the director of its Institut d'Histoire des Civilisations Comparées (IHCC). She is the author of *Djibouti 1888–1967: Héritage ou Frustration?* (1996).

Hala Fattah is an Independent Scholar and a Fellow of the Royal Institute for Inter-faith Studies of Amman, and was formerly a visiting assistant professor at Georgetown University in both the Center for Contemporary Arab Studies and the History Department. She is book editor for the *Bulletin of the Royal Institute for Inter-Faith Studies* and the author of *The Politics of Regional Trade in Iraq, Arabia, and the Gulf, 1745–1900* (1997).

Leila Fawaz is Issam M. Fares Professor of Lebanese and Eastern Mediterranean Studies and director of the Fares Center for Eastern Mediterranean Studies at Tufts University. Her publications include *Merchants and Migrants in Nineteenth-Century Beirut* (1983); and *An Occasion for War: Ethnic Conflict in Mount Lebanon and Damascus in 1860* (1994).

Robert Ilbert is Professor of History and director of the Maison Méditeranéenne des Sciences de l'Homme at the Université de Provence at Aix-en-Provence. He is a member of the Institut Universitaire de France and of the European Science Foundation. His publications include *Heliopolis, Le Caire 1905–1922: Genèse d'une ville, 1905–1922* (1981); and *Alexandrie 1830–1930: Histoire d'une communauté citadine*, 2 vols. (1996).

Ayesha Jalal is a Professor of History at Tufts University. She currently holds a five-year MacArthur fellowship. Her publications include *The Sole Spokesman: Jinnah, the Muslim League, and the Demand for Pakistan* (1986); *State of Martial Rule: The Origins of Pakistan's Political Economy of Defense* (1990); with Sugata Bose, *Modern South Asian History, Culture, Political Economy* (1998); and *Self and Sovereignty: Individual and Community in South Asian Islam since 1850* (2000).

Reşat Kasaba is a Professor at the Jackson School of International Studies at the University of Washington, and the chair of its International Studies program. He co-edited (with Sibel Bozdoğan) *Rethinking Modernity and National Identity in Turkey* (1997); and is the author of *The Ottoman Empire and the World Economy* (1998).

Elisabeth Kendall is Arabic Lector at the Oriental Institute of Oxford University, teaching language and literature. Her publications in English and in Arabic include articles on modern Arabic literature. She is currently working on a book, "The Cultural History of Modern Arabic Literature."

Kenneth McPherson is Adjunct Professor at Curtin University in Perth, Australia. He was the founding director of the Indian Ocean Centre at Curtin University and has been an adviser to the Australian government on Indian Ocean issues since 1995. His recent publications include *The Indian Ocean. A History of People and the Sea* (1993), as well as numerous articles. Currently he is working on histories of Indian Ocean regionalism and Indian Ocean port cities from the seventeenth century.

Robin Ostle is Official Fellow and Tutor in Modern Arabic at St. John's College, Oxford University. He was one of the founding editors of the journal *Arabic and Middle Eastern Literatures* and was its editor for the modern period from 1998 to 2000. His recent publications include, as editor, *The Quest for Freedom in Modern Arabic Literature*, a special number of the *Journal of Arabic Literature* (1995); and *Marginal Voices in Literature and Society* (2000); and as co-editor with Ed de Moor and Stefan Wild, *Writing The Self: Autobiographical Writing in Modern Arabic Literature* (1998).

Abdul-Karim Rafeq is William and Annie Bickers Professor of Arab Middle Eastern Studies at the College of William and Mary. He was formerly professor of modern Arab history and chairman of the Department of History at the University of Damascus. He has written numerous articles and a book, *The Province of Damascus 1723–1783* (paperback ed., 1970) in English, and several books, notably *The Arabs and the Ottomans, 1516–1916* (2d ed., 1993) in Arabic.

André Raymond is professor emeritus at the Université de Provence at Aix-en-Provence. He has served as director of the Institut Français d'Études Arabes de Damas and of the Institut de Recherches et d'Études sur le Monde Arabe et Musulman at Aix-en-Provence. His publications include *The Great Arab Cities in the 16th–18th Centuries: An Introduction* (1984); *Egyptiens et Français au Caire 1798–1801* (1998); *La ville Arabe, Alep,* à l'époque Ottomane (XVIe–XVIIIe siècles) (1998); Cairo (2000); and as editor of Le Caire (2000).

May Seikaly is an Associate Professor of History in the Department of Near Eastern and Asian Studies at Wayne State University in Detroit. She is the author of Haifa: Transformation of an Arab Society (1995 and 2001) and of articles on Palestinian oral history, Gulf history, and on gender studies. Her current work is on the oral testimony of Palestinian displacement.

Peter Sluglett is a Professor of Middle Eastern History and former Director of the Middle East Center at the University of Utah. His books include Britain in Iraq, 1914–1932 (1976); and with Marion Farouk-Sluglett, Iraq since 1958: From Revolution to Dictatorship (1987).

Michel Tuchscherer is Maître de Conference Habilité at the Université de Provence at Aix-en-Provence. His publications include Imams, notables et bedouins du Yemen au XVIIIe siècle: Présentation et traduction de la chronique de 'Abd al-Rahman al-Bakhal; Quintessence de l'or du règne de cherif Muhammad b. Ahmad (1992); as editor (with Sylvie Denoix and Jean-Charles Depaule), Un centre commercial et artisanal du Caire du XIIIe au XX siècle: Le khan al-Khalili et ses environs (1999); and Le commerce du café avant l'ère des plantations commerciales: Espace réseaux, société (XVe–XXe siècle) (2001).

Modernity and Culture

Introduction: The Connected World of Empires

C. A. Bayly and Leila Fawaz

This collection of essays brings together work on the Mediterranean–Middle East and Indian Ocean–South Asian areas in order to create a comparative framework for the study of the impact of global modernity in the region between the 1890s and the 1920s. The book investigates the cultural dimension of life without losing sight of the economic context. The focus on intellectual and political culture yields new perspectives on the way business was conducted in the increasingly cosmopolitan and complex cities of the time, where both commodities and ideas were exchanged. Contributors to this volume have paid attention to political ideas, such as shifts in the concepts of autonomy and sovereignty that emerged through the dialectic of domination and resistance in power relations at the international, regional, and local levels.

The essays examine how peoples of the Middle East and South Asia appropriated, adapted, or resisted the onset of European modernity. The comparative analysis of culture and society in the Mediterranean and Indian Ocean they present provides a complex picture of contested versions of modernity and reveals both the contradictions that sharpen and the overlap that blurs the distinctions between West and East, elite and popular, urban and rural. The essays revisit the culture of cities, not in the usual terms of the influence of Europe on the Middle East or South Asia, but as a set of relationships between Europe, the Middle East, and South Asia. This shift in emphasis provides new insights into how the peoples of the Mediterranean and the Indian Ocean sought to discover new ways to negotiate the problems of cultural difference.

The volume begins by sketching a historical background of long-term trends before concentrating on the decades between the 1890s and the 1920s. The decision to take into consideration the *longue durée* reflects the conviction that such an approach would clarify continuity and change from the seventeenth to the nineteenth centuries, particularly as the cities of the Red Sea region did not undergo the same degree of change as the cities of the Mediterranean and Indian Ocean, which were more directly affected by new economic, cultural, and political interactions with Europe. Between the 1890s and the 1920s, both the Mediterranean and Indian Ocean regions were in ferment as a result of the political, social, economic, and cultural changes that had been set in motion around the beginning of the nineteenth century. As the age of empires gave way to nation-states, there was a sense that a particular inclusiveness of culture and economy had been irretrievably lost to a more intolerant age. Scholars of the late twentieth and early twenty-first century do not necessarily share this sense of nostalgia for the past and fear of the future, but they help us understand and explain the attitudes and beliefs of a critical turning point in modern history.

The Rise, Decline, and Revival of Area Studies

Most of the essays published here were originally presented at a conference organized and funded by the American Social Science Research Council (SSRC) in Aix-en-Provence, France, in September 1998. The policies of the patron of the meeting and the link with the French academic world provided insights into what was attempted and why. For much of the twentieth century the SSRC was at the forefront of the promotion of the idea of area studies throughout Western academia. This was a conference that sought to bring into dialogue the agenda of two distinct area studies groups.

It is worth reflecting at the outset on the origin and meaning of area studies. The concept arose from an application of the ideas of the social science modernization theory of the 1950s to the cultural forms and experience of economic development in particular regions. In the late 1950s and 1960s, most social scientists, including historians, expected the rest of the world to blossom into modern societies as the nation-states of Western Europe and North America had once done. The universality of social changes such as urbanization, industrialization, the emergence of capitalism, the rise of the nuclear family, and the de-mystification of society were taken for granted. These solvents of society had appeared in seventeenth- and eighteenth-century England and France and were expected to spread across what was then called the Third World. Theorists such as Shmuel Eisenstadt[1] had perceived the traces of these great transformations in Asia and Africa, yet it was already clear that change would proceed unevenly because societies had inherited different social and political organizations and cultural systems. Anthropologists, economists, and historians therefore insisted that the study of the modernization process should be firmly located in particular areas and periods. They made sure that graduate students trained in the major academic subjects acquired appropriate language skills and an understanding of the cultures of the regions supposedly now on the brink of modernity. Area studies centers, graduate programs, periodic conferences, and academic journals dedicated to particular regions were founded in many North American universities.

Before World War II, non-European regions had been studied through broad social and religious categories—Islam, Buddhism, and Hinduism, in particular. In this way, Islamic history had become part of a more general category of "Islamic studies," which also included comparative philology, Biblical criticism, and the science of religion, until Ignaz Goldziher (d. 1921), Christiaan Snouck Hurgronje (d. 1936), Carl Heinrich Becker (d. 1933), and W. Barthol'd (d. 1930) introduced a more historical approach, although one still heavily dependent on literary sources.[2] In the 1960s, graduate students began to consider the social structure of regions as bounded entities that displayed particular characteristics. These were expected to resist or expedite modernization. Typical works of this period include the studies by Burton Stein[3] and Bernard Cohn[4] of the Indian "little kingdom," the "levels" of the precolonial Indian state, and the entrepreneurial characteristics of castes that were supposed to impart a particular character to the subcontinent's development under colonialism. Scholars of the Middle East, such as those invited to a conference in 1966 at the University of Chicago's new Center of Middle Eastern Studies, traced the beginnings of modernization in the Middle East, began to map out the character of the medieval, classic Ottoman, and nineteenth-century Arab cities, and relied more and more on diplomatic, legal, and commercial documents, in addition to literary sources, numismatics, and Islamic art and architecture. These scholars carried out anthropological fieldwork in local languages, but also used the colonial archives to give their work a sense of change over time.[5]

The swing to area studies took place in other English-speaking countries as well. In Britain, the School of Oriental and African Studies emerged from World War II as a college for general education in African and Asian studies rather than as a specialist language institute. Influential figures such as Hamilton Gibb and, in the younger generation, Bernard Lewis and Albert Hourani insisted on interdisciplinary area studies training. In Oxford, St. Antony's College fortuitously emerged as a center of Middle Eastern and South Asian studies. Canadian universities responded to the American precedent, and in Australia the dawning realization that the country was closer to Asia than to Great Britain resulted in the foundation of South and Southeast Asian studies centers at Canberra and other large universities.

As early as the 1970s, the area studies literatures, though often introverted and uncommunicative with the wider academy, had begun to influence each other. The studies of Albert Hourani in Oxford on the notable class in the Arab provinces of the Ottoman Empire[6] and on Syria and Lebanon[7] were imported into the work of Indian historians examining Indian urbanization and the beginnings of nationalism. The work of Ira Lapidus[8] and other Gibb students on Middle Eastern cities was also referred to by the new generation of Indian social historians in the United States. Generally, however, the institutionalized distinctions between the area studies centers made it difficult for scholars working on the different regions to talk to each other. Area studies, barring perhaps the massive East Asian Studies complex at Harvard, generally failed to lodge themselves effectively in departments of history, economics, or anthropology, and consequently suffered when grand theoretical constructs returned to the social sciences in the late 1980s.

The situation in France, which had long been a major player in Middle Eastern studies, was rather different. What can broadly be described as area studies had a much longer history in the French academy, which was more closely related to the central concerns of metropolitan intellectuals. Even before the foundation of the journal *Annales* in 1936, historical geography as a dimension of the study of mechanical human collectivities had achieved respectability.[9] The integration of geography, demography, history, economy, and society was thus evident in the monographs of urban historians and of geographers of the Middle East beginning in the 1930s.[10] After the 1960s, it became particularly characteristic of what is commonly referred to as "the school of Aix-en-Provence,"[11] which gathered around the historians André

Raymond and Robert Mantran.[12] The concept of *terroir*, a unit of human geography defined by certain characteristics of culture and production, was applied to France itself. The idea of "Mediterranean Man" became common currency among both conservatives and the Durkheimian left, who believed that the Mediterranean zone merged into, but was distinct from, the Moyen Orient. These French ideas were influential in Anglo-American historiography as well, but indirectly. They were absorbed into early modern European history in the English-speaking world through the work of Fernand Braudel.[13]

Braudel's insistence on the importance of the sea as a zone of economic and cultural interconnection was soon echoed in other regional historiographies. Parallel and overlapping with the study of South Asia, Indian Ocean studies became a field in its own right. The empirical work of Ashin Das Gupta, Tapan Raychaudhuri, S. Arasaratnam,[14] and various historians of Southeast Asia was thrown into sharper theoretical focus by the grand model building of K. N. Chaudhuri, who brought a specifically Braudelian perspective to his work on the Indian Ocean.[15] Similar influences permeate the research of scholars of the Arab world such as Mohammad Amin, Abdul-Karim Rafeq, Nelly Hanna, Mohammad Naciri, and Abdeljelil Temimi, and of scholars of the Ottoman Empire and Turkey trained in Chicago or affiliated with the State University of New York in Binghamton, and others.[16]

By the 1980s, the original modernization paradigm that had presided over the separate area studies agendas was modified by the growing importance of neo-Marxist theories of economic dependency. As geographically distant fields absorbed the work of the Latin American *dependista* scholars, faith in the universal but patchy progress toward modernization was replaced with the conviction that Western expansion had brought various degrees of economic dependency to the non-European world. Modernization was replaced with the "development of underdevelopment." Area studies now seemed to be more often a process of charting the progressive underdevelopment of the rest of the world, and Immanuel Wallerstein's world systems theories professed to provide a general historical scheme with which to understand these degenerative changes.[17] The Middle East and Indian Ocean regions were now seen as former world empires converted in the eighteenth century to the status of semi-peripheral zones of the emerging world capitalist economy. The region remained, however, a legitimate unit of analysis.

In the late 1980s and 1990s, however, more radical and, to some, more corrosive intellectual influences began to throw doubt on the whole agenda of area studies that had held sway since the 1960s. Studies published in the wake of Edward Said's *Orientalism* and the emergence of postcolonial discourse theory seemed to imply that the area studies agenda was a come-lately offshoot of the old imperialist project of "dominating and having mastery over the orient."[18] Ronald Inden's parallel work, *Imagining India*,[19] carried similar implications. It seemed to suggest that the Indian studies agenda, which had been centered on caste, dominant peasantry, village, community, and "little kingdom," was little more than a modernized version of the British imperialist vision of society propagated in the old gazetteers, settlement reports, and parliamentary blue books. More radical voices yet insisted that nothing could be known about the history of non-European peoples except by their own self-representation as oppressed "fragments."[20] Area studies were simply a sociological version of the malign enlightenment project of reducing the world to Western ordering, itself a handmaiden of global capitalism, and contemporary events such as the Iranian revolution or the rise of radical Islamist movements confirmed the fear that the West had always misunderstood and caricatured the East.

At the same time, the concept of areas studies came under attack, if only implicitly, from positions inside the various disciplines that comprised it. In the field of economics, economic history and the study of economic institutions, it lost ground at the expense of mathematical and quantitative economic testing that often eschewed any form of microanalysis. Ironically, most of the social sciences moved in the direction of more rigidly generalizing and universal theorizing at the very time that some branches of cultural studies became ever more relativistic. At all events, the study of particular times and places, especially if these were outside Europe, became less fashionable. Postmodernist analysis and social science theory provided yet another justification for European and American parochialism, perhaps unsurprisingly in view of the history of Western thought.

The issue for the contributors to this volume (and for the SSRC more generally) was how, at the end of the twentieth century, to preserve and enhance the considerable gains in knowledge and theory that the area studies literature of the 1950s to 1980s represented. How could these writings be made to speak to contemporary concerns with globalization and shifting identities? How could the substance be made useful while the static, introverted feel of some of this work was dispelled? In essence, the Aix meeting sought, by putting together two regions that had largely been studied in isolation, to interrogate the boundaries between them. In some cases this made it clear that the Mediterranean–Middle East and Indian Ocean–South Asia zone was, in fact, a unity constructed by a myriad of long-range connections of migrant communities, trade links, and religious doctrines. The absence of rigid boundaries among the great multinational empires aided the movement of people and ideas. The institutions that grew up around the Hajj promoted an equally important flow of cultural forms and ideologies across the entire region from the borders of China to the Maghreb.[21]

Yet there appeared to be other ways in which even precolonial and premodern social systems were fragmented by significant linguistic, cultural, and political barriers. This is an important finding because much postmodernist and cultural studies literature takes it as axiomatic that the early modern world was one of seamless cultural interpenetration. Only European imperial hegemony broke down these happy unities into rigid, racially based hierarchies. In this interpretation, the distinction between the Middle East and the Indian Ocean area was itself a product of colonial domination. But the SSRC meeting began to throw doubt on this.

For instance, French scholars of the early modern Mediterranean and Indian Ocean had no difficulty in conceding that commodity trades linked the Southeast Asian archipelago through the Middle East and Egypt to the Maghreb. Indian calicoes and Chinese silks passed along the whole of this route, exchanged in a series of great marts stretching from Ahmedabad and Surat, through Jiddah to Cairo and on to the cities of North Africa.[22] The French scholars insisted, however, that the transfer of goods did not mean that there was a significant migration of commercial personnel. Indian merchants were not found in the early modern period in Middle Eastern or North African bazaars. Instead, the Indian Ocean formed a distinct and more or less impenetrable zone of fracture. It is not clear whether this fracture represented a political or cultural boundary, but it certainly appears that Indian merchants, whether Hindu or Muslim, did not participate in the networks of trust that linked together the bazaars and merchant communities of the Arab and Mediterranean worlds. Ironically, perhaps, Indian merchants (Sindhis and Gujaratis in particular) made a much more direct impact on Middle Eastern trade in the nineteenth century, when they expanded their activities to Aden, Basra, Baghdad, Jiddah, and Cairo under the aegis of British commercial and political representatives.[23] Some of the papers on the Mediterranean cities also imply that a subtle and shifting boundary divided the world of the Mediterranean from that of the Ottoman and Arab interior both under the old order and after European influences had consolidated themselves more firmly in Alexandria, Haifa, and Beirut.[24]

Similar boundaries bonded subregions in other parts of the premodern eastern world. Beyond Astrakhan in southern Russia, Indian merchants were not to be found.[25] The story of Indian mercantile activities in premodern Southeast Asia is similarly sketchy. There is no doubt that Indian goods reached Sumatra and Java, but the idea of a great eastern Indian cultural zone beloved by Coedes and the anthropologists of the Ecole Française de l'Extrême Orient at the beginning of the twentieth century is difficult to sustain. It was colonial power that brought the South Indian Chettiars to Burma and Cochin China in numbers.[26]

In this way the study of boundaries and people who crossed boundaries and transform their identities, which is a staple of postmodern study, can still be pursued under the rubric of areas studies. What is required is that the meaning of boundaries should be questioned and not simply taken for granted.

The same is true of representations, the study of images and their production. The word "representations" is usually taken as emblematic of postmodernity and is deeply unsettling to the empirical area studies agenda. But the problem was that in the past the existence of regions or communities or large intellectual constructs was taken as self-evident in the writing on both regions. The study of the construction of representations was not part of the academic agenda in subjects such as history and anthropology, so concepts such as caste, tribe, or Islamic society were drawn directly from the literature of late colonialism. Yet there is no reason why today's students of the Middle East or Indian Ocean region should not take seriously the way that both the colonial powers and indigenous nationalists and modernizers portrayed themselves and each other. The politics of representations should be taken as a form of political activity; discursive innovation is just another form of social change. Several essays in this volume deal with representations viewed from different perspectives. Sugata Bose shows that the Indian Ocean was not only a zone of economic and labor exchange, but also one reflected in indigenous literature and poetry.[27] Other papers show how Western and imperial perceptions of Middle Eastern and Indian society were built and used to enshrine the politics of divide and rule.[28] But crucially, the papers also show how indigenous leaderships—of Copts and Indian Muslims, for instance—were able to manipulate and use these representational themes in pursuit of their own identities. Susan Bayly's essay shows that Western representations of the Orient were by no means always conservative or demeaning. The French scholars of the turn of the century associated with the *Revue du monde musulman,* for instance, were favorable to the dynamic and progressive elements within the contemporary pan-Islamic movements.[29] They clearly perceived the connections between West Asia and the East, giving weight to intellectual innovations in the Indian world that were often seen, even by contemporary Arabs, as somehow degraded and second rate. Even where European theories of racial evolution were invoked, it was often possible for liberal Westerners and local literary figures to invert them and turn them back against the purveyors of European power.

Other essays insist that Indians and Arabs of the later nineteenth century fashioned their own modernities to face the global social and economic changes confronting them. Through literature and cinema, the middle-class inhabitants of Alexandria sought to portray themselves as heirs to a polyglot Mediterranean civilization that had been in the vanguard of modernity since the days of the confluence of Egyptian and Hellenistic civilization.[30] This perspective suggests a refreshing change from some of the older area studies assumptions, which constantly sought the regionally authentic and consequently marginalized the hybrid Euro-Oriental cities and their middle-class inhabitants. This is a case where the postmodernist emphasis on hybridity can help to rejuvenate a neglected facet of the earlier literature.

An important arena in which the classic concerns of social history come together with the contemporary interest in representations is the study of the public sphere and especially of printing. J.R.I. Cole's essay in the volume compares and contrasts the history of printing in the Indian and Middle Eastern worlds.[31] He insists that there were many continuities in these societies from early oral and scribal cultures to the age of printing, but there were also profound ruptures. Cole acknowledges the way Western ideas could be disseminated from the new port cities and centers of modern commerce, but more important, he shows that Delhi, Lahore, and Cairo became major centers of publishing of the Qur'an and orthodox religious texts. Even if the interior cities were at the margins of the world of high imperialism, they remained culturally vital.

A third area that came into focus when the two area studies traditions were put together were the interregional linkages that had been marginalized in both fields. However impenetrable some of the boundaries that ruptured the world of interconnected communities, even in the premodern age, there were always communities and intellectual currents that transcended them.

The role the sayyids of the Hadramawt played in southwest India and the East Indies as sponsors of a particular style of purist Islam was recognized in the historical writing of the 1950s and 1960s, but many other such connections achieved new visibility in the discussions surrounding the Aix-en-Provence meeting. Even if Indian merchants played only a small role in West Asian trade before 1860, Indian Muslim clerics came to Mecca, Medina, and the Cairo seminary of al-Azhar in great numbers. Muslim teachers and clerics on the run from the British in India stimulated a purist revolt in southern Egypt in the 1860s. The connections of Arab merchants stretching down from the Arabian peninsula to southeast India and up into Cairo, the so-called Tamil-Arabic communities, provided a link along which could pass the influence of the great pan-Islamic teachers, Jamal al-Din al-Afghani and Muhammad Abduh.[32] Once the British consolidated control in Egypt, the links became even stronger. Syrian Christians and Indian Muslims went to work for the British authorities in Egypt; the former spurred a great expansion of the Egyptian popular press. Much of the police and administration of occupied Egypt was recruited from India.[33] Here social history and the history of representations came together as the Anglo-Indians brought decisive and well-developed stereotypes to bear on their new territories; Cromer's *Government of Subject Races* viewed the Middle East in clearly Indian terms. The social history of the press and publicity in the two societies can help to remind us that Cromer's intervention was both a failure and in itself a reaction to a powerful and well-developed nationalist debate. This was not triumphant Orientalism but a belated response to a strong critique of European intervention in West Asia already evident in the slogan "Egypt for the Egyptians."[34] Bringing the two regions together, it is possible to see that to study nationalism in one area was always inadequate. Nationalism was globalized after the 1850s along the lines of the telegraph and the steamship. It was precisely nationalism as a newly international phenomenon that forced the imperial powers to the publicity and propaganda offensive that we now call Orientalism, or the new imperialism.

Finally, by juxtaposing two area studies literatures, it is easier to appreciate the lacunae in the respective regional agendas. The study of Indian cities and their morphologies flourished in the 1960s. After that, however, the contemporary East Asian emphasis on the peasant pushed Indian scholarship in a rural direction; cultural studies and the concept of the subaltern further marginalized the older interest in urban social history.[35]

Because of the importance of the city in Arab and Middle Eastern thought, both as a place of interchange and as a medina, a center of politics

FIGURE I.1 The Lighthouse at Alexandria. *Photograph by Languki. Fonds Dumoulin. Courtesy Archives d'Outre Mer (CAOM)*

and administration, that could never happen in the other region. Thus although it can reasonably be argued that studies of peasant movements are
underdeveloped in the Middle Eastern case, in India, urban history has
generally withered since the 1960s, except in the field of labor history. In
the case of the Middle East, the study of cities as pivotal to Arab or Ottoman
governments set on imposing their will on, and if possible settling, the
countryside was given new life with the increasing use of law-court registers,
probate inventories, biographical dictionaries, and other local sources that
provided a window into civil society. Scholars investigated the role of the
a'yan, notables who served as middlemen between the rulers and the ruled.
It even proved possible to begin to reconstruct the world of the wider urban
population through the court records and biographical dictionaries that
chart the social structure of cities. These records also shed light on disparities
of urban wealth, the origins of riots, and the movement of displaced rural
populations to city suburbs.[36]

European penetration of the Middle East in the nineteenth and early
twentieth centuries gave another impetus to Middle East urban history,

FIGURE I.2 Quay, Port Said. *Photograph attributed to Hyppolite Arnoux (French photographer active 1860–1880). Fonds Dumoulin. Courtesy Archives d'Outre Mer (CAOM)*

marked by a new interest in its absorption into the world economy. In the case of Egypt, the growth of Alexandria did not affect the political centrality of Cairo, but in the *Bilad al-Sham*, or Syrian lands, the rise of ports and middle-sized towns in Mount Lebanon that served as centers of exchange for the new trade was accompanied by the decline of the great cities of the interior such as Aleppo and Damascus, as both Ottoman and European powers shifted their bases of control from the inland cities to the Mediterranean.

The conference in Aix-en-Provence was confronted by a series of excellent detailed studies of towns, notably Beirut, Aleppo, Haifa, Damascus, Basra, and Alexandria, which found no match in the recent Indian literature, but point up the need for a reevaluation of Indian colonial urbanism. The materials for this could easily be assembled. The study of Damascus's role in the organization of the Hajj pilgrim trade could be replicated by a study

FIGURE I.3 Port Said, Egypt. *Photograph by Hyppolite Arnoux. Fonds Dumoulin. Courtesy Archives d'Outre Mer (CAOM)*

of the importance of nineteenth-century Indian pilgrimage places of Ajmer, Gaya, Allahabad, or Banaras. So too the study of Basra as an Indian bridgehead in Iraq could parallel a study of the trade and society of Cambay, Surat, or Cochin, which still had important Red Sea and Indian Ocean trading communities in the nineteenth century.[37]

One area where Indian history has not abandoned urban studies is in the field of intercommunal relations and communal violence. Here Reşat Kasaba's study of İzmir when the Greek and Turkish populations fell into a terrible bout of mutual killings was painfully echoed in the Indian literature.[38] As with the Ionian coast, so in eastern India the communities had lived peacefully together throughout the nineteenth century. In İzmir, it was the intervention of an international struggle that suddenly ruptured those links by confronting a half-formed Turkish nationalism with an emerging Greek one. In Calcutta, the great killings of 1946 marked the beginning of an international struggle for succession in the region consequent on the

FIGURE 1.4 View of Ismailia, Egypt. *Photographer unknown. Fonds Dumoulin. Courtesy Archives d'Outre Mer (CAOM)*

massive turmoil of World War II. Here communal antagonism could not easily be read out of the region's earlier history. But elsewhere in the Indian Ocean and in the Middle East there were cases where an older history of conflict certainly provided legends and histories that could be enlisted in the struggles of the present. The juxtaposition of two historical regions could thus help break down the uniformity of the picture on both sides. It could be an aid to de-essentialization by internal contrast and comparison as much as through external ones.

At the broadest level, an overview of the historiography of the two regions suggests that there was a long-term cycle by which power shifted from the old imperial cities of the interior to new European and local entrepreneurs who dominated coastal cities such as Beirut, Alexandria, and Madras. In the second part of the cycle, however, the interior reasserted itself: Ankara, Delhi, Cairo, and Damascus regained their preeminence. A symbolic act here was the British moving their capital from Calcutta to Delhi in 1911.[39]

The colonial rulers were trying to cement alliances with the great notables and peasant communities of upper India and push the middle-class nationalists of Bengal to the margins. We can see a limited parallel in the case of Damascus;[40] reassertion of central control in the Ottoman Empire and the expansion of communications foreshadowed a process by which the Anatolian and Syrian interiors and the great rural clans gradually took back power from the polyglot trading cities of the coast in the course of the twentieth century.[41] Since the 1950s, the cultural and economic supremacy of Alexandria has all but vanished. By the 1980s, even the century-old ascendancy of Beirut over Damascus had been reversed.

Another area where the two historiographies have moved at different paces and where comparison can help fill in lacunae relates to the area of regional identities or patriotism. Historians of the Middle East have been rightly concerned not to create a teleological narrative that constantly seeks to find the historical origins of contemporary nation-states. After all, this is what early nationalists themselves mined history for. In recent years, there has been great stress on the continuing importance of a sense of an Ottoman world culture for elites throughout the Middle East, Turco-Circassian, and even Arab regions. In particular, some scholars have argued that the Egypt of Muhammad 'Ali should be seen more as a continuation of Ottoman statecraft by other means than as the emergence of a new Egyptian-Arab nation state.[42] Nevertheless, an analysis of the emergence of a stronger sense of regional identity—sometimes in contest with this Ottomanism, sometimes complementing it—in Syria, Egypt, and Palestine, in particular, has continued to seem a legitimate enterprise for many historians. Even in the eighteenth century, while operating within an Ottoman framework, Syrian notables were identifying themselves as "Arabs."[43] Early in the nineteenth century, Muhammad 'Ali found it worthwhile to try to foster a more specifically Egyptian identity that could, ironically, provide legitimation for his Turco-Circassian regime. Several of the Middle East papers given at the Aix conference sought to discern the beginnings of such regional identities in the declining Ottoman system, whereas others concluded that the case was unproven. The strength of this literature in recent years has been to show that identities remained open and contested. The beginnings of pan-Arabism, pan-Islamism, and regional patriotisms could coexist in tension with the older sense of Ottoman or Mediterranean identity.

By contrast, Indian literature has retreated from the notion of regional identity. It has proved unacceptable both to subaltern studies and to studies of nationalist ideology, which have normally been preoccupied by the issues of modernity, gender, and religion. The Aix conference took place at a point when this attitude was apparently changing. A new generation of research students in the United States, India, and Europe has begun to ask questions about the origin of the notion of regional patriotisms in locations as varied as Assam, Orissa, and Kashmir.[44] None of the studies start from the assumption that these were organic or natural entities. Instead, they emphasize the overlapping of processes of linguistic uniformity and colonial government to produce a newly invented regional identity. But most also give some weight to an inheritance from the past: the sense of sacred landscape, or ancient institutions, or stories, legends, and heroes, which help root and give meaning to these invented traditions of the nineteenth century. Here the findings of Middle Eastern scholars provide important comparative insights. For instance, the pervading sense of Ottoman culture has clear parallels in the continuing charisma of the ideal of Mughal gentry culture in nineteenth-century India. Once denounced as a dying "husk culture" or as a precursor of malign antinationalist Muslim separatism, Indo-Islamic life and thought in the nineteenth century needs to be reassessed. Ayesha Jalal's paper in this volume considers this issue.

The conclusion of the Aix conference was perhaps more optimistic about the future of area studies than one might expect. Areas are not things in themselves, and even at the time of their origin, area studies were intended to be techniques for testing general propositions against particular bodies of knowledge rather than bounded disciplines. Provided area studies are in constant dialogue with each other and with the general developments in the larger disciplines, they will continue to produce valuable insights.

Convergences and Divergences: The Middle East and India, circa 1600–1920

To have meaning, comparative history must also be a history of connections; history, to distinguish itself from other disciplines, needs to account for change. The Aix conference found that its attempts at inter-area comparison were of most use and most revealing about how the two historiographies might develop when divergent and convergent historical trends over the long term could be identified. The picture of burgeoning seventeenth-century trade in the Red Sea and eastern Mediterranean painted by the

French scholars of the Maison Méditerranéene des Sciences de l'Homme[45] fits well with the impression gained by scholars of the Indian Ocean during the height of the Mughal hegemony. This was an era when the Ottoman, Safavid, Mughal, and Deccan Sultanate polities were reaping vast rewards from a great reduction in the costs of production in their large realms when peace was imposed on local warlords and factions.[46] Internecine warfare had increasingly given way to elite consumption and display, benefiting the textile industry, all forms of smithing, leathermaking, and specialist agricultural production. This great expansion of production, only marginally dented by the so-called Southeast Asian crisis of the seventeenth century, was also powered by a world expansion in the circulation of precious metals that followed the silver exports from Latin America and a boom in the North Atlantic slave and sugar economies, both of which increased world liquidity and gave rise to considerable economies of scale in world shipping. The Islamized kingdoms of the east (these included formally Hindu ones such as Vijayanagara) had pioneered successful systems to incorporate diverse ethnic and religious groups under the umbrella of Islamic kingship, if not of shari'a. Studies of Istanbul, eastern Mediterranean seaports such as İzmir, Alexandria, and Beirut, and Indian Ocean ports such as Bandar Abbas, Surat, Cambay, Cochin, and Hughli show that merchant groups and entrepreneurial nobles retained great local influence under the aegis of Muslim law officers. Even if the Red Sea provided a formidable barrier to personnel moving from east to west, trade cycles and systems of government across this large Ottoman-Safavid-Mughal area were very closely correlated. As Sanjay Subrahmanyam has shown, administrators, military dynasties, and even intellectual currents moved across the whole region.[47] It is an obvious point, but still sometimes forgotten, that the dominant elites in seventeenth- and eighteenth-century India were Turks and Persians. Their relations with the local Rajput magnates bore a family resemblance to the relations of cultural assimilation and occasional coercion sustained between the Ottoman rulers and the Balkan Christians.

The eighteenth century saw both a crisis in the internal governance of the two regions and a disruption and militarization of the trade relations with the European-Atlantic economies. This resulted in a similar pattern of warfare, political decentralization, and patchy European conquest. The internal reasons for the decline of the Islamic empires are still a matter of dispute. The costs of warfare following the so-called military revolution affected all these regimes whether they faced European competitors directly,

as in the case of the Safavids and Ottomans, or indirectly, as in the case of
the Mughals. Revenue pressure on landowners and peasants produced an
inevitable concatenation of revolts from the Balkans to the Sikh and Maratha
revolts in India. Tribal groups, whether the Wahhabis, Persian nomads, Afghan invaders, or western Indian Bhils, kept the imperial forces on the defensive. Yet the most obvious cause of the decline and decentralization of
the imperial centers was that their hold was always fragile. It was almost
inevitable that the regional nobles and merchant coalitions would assert
some degree of independence from Istanbul, Isfahan, or Delhi; thus there
was not a revolt of the Ottoman *a'yan* and the Egyptian mamluks or the
nizams of Hyderabad and nawabs of Bengal. In many cases all that happened
was that these rulers amalgamated offices and built up local coteries within
the shell of the older imperial institutions.[48] Thus the much-vaunted decline
of the Islamic empires can better be seen as a diaspora of its leading citizens
along the frontier of empire, something that affected Western European
empires to an equal degree. This meant that in the nineteenth century, the
social politics of the successor regions was always most complex. Turko-
Circassians looking to Istanbul remained key figures in the social and intellectual history of the Middle East into the twentieth century. Equally, the
Mughal aristocrats, often in economic decline and scattered throughout
India's cities, remained important figures in nineteenth-century Indian politics and thought. Sir Sayyid Ahmad Khan, a leading Islamic modernist and
supposedly leader of Muslim separatism in India, was one such displaced
Delhi Mughal noble.

Clearly it was in the eighteenth century that the influence of European
trade and warfare became, if not a dominant, at least an important factor
working on the eastern Mediterranean, Red Sea, and Indian Ocean areas.
As André Gunder Frank points out,[49] Europeans were great innovators in
the alliance between commerce and force. Even in the seventeenth century,
Indian and Ottoman rulers had lagged behind in the creation of armed
shipping; Europeans brought to the balance of trade at world level the skills
of the arms dealer and the military expert. As Niels Steensgaard argued in
the 1960s, they were able to internalize protection costs.[50] Thus even while
the bulk of Asian and Middle Eastern trade remained in indigenous hands,
by the mid-eighteenth century Europeans had seized control of its most
valuable products. The Bombay marine was the dominant fleet in the Indian
Ocean, and French and allied Syrian Christian, Greek, and Maltese traders
became dominant in the Mediterranean. At the same time, the textile and

specialist products of the Middle East and India were already fading on the world market before Europeans forced open the barriers of trade and devastated the local textile and other artisan industries. Although the simplistic idea that Europeans initiated the Industrial Revolution and transformed world trade can no longer be maintained, it is idle to pretend that Europeans did not devise successful measures to maintain their industries at the world level, which the Middle East and the Indian Ocean area could not do. European governments were adept at protecting their industries, and European capital and labor markets were evidently freer and more flexible than the Eastern ones. Narrow measures of standard of living cannot do justice to the great variations in institutional economic structures revealed here.

On the other hand, it is a shallow history that does not recognize that some of the economic institutions and political forms that emerged from the Asian and Middle Eastern eighteenth century were both viable and relatively successful. The regional kingdoms that emerged from the decline of the imperial polities did much to shape the society and thought of the nineteenth century. Enlightened despots of the region did much to foster a sense of regional identity and to preserve local independence almost to the point where the new generation of nationalists could step in to articulate resistance. Muhammad 'Ali's Egypt had, in this respect, quite a lot in common with the Punjab of the Sikh ruler Raja Ranjit Singh, who brought in European military and technical advisers, built a new model army, and revived the agricultural prosperity of the Mughal Punjab.[51] Even in regions where political independence was snuffed out earlier, as in Awadh or the Maratha territories, or the Ottoman lands conquered by the Russians, the period of the precolonial kingdoms gave rise to traditions, legends, and institutions that could be reinvented and promulgated by later nationalist writers and ideologues. Above all, as Engin Akarlı's paper shows, the post-Tanzimat Ottoman Empire offered for a time the possibility of an alternative modernity for the Middle East, where older norms of social integration and imperial government might subsist with techniques and ideas derived from European sources.[52] The new aggression of the European powers, as well as the incapacity of the Ottoman military system to transform itself into a disinterested civil bureaucracy, aborted these developments.

The close parallels in historical change through time between much of the Middle East and the Indian Ocean rim persisted into the late nineteenth century and the first era of global capitalism. Of course, Egypt maintained formal independence until 1882, and much of the rest of the region until

1917, whereas India had been largely conquered by the British as early as 1818. But the intensification of colonial pressures, both economic and political, began after the opening of the Suez Canal and the coming of the electric telegraph and the steamship. The era of the American Civil War cotton boom ensured the incorporation of Egypt and a large part of the Levant and western India into the international economy, and the vicissitudes of that economy were calibrated quite closely with the emergence of colonial nationalism. Many historians of empire have poured scorn on the Hobson-Lenin thesis that there was a new imperialism at the end of the nineteenth century and that it was related to the attempt by governmental financial interests to re-divide the world's resources. But historians of the Middle East and of the Indian Ocean should be more favorable to this position than most of their peers. It cannot be doubted that between them the Ottoman Bank, the Egyptian bondholder interests, and the Bombay- and Calcutta-based British export firms successfully used the European powers to maintain and expand their interests. Equally, it seems clear that the rise of nationalisms in the Young Turk Movement, pan-Islamism, and the so-called extremist party of the Indian National Congress all related to a quickening of colonial exploitation and the rise of military competition among the great powers that signaled the onset of war. Those particular nightmares of the twentieth century, intercommunal and state-sponsored massacres, were also in evidence before the end of the period. The riots over the Kanpur mosque in India and the pressures on the Armenian populations in the Ottoman Empire were early warnings of the fate of İzmir, or of Calcutta later in the twentieth century.

Putting the two area studies agendas together at Aix had the desirable effect of unsettling them both and reminding us how much historiographical convention determined outcomes in history writing. By forcing us to think beyond the region, it also made us come to terms with places where the histories of the regions converged and diverged. It made clear that regional histories could only be one way of writing world history, and that radical relativism, the emphasis on the fragment, the decontextualized discourse, or the shallowly researched representation could never be enough. Merely identifying the appropriate fragment or the submerged voice requires, of course, an act of selection and an implicit contextualization. For this reason, the study of economic change, urbanization, and the colonial and paracolonial state will inevitably remain the staple of Middle Eastern and Indian Ocean historians. Research in archives and private collections, the strengths of postwar scholarship, will have to continue even if we all believe that we can do no more than find traces of the past in the present world and not really reconstruct the past with any sense of finality.

Notes

1. Shmuel Noah Eisenstadt, *Revolution and the Transformation of Societies: A Comparative Study of Civilization* (New York: Free Press, 1978); Eisenstadt, *Modernization: Growth and Development* (Bloomington: Indiana University Press, 1963).

2. Albert Hourani, "The Present State of Islamic and Middle Eastern Historiography," in *Europe and the Middle East,* ed. Albert Hourani (London: St. Antony's/Macmillan Series, 1980), pp. 161–96, 209–16. See also André Raymond, "Islamic City, Arab City: Orientalist Myths and Recent Views," *British Journal of Middle Eastern Studies* 21, 1 (1994): 3–18.

3. Burton Stein, *All the Kings' Mana: Papers on Medieval South Indian History* (Madras: New Era Publication, 1984); Stein, *Peasant State and Society in Medieval South India* (Delhi: Oxford University Press, 1985).

4. Bernard Cohn, *The Chamars of Senapur: A Study of the Changing Status of a Depressed Caste* (Ithaca: Cornell University Press, 1967); Cohn, *Notes on the History of the Study of the Indian Society and Culture* (Chicago: University of Chicago, Committee on South Asian Studies, 1968).

5. William R. Polk and Richard L. Chambers, eds., *Beginning of Modernization in the Middle East: The Nineteenth Century,* Publications of the Center for Middle Eastern Studies, no. 1 (Chicago: University of Chicago Press, 1968); Albert H. Hourani and S. M. Stern, eds., *The Islamic City* (Oxford: Cassirer, 1970); Ira Lapidus, *Muslim Cities in the Later Middle Ages* (Cambridge: Harvard University Press, 1967); Richard Bulliet, *The Patricians of Nishapur: A Study in Medieval Social History* (Cambridge: Harvard University Press, 1972); Roy P. Mottahedeh, *Loyalty and Leadership in an Early Islamic Society* (Princeton: Princeton University Press, 1980); Janet L. Abu-Lughod, *Cairo: 1001 Years of the City Victorious* (Princeton: Princeton University Press, 1971).

6. Albert Hourani, *Syria and Lebanon* (London: Oxford University Press, 1954). This work influenced C. A. Bayly's work on Allahabad, though only indirectly; see C. A. Bayly, *The Local Roots of Indian Politics* (Oxford: Clarendon Press, 1975).

7. Albert Hourani, "Ottoman Reform and the Politics of the Notables," in *The Emergence of the Modern Middle East,* ed. Albert Hourani (London: Macmillan, 1981), pp. 36–66.

8. Lapidus, *Muslim Cities*; Lapidus, *Islam, Politics and Social Movements* (Berkeley: University of California Press, 1988); Lapidus, *A History of Islamic Societies* (Cambridge: Cambridge University Press, 1991).

9. Peter Burke, *The French Historical Revolution: The Annales School* (Stanford: Stanford University Press, 1990).

10. Robert Ilbert, "Méthodologie et Idéologie: La recherche française sur les politiques urbaines en Egypte," in *Middle Eastern Cities in Comparative Perspective: Points de vue sur les villes du Maghreb et du Mashreq*, ed. Kenneth Brown, Michèle Jolé, Peter Sluglett, and Sami Zubaida (London: Ithaca Press, 1986), pp. 103–14, mentions the works of Marcel Clerget, *Le Caire: Etude de géographie urbaine et d'histoire économique*, 2 vols. (Cairo, 1934); Jean Sauvaget and J. Weulersse, *Introduction à l'histoire de l'Orient musulman* (Beirut, 1950); Jean Sauvaget, *Inventaire des monument musulmans de la ville Alep* (Paris, 1931); Sauvaget, *Alep* (Paris: P. Geuthner, n.d.). See also the works of William and George Marçais, Jacques Weulersse, Roger Le Tourneau, and others. For a concise and useful survey of French historiography of Egyptian cities, consult Ilbert, "Méthodologie et Idéologie," pp. 105–6, citing J. Besançon, "Une banlieu du Caire, Héliopolis," thèse annexe de doctorat d'état, 1955; Pierre Marthelot, "Le Caire: Nouvelle métropole," *Annales Islamologiques* 8 (1969); and others. See also Louis Massignon, *L'Islam et l'Occident* (Paris: Cahiers du Sud, 1947); Dominique Sourdel et Janine Sourdel-Thomine, *La civilisation de l'Islam classique* (Paris: Arthaud, 1976); Jacques Berque, *Histoire sociale d'un village égyptien au XXe siècle* (Paris: Mouton, 1957); Claude Cahen, *Mouvements populaires et autonomisme urbain dans l'Asie musulmane du Moyen Age* (Leiden: E. J. Brill, 1959); Cahen, *L'Islam: Des origines au début de l'empire ottoman* (Paris: Hachette, 1995).

11. Ilbert, "Méthodologie et Idéologie," p. 111, n. 6, mentions that the expression "l'école d'Aix-en-Provence" was coined by Pierre Marthelot in *Hérodote* 29–30 (April 1983).

12. André Raymond, *Artisans et commerçants au Caire au XVIIIe siècle* (Cairo: Institut Français d'archéologie orientale, 1973); Raymond, *The Great Arab Cities in the 16th–18th Centuries: An Introduction* (New York: New York University Press, 1984); Raymond, *Le Caire* (Paris: Fayard, 1993); Raymond, *Egyptiens et Français au Caire 1798–1801* (Cairo: Institut Français d'archéologie orientale, 1998); Robert Mantran, *Istanbul dans la seconde moitié du XVIIe siècle* (Paris: Maisonneuve, 1962); Jean-Claude Garcin, *Etats, sociétés et cultures du monde musulman médiéval: Xe–XVe siècle* (Paris: Presses Universitaires de France, 1995); Colette Establet et Jean-Paul Pascual, *Familles et fortunes à Damas: 450 foyers damascins en 1700* (Damascus: Institut Français d'études arabes de Damas, 1994); Robert Ilbert, *Alexandrie 1830–1930*, 2 vols. (Cairo: Institut Français d'archéologie orientale, 1996); Brigitte Marino, *Le faubourg du Midan à Damas à l'époque ottomane: espace urbain, société et habitat (1742–1830)* (Damascus: Institut Francais d'études arabes de Damas, 1997); Daniel Panzac, *La peste dans l'Empire ottoman, 1700–1850* (Louvin: Peeters, 1985).

13. Fernand Braudel, *La Méditerranée*, vol. 1: *L'espace et l'histoire*, vol. 2: *Les hommes et l'héritage* (Paris: Flammarion, 1985). The influence worked in the opposite direction, e.g., the work of André Raymond, though rooted in the French tradition, was influenced by the supervision of Albert Hourani at Oxford.

14. Ashin Das Gupta, *Indian Merchants and the Decline of the Surat: 1700–1750* (Wiesbaden: Steiner Verlag, 1970); Ashin Das Gupta and M. N. Pearson, eds., *India and the Indian Ocean 1500–1800* (New Delhi: Oxford University Press, 1987); Tapan Raychaudhuri, *Jan Company in Coromandel 1605–1690* (The Hague, 1962); Sinnappah Arasaratnam, *Indian Merchants and Their Trading Methods (c. 1700)* (New Delhi: K. A. Naqvi, 1966); Arasaratnam, *The Dutch East India Company and Its Coromandel Trade 1700–1740* (The Hague: Martinus Nijhoff, 1967); Arasaratnam, *Maritime India in the 17th Century* (Oxford: Oxford University Press, 1994).

15. K. N. Chaudhuri, *Asia before Europe: Economy and Civilization of the Indian Ocean from the Rise of Islam to 1750* (Cambridge: Cambridge University Press, 1990); Chaudhuri, *Trade and Civilization in the Indian Ocean* (Cambridge: Cambridge University Press, 1985); Chaudhuri, *From the Atlantic to the Arabian Sea: A Polyphonic Essay on History* (Florence: K. N. Chaudhuri, 1995).

16. Nelly Hanna, *An Urban History of Bulaq* (Cairo, 1983); Hanna, *Making Big Money in 1600: The Life and Times of Isma'il Abu Taqiyya Egyptian Merchant* (Syracuse: Syracuse University Press, 1998); Abdul-Karim Rafeq, *The Province of Damascus, 1723–1783*, 2nd ed. (Beirut: Khayats, 1970); Dominique Chevallier, ed., *L'espace social de la ville arabe* (Paris: Maisonneuve et Larose, 1979); Mohamed Naciri, *Succès de la ville, crise de l'urbanité* (Paris: Éditions l'Harmattan, 1991); Mohamed Naciri and André Raymond, eds., *Sciences sociales et phénomènes urbains dans le monde arabe* (Casablanca: Fondation du Roi Abdul-Aziz Al-Saoud, 1997); Reşat Kasaba, Caglar Keyder, and Faruk Tabak, "Eastern Mediterranean Port Cities and Their Bourgeoisie: Merchants, Political Projects, and Nation States," *Review* 10 (1986): 121–35; Daniel Goffman, *İzmir and the Levantine World, 1550–1650* (Seattle: University of Washington Press, 1990).

17. Immanuel Maurice Wallerstein, *The Modern World-System* (San Diego: Academic Press, 1989); Wallerstein, *The Rise and Future Demise of World Systems Analysis* (Binghamton, N.Y.: Fernand Braudel Center for the Study of Economics, Historical Systems and Civilization, 1996).

18. Edward Said, *Orientalism* (New York: Vintage Books, 1994); Gyan Prakash, "Writing Post-Orientalist Histories of the 3rd World Perspectives from Indian Historiography," *Comparative Studies and History* (April 1990).

19. Ronald Inden, *Imagining India* (Oxford: Basil Blackwell, 1990).

20. Greg Dening, "The Theatricality of Observing and Being Observed: Eighteenth-century Europe 'Discovers' the 'Pacific,'" in *Implicit Understandings. Observ-*

ing, Reporting and Reflecting on the Encounters between Europeans and Other Peoples in the Early Modern Era, ed. Stuart Schwartz (Cambridge: Cambridge University Press, 1994), pp. 451–83. See also Dale F. Eickelman, *The Middle East: An Anthropological Approach*, 2d ed. (Englewood Cliffs, N.J.: Prentice Hall, 1989); Dale F. Eickelman and Jon W. Anderson, eds., *New Media in the Muslim World: The Emerging Public Sphere* (Bloomington: Indiana University Press, 1999).

21. Barbara Daly Metcalf, *Islamic Revival in British India: Deoband, 1860–1900* (Princeton: Princeton University Press, 1982); Marshall G. S. Hodgson, *The Venture of Islam: Conscience and History in a World Civilization*, 3 vols. (Chicago: University of Chicago Press, 1974); Rafeq, *The Province of Damascus*, pp. 52–76; Rafeq, "New Light on the Transportation of the Damascene Pilgrimage during the Ottoman Period," in *Islamic and Middle Eastern Societies*, ed. Robert Olson (Brattleboro, Vt., 1987), pp. 127–36; Suraiya Faroqhi, *Pilgrims and Sultans: The Hajj under the Ottomans, 1517–1683* (London: St. Martin's, 1996); Dale F. Eickelman and James Piscatori, eds., *Muslim Politics* (Princeton: Princeton University Press, 1996); Colette Establet and Jean-Paul Pascual, *Ultime voyage pour la Mecque: Les inventaires après décés de pèlerins morts à Damas vers 1700* (Damascus: Institut Français d'études arabes de Damas, 1998).

22. Chaudhuri, *Asia Before Europe*.

23. See Sugata Bose's essay in this volume and chapter 3 of his forthcoming work, *The Indian Ocean Rim: An Inter-Regional Arena in the Age of Global Empire*; Claude Markovits, of the CNRS, Paris, on Sindhi merchants worldwide, entitled *The Global World of Indian Merchants, 1750–1942* (Cambridge, Eng.: Cambridge University Press, 2000); and Hala Fattah's paper in this volume.

24. See May Seikaly's and Robert Ostle's papers in this volume; Leila Fawaz, *Merchants and Migrants in Nineteenth-Century Beirut* (Cambridge: Harvard University Press, 1983); Ilbert, *Alexandrie*; May Seikaly, *Haifa: Transformation of an Arab Society, 1918–1939* (London: I.B. Tauris, 1995).

25. Stephen F. Dale, *Indian Merchants and Eurasian Trade* (New Delhi: Foundation Books; Cambridge: Cambridge University Press, 1994).

26. C. J. Baker, "Economic Reorganization and the Slump in South and Southeast Asia," *Comparative Studies in Society and History* 23, 3 (1981); Sugata Bose, *The Indian Ocean Rim* (forthcoming).

27. See Sugata Bose's paper in this volume.

28. See C. A. Bayly's and Ayesha Jalal's papers in this volume.

29. See Susan Bayly's paper in this volume.

30. See Robin Ostle's and Elisabeth Kendall's papers in this volume.

31. See Juan Cole's paper in this volume.

32. See C. A. Bayly's paper in this volume.

33. Robert L. Tignor, "The 'Indianization' of the Egyptian Administration under British Rule," *American Historical Review* 68 (1963): 636–61; Roger Owen, "The Influence of Lord Cromer's Indian Experience on British Policy in Egypt, 1883–1907," *St Antony's Papers* 17 (1965).

34. Alexander Schölch, *Egypt for the Egyptians!: The Socio-Political Crisis in Egypt 1978–1882* (Oxford: Middle East Centre, St. Antony's College; London: Ithaca Press, 1981); Juan Cole, *Colonialism and Revolution in the Middle East: Social and Cultural Origins of Egypt's 'Urabi Movement'* (Cairo: American University in Cairo Press, 1999).

35. See Ranajit Guha, ed., *Subaltern Studies: Writings on South Asian History and Society*, 6 vols. (New Delhi: Oxford University Press, 1982–89).

36. For example, consult the works of André Raymond, Jean-Claude Garcin, Nelly Hanna, Janet Abu-Lughod, Thomas Philipp, and others for premodern and modern Cairo, and the works of Robert Ilbert, Michael Reimer, and others for studies on nineteenth- and early-twentieth-century Alexandria. Consult the works of Abdel-Karim Rafeq, Jean-Paul Pascual and Colette Establet, Linda Shilcher, Philip Khoury, James Reilly, Brigitte Marino, Elizabeth Thompson, and others for premodern and modern Damascus.

37. Kenneth McPherson's paper in the volume provides a valuable overview of comparative issues of this sort.

38. See Reşat Kasaba's article in this volume. It must be noted, however, that although the great Calcutta massacre of August 1946, which left some 4,000 Hindus and Muslims dead, was an urban phenomenon, the worst of the partition violence in 1947 involving the massacre of several hundred thousand people occurred in rural Punjab. See Ayesha Jalal, *Self and Sovereignty: The Muslim Individual and the Community of Islam in South Asia since 1850* (London: Routledge; New Delhi: Oxford University Press, 2000), chap. 9.

39. Robert Grant Irving, *Indian Summer: Luytens, Baker and Imperial Delhi* (New Haven: Yale University Press, 1981).

40. See Abdul-Karim Rafeq's article in this volume.

41. Leila Fawaz, "The Changing Balance of Forces between Beirut and Damascus in the Nineteenth and Twentieth Centuries," *Revue des Etudes du Monde musulman et de la Méditerrannée*, 55–56, 1–2 (1990): 209–14.

42. Khaled Fahmy, *All the Pasha's Men: Mehmed Ali, His Army and the Making of Modern Egypt* (Cambridge: Cambridge University Press, 1997). For Ottoman-Arab relations, consult the works of Abeljelil Temimi and of scholars affiliated with the Temimi Center in Zaghouan, Tunisia; Dina Rizk Khoury, *State and Provincial Society in the Ottoman Empire: Mosul, 1540–1834* (Cambridge: Cambridge University Press, 1997); Hasan Kayali, *Arabs and Young Turks: Ottomanism, Arabism, and Islamism in the Ottoman Empire, 1908–1918* (Berkeley: University of California Press, 1997).

43. Abdul-Karim Rafeq, "The Syrian 'Ulema, Ottoman Law, and Islamic Shari'a," *Turcica* 26 (1994): 9–29; Rafeq, "Social Groups, Identity and Loyalty, and Historical Writing in Ottoman and Post-Ottoman Syria," in *Les arabes et l'histoire créatrice*, ed. Dominique Chevallier (Paris: Presses de l'Université de Paris-Sorbonne, 1995), pp. 79–93; Rafeq, "Identity and Communal Coexistence in Ottoman Syria," paper presented at a seminar of the Syria study group, Center for Contemporary Arab Studies, Georgetown University, February 2000; Thomas Naff and Roger Owen, eds., *Studies in 18th-Century Islamic History* (Carbondale: Southern Illinois University Press, 1977).

44. C. A. Bayly, *Origins of Nationality in South Asia: Patriotism and Ethical Government in the Making of Modern India* (New Delhi: Oxford University Press, 1988). See also Sugata Bose,"Nation, Reason and Religion: India's Independence in International Perspective," *Economic and Political Weekly*, 1–7 August, 1998; and Ayesha Jalal, "Nation, Reason and Religion: The Punjab's Role in the Partition of India," *Economic and Political Weekly*, 8–15 August, 1998. Two recent dissertations on the history of Kashmir, a region that dominates news from the subcontinent but that hardly figured on the map of South Asian historiography, are particularly noteworthy: Mridu Rai, "The Question of Religion: Sovereignty, Legitimacy and Rights in Kashmir, 1846–1947," Ph.D. diss., Columbia University, 1999; and Chitralekha Zutshi, "Community, State and Nation: Regional Patriotism and Religious Identities in the Kashmir Valley, c. 1880–1953," Ph.D. diss., Tufts University, 2000.

45. See the articles of Michel Tuchscherer, André Raymond, and Colette Dubois in this volume.

46. John F. Richards, *The Mughal Empire* (Cambridge: Cambridge University Press, 1993); Tapan Raychaudhuri and Ifran Habib, *The Cambridge Economic History of India* (Cambridge: Cambridge University Press, 1931); Suraiya Faroqhi, Halil İnalcık, and Donald Quataert, *An Economic and Social History of the Ottoman Empire* (Cambridge: Cambridge University Press, 1994); Suraiya Faroqhi, *Peasant, Dervishes and Traders in the Ottoman Empire* (London: Variorum Reprints, 1986); Cemal Kafadar, *Between Two Worlds: The Construction of the Ottoman State* (Berkeley: University of California Press, 1995).

47. Sanjay Subrahamayam, et al., *L'Empire portugais d'Asie, 1500–1700: histoire politique et economique* (Paris: Maisonneuve et Larose, 1999); Sanjay Subrahmayam, *Sinners and Saints: The Successors of Vasco de Gama* (New Delhi: Oxford University Press, 1998); Subrahmayam, *Merchant Networks in the Early Modern World* (Aldershot: Variorum, 1996); Subrahmayam, *The Political Economy of Commerce: South India, 1500–1650* (Cambridge: Cambridge University Press, 1990).

48. This remains a source of conflict. See M. Athar Ali, "The Passing Empire: The Mughal Case," *Modern Asian Studies* 9 (1975): 385–96; Ali, "Some Recent

Theories of Eighteenth Century India," *Indian Historical Review* (1989): 102–10; C. A. Bayly, *Indian Society and the Making of the British Empire* (Cambridge: Cambridge University Press, 1990); Naff and Owen, eds., *Studies in 18th-Century Islamic History*. For an analysis of the issue from a sociological perspective, see Andrea Hintze, *The Mughal Empire and Its Decline: An Interpretation of the Sources of Social Power* (Aldershot: Ashgate Publishing, 1997); P. J. Marshall, "Reappraisals: The Rise of British Power in Eighteenth-Century India," *South Asia* 19, 1 (1996).

49. André G. Frank, *Reorient Global Economy in the Asian Age* (Boulder: Nett Library, 1999); Frank, *Asian Age: Reorient Historiography and Social Theory* (Amsterdam: Center for Asian Studies, 1998). See also David Landes, *The Wealth and Poverty of Nations: Why Some Are So Rich and Some So Poor* (New York: W. W. Norton, 1998).

50. Niels Steensgaard, "Carracks, Caravans and Companies: The Structural Crisis in the European-Asian Trade in the Early 17th Century," *Scandinavian Institute for Asian Studies*, Monograph series 17 (1973).

51. J. S. Grewal, *The Sikhs of the Punjab* (Cambridge: Cambridge University Press, 1998); Afaf Lutfi al-Sayyid Marsot, *Egypt in the Reign of Muhammad Ali* (Cambridge: Cambridge University Press, 1984).

52. See Engin Akarlı's paper in this volume.

1 Trade and Port Cities in the Red Sea– Gulf of Aden Region in the Sixteenth and Seventeenth Century

Michel Tuchscherer

A favored trade route between the regions surrounding the Mediterranean and the Indian Ocean, the Red Sea–Gulf of Aden area permitted contact between Mediterranean and Asiatic networks onto which regional and local networks were grafted. Port cities developed where these various networks came together as a result of both regional and more distant changes. Here I propose to analyze the elements that made the coherence of this area possible, as well the functions provided by the port cities, and then provide a chronology for this region's evolution in the sixteenth and seventeenth centuries.

The Diverse Function of Port Cities over Time

The area comprising the Red Sea and the Gulf of Aden and their hinterlands forms a coherent environment organized around two complementary waterways, long and narrow appendages of the Indian Ocean oriented toward the Mediterranean. This interior sea separates the African shore from the Arabian Peninsula, though the opposite shores are never far apart. It is also inhospitable to shipping, as it provides few anchorages or harbors. The littoral borders desert and is usually narrow and sparsely populated, mostly by nomads. This region is poor in men, food, and resources, and as such not well suited to the development of either ports or cities.

Behind these coastal zones so ill-suited to human activity, there are relatively well-watered mountains and fertile oases where people have settled and states whose resources are essentially agricultural have developed. Though not attuned to the sea, these political entities have not been able to live in total autarky. With their continental borders on vast desert wastes or, in the case of Ethiopia, on vast marshes, they have always been keen to maintain the outlets to the sea to ensure communication with the outside world.

This physical coherence is reinforced by a certain number of common cultural traits shared by the region's inhabitants. They almost all speak Semitic languages; they have maintained close relations since ancient times, to the north and south as well as from shore to shore; and they are marked by the three great monotheistic religions that developed near the Red Sea.

Commercial Activities

Although this region is coherent at both the physical and cultural levels, its trade displays a hierarchical pattern. At the highest level is long-distance trade, often dominated by networks of usually foreign merchants who have adopted sophisticated commercial practices. In ancient times this trade followed two routes: a sea route between the Mediterranean and the Indian Ocean south of the Red Sea and along the Arabian coast, and a land route in the north following the caravan routes in the Arabian Peninsula or the Nubian Desert. Until the nineteenth century, there was an almost continuous flow of gold and silver along this route from the Mediterranean to India and China to compensate for the consistently limited flow of goods. This trade was based on hard cash. The Ottoman dinar and Venetian ducat dominated transactions right up to the end of the sixteenth century, but during the first quarter of the seventeenth century American silver minted into Sevillian piasters or Dutch guilders also became common.

Until the middle of the nineteenth century, this long-distance route remained subject to the implacable whim of the winds — the monsoons of the Indian Ocean and Gulf of Aden, the trade winds over the Red Sea. Isthmuses and straits were a hindrance, as well. In the vicinity of Bab al-Mandab, shifting from navigation on the high seas to coastal trade generally required the transfer of merchandise to other ships. The incoming ships preferred to discharge their cargo at Shihr or Aden, and, after the second half of the sixteenth century, at Mokha, rather than to undertake the long and risky voyage on the Red Sea. Near the Sinai Peninsula, shifting from sea to land required another transfer. In the upper latitudes of the 20th and 22nd parallels, a change in the prevailing winds often imposed another transfer.

From the eleventh century under the Fatimids until the end of the fourteenth century under the Mamluks, ships unloaded their cargoes at Aydhab[1] on the African shore or sometimes at Suakin. From there, caravans carried the merchandise to the Nile Valley and then down the Nile River by felouque to Cairo, where it was carried by ship again to the ports of the Mediterranean.

When Jiddah later secured control of most of the trade,[2] two different routes were possible. Ships carried merchandise by sea up to the tip of Sinai, where it was brought ashore at Tur[3] and transported to Cairo by caravan. This avoided risking the difficult journey up the Gulf of Suez against winds that were almost always contrary. The port of Qusayr was also popular for the same reasons: from there, merchandise could be brought up the Nile Valley to Cairo.[4] In the other land route, from Jiddah, caravan merchandise went across the Arabian Peninsula to either Cairo or Damascus before reaching the Mediterranean.[5]

Although large-scale commerce crossed the entire zone from the Mediterranean to the Gulf of Aden, other commercial activity developed at a lower level among different regional entities built around political units that had formed in the hinterland beyond the inhospitable desert coasts. At the beginning of the sixteenth century, the Mamluks still controlled Egypt. Ethiopia was divided into a Christian kingdom established on the high plateau and a Muslim emirate in the southeast.[6] In the Arabian Peninsula, the sharifs of Mecca controlled the Hijaz, but Cairo was under the suzerainty of the Mamluks.[7] The Yemen was divided among the Zaydite imams on the high plateau, the weakened Tahirid state in the southern part,[8] and the Kathiri sultanate consolidating in the Hadramawt.[9] These entities carried on an active bilateral trade to alleviate chronic food shortages resulting from the arid climate. In Arabia, which was largely desert, the rare oases in the north and mountains of the south with very irregular rainfall were never able to meet food needs, especially of the coastal cities that could not be nourished by the meager resources of the local hinterland. The African shore, however, was in a much better position, and the immense Nile Valley nourished the holy cities of the Hijaz, mainly through waqfs.[10] The Ethiopian steppes and high plateau also produced abundant quantities of grain and animal products for the Hijaz, as well as for the Yemen.[11] The African side could thus support the needs of the people on the opposite shore.

This regional commerce was largely run by local merchants. Products supplied by the African side were exchanged for the plentiful merchandise coming from the large-scale transit commerce from the port cities of the Arabian side. Money, which was common in the ports, yielded to barter or nonmetallic money in remote areas: peppercorns in Hadramawt,[12] salt or cloth in Ethiopia.[13]

Trade in the Red Sea–Gulf of Aden area was also stimulated by the pilgrimage routes, especially those that carried the faithful of the Muslim world to the holy sites of the Hijaz.[14] But Christians from Ethiopia and the Nile Valley also went to Jerusalem,[15] and numerous saints' tombs attracted far-flung pilgrims, such as Isma'ili Indians going to Haraz in the mountains of Yemen, and Muslims traveling to Mecca.[16] The Mecca pilgrimage, held according to the calendar of the Hegira, only rarely coincided with the arrival in Jiddah of ships from Egypt, India, or Yemen, whose movements were determined by the seasonal patterns of the winds, and so even if the coming of thousands of pilgrims to the Hijaz greatly stimulated commerce, trade was still governed by natural factors such as the monsoons of the Indian Ocean, the harvest seasons of spices in Malabar and Sumatra, the manufacture of textiles in Gujurat,[17] and, at the end of the sixteenth century, by the coffee harvest in the mountains of Yemen.

Transfer, Taxation, Distribution, and Export

Large-scale transit commerce and regional exchanges gave rise on both shores to port cities that performed specific functions. They were junction points between the caravan routes and sea lanes, or between sea routes and interior-coastal trade. Grain and animal products or dried fruits and pulses went to the inhabitants of the Arabian Peninsula; incense, gum, ivory, gold dust, horses, slaves, and madder joined the flow of merchandise crossing the Mediterranean and the Indian Ocean.[18] Some of the port cities served as markets for the local distribution of goods. Jiddah, Aden, and Mokha, in particular, lay at the intersection of multiple merchant networks.

The port cities also contributed to the financing of the state apparatus in the hinterland. Rulers would levy taxes and assorted fees on transiting merchandise, which permitted them to enforce their superiority over their subjects. The sharif of Mecca split the revenue with the pasha of Jiddah,[19] thereby managing to calm the ambitions of rival clans by granting them important subsidies. In Yemen, revenue from ports made up one-fourth of the income of the Ottoman administration at the end of the sixteenth century.[20] After the expulsion of the Turks from Yemen in 1635, the Qasimite imams derived most of the revenues needed to pay their tribal troops and mercenaries from ports, particularly Mokha.[21] The Ottomans maintained their presence on the coasts of Ethiopia by relying entirely on the revenues from Massawa and Suakin.[22]

Most port cities did not provide all these functions, however; Suez and Tur were hardly more than transshipment points, with trade and taxation taking place mostly in Cairo.[23] Jiddah was an important redistribution market and taxation point for rulers of Cairo and the sharif of Mecca, but it offered almost no production for export from its own hinterland. Zayla' was only a transit and taxation point.[24]

Cities with Transient Populations

Most port cities had very cosmopolitan but unstable populations. A motley mix of traders from the regional shores or more distant lands of the Mediterranean and Indian Ocean filled the streets, the markets, and the ports of Mokha,[25] Jiddah,[26] Massawa, and Zayla'. When the trading season came to an end, most of them returned to Egyptian or Indian cities, or the cities and towns of the hinterlands. In addition to the merchants, these ports attracted Yemeni sailors, Turkish captains, Egyptian oarsmen and masons, Bedouin caravaniers, Somali porters, Anatolian carpenters, Indian money-changers, and many others. The population of these ports varied considerably, both over the course of the year and from year to year. The cities of Qusayr and Berbera were practically deserted during the off-season: in Suez, traders and their agents would retire to Cairo during the summer, which was a slow season for sailing in the northern part of the Red Sea. The heart of the trading networks was not, therefore, in the Red Sea–Gulf of Aden area, but elsewhere, in Cairo, in Gujurat, or some other city. The Red Sea was only an extension.

There was also instability over the long run. Ports would rise, develop, and decline at the whim of political, economic, or technological changes. Aydhab probably disappeared at the end of the fourteenth century, a victim of the northward shift of the great trading routes. This not only made it possible to avoid the growing insecurity of Upper Egypt,[27] but also reinforced the monopoly of the spice trade instituted by the Mamluk sultans in the first quarter of the fifteenth century. If Mokha developed rapidly from the second half of the sixteenth century, it was because the Ottomans wanted to make it a naval base,[28] and because their governor in San'a diverted trade to the port to obtain the benefits of customs duties.[29] The prosperity of Tur, at the extreme end of the Sinai Peninsula, was short-lived; it declined in the sixteenth century as traders began to go up the Gulf to Suez without difficulty.

Crisis in the Pepper Trade and Struggle Against the Portuguese

Trade between the Mediterranean and the Indian Ocean declined abruptly at the end of the fifteenth century. By the first quarter of the next century, traffic had declined by 50 to 75 percent.[30] The trouble began in 1496 with a shortage of gold and silver, which seriously hampered trade in the eastern Mediterranean and the Red Sea.[31] This was aggravated by the arrival of the Portuguese in the Indian Ocean, where they tried to influence the flow of spices through the Red Sea.

The difficulties were not just economic. In the eastern Mediterranean, Mamluks, Ottomans, and Safavids were engaged in a life-and-death struggle that ended with the Ottoman conquest of Egypt and the development of new Muslim empires. The Mughals and Safavids were continental powers, but the Ottomans had both a powerful modern army and a powerful navy,[32] and were thus the only ones with the necessary means to combat the Portuguese in the Indian Ocean. The Ottomans helped the Mamluks construct a fleet in Suez (1504–15) and lead an expedition against the Portuguese in India. The Ottomans renewed their efforts against the Portuguese after they took Egypt in 1517, but in the end they committed relatively few resources to it.[33] Until 1529, Süleyman the Magnificent was too intent on fighting the Hapsburgs, mobilizing all the forces of the empire on the European and Mediterranean front; it was only after 1530 that his galleys turned to the southern Red Sea and the coasts of southern Arabia.

The defeat of the Ottoman fleet before Diu on October 1538 and the failure of the retaliatory Portuguese expedition in the Red Sea of 1541 created a new situation in the Indian Ocean. The Ottomans realized they did not have the means to expel the Europeans from the region, and the Portuguese were compelled to cope with the presence of the Turks in the Indian Ocean,[34] because the Ottomans were asserting their authority not only in Yemen as far as Shihr, but also in the southern part of the Gulf. The sultan's agents were reported as far away as the court of the sultan of Acheh, at the western end of Sumatra.[35] A delicate but durable balance was maintained between the Portuguese and the Ottomans.

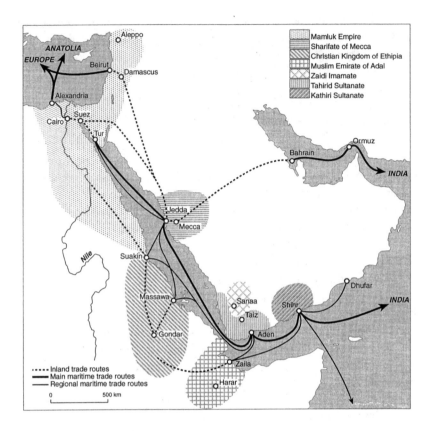

FIGURE 1.1 The Red Sea area around 1510.

The Ottoman Red Sea (1547–1626)

The conquest of San'a by the Ottomans consolidated their hold on the southern Red Sea and the Gulf of Aden. A few years later, around 1554, Mokha became the seat of a second Ottoman admiralty, after that of Suez.[36] Control of the Red Sea was completed between 1555 and 1557 with the creation of the province of Habash and the Ottoman conquest of the entire Ethiopian coast up to Bab al-Mandab.[37] The Red Sea was thus transformed into an Ottoman lake closed to any Portuguese incursion, and for the first time in its history all the coastal regions were subject to a single authority.

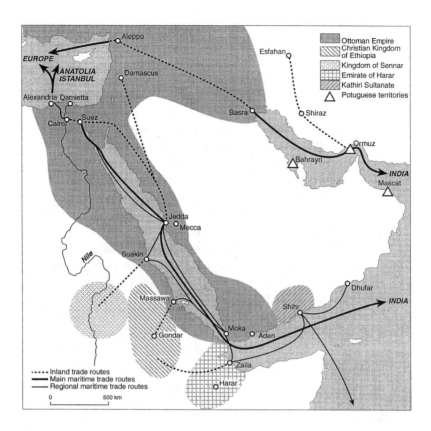

FIGURE 1.2 The Red Sea area around 1600.

The closing of the Red Sea and the establishment of a real, if precarious, balance of forces in the Indian Ocean created favorable conditions for a renewal of vigorous trade between the Mediterranean and southern Asia. According to European sources, by 1543, pepper and spices were plentiful in the Levantine ports,[38] though the revival probably took place earlier. The Portuguese had understood that they did not have the means to prevent spices from reaching the Mediterranean, but they also understood it was in their interests to allow a certain amount to make its way to the Ottomans because they did not have the means to furnish the coral, the gold dust, the copper, the gold and silver specie, the opium, the madder, or the brocades needed by India and that Indian merchants could not obtain elsewhere than at the ports of the Red Sea.[39] Nor were the Portuguese in a position to finance the administration, the garrisons, and the ships of the Estado da India other than by levying a tax on Asiatic commerce. That is why, from the middle of the sixteenth century, they multiplied the *cartazes*, or passes, granted to ships going to the Red Sea or the Gulf.[40] Finally, the Portuguese were unable to prevent the development of direct navigation from Sumatra all the way to Arabia.[41] In 1550, the amount of pepper and spices shipped through the Red Sea equaled the high point of the trade a hundred years earlier.

This revival was accompanied by a restructuring of the old networks. Near Bab al-Mandab, Mokha developed rapidly. It was an insignificant anchorage around 1520; a century later, it was a prosperous port.[42] It was a safe place, sheltered from the ever-possible Portuguese attack. It was also a market in which merchants enjoyed a great measure of autonomy in the conduct of their business. Non-Muslim communities, Indian or European, could set up there without local objection. The authorities, content with collecting taxes to finance the administration of Yemen, hardly interfered with their commercial activities. After 1570, coastal trading in the Red Sea was centered at Mokha, which brought about the decline of Aden and probably of Shihr. Most transshipments came from the Indian Ocean. Mokha also attracted regional traffic, especially with neighboring Ethiopia. When the merchants of Gujurat relocated their activities on the western side of the Indian Ocean around 1600, Mokha naturally became their base for their Red Sea trade.[43]

Mokha was in a special situation at the end of the sixteenth and beginning of the seventeenth centuries. A veritable emporium,[44] it was also the hub where various networks of the Mediterranean and the regions of the Indian Ocean met. The city was the heart of a vast transoceanic network reaching from Suez to East Africa, India, and Sumatra, involving all the ports of the Red Sea and the Gulf of Aden.[45]

At the other end of the Red Sea, Suez also grew. At first the Ottomans developed transport to bring troops, materiel, and foodstuffs to the Hijaz, Yemen, and Ethiopia, but these new facilities soon captured part of the caravan traffic as well, which had previously used routes emanating from Jiddah. Direct maritime links with Mokha also developed.[46] Every year, at least one large ship belonging to the sultan left Suez loaded with large sums of money and merchandise. At Mokha, these were exchanged for spices and drugs from South Asia, textiles from India, and porcelain from China. The development of Suez and especially Mokha was responsible for the sharp decline of Jiddah, as the sharif reported in the 1580s to the authorities in Istanbul, complaining of a substantial fall in revenues.[47]

Ottoman expansion into the Mediterranean and the Red Sea and the increase in trade traffic was of considerable benefit to Cairo.[48] The city was at the crossroads of networks that extended to the Maghreb, Anatolia, Istanbul, Rumelia, and Syria. These networks were controlled by traders native to the regions involved; they established themselves in Cairo, but in separate communities in the city.[49] Their business extended to the Red Sea, but rarely further than Mokha.

Rare indeed were the traders whose commercial operations reached as far as the Indian ports during the second half of the sixteenth century and the beginning of the seventeenth century. From then on, the Cairene network in the Indian Ocean began to lose the power it had known under the *karimi* merchants in the Middle Ages and to shrink to the benefit of Muslim India. As indicated by documents in the Cairo archives, the Ottoman governing elite—provincial governors and military officers in particular were heavily into commerce in the Red Sea as early as the last quarter of the sixteenth century. An example is Hasan Pasha, governor of Yemen in 1597, who sent from Mokha to Simon Borreo, the French consul in Alexandria, various goods (pepper, spices, indigo, muslins, and even coffee beans) for the goodly sum of 10,000 dinars.[50]

The renewal of commerce in the Red Sea, which depended for the most part on the revival of the spice trade, remained fragile and in the end ephemeral. During the second half of the sixteenth century, the Portuguese were in a position to hamper the arrival of ships in the area near southern Arabia. To this was added, from the last quarter of the sixteenth century, danger from pirates—at first Malabars, Baloutches, and Arabs,[51] and, from the second decade of the seventeenth century, Europeans. But the most important factor was the development of an alternate route, when the growing presence of the Ottomans in the northern Gulf after 1546 and the end of the wars with the Safavids in 1555 allowed trade there and siphoned off part of the traffic through the Red Sea. Aleppo, located at the end of caravan routes bringing silk from Iran, rapidly expanded during the second half of the sixteenth century.[52] The route through the Red Sea still had many advantages however, foremost of which was that it was less expensive than the Gulf.[53]

Starting in 1580, there were signs of decline in the spice trade. Ottoman merchants, especially in Cairo,[54] had difficulty obtaining pepper from Malabar and Kannara in southern India; it increasingly went to East Asia and

China instead.[55] The problem increased in the seventeenth century with the establishment of new European companies. In less than a quarter century, the Verenigde Oost-Indische Compagnie succeeded in capturing all of the pepper and spice trade for the European market. After 1625, only the domestic Ottoman market was supplied from the Red Sea and the Gulf of Aden.[56]

Meanwhile, coffee from Yemen had become an important enough commodity to compensate for the declining trade in spices. Even before the fall of the Mamluks, coffee drinking had spread from Yemen to the Hijaz and Cairo. By about 1545, coffee cultivation had been introduced into the mountains of Yemen from southern Ethiopia, perhaps by the Ottomans, but its consumption increased only slowly in the Ottoman Empire, partly because of religious proscriptions.[57] It did not become fashionable until 1570–80, when it spread through all the social classes in the principal cities of the empire, and even reached isolated hamlets in Anatolia.[58] Demand then grew rapidly, and coffee became the object of intensive trade with Yemen, at that time its almost exclusive provider. Taxes on coffee were introduced to the trade in Suez in 1573.[59] By the end of the sixteenth century, the coffee trade equaled spices and Indian textiles in importance among the Cairene merchants.[60]

The Red Sea under Ottoman Control and the Indian Ocean under Gujurati Influence (1626–1700)

The fighting between the Ottomans and the Zaydites in Yemen in 1626 led to the total withdrawal of the Ottomans from the country nine years later. After that, the Qasimite imams soon extended their domination over a vast territory from Najran to the Hadramawt, which was for the first time in its history united under a native dynasty. On the African shore, the port of Zayla' also fell under the domination of the imams of Yemen.

Despite the loss of Yemen, the Ottomans were able to stay on the Ethiopian shore, but only to serve as protectors against the West. When the new emperor Fasiladas decided to expel all the Catholic missionaries in 1632, he required the Ottomans to forbid passage through his territories to Europeans on pain of death.[61] Further north of Suez, Ottoman power was also showing signs of decline. The number of ships was shrinking, and the condition of the fleet deteriorating.[62] After the fall of Mokha, the Ottomans no longer had any authority in the southern half of the Red Sea.

Important changes also took place in the Indian Ocean. Gujurat, a part of the Mughal Empire since 1573, redirected its commercial activities to the ocean's western basin after the arrival of the Dutch and English in the region. After 1618, Gujurati traders ceased to visit Acheh,[63] but at the same time they became the principal commercial power in western India by eliminating most of their rivals, in particular those of Dabhol.[64] In a few years they made the Red Sea their major market for the ordinary cottons produced by the rapidly growing Indian textiles industry, which they traded for gold and especially the silver coins that were in great demand in the Mughal Empire after the monetary and fiscal reforms undertaken by Emperor Akbar. In their turn, the European trading companies lost no time in looking to the Red Sea. In 1618, the English East India Company established a counter in Mokha, and in 1621, the Verenigde Oost-Indische Compagnie followed. They hoped to obtain part of the specie needed to finance their Asiatic purchases of Indian printed fabrics, Javanese spices, and Chinese porcelain destined for European markets.[65]

All these changes taken together resulted in the division of the Red Sea–Gulf of Aden maritime region into two clearly defined zones. Jiddah, a mandatory stop since the Ottoman retreat from Yemen, became the point of contact. To the north, the Cairene traders tried to maintain their nearly absolute monopoly between Suez and Jiddah by relying on Ottoman authority, which remained uncontested. With a fleet of about forty ships, in part built in Suez with materials from Anatolia and in part purchased from Indian merchants[66] in Jiddah, they dominated trade between Egypt and the Hijaz. They were able to exclude Europeans from the zone behind Jiddah until 1773 on the grounds that they were too near the holy sites. They were just as intransigent toward Indian traders. In 1699, a rich Muslim merchant from Surat, Mullah Abd al-Ghafur, sent one of his ships directly to Suez; authorities, at the instigation of the Cairene merchants, discouraged him from repeating this initiative.[67]

Beyond Jiddah, the southern parts of the Red Sea and the Gulf of Aden had fallen under the domination of Gujurati merchants of Surat. Based in Mokha, they commanded a network of commercial agents, often Hindus or Jains, and compromised a commercial class known under the Sanskrit name of Banians. They could be found not only in all the port cities, but often also in the hinterland, especially in Yemen. Nonetheless, the Gujurati merchants did not enjoy hegemony in the region; they had to contend with competition from numerous Indian merchants, and especially with the thousands of Indian pilgrims who brought with them a few bales of cotton stuffs to pay their expenses for travel to the holy sites.[68] Less threatening was the competition from the European companies. Up to the end of the seventeenth century, the English and the Dutch were hardly in a position to compete with Indian merchants, whose costs could be kept low and who could also rely on highly efficient local networks. Faced with disappointing returns, the English closed their counter in 1664, followed twenty years later by the Dutch. Europeans did not return to Mokha until the end of the century, when demand for coffee in London and Amsterdam made direct purchases from Yemen profitable.

Indian merchants had to take into account regional and local networks in the hands of native merchants. During the second half of the seventeenth century, a large part of the commerce between the Red Sea and the Gulf passed through the hands of Omanis and coastal trade between the African and Arabian shores was in the hands of Yemeni sailors who used numerous small boats or *djalbas*[69] to bring coffee to Jiddah from the Yemeni ports of Hodeida and Luhayya, which grew rapidly in the seventeenth century as a result. Commerce from Massawa with the kingdom of Ethiopia seems to have been in the hands of Christian Abyssinians and Yemenis, but from Zayla' and the interior it was in the hands of Muslim Ethiopia, at least as far as the borders of the Christian kingdom.[70]

The retreat of the Ottoman fleet to the northern part of the Red Sea left the field open to pirates near the straits of Bab al-Mandab. Whether European or Omani, piracy reached such proportions that the Mughals were forced to place their ships under the protection of the Dutch fleet after 1698.

The establishment of Ottoman hegemony in virtually all the Red Sea–Gulf of Aden area and of a balance of power in the Indian Ocean allowed the vigorous recovery of commerce between the Mediterranean and Indian Ocean toward the middle of the sixteenth century. The particular geography of the Red Sea, however, mandated two emporia: to the north, Cairo asserted itself anew as the terminal for all the Mediterranean networks; to the south, Mokha underwent spectacular development at the expense of Aden and Shihr.

The military retreat of the Ottomans from Yemen had the immediate effect of shrinking the network of Cairene merchants and reinforcing the Indian, especially Gujurati, presence in the Red Sea. The decline of the pepper and spice trade after the end of the sixteenth century hardly affected commercial activity, at least in the long term, as other products took up the slack. However, the nature and the flow of goods changed. Luxury items, small in size but high in value, were replaced by heavy goods, especially coffee, but also indigo and ordinary goods such as Indian cottons, used as much by a Yemeni coffee-tree planter as by a sailor in Suez, an Ethiopian shepherd, or a Bedouin in the Sinai. A single long-distance trade flow between Asia and the Mediterranean was replaced by more limited traffic, such as Yemeni coffee to the Mediterranean or Indian textiles to the Red Sea or Egypt. Massive cash purchases at Mokha of coffee by the European companies was a harbinger of later changes. They made it more difficult to supply coffee to the Ottoman Empire, which retaliated by forbidding export from Alexandria to Europe, thus throwing into doubt the flow of specie from Europe and the Mediterranean to southern Asia and the Far East. This anticipated the decline, or at least stagnation, of commercial activity in the Red Sea.

Notes

1. Jean-Claude Garçin, *Un Centre musulman de la Haute-Egypte médiévale: Qus* (Cairo: IFAO, 1976), pp. 96–102, 135–40, 210–30, 425–35; Labib, *Handelsgeschichte Ägyptens im Spätmittelalter, 1171–1517* (Wiesbaden: Franz Steiner Verlag, 1965), pp.124–27.

2. Garçin, *Un centre musulman*, pp. 413–25; "Jean Leon l'Africain et 'Aydhab," *Annales islamologiques* 11 (1972): 189–209; Labib, *Handelsgeschischte Ägyptens im Spätmittelalter*, p. 130.

3. Ibid., p. 128; Garçin, *Un centre musulman*, p. 415.

4. Labid, *Handelsgeschichte Ägyptens im Spätmittelalter*, p. 417.

5. Halil İnalcık, with Donald Quartaert, *Economic and Social History of the Ottoman Empire 1300–1918* (Cambridge: Cambridge University Press, 1994), p. 345.

6. John Spencer Trimingham, *Islam in Ethiopia* (Oxford, 1952), pp. 82–90; Joseph Cuoq, *L'Islam en Ethiopie des origines au XVIe siècle* (Paris: Nouvelles Editions latines, 1981), pp. 147–88.

7. Richard Mortel, *al-Ahwāl al-siyāsiyya wa-l-iqtisādiyya fi Makka* (Riyadh, 1983); "Aspects of Mamluk Relations with Jedda during the 15th Century: The Case of Tunraz al-Mu'ayyadi," *Journal of Islamic Sudies* 6, 1 (1993): 1–13.

8. R. B. Serjeant and Ronald B. Lewcock, *San'a': An Arabian Islamic City* (London, 1983), pp. 64–67.

9. Salih al-'Alawi, *Tarīkh Hadramawt* (Jiddah, 1968), vol. 2.

10. For the Mamluk period, see Heinz Halm, *Ägypten nach den mamlukischen*

Lehensregistern, vol. 1: *Oberägypten und das Fayyum*: vol. 2: *Das Delta*, Tüb-inger Atlas der Vorderen Orients, Beihefte II, Geisteswissenschaften, no. 38.1 and 38.1 (Tübingen, 1979, 1982); for the Ottoman period, see Stanford Shaw, *The Financial and Administrative Organization and Development of Ottoman Egypt 1517–1798* (Princeton, 1962), pp. 253–72; Michel Tuchscherer "Ap-provisionnement des villes saintes d'Arabie en blé d'Egypte d'après des docu-ments ottomans des années 1670," *Anatolia Moderna* 5 (1994): 79–99.

11. Emerich Van Donzel, *Foreign Relations of Ethiopia 1642–1700: Documents Relating to the Journeys of Khodja Murad*, vol. 46 (Istanbul: Dutch Institute, 1979), p. 203, n. 21; Evliya Çelebi, *Siyahatnamesi*, vol. 10: *Misr, Sudan, Habes* (Istanbul, 1938), p. 942.

12. R. B. Serjeant, *The Portuguese off the South Arabian Coast. Hadrami Chronicles* (Oxford: Clarendon Press, 1983), p. 77.

13. Van Donzel, *Foreign Relations of Ethiopia*, pp. 18, 93.

14. For routes in the Ottoman period, cf. Suraiya Faroqhi, *Pilgrims and Sultans: The Hajj under the Ottomans* (London: I. B. Tauris, 1994), pp. 32–45.

15. Cuoq, *L'Islam en Ethiopie des origines au XVIe siècle*, pp. 215–16, mentions the pillaging near Massawa of a caravan of Ethiopian pilgrims on their way to Jerusalem.

16. For this fair, see Faroqhi, *Pilgrims and Sultans*, pp. 166–70; for trade and pil-grims, see Colette Establet and Jean-Paul Pascual, *Ultime voyage pour la Mecque: Les inventaires après décès de pèlerins morts à Damas vers 1700* (Da-mascus: IFEA, 1998), pp. 148–62.

17. Ashin Das Gupta, *Indian Merchants and the Decline of Surat c. 1700–1750* (Wiesbaden: Franz Steiner Verlag, 1979), pp. 68–69.

18. Vittorino Magalhaes-Godinho, *L'économie de l'Empire portugais aux XVe et XVIe siècles* (Paris: SEVPEN, 1969), pp. 309–12, 758–59.

19. Faroqhi, *Pilgrims and Sultans*, pp. 200–1; Inalcik and Quartaert, *Economic and Social History of the Ottoman Empire*, p. 333.

20. Ibid., pp. 85, 335.

21. Carsten Niebuhr, *Description de l'Arabie* (Paris: Brunet, 1779), 2: 37–44.

22. Van Donzel, *Foreign Relations of Ethiopia*, pp. 101–3.

23. Shaw, *Organization and Development of Ottoman Egypt*, pp. 104–5.

24. Van Dozel, *Foreign Relations of Ethiopia*, pp. 101–3.

25. C. G. Brouwer, *Al-Mukha, Profile of a Yemeni Seaport* (1997), pp. 201–55.

26. Evliya Çelebi, *Siyahatname*, vol. 9: *Anadolu, Suriye, Hicaz* (1671–1672) (Is-tanbul, 1935), pp. 795–97.

27. Jean-Claude Garçin, "La Mediterranéisation de l'Empire mamelouk sous les Sultans bahrides," *Rivista degli Studi Orientali* 48 (1974): 112–16; "Transport des épices et espace égyptien entre le XIe et le XVe siècle," *Annales de Bretagne* 85/2 (1978): 311–12.

28. Salih Özbaran, "Osmanlı Imparatorluğu ve Hindistan Yolu," in *Tarih Dergisi* 31 (1977): 138.

29. Faroqhi, *Pilgrims and Sultans*, p. 162.

30. Magalhaes-Godinho, *L'économie de l'Empire portugais aux XVe et XVIe siècles*, pp. 725–26.

31. Ibid., p. 717; Labib, *Handelsgeschichte Ägyptens im Spätmittelalter*, p. 476.

32. Palmira Brumett, *Ottoman Seapower and Levantine Diplomacy in the Age of Discovery* (New York: New York University Press, 1994), pp. 21–22.

33. İnalcık and Quataert, *Economic and Social History of the Ottoman Empire*, pp. 319–27.

34. Magalhaes-Godinho, *L'économie de l'Empire portugais aux XVe et XVIe siècles*, pp. 770–72; Salih Özbaran, *The Ottoman Response to European Expansion: Studies on the Ottoman-Portuguese Relations in the Indian Ocean and Ottoman Administration in the Arab Lands during the 16th Century* (Istanbul: Isis, 1994), p. 67, no. 119.

35. Anthony Reid, "Sixteenth-Century Turkish Influence in Western Indonesia," *Journal of Southern Asian History* 10, 3 (1969): 395–414.

36. Özbaran, "Osmanlı Imparatoluğu ve Hindistan Yolu," p. 138.

37. Cenghiz Orhonlu, *Osmanlı Imparatoluğu güny siyaseti. Habeş eyaleti* (Istanbul: Edebiyat Fakultesi, 1974), pp. 31–42.

38. Özbaran, "Osmanlı Imparatoluğu ve Hindistan Yolu," pp. 103, 133; Fernand Braudel, *La Méditerranée et le monde méditerranéen à l'époque de Philippe II* (Paris: Armand Colin, 1985), pp. 495–98.

39. Megalhaes-Godinho, *L'Economie de l'Empire portugais aux XVe et XVIe siècles*, p. 758.

40. Niels Steensgaard, *The Asian Trade Revolution of the Seventeenth Century: The East India Companies and the Decline of the Caravan Trade* (Chicago: Chicago University Press, 1974), pp. 87–91.

41. Boxer, "A Note on Portuguese Reactions to the Revival of the Red Sea Spice Trade and the Rise of Acheh, 1540–1600," *Journal of South East Asian History* 10 (December 1969): 415–28; Ashin Das Gupta, "Changing Faces of the Maritime Merchant," in *Emporia, Commodities, and Entrepreneurs in Asian Maritime Trade*, c. 1400–1750, ed. Roderich Ptack and Dietmar Rothermund (Stuttgart: Franz Steiner Verlag, 1991), pp. 357–58.

42. Brouwer, *Al-Mukha, Profile of a Yemeni Seaport*, pp. 25–44.

43. Ashin Das Gupta, "Indian Merchants and the Trade in the Indian Ocean, c. 1500–1750," in *Cambridge Economic History of India* (1981), pp. 416–17.

44. Ptak and Rothermund, *Emporia, Commodities, and Entrepreneurs in Asian Maritime Trade, c. 1400–1750*, p. 3.

45. C. G. Brouwer, "Non-Western Shipping Movements in the Red Sea and Gulf of Aden during the Second and Third Decades of the 17th Century According

the Records of the Dutch East India Company," *Die Welt des Islams* 32, 2 (1992): 7–16.

46. C. G. Brouwer and A. Kaplanian, *Early Seventeenth-Century Yemen: Dutch Documents Relating to the Economic History of Southern Arabia, 1614–1630* [in Arabic] (Leiden: E. J. Brill, 1988), p. 136.

47. Faroqhi, *Pilgrims and Sultans: The Hajj under the Ottomans*, pp. 162–64.

48. Nelly Hanna, *Making Big Money in 1600: The Life and Times of Isma'il Abu Taqiyya, Egyptian Merchant* (Syracuse: Syracuse University Press, 1998), pp. 73–75.

49. André Raymond, *Artisans et commerçants au Caire au XVIIIe siècle*, 2 vols. (Damascus: IFEA, 1974), 1:464–80.

50. Mahkama Salihiyya Najmiyya, register 474, document 330, 7 Dhu'l-qa'da 1005/22 June 1597, p. 92.

51. Özbaran, *Ottoman Response to European Expansion*, pp. 139–40.

52. André Raymond, "Alep à l'époque ottomane (*XVIe–XIXe siècle*)," *Revue du Monde musulman et de la Méditerranée* 62 (1991): 94–98.

53. Steensgaard, *Asian Trade Revolution of the Seventeenth Century*, pp. 39–40.

54. Nelly Hanna, "Coffee and Coffee Merchants in Cairo 1580–1630," in *Le Café avant l'ère des plantations coloniales: espaces, réseaux, sociétés (XVe–XVIIIe siècle)* (Cairo: IFAO, 2001), pp. 91–102.

55. Magalhaes-Godinho, *L'économie de l'Empire portugais aux XVe et XVIe siècle*, p. 777.

56. Braudel, *La Méditerranée et le monde méditerranéen à l'époque de Philippe II*, 1:510.

57. Ralph Hattox, *Coffee and Coffeehouses* (Seattle: University of Washington Press, 1985), pp. 29–45.

58. Suraiya Faroqhi, "Coffee and Spices: Official Ottoman Reaction to Egyptian Trade in the Later Sixteenth Century," *Wiener Zeitschrift für die Kunde des Morgenlands* 76 (1986): 89.

59. Ibid., p. 92.

60. Michel Tuchscherer, "Production et commerce du café en Mer Rouge au XVIe siècle," in *Le Café avant l'ère des plantations coloniales: espaces, réseaux, sociétés (XVe–XVIIIe siècle)* (Cairo: IFAO, 2001), pp. 69–90.

61. Donzel, *Foreign Relations of Ethiopia 1642–1700*, p. 1.

62. Shaw, *Financial and Administrative Organization and Development of Ottoman Egypt*, p. 262.

63. Das Gupta, "Indian Merchants and the Trade in the Indian Ocean," p. 431.

64. Ashin Das Gupta, "Indian Merchants and the Western Indian Ocean: The Early 17th Century," *Modern Asian Studies* 19 (1985): 496–99.

65. Hans van Santen, Das Verenigde Oost Indische Compagnie in Gujurat en Hindustan 1620–1660," Ph.D. diss., University of Leiden, 1982, pp. 49–76.

66. Tuchscherer, "Approvisionnement des villes saintes," pp. 79–99; "La flotte impériale de Suez de 1694 à 1719," *Turcica* 29 (1997): 47–69.

67. Das Gupta, *Indian Merchants and Decline of Surat*, p. 70.

68. Hans van Santen, "Trade between Mughal India and the Middle East, and Mughal Monetary Policy, c. 1600–1660," in *Asian Trade Routes, Continental and Maritime*, ed. Karl Haellquist (London: Curzon Press, 1991), p. 90.

69. Donzel, *Foreign Relations of Ethiopia 1642–1700*, pp. 54–60.

70. Ibid., pp. 70–71.

2 A Divided Sea: The Cairo Coffee Trade in the Red Sea Area during the Seventeenth and Eighteenth Centuries

André Raymond

We can find information about the important merchants (*tuggâr*) of coffee and spices in probate documents preserved in the archives of both the military ('*askariyya*) and civilian ('*arabiyya*) tribunal (*mahkama*) of the Bab al-'Ali in Cairo. The best information comes from the former source, as virtually all the *tuggâr* were affiliated with an ojaq beginning around the year 1650. Fifteen of these *tuggâr* successions date from the years 1624–33; 283 more date from 1661–1798. These two groups form the basis of this study.[1]

These documents give a clear picture of the wealth and influence of the merchants who dealt in Yemeni coffee, a trade that was at its zenith in the last decades of the seventeenth century and the first decades of the eighteenth.[2] For the 80 *tuggâr* studied in the first period (1679–1700), the total of their combined estates amounted to 41.7 million "constant" paras, as against a total of 64.7 million paras for 468 artisans and merchants.[3] In the period 1776–98, a time when the coffee trade had started to decline, 28 coffee *tuggâr* (accounting for 4.9 percent of the total of 567 estates studied in this period) left estates amounting to 24.6 million paras.

Sixty-two caravanserais (out of the 360 then existing in Cairo) carried out the coffee trade in Cairo; coffee represented a third of Egypt's foreign commerce, thus making it the single most important economic activity in the country. Some of the 100,000 hundredweight of coffee imported annually from Yemen to Cairo was reexported to countries in the Ottoman Empire and Europe. The 500 *tuggâr* involved in the business consisted largely of

North Africans, Turks, and Syrians (30 out of the 80, and 15 of the 28 in the two periods studied), which demonstrates the international nature of the business.[4]

One of the characteristics of the coffee trade was that the trading area for the Cairo *tuggâr* was limited to the Hijaz southward—a line of demarcation that also formed the northern frontier for traders from the Yemen and India. This clear geographic boundary dividing the Red Sea into two distinct commercial zones is the subject of the following analysis, based on the *mahkama* documentation and backed by other evidence, notably observations from consuls and Western travelers.

The Delimitation of Cairo *Tuggâr* Business Activities

There is an enormous contrast between the accepted limits on area of trade of the Cairo *tuggârs* during the Ottoman era and the far-flung

FIGURE 2.1 Wakala (Caravansarai) of Dhulfiqar Kathuda (1673): The main center for coffee trade in Cairo. From Pascal Coste, *Architecture arab, ou Monuments du Kaire, mesures et dessins, de 1818 à 1826* (Paris, 1839).

commerce of the great traders (*kârimî*) of Mamluk times, whose activities stretched to India and Southeast Asia.[5] The situation is even more striking when one considers the importance of the coffee business to the economy of Ottoman Egypt. This demarcation has inevitably been interpreted as a consequence of the great discoveries that opened up to the Europeans an area which had hitherto been monopolized by eastern shipping and trade and aggravated by the Ottoman conquest, whose effects were to add to the economic decline of the final Mamluk century. Nevertheless, it is not clear how the restriction to the south of the Hijaz developed or the time it took to develop.

In her work on the great Cairene merchant Isma'il Abu Taqiyya, who was commercially active between 1590 and 1624, Nelly Hanna suggests that many of the characteristic features of the commercial dynamism of the kârimî were still noticeable among the great Cairo traders at the beginning of the seventeenth century. Contemporary foreign accounts confirm this view. During his stay in Mokha in 1611, Henry Middleton witnessed a large caravan of merchants from Suez, Damascus, and Mecca coming to trade with Indian merchants. In his work on Mokha, C. G. Brouwer mentions the presence of Egyptians in the port between 1614 and 1640. However, relations between Mokha and Egypt seemed to be breaking down: the German traveler Albert Schelling arrived in Mokha in the spring of 1623 to wait for a Suez boat to take him to Egypt, but by 2 September, Schelling still had had no success; he gave up and returned to Surat. The shipping figures give the same picture: according to Brouwer, between 1614 and 1640, out of the 256–279 boats docking in Mokha, only 11 came from the Red Sea and Aden, compared with 155–169 originating in the West Indies.

The line of demarcation that governed the Cairene *tuggâr* trade in the Red Sea began only about 1650. An analysis of the *tuggâr* successions does not contradict this chronology, but a study of the period 1620–60 is needed to confirm it.[6]

Useful clues are provided by a study of the cases of *tuggâr* who died while on journeys—not an altogether unusual occurrence as 31 of the 298 probate papers examined fell into this category.[7] Of this group of 31, very few had gone south of the Hijaz: three had died in South Arabia, 11 on the pilgrimage road, 14 in the Hijaz (one in Yanbu, five in Mecca, four in Jiddah), and three had drowned at sea. That the vast majority of these *tuggâr* (25 of 31) had died on pilgrimage or in one of the holy towns involved in it, suggests that the hajj was useful for commercial as well as religious ends (fig 2.2).

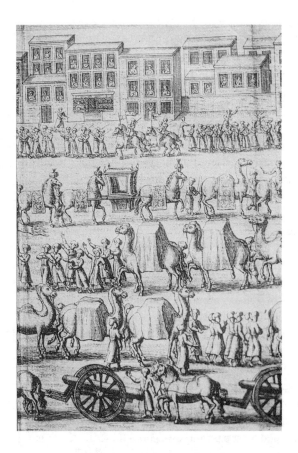

FIGURE 2.2 Hajj (pilgrimage) caravan in Cairo. From Paul Lucas, *Voyage du Sieur Paul Lucas au Levant* (the Hague, 1705).

There are only three cases of *tuggâr* dying further south than Mecca. In 1626, Khalil Basha died in the town of Muscat, leaving behind in the Khan al-Hanna (Khan al-Khalili, in Cairo) 74.5 *qintâr* of coffee, with a (relatively modest) total estate of 50,794 paras. In 1685, Ahmad al-Sharib died in Luhayya in the Yemen. His estate—composed mostly of coffee bonded in warehouses in Jiddah (118 loads) and in Luhayya (192)—amounted to the considerable sum of 1,023,750 paras. Finally, in 1700, Hajj 'Ali al-Ghazzi died in the Yemen, leaving his wife and daughter, who lived in Ghazza, a small amount of coffee and incense from the Hijaz warehoused in the Wakala al-Bahar in the Bunduqaniyyin quarter in Cairo; its total worth came to 26,006 paras.[8] These three cases date from 1626–1700. After 1700, no reports mention any *tâgir* dying outside the area between Suez and the Hijaz. Although the sample is admittedly small, it still seems to confirm progressively more limited travel by the Cairo *tuggâr*.

One can draw the same conclusion from indications emerging from our sample on the activities of the coffee merchants. Of the 67 cases where the origins of the coffee are mentioned in the probate documentation, in 62 the coffee came from the Hijaz (one from Yanbu, 25 from Jiddah, two from Mecca, the other 34 unspecified); one came from Luhayya, and four from Qusayr. As these figures show, Qusayr played a minor part in Red Sea commerce; purchasing direct from the Yemen was even less common—the only recorded case took place in 1685. The coffee trade passed almost exclusively through the Hijaz, principally via Jiddah, and mainly by sea; the overland pilgrimage route was of only secondary importance.

It is not surprising, then, that references to remittances (*irsâliyya*) sent to the Yemen for purchases of coffee and other oriental merchandise are extremely rare in our documentation. We have so far turned up only two examples. In 1688, when the estate of Khawaja Ahmad b. Hasan al-Wafa'i (who dealt in sugar and coffee) was wound up, he had funds in the Yemen and Jiddah totaling 125,000 paras. A 1692 document relating to the affairs of Hasan al-Baqi al-Bursali, a Turkish merchant, lists coffee, gum lac (*lukk*), and fabric worth 149,184 paras on an inventory of possessions in Mecca, and also a sum of 6,000 riyals (348,000 paras) in the Yemen—a considerable amount, presumably destined for the purchase of goods there. But here again it is worth noting that these two documents date from the end of the seventeenth century.[9]

The virtual nonexistence of direct commercial relations between Cairo traders and the Yemen can also be inferred from the absence of any reference to *tuggâr* agents (*wakîl*) in the ports or markets of the Yemen in the eighteenth century. There are many references to such agents in the Hijaz: 16 cases between 1673 and 1753. Fifteen of these cases concern Jiddah, which acted as the main commercial center for the Cairo *tuggâr* in the Hijaz; there was also one case in Yanbu. By contrast, I found no documentation indicating that the *tuggâr* were represented in any of the main coffee trade centers (even Bayt al-Faqih), nor in its main ports of embarkation (Luhayya, Mokha). That no evidence has been uncovered, of course, does not prove the absolute absence of relations, but it does indicate their exceptional nature, especially in the light of the closeness of the business ties between Cairo and the Hijaz.

References to the presence of Cairenes in Yemeni ports by European travelers such as that made by Niebuhr in 1762 regarding Luhayya doubtless reflect a fairly rare occurrence, and it could be one of those stereotypes they customarily believed. A *fortiori*, the archives show no trace of permanent installations of merchants with their families in the Yemen, as was so often the case in the Hijaz, where residing locally not only made sound economic sense, but also afforded the added benefit of proximity to the holy places of Islam.[10] 'Ali al-Ghamrawi, who died around 1685, had lodgings in Cairo in a depot (*hâsil*) of the Wakala Murgan 'Arab, but his wife, children, and father lived in Mecca; the wife and three sons of Hajj Ahmad al-Karim, who died in 1715, lived in Jiddah.[11] The absence of such information for the towns and ports of the Yemen confirm that this area was outside the normal sphere of commercial activity for the Cairo *tuggâr*.

The Absence of Eastern Muslims in Cairo

The almost total confinement of Egyptian business interests to within the northern part of the Red Sea up to and including the region of the holy places was logically complemented by the virtual absence in Egypt of Arabs and Muslims from the southern regions of Arabia and the eastern areas of the *ummah* (Mesopotamia, Iran). This is especially striking because Turkish, Syrian, and North African traders were both numerous and active in the commerce of Cairo (as shown in the statistics I provided in *Artisans et Commerçants*); the world of the ulama was characterized by its universality: al-Azhar had a *riwâq* for the Kurds, Iraqis (Baghdâdiyyîn), Indians (Hanâdwah), and the people of southern Arabia (al-Yamaniyya).[12]

The absence of Yemeni traders in Cairo can be explained by the division of the Red Sea into trading spheres and by the marked desire on the part of the Egyptian merchants to exclude from Cairo competition coming from a region where they themselves did not go. More remarkable, perhaps, from this point of view, is the very small number of references to merchants coming from the Hijaz in the *mahkama* documents I studied. I could only find four traders who might have come from this region; this is merely an assumption[13] in the case of Muhammad al-Makkî, a *tâgir* in the Khan al-Khalili, who died about 1631, leaving a modest estate of 34,747 paras, or of

Ahmad al-Makkî, *tâgir* in the Wakala al-Khurnub of Bulaq, whose estate amounted to 646,924 paras in 1686. It is certain in the case of al-Hajj 'Abd al-Karim b. 'Umar, referred to as "an inhabitant of Yanbu" (*min ahâlî bandar Yanbu'*), where he had a wife and four children. His estate (26,619 paras) was settled in 1721; it consisted of diverse merchandise—flour, beans, and biscuit (*buqsumât*)—in Suez, destined to be shipped to Yanbu. We do not know which products he actually brought with him to Cairo. But we do know that Hajj Gawhar b. 'Abdallah al-Asmar, an emancipated slave of Husayn al-Makki and resident of Jiddah, was a coffee trader, living perhaps at the Wakala Dhu' l-fiqar Katkhuda (which was to be the usual lodging place for people from the Yemen and the Hadramawt in the nineteenth century). In 1766, he left an estate worth 167,164 paras.[14] This is without question a very small group, especially when compared with the 54 North Africans, 34 Turks, and 23 Syrians to be found in the corpus of the 298 *tuggâr* documents studied. In this same corpus, there was only one Baghdadi.

The limited presence of Indian traders is no less surprising in the light of the considerable role played by the "Banians" in the commercial marketplaces in the southern regions of the Red Sea. Things were perhaps different at the beginning of the seventeenth century. De Stochove writes (in 1631) that Indians used to visit Egypt via the Red Sea but that "they no longer dare come because of the Pashas who often seized their ships and cargo, and imprisoned them." This same traveler claimed to have seen at Tore (Tûr) three or four great galleons "which go once a year to the Indies." He described them as "badly built" but very large (1,000–1,200 tons).[15] In the eighteenth century such cases are very rare indeed. In 1712, Muhammad b. 'Ali "al-Hindi" left an estate worth 147,098 paras, made up, for the most part, of 122 *qintâr* of coffee. The estate of al-Hajj Hasan al-Hindî in 1716, amounting to 1,193,676 paras, was comprised of coffee (235,950 paras) and Indian cloth (784,180 paras).[16] Significantly, the merchandise was in Jiddah at the finalization of the succession, and had certainly been bought in that market, where the associates of al-Hajj Hasan operated. It would appear, then, that it was by no means a transaction effected directly between the Yemen and India, where the goods had originated.

Visits by dealers from such faraway places were so exceptional that the sources commented on when they occurred. In 1698, an Indian ship arrived in Suez, and was noted in an account by the French consul De Maillet; an account in almost identical terms appears in the chronicle of Ahmad Chelebi. Both writers were struck by the exceptional nature of the event. The boat belonged to a great Hindu trader (*khawâjâ*), 'Abd al-Ghafurj, who owned a fleet of 17 boats. Selling this cargo must have proved difficult; it took a year, which would seem somewhat at odds with De Maillet's comments on the positive reception the ship received in Cairo and the encouragement given for another voyage. Das Gupta is of the opinion that the arrival of the ship "endangered the lucrative monopoly the Cairenes held over the Jiddah-Suez route" and that a heavy tax levied on his merchandise in Jiddah the following year "dissuaded him from renewing efforts at further business in Suez"—a very probable conclusion. Whatever the case, there is no evidence of such attempts in later years.[17]

The Division of the Red Sea

The *mahkama* documents show clearly that after 1650, the Red Sea was strictly divided up into a northern sector reserved for Egyptian navigation (about 40 vessels at the turn of the century) and a southern sector where small Yemeni craft sailed, along with Hindu and Western ships. The dividing line between the two zones was at Jiddah, where in 1762 Niebuhr saw "richly charged" boats arriving from Suez and the Indies—some of them English ships—and witnessed the arrival of merchandise from Europe, in addition to Egyptian products, Yemeni coffee, and cloth and spices from the Indies.[18]

The Muslim pilgrimage to the holy places explains the links between Egypt and the Hijaz. Egypt's traditional control over the Mecca/Medina area had been strengthened by the Ottomans, who promoted the legitimacy of their sovereignty by emphasizing the interest and care they took over the pilgrimage and its organization. They had delegated to the Egyptian pashas the main responsibility for the organization and protection of the hajj caravan, together with the supply of essential provisions to the holy places (in particular 100,000 hundredweight of grain), which were transported by sea.[19]

Virtually all the trade in coffee—the bulkiest product traded—was conveyed by sea because of its volume, and also because of the discrepancies among the religious calendar (lunar months and the 13-day short year) that ruled the pilgrimage, the agricultural calendar (the date of the coffee harvest), and the maritime calendar (which determined the seasons when winds were most favorable to navigation and traffic flow in both directions).

After a period of trying to occupy the Yemen on a more permanent basis, in 1635, the Ottomans gave up their hold on this distant possession just as the coffee market began a boom that was to last a hundred years. Well established in the Hijaz, the Ottomans resigned themselves to sharing the Red Sea both politically and militarily, because their main objective was to remain firmly in control of the pilgrimage. It is probably for that reason as well that the right to navigate on that side of Jiddah was reserved to the Egyptians. The prohibition of entry by foreign vessels was confirmed in a decree from the Turkish government in 1774, and Parsons, a traveler in the area in 1778, wrote that "the ships belonging to Suez have an exclusive right to the trade, as no ship from Mocha, Muscat or India is allowed to enter any port in the Red Sea beyond Jedda, on pain of confiscation." The Turks were active in protecting the major Red Sea routes, as Michel Tuchscherer has noted.[20]

Such a system was illogical, however, and led to serious inconvenience. In Jiddah, coffee had to be transferred either to other ships or, in the case of no more than 10 percent of the tonnage, hauled overland by caravan. It would clearly have been easier for the Egyptian ships to continue their routes in a region where navigation conditions were the same as they were from Suez to Jiddah. Breaking a voyage in Jiddah meant delay and extra cost.

But it also had its advantages, which explains why the concerned parties made certain the system was not changed for a century and a half. First, it ensured the equilibrium of traffic between Suez and Jiddah in both directions: from Suez to Jiddah boats carried 100,000 hundredweight of grain, and from Jiddah to Suez, the same weight in coffee. Egyptian trade between Suez and Jiddah benefited from Ottoman protection, which was particularly vigilant in a region of such political and religious significance. The pilgrim caravans were subject to frequent Bedouin attacks, but travel by sea was much less risky. By not continuing south from Jiddah, the Muslims who traded with the holy cities could avoid contact with the numerous Europeans and Banians whose presence in the ports of Yemen was often a source of difficulty. Niebuhr, who estimated the number of the Banians at 600–700 in Mokha and 120 at Bayt al-Faqih, remarked that they were "bothered" in the Yemen where they were despised and considered to be infidels. He notes that they were forbidden to cremate their dead or to have their wives accompany them; he further states that they were not found in any of the regions under Turkish rule, such as Baghdad, Jiddah, or Suez.[21] The cosmopolitanism of places like Bayt al-Faqih and Mokha would certainly have made the Muslim merchants of Cairo uncomfortable. Finally they perhaps preferred a monopoly that allowed them to make a good profit in a limited part of the

Red Sea to a more open market where greater competition might have affected their position, as in the Mediterranean where Western navigation overwhelmingly predominated.

The division of the Red Sea trade that left the Egyptians with exclusive control over the northern part satisfied all parties concerned—the Ottoman government, the pashas of Cairo, and the Janissary officers. With this strong support the Cairo *tuggâr* vigorously defended the monopoly that afforded them so many advantages at the price of limiting their commercial horizons. This demarcation was not called into question until the eighteenth century, when the Europeans decided to try and gain free access for their shipping as far as Suez, first, to cast a wider commercial net in the direction of Egypt and, second, to further their strategic interest in establishing as direct a connection as possible with India. Their attempts at breaking the monopoly did not begin to bear fruit until much later, with draft treaties for opening navigation routes to Suez to the English (1775, 1794) and French (1785).[22] The explanation for this change in attitude in Egypt and the relative success of these attempts can be explained in part by the predominance of the Mamluk beys who were beginning to define an autonomous external policy; by the complete collapse of the Janissary *ojaq*—the traditional protectors of the Cairo *tuggâr* (and themselves active participants in the trade with the East); and certainly by the weakening in the importance of the coffee *tuggâr*, due to the crisis that began in the 1760s. The inroads made by Christian Syrians into the Egyptian economy also played a part. But in the end, all these projects came to naught, mainly because the Ottoman government remained firmly opposed to opening up the Red Sea to Western influence, the dangers of which they both understood and feared. This opposition led the interested European governments to dampen the enthusiasm shown by their consuls for concluding treaties with the Egyptian beys. The prevailing anarchy in Egypt was also hardly conducive to allowing the Mamluks to engage in such a radical new policy that was strongly opposed by the population and that would had been difficult to enforce. In 1779, the Bedouins seized the cargoes of Danish ships carrying English merchandise. It can be assumed that the expedition launched by the Ottoman government against the Egyptian beys in 1786 was also a response to their recent initiatives in this area, which probably met with severe criticism in Istanbul.

In 1798, the situation still had not changed, and the Red Sea remained a divided sea, closed in its northern part to international shipping. It was not until Bonaparte's expedition in 1798, followed after 1805 by the opening up

of Egypt by Muhammad 'Ali, that the lock the Ottomans had kept bolted
for nearly three centuries was finally broken for good.

Notes

1. See André Raymond, *Artisans et commerçants au Caire*, 2 vols. (Damascus: Institut français de Damas, 1974), xxii–xxiv; reprinted in Cairo, IFAO, 1999.

2. On Yemen coffee and its trade, Raymond, *Artisans et commerçants*; Raymond "Les problèmes du café en Egypte au XVIIIème siècle," in *Le café en Méditerranée*, ed. J.-L. Miège (Aix: CNRS, 1981), pp. 31–71; Raymond, *Le Caire des Janissaires* (Paris: CNRS, 1995). Michel Tuchscherer, "Le commerce en mer Rouge aux alentours de 1700," *Res Orientales* 5 (1993): pp. 159–78; Nelly Hanna, *Making Big Money in 1600* (Syracuse, N.Y.: Syracuse University Press, 1998).

3. The para was a small silver coin which was used in daily transactions. In *Artisans et commerçants*, I determined a "constant" para with a value calculated for the years 1681–88. It is in these "constant" paras that the amounts involved in the estates are rendered.

4. On the Turkish traders, see Michel Tuchscherer, "Activités des Turcs dans le commerce de la mer Rouge au XVIIIème siècle," in *Les villes dans l'empire ottoman*, ed. D. Panzac (Paris: CNRS, 1991), pp. 321–64.

5. On the Karimi merchants, see the classical studies of W. Fischel, S. Labib, G. Wiet, E. Ashtor, and S.-D. Goitein.

6. Hanna, *Making Big Money*, passim; Carsten Niebuhr, *Description de l'Arabie*, 2 vols. (Paris, 1779), 2:127; C. G. Brouwer, *al-Mukhâ* (Amsterdam, 1997), pp. 46, 48, 205, 357.

7. In their recent book, *Ultime voyage pour la Mecque* (Damascus: Institut Français de Damas, 1998), Colette Establet and Jean-Paul Pascual found 135 inventories of pilgrims who had died on the *hajj* in a corpus of 628 probate inventories dating from between 1686 and 1717.

8. Archives of the Mahkama, Cairo, Bâb al-Âlî, *qisma 'askariyya*, vol. 28, p. 366, 1 March 1626; vol. 78, p. 222, 15 August 1685; *qisma 'arabiyya*, vol. 73, p. 57, 3 August 1700.

9. Mahkama, *qisma 'askariyya*, vol. 81, p. 181, 26 February 1688; vol. 86, p. 73, 23 November 1692.

10. M. Tuchscherer remarks that 11 out of the 56 Turks he studied (20 percent) were more or less permanently established in the Hijaz ("Activités des Turcs"); see also C. Niebuhr, *Voyage en Arabie*, 2 vols. (Amsterdam, 1776), 1: 236.

11. Mahkama, *qisma 'askariyya*, vol. 78, p. 191, 19 May 1685; vol. 106, p. 402, 6 February 1715.

12. See Raymond, *Artisans et commerçants*, 1:283–87; J. Heyworth-Dunne, *Introduction to the History of Education in Modern Egypt* (London, 1938), pp. 25–26.

13. The geographic *nisba* gives only a presumption of origin because it can be inherited.

14. Mahkama, *qisma 'arabiyya*, vol. 32, p. 149, 6 December 1631; vol. 63, p. 203, 26 March 1686; *qisma 'askariyya*, vol. 118, p. 575, 6 August 1721; vol. 178, p. 63, 25 February 1766; A. A. Paton, *A History of the Egyptian Revolution*, 2 vols. (London, 1863), 2: 312.

15. De Stochove, *Voyage du Levant* (Brussels, 1662), pp. 418, 467.

16. The remark in n. 13 is naturally also valid for the "Hindî." Mahkama, *qisma 'askariyya*, vol. 103, p. 6, 12 November 1712; vol. 109, p. 18, 30 August 1716.

17. De Maillet, "Mémoire sur le commerce de la mer Rouge," B.N. Paris, fonds français, 9095, 139a (1698). Ahmad Chelebî, *Awdah al-Ishârât*, ed. A. A. 'Abd al-Rahîm (Cairo, 1978), p. 205; Tuchscherer, "Le commerce en mer Rouge," p. 170, quoting Das Gupta, *Indian Merchants*, p. 70.

18. Niebuhr, *Voyage en Arabie*, 1: 224. See on this problem, Tuchscherer, "Le commerce en mer Rouge."

19. This question is studied by Michel Tuchscherer, "Approvisionnement des villes saintes de l'Arabie," *Anatolia Moderna* 5 (1994): 79–99.

20. Abraham Parsons, *Travels in Asia and Africa* (London, 1808), p. 285; Daniel Crecelius, "A Late-Eighteenth-Century Austrian Attempt to Develop the Red Sea Trade Route," *Middle Eastern Studies* 30, 2 (1994): 262–80. M. Tuchscherer, "La flotte impériale de Suez," *Turcica* 29 (1997): 47–49.

21. Niebuhr, *Description*, 1: 37; *Voyage* 1: 253, 287.

22. On these (unsuccessful) attempts, see Daniel Crecelius, "Unratified Commercial Treaties between Egypt and England and France, 1773–1794," *Revue d'Historie Maghrébine* 37–38 (1985): 67–104; "A Late Eighteenth-Century Austrian Attempt"; also Raymond, *Artisans et commerçants*, 1:151–54.

3   The Red Sea Ports During the Revolution in Transportation, 1800–1914

Colette Dubois

Crisscrossing the Red Sea in a rickety boat is obviously a perilous enterprise. Joseph Kessel, a famous French writer, describes some of its perils in the following passage of *Fortune Carrée*:

> The storm had reached the dhow Ibn el-Ribèb. The dhow tipped under the wind and the waves, rolled beam aport. Mordhom and Philippe saw flashing light, feeble and distant, then a multitude of lights suspended over the water. Mordhom growled, "liner." The enormous mass passed right next to them, tranquil, sparkling, ignoring this boat pushed ahead by the storm.[1]

The description reminds us that among the innumerable dangers facing boats and their crews in the straits of Bab al-Mandab was the passenger liner, whose size and powerful engines mocked the furious elements, and the contrast is a tangible demonstration of the upheavals in transportation over the course of the nineteenth century. How did these technological changes affect the ports in the Red Sea?

In the eighteenth century, as André Raymond has shown, the Red Sea was divided into two spheres of influence: the northern part above Jiddah became the preserve of Ottoman and Egyptian sailors and merchants; the southern part was largely open to Arabs, Indians, Europeans, and Africans. By the nineteenth century, this was no longer true. The Red Sea regained the unity it had had in the sixteenth century.

In 1869, the Suez Canal eliminated the obstacle of the Isthmus of Suez. The Red Sea, hitherto half-closed at its northern end, was now connected directly to the Mediterranean, eliminating the need to transship cargoes at Suez overland, either carrying them to Cairo or Alexandria, or, after 1859, sending them by rail.

In the 1880s, the European governments took advantage of the canal, which reduced the distances between the Western ports and the East. The route to India, of primary importance to Britain, was protected in the Mediterranean by Gibraltar and Cyprus; Aden, acquired in 1839, and the Perim Islands, acquired in 1857, guarded the southern outlet of the Red Sea. Several nations were competing for colonies including the regional power of Egypt, as well as Britain, France, and Italy, and to a lesser extent and without success, Russia and Spain. This competition coincided with the appearance of steamships, which revolutionized maritime transportation, and the building of railroads, which revolutionized land transportation.[2]

Starting in the 1830s, sailing ships were used along with steamships. Fleets became still more diversified when the internal combustion engine was introduced in the first half of the twentieth century. Aden, which benefited from the naval superiority of the British as well as from traditional commercial links with India and Arabia, remained an international port and a favored stop on the Mediterranean–Indian Ocean route; it also fed regional distribution channels. Its supremacy came at the expense of regional ports. However, rather than comparing their activities, it is more important to realize that, during the nineteenth century, the function of ports had changed as a result of the revolution of transportation. It is possible to distinguish three phases.

The First Phase: 1800–1860

In the first half of the nineteenth century, the two shores of the Red Sea complemented each other. Sea routes running lengthwise down the Red Sea linked the India Ocean to the Mediterranean. Products from the Hijaz, Sudan, Ethiopia, and Somaliland were brought by caravans to international or regional depots and redistribution centers in the ports of Qusayr, Massawa, Tajura, and Zula on the African shore, and of Hodeida, Mokha, and Luhayya on the Arabian side.

Using Fernand Braudel's approach of differentiating among geographic, social, and personal time, we can characterize the period from 1800 to 1860 by the preservation of features of both geographic and social time—sailing ships and land routes depending on political and economic conditions— and by the fundamental changes caused by the Industrial Revolution, which had just begun. Among the permanent features that, according to Braudel, would be part of "immovable time," time that links man to his environment, were the geographic and climatic conditions that determined the ancient port sites.

From Suez to the Bab al-Mandab, the African shore stretched for over 2,400 kilometers. This long shoreline, virtually devoid of vegetation and water, was home to nomadic shepherds and caravans. The more clement weather of the Abyssinian plateau allowed crop cultivation. In spite of the shore's hostility at some locations, small craft could find a natural shelter, and sailors could find fresh water and food. Where there were routes to the hinterland, men created ports; where caravan routes ended, merchants stored local products and foreign goods.

Over the centuries, the ports underwent changes brought about by social time. In the seventeenth century, Mohka, stimulated by the worldwide de- mand for coffee, became an international port visited by sailing ships arriving from every direction. But in the first half of the nineteenth century, the French traveler Théophile Lefebvre, who frequented the port in 1840, ob- served that Mohka declined every day, while Jiddah progressed.[3]

There were numerous small coastal ports on both shores and the islands, but they were dominated by Jiddah.[4] Jiddah performed three functions: it was the holy port, welcoming thousands of pilgrims from all over the world, who brought products they could sell to pay their expenses. It was also the regional port of the Hijaz, importing foodstuffs (grain, sheep, butter, honey, dates, etc.), wood for construction, and finished products (textiles), and ex- porting the riches of the Arabian Peninsula as well as that of neighboring Africa (coffee, gum, slaves, ivory). Finally, it was an international port, ac- commodating two kinds of trade: sailing ships went to the Indies and to the Persian Gulf and back, thanks to the monsoon winds, carrying spices, cotton fabrics, silk, rice, and so on; others went to Qusayr to deliver Arabian, Afri- can, and Asia products and bring back foodstuffs and Egyptian and European products.

In 1837, steamships began to appear amid these fleets of sailing ships. The first steamship was owned by a British company, the Peninsular and Oriental; it was followed in 1858 by a ship from an Egyptian company. The drawback of steam over sail was that the ship had to carry its own fuel to the detriment of potential cargo, so the first generation of steamships had a very limited cargo capacity. In the 1850s, their range without refueling was from 1,000 to 1,200 kilometers. Starting in 1860, Jiddah, halfway between Suez and Aden, became a coal depot where steamers could stock up on water and fuel before continuing to India.

Jiddah was connected to Egypt by a network of Arab and Egyptian merchants and to Aden and Bombay by a network of Indians and Europeans. Jiddah became a center of international trade: between 1843 and 1875, steamships on their regular run would deposit cargo there before continuing on. Coastal shippers redistributed this supply of Indian, European, and African goods throughout the Red Sea region. They would also pick up passengers and regional products on their numerous stops. Jiddah's role as redistribution port revitalized the economy of all the coastal ports.

In the 1860s, the four most important ports along the 2,200 kilometers of the African coast were Qusayr, Suakin, Massawa, and Zula. Islands well placed at the intersection of longitudinal and transversal routes such as Dahlak also functioned as ports. From Suez to Qusayr, relations between the northern semiarid coast and Lower Egypt were hampered by the presence of a mountain barrier with only a single valley passage, at the end of which was Qusayr (latitude 27°N). Grain from Egypt was sent from there to Jiddah or to Yanbu, where it was exchanged for fabric and spices from India.

From Qusayr south, the treacherous coast offered only one favorable site, the round island of Suakin, located at the end of a bay with an excellent harbor for sailing ships.[5] In 1864, French consul Guillaume Lejean wrote:

> Suakim (latitude 19°8′N) fills an island which is almost round. One comfortable quarter. Behind the Great Mosque, around the customs plaza, we see the governor's palace, customs, the office of the Egyptian steamers and finally, the pride of Suakin, the telegraph office. The anchorage for large steamships is to the north-northeast, that of Arab boats opposite the island at the custom dock.[6]

This island had maritime links with Jiddah and with Egypt through Suez. Construction of a telegraph line to Cairo in 1864 improved communications. It was connected a few years later to the Egypt-India cable via Aden, giving traders an efficient means of communication. The port was linked by two caravan routes to the Sudanese and Abyssinian hinterlands. The first

linked Suakin to Kassala and Guadaref, where there were routes to Gallabat
on the border with Abyssinia, and to Khartoum, the capital of Egyptian
Sudan. The second went directly to Berbera on the Nile. Suakin thus became the supply point for the commerce of Nubia, of Sennar, and of Abyssinia, and a center for the redistribution of Indian and European goods.
In the 1850s, its 5,000 inhabitants traded material from Bombay for foodstuffs, via Jiddah.

Further south, not far from the Dahalak Islands, the island of Aslak and
Cape Abdel Kader formed a natural harbor, the port of Massawa, opposite
the Arabian port of Luhayya. The most direct caravan route to northern
Abyssinia left from Massawa. It was the route for slaves, ivory, gums, civet
musk, honey, hides, and grain. Massawa exported ivory to India and imported
cottons, silks, rice, sugar, and so on. Because of its position to the south of
Suakin, it had close ties with Jiddah as well as with Aden.

Both Suakin and Massawa had natural harbors that could accommodate
small boats and steamships of less than 6,000 tons without extensive improvements. The bazaars and merchant quarters were small, but once am-
icable relations were established with the coastal population, suburbs were
built on the mainland at the end of the caravan routes. Water supply remained a problem; water was expensive and brackish, which made it unsuitable for steamship boilers.

After passing through Bab al-Mandab, the next ports were Tajura, Zula,
and Berbera. Zula was located in the southern part of a bay with an opening
six leagues wide and as many deep, on an island separated from the mainland
by a narrow stretch of sea. It was surrounded by a wall. Its greatest weakness
was the lack of water. Caravans from Abyssinia and the Oromo country
brought coffee, gold, incense, and slaves, which were shipped by vessels from
Yemen, Muscat, Oman, and Jiddah.[7]

For the first half of nineteenth century, fragmentary data exist from Egyptian and Ottoman customs administrations—as well as from European consuls—that make it possible to estimate traffic. Slaves were an important part
of the trade for which Jiddah was the principal market.[8] Elimination of the
slave trade by Great Britain in 1848 did not end this commerce. Coffee,
ostrich feathers, ivory, gums and resins for perfume, wax, and hides were
also exported. Arabia imported foodstuffs (grain, animals, butter, honey, salt,
dates), wood, and leather; the African ports traded in manufactured articles
(silk, cotton, weapons and munitions) and pearls. The ports had commercial
links with continental markets, such as Bayt al-Faqih in Arabia, and Khartoum or Harrar on the African Horn.

At the beginning of the second half of the nineteenth century, the Somali port of Berbera had close trade links with Aden, a British port, delivering foodstuffs and livestock. In addition, it traded with the other ports along the Red Sea and the India Ocean from Zanzibar to Bombay.

All these exchanges required intermediaries for transporting, selling, and collecting products. Certain communities specialized in transport; others guaranteed the safety of the caravans and assumed administrative tasks.[9] Some people were both bankers and traders and sold wholesale. There were many networks, including Arabs, Africans, Europeans, and Banians,[10] who took part in exchanges and helped to boost the regional economy. The ancient structures were suitable for the economic conditions that prevailed during the 1850s. Sailing ships, in spite of unstable and sometimes violent winds and dangerous coral reefs, crisscrossed the sea, finding shelter and cargoes in the ports. Both coastal vessels and those designed for the high seas were built in Arabian shipyards[11] with well understood naval construction techniques. Teak wood, which was unavailable locally, was imported from Asia or Africa for naval construction. In 1856, French captain Antoine Guillain wrote:

> The Beugli, ships of the first category bigger than dhows, have high decks and can displace up too 250 tons. They navigated the seas between Bombay and Jiddah (or between Jiddah and Qusayr or between Jiddah and Suez). They have two triangular sails, the rear sail being the smaller. In spite of the enormity of the mast and of the sail it supports, these craft seldom have accidents and their teak mast stands up to the strains of sailing close to the wind. Dhows differ from this sailing ships only in size. They displace from 30 to 100 tons. The "saya" is longer, narrower, and better for the high seas and originated in the Persian Gulf. These sailing ships take refuge in the ports or the islands when a storm arises. Several sailors are needed. The captain's role is vital, as he has the responsibility for the ship, and the journey is extremely dangerous; Suez-Jiddah can take 12 to 20 days with an easier return in 2 to 8 days.[12]

In 1837, steamships of European manufacture with metal hulls began to ply the north-south route. Technological progress made possible the construction of larger and faster vessels. In 1867, the steamers of the British company, the Peninsular Oriental, on the Suez-Bombay or on the Suez—Hong Kong route, with their 200 horsepower motors, could cross the Red

Sea in seven days, with a brief stop at Jiddah, a trip that ten years earlier had taken 11 to 13 days.[13]

At the beginning of the 1870s, the fleets stopped at the same ports, with their outmoded facilities. With the advent of the steamships, Jiddah and Aden became international ports; the others remained regional ones. Would this balance be maintained in the face of the upheavals resulting from the irreversible introduction of the steamships? The intrusion of technological Europe, which envisaged eliminating the northern barrier to the Red Sea by a rail link and then by a water link, brought improvements.[14]

The Second Phase: 1860–1880

The years from 1865 to 1875 were particularly decisive for Egypt, which sought to expand both toward the Upper Nile and toward the African shore of the Red Sea, then still part of the Ottoman Empire. The new viceroy Isma'il (1863–79), a worthy successor to Muhammad 'Ali, wanted to control the Red Sea ports, which were expanding with increasing trade, and the African regions, where products were collected for export.

Ismail began by taking administrative control of the ports of Suakin and Massawa. After negotiations with the Sublime Porte, an accord was reached by which the sultan yielded to the viceroy the administration of the districts of Suakin and Massawa. A year later, they became part of the Egyptian khedivate. A firman of June 1873 confirmed this cession of sovereign rights and extended the zone of Egyptian influence to the dependencies of Suakin and Massawa. Egypt then renewed coastal expansion beyond Bab al-Mandab, where the Porte's influence was weaker. Zula paid tribute to the amir of Yemen; elsewhere the coastal chiefs, Afars, and Somalis, had maintained their independance.[15]

This southern expansion beyond the Bab al-Mandab straits to Cape Guardafui was not just a function of economic-strategic interests. Though the dhows were more numerous, with the opening of the Suez Canal, steamships, whose tonnage was increasing steadily, had a more important role. They were superior, less expensive, bigger, and could travel without refueling for 2,000 kilometers. This development made the southern outlet strategically more important, making the availability of a coal supply imperative to avoid dependence on the British facilities at Aden.

When a stop at Jiddah was no longer necessary, Aden's supremacy was established. Its transactions rapidly overshadowed those of Jiddah, whose commercial activities had declined by 1887.[16] In Aden's wake, Hodeida also grew, as did Massawa on the opposite shore. An indication of this growth was the attempt by two traders from Marseilles, Bazin and Rabaud, to make the island of Sheikh Saïd into a French port to compete with Aden. At the outlet of Red Sea, Berbera changed profoundly. We have a very good description of this port in 1873:

> The annual fair is the most interesting spectacle on the coast. From April until October, the place is completely deserted and the only testimony of prior human occupation are the frames of the native huts. But as soon as the monsoon wind changes the interior tribes come to the coast and with delicate mats, blankets and fabrics they prepare the huts for themselves and their expected guests. Regional boats coming from Aden, from the Red Sea, from Muscat, from Basrah, from Bombay begin to arrive. 10,000 to 20,000 people congregate and the village, previously deserted, becomes a babel of languages. Towards the end of March, the fair ends. The boats, heavily laden, begin their return trip.[17]

Thus, Berbera lived by a seasonal rhythm of fairs and winds, welcoming the caravans from southern Ethiopia and numerous sailing ships from the Indian Ocean, the Gulf of Aden, and the Red Sea. The inhabitants delivered fresh supplies to Aden.[18] The port was well integrated into the international network, and Berbera's importance drove Khedive Isma'il to add it to his zone of influence. In 1869, diplomatic maneuvering with local sultans and the British, who were concerned about supplying Aden, allowed the Egyptians to occupy Berbera, as well as other sites such Sagallo, on the Gulf of Tajura, in 1873. The British also seized Guardafui, at the tip of the Horn of Africa, to limit Egyptian expansion. Seizing control of the coast was easy, but taking control of the African hinterland was difficult.

Revitalizing the activities of Suakin and Massawa required linking them to the continent.[19] Suakin, the principal outlet for Sudanese products, was linked with Berbera by caravan route, and was subject to competition from Khartoum, an interior market that exported African products to Egypt down the Nile. In 1870, the cosmopolitan European community of Khartoum, shaken by an economic crisis (1864–65), proposed building a rail line between the capital of the Sudan and Suakin. This modern transport would strengthen the links between the two cities and would help bind the Sudan to the Red Sea. Studies of the proposed route and possible termini, however,

showed the cost of the project to be beyond the resources of the Sudan and
the Egyptian finance ministry, which was heavily burdened by other expenses. It was only possible to improve what already existed: running the
province of Taka more efficiently and making Kassala a market-staging point
linked with the rich Gallabat region to ensure the security of the existing
routes.

Egypt, after having abandoned the idea of annexing Gallabat, particularly
the rich city of Metammah, tried to take advantage of the internal dissension
in Ethiopia to conquer Tigre, the hinterland of Massawa. In 1875, after
having taken Keren, it met unexpected resistance. The end of reign of Khedive Isma'il was tarnished by this costly failure. A weakened Egypt began to
pull back from the Horn of Africa.

Egypt controlled the collection zones for African products and ports and
stimulated maritime trade with its own steamship companies. Traffic between Suakin and Massawa, which maintained relations with Jiddah and
with Egypt through Suez,[20] as well as with Aden and the Indian Ocean,
continued to grow. This increased customs receipts. Trade in goods made
up for the initial effects of international pressure to repress the slave trade
in the Egyptian Sudan.

Land and sea trade depended on the existing economic infrastructure.
The island ports were not abandoned; the Egyptians were satisfied with
improving them. The goal was to make the economic tools more effective
by improving the existing docks, which had been neglected in the later
Ottoman years, and urban structures (mosques, stone houses, hospitals). Providing infrastructure made the cities more livable, and improved living conditions stimulated urban growth: the population of Suakin rose from 5,000
to 8,000 between 1860 and 1880. By 1880, Massawa had also been transformed. Among numerous descriptions, we have one written by a naval
officer:

> The city, which takes up half the rock, is comprised of stone houses
> built in a Moorish style. By the port is one vast house which is the
> governor's, a barracks, and even a jail. In several places, particularly
> near the sea and around the market street, instead of stone houses,
> there are shacks, in the middle of a courtyard itself encircled by a
> fence of mats. Not one tree, not one leaf, absolute aridity and barren-
> ness. The sea wall, also under construction, built of calcareous stone
> and coral, was equipped on the lee side with a layer of stone, brought

from the island of Dissye. Even more spectacular was the construction of a 7 km aqueduct, which was entrusted to the Frenchman Volant.[21]

The description of Zula was less impressive. It was a cluster of houses, made of whitewashed coral and straw huts able to house 1,800–2,000 inhabitants, on a small sand spit with neither water nor wood. A fire almost destroyed the entire town in 1879. The port sheltered 200 dhows that plied the Gulf of Aden and the Red Sea. The level of commerce was lower than that of Berbera because unloading at low tide was difficult.

The Egyptians were also content to maintain and improve what already existed beyond the Strait of Bab al-Mandab. But in the Gulf of Aden, devoid of facilities, they innovated, as they had a half-century before in the Sudan in building Khartoum.[22] During the ten years of Egyptian presence (1874–84), Berbera was an establishment much admired by sailors. In 1880, a French captain wrote:

> The description of Berbera given in 1873 no longer applies. Berbera is the only port worthy of the name on the Somali coast. The monthly export from Berbera to Aden sometimes rises above 8,000 sheep, 300 cattle. Aden consumes part and exports the rest. The fair begins in October, ends in May, with the high points in January and February. At that time, numerous caravans come to trade. For the last 5 years, Berbera has not been abandoned during the hot season (May to October). The perfectly sheltered harbor is visited every month by numerous dhows, coastal traders who keep Aden supplied. There are two cities, that of the Somalis and traders from Aden at the eastern end of the bay, and the Egyptian city, 1 km southwest of the other, on the mainland, opposite the deep sea port. At the end of a long stone jetty is a loading bridge on an iron frame, in deep water, ensuring easy communication between the city and the harbor. Examination of the works undertaken by the Egyptians (especially the aqueduct) show the importance of the commercial station.[23]

In addition to its innovative urban and port policy, Egypt participated in maritime activities through its steamship company with regular service between the two shores of the Red Sea, taking pilgrims to Jiddah and picking up ever increasing cargoes in various ports of the Red Sea and Gulf of Aden. This dynamic enterprise ceased with a financial crisis linked to the fall in

the price of Egyptian cotton and the costs of war and external threats from
Ethiopia and from the revolt of the Mahdi (1882–98) in Sudan. Egypt abandoned the Horn of Africa at the very moment when the European powers
embarked on an ambitious policy of expansion and were looking for refueling points on the route to Asia via Suez. After ten years of difficulties, the
Suez Canal was finally becoming viable, at the very moment when steamers
were displacing sailing ships. With these political and technological
changes, new ports were created.

The Third Phase: European Colonial Innovations

Starting in 1884, the Europeans colonized the African shore of the Red
Sea on both sides of the strait of Bab al-Mandab. Except for Aden, the
Arabian shore stayed within the Ottoman orbit. In 1884, France decided to
occupy Obock, which it had purchased in 1862. An Italian expedition took
Massawa in January 1885. In 1884, the British, who were more diplomatic
and had better contacts in the court of the Khedive after the famous Alexandrian incidents of 1882, bought Berbera.

Europeans continually searched for the refueling ports their commercial
and military fleets required. Steamships, which by 1880 exceeded 5,000 tons,
needed deep harbors, accessible day and night, far from dangerous coral
reefs. Freed of dependence on the seasonal winds, these ships now were
dependant instead on the availability of expensive port infrastructure. Suitable ports were few. Time to load and unload cargoes decreased. Land transport by camel or mule caravan passing through territory where raids were
endemic could no longer satisfy the increasing demands of the steamers.
Innovation was necessary to cope with those new demands. Without killing
off the old port centers, new ones developed. Some became terminals for
internal land routes (railroads, passable roads), and enjoyed population and
commercial growth never seen by their older rivals. These changes mani-
fested themselves both in their urban shape and their location. Port Sudan
and Djibouti illustrate this development.

Port Sudan[24] rapidly took over the large-ship trade from Suakin, which
could not handle ships greater than 5,500 tons. During the struggle against
the Mahdist insurrection, the Anglo-Egyptian forces benefited from the construction of rail lines.[25] When peace was restored, these links were converted
into economical railroads. The British decided to promote commerce in the
Sudan, which in 1898 had become an Anglo-Egyptian condominium, by

creating economically useful infrastructure. The idea resurfaced of grafting onto the Wadi Halfa—North Khartoum line a branch linking the Nile to the Red Sea. The study for the Berbera—Kassala—Tokar—Suakin line was entrusted to Kitchener in 1899. The route, in spite of the obstacle of crossing the Atbara, was approved at the turn of the century.

Suakin remained a problem, however. It was a small and poor port usable only by day and by only a few ships at the same time. Improving it would be very expensive. The city did not have enough space to grow and could no longer ensure its supply. However, the site of Shaykh Barhut had a dependable spacious harbor, usable night and day, and whose improvement would be less expensive. There was ample room for a well-designed city.[26]

Sir Reginald Wingate, governor of the Anglo-Egyptian condominium, named a committee to monitor the progress of the project, which was to cost an estimated £940,000. In spite of difficulties caused by the lack of water and building materials, by the end of 1907, the administrative quarter and the customs houses had been built on solid ground, on a checkerboard pattern. The built-up space faced the port. A jetty 650 meters long made double docking possible. Water tankers fed the reservoirs of Port Sudan, from which ran the urban distribution network.[27] In April 1909, this modern port went into service[28] and controlled trade with the Sudan, as its geographical name suggests.[29]

In 1884, the French in Somalia faced the same problem, the inadequacy of the port of Tajura for steamships. The French traders and naval officers proposed Obock, then a haven for dhows, where the coast was healthy and easily accessible, where without improvements only one large ship could dock, and where there were several wells.[30] It was destined to become the port of transit for Abyssinian products and the strategic stop on the route to Indochina and to Madagascar.[31] In addition, the Jules Mesnier company, affiliated with Poingdestre of Le Havre, which ran steamers on the Orient line linking Zanzibar to the Persian Gulf, would establish a coal depot only on condition that warships be ordered to obtain their fuel at Obock instead of Aden.[32] In a context of bitter rivalries between France and Great Britain, and in an emergency, Paris consequently chose Obock as a maritime and economic port. Besides, it would permit French ships to avoid refueling at Aden.

The limitations of the site rapidly became apparent.[33] Obock was not a terminus of Ethiopian caravans, not a favorable stopping point. Swimmers had to bring casks of sulfurous water to the ships anchored offshore; delivery of coal and water was more expensive than at Aden; the presence of coral reefs made access to the harbor perilous. Only the few steamers of the Messageries Maritimes company, which enjoyed a government subsidy, stopped there.

Sailors and civilians, in particular the first governor Léonce Lagarde, who concluded numerous peace and friendship treaties with the traditional Afar and Somali chiefs, complained about the site:

> My passage by Djibouti, little frequented up till now by vessels of the size of my steamer, the *Primauguet*, permitted me to compare this harbor with that of Obock. It is obvious that Djibouti's is in every way superior to that of Obock in extent and as a harbor. The space at Obock, near the rocks, is a square 500 meters to a side, or 25 ha. In Djibouti there are 80 ha with a minimum depth of 7 m. at low tide. From a commercial point of view, it seems to me Obock is a complete mistake. I observe that products come from Ethiopia via Harrar embark at Zayla', not far from Djibouti, instead of taking the detour to go to Tajurah, in difficult country with bellicose inhabitants.[34]

In October 1891, Léonce Lagarde determined the location of the lighthouse of the new port, which would make it accessible by night. To make Djibouti a practical commercial port with easy access, "there must be two or three lights, buoys in the channel, several deadmen in the harbor, and a coal depot."[35]

After a decade of effort, France abandoned Obock for Djibouti, on the other shore of the Gulf of Tajura, at a place known by a few fishermen and sailors looking for water.[36] By 1892, a rudimentary port infrastructure had been constructed on a site comprised of four low plateaus linked to one another by spits of low land, partly covered at high tide. All this formed a peninsula. Thus the fleet had a naturally protected harbor without strong currents; it could depend on the springs of Ambouli, even though they produced water with a high salt content (1.6 to 2 g.) unsuitable for use in ship boilers unless treated.

A sea wall about 800 meters long was built at the end of the natural bay to accommodate lighters, because Djibouti was not a deep-water port. The Messageries Maritimes company established a coal depot. Immediately after its creation, steamships of French companies (Messageries Maritimes, Chargeurs réunis, Compagnie péninsulaire havraise) refueled there before continuing on their way to Indochina and Madagascar, complaining at times of the prohibitive tariffs, while praising the better service at Aden.

Tajura, the old port of the Dankalie coast, fell asleep, while first Obock, then Djibouti, received sailing ships and small coastal steamers. The graft of material civilization imposed by colonial France took root and grew; however, foreign ships continued to go to Aden, instead of Obock or Djibouti.

In this ever-changing situation, Berbera, which had been purchased by the British in 1884, distanced itself from Djibouti and Port Sudan. There were various reasons for this: its mainland site, its recent, quite modern improvements, the interpenetration of land and sea networks, and its links with Aden that made it as effective as the new generation of sites established by the colonizers. Thus, where Egypt had implemented a deliberate policy of innovation, success was possible; Britain had only to reap the benefit they had inherited.

A naval report written in 1888 described the new context:

> In exchange for a large financial indemnity, the Egyptians ceded Berbera to the British in October 1884 and the Egyptian garrison returned home on ships of the India fleet. This port, which exports African products, is the best on the entire southern coast of the Gulf of Aden. The market is supplied on the one side by caravans from Oromo country, Choa, Harrar and the fertile plains 4 or 5 days' walking distance. On the other side, by dhows from the Hijaz, Yemen, the Persian Gulf and India. In addition, a small steamship passes weekly through Berbera, Boulhar, Zayla'. All this traffic is performed exclusively by Banians, Arabs, and Somalis who form a permanent population of several thousand souls and not a single European.[36]

The Italians profited from the infrastructure at Massawa that they modified to handle steamers, while launching a new port at Assab. With the railway inaugurated in 1917 linking Djibouti to Addis-Ababa, the French port on the Somali coast became the main port of Ethiopia. At the dawn of the twentieth century, Djibouti, rather than Assab or Massawa, was the outlet of Ethiopia. Its traffic increased without, however, eclipsing Aden.

Conclusion

The fortunes of the ports in the Red Sea changed greatly during the nineteenth century, the result of the revolution in transport. The old markets, based on sailing ships and caravan routes, continued to do well until the beginning of the twentieth century, when Suakin and Hodeida sank into decline. However, a new generation of ports (Port Sudan, Djibouti) came into being, having overcome start-up difficulties. These ports, terminals for interior railways, had advantages they could assert at the end of World War I. But Aden, well situated on the maritime route between the Indian Ocean and the Mediterranean via the Suez Canal, maintained its primacy, its traffic competing with that of other regional ports.

Notes

1. Joseph Kessel, *Fortune Carrée* (Paris: Gallimard, 1931). Kessel investigated the slave trade in East Africa in 1930, using the knowledge of the French adventurer Henry de Monfreid, a well-known novelist.
2. Daniel Headrick has written two excellent studies on this subject in *The Tools of Empire: Technology and European Imperialism in the 19th Century* (New York: Oxford University Press, 1981); and *The Tentacles of Progress: Technology Transfer in the Age of Imperialism 1860–1940* (New York: Oxford University Press, 1988).
3. Archives Nationales, Paris Fonds Marine, 3JJ/359. Rapport sur la navigation de la mer Rouge de Th. Lefebvre au ministre Beaupré de Freycinet, Paris, 20 juillet 1840.
4. Among numerous studies on this subject, see William Ochsenwald, "The Commercial History of the Hijaz Vilayet 1840–1908," *Arabian Studies* 6 (1982): 57–77; J.-L. Miège, "Jiddah Port d'Entrepôt," *Les ports de l'Océan Indien aux XIXème et XXe siècles* (Aix-en-Provence: IHPOM, 1982), pp. 93–108.
5. J. F. E. Bloss, "The Story of Suakin," *Sudan Notes and Records* 19 (1936): 271–300 and 20 (1937): 247–80.
6. G. Lejean, *Voyage aux deux Nils, exécuté de 1860 à 1864 par ordre de l'Empereur* (Paris: Hachette, 1865).
7. Archives nationales, Paris Fonds Marine, 3JJ/359.
8. Foreign Office, 84–1305, Arthur Raby to Lord Palmerston, Jiddah, 10 December 1869. The British consul estimated the number of slaves unloaded annually in the vicinity of Jiddah at 2,000 to 2,500. Of this number, 500 to 600 came directly from Massawa and Suakin, and the rest from Hodeida, a maritime staging point for slaves coming from Zula. The trade seemed to have been diminishing over the previous five years; the totals in 1863 were 12,000 to 15,000 slaves.
9. A.N.P., Affaires Etrangères, Commercial correspondence, vol. 2, (1864), fols. 34–35. Guillaume Lejean had been interested in the *hardaba* (merchants) of

Suakin, who had a branch at Messalamiye and intermediaries in Khartoum, Berbera, Kassala, and Jiddah. Through the last port, they traded with India.

10. R. Pankhurst, "The Banyan or Indian Presence at Massawa, Dahklak Island and the Horn of Africa," *Journal of Ethiopian Studies* 9 (January 1974): 185–212; "Ethiopia and the Red Sea and Gulf of Aden Ports in the XIXth and XXth Century," *Ethiopia Observer* 8 (1964): 37–101.

11. Around 1850, the shipyards at Jiddah were turning out six dhows of about 80 tons each every year. The decline in the production sailing vessels perceptible by the end of the nineteenth century, halted by the beginning of the twentieth: in 1901, only two dhows were built.

12. Archives nationales, Paris Fonds Marine, 3JJ/359.

13. Technological questions are partly treated in R. J. Gavin, *Aden under British Rule 1839–1967* (London, 1975).

14. D. A. Farnic, *East and West: The Suez Canal in History, 1854–1956* (Oxford: Clarendon Press, 1969).

15. Indian Record Office, Political and Secret Department. Letters of Aden-Zanzibar, vol. 39, Playfair to K. Forbes, 14 May 1861, pp. 85–86.

16. See above, n. 4.

17. Indian Record Office, Correspondence from Aden, vol. 193, letter from Coghlan to Anderson, 15 November 1873.

18. The proximity of Aden was decisive in Berbera's growth.

19. Ghada H. Talhami, *Suakim and Massawa under Egyptian Rule 1865–1885* (Northampton, MA: University Press of America, 1987); D. Roden, "The Twentieth Century of Suakin," *Sudan Notes and Records* 60 (1970): 1–22.

20. L. Dori, "Esquisse historique de Port Saïd," *Cahiers d'Histoire Egyptienne* 6 (1954): 180–219; (1955): 1–46; and, (1956): 311–42.

21. Archives Nationales de Paris, Fonds Marine, 3 JJ/360; excerpts from the report by Commandant du Laclocherie, Aden, 12 April 1880.

22. Colette Dubois, "Morphologie de Khartoum: conflits d'identité (1820–début du XXe siècle," *Soudan. Histoire, identité, idéologies,* ed. H. Bleuchot, Ch. Delment, and D. Hopwood (Reading: Ithaca Press, 1991), pp. 13–32.

23. Archives nationales, Paris Fonds Marine, 3JJ/360 (cited above, n. 21).

24. Kenneth J. Perkins, *Port Sudan: The Evolution of a Colonial City* (Boulder: Westview Press, 1993); *Abd al-Rahim Mahmud, Maskakil mima BurtSudan w'al sikkah hadid* (Khartoum: National Council of Economic and Social Research, 1977).

25. Martin Daly, *Empire on the Nile: The Anglo-Egyptian Sudan 1898–1934* (Cambridge: Cambridge University Press, 1986).

26. "Report of Captain Kennedy, April 1904," E.W.C. Sandes, *The Royal Engineers in Egypt and the Sudan* (Chatham, 1937). Officers of the Royal Navy praised the site of Shaykh Barhut, north of Suakin.

27.   These problems are discussed by H. E. Hebbert, "The Port Sudan Water Supply," *Sudan Notes and Records* 60 (1970): 33–42.

28.   Until 1899, the statistics of the Foreign Office concerned traffic only through Suakin (Diplomatic and Consular Report, Egyptian series, no. 2247); after 1911, only Port Sudan appears (Egypt, no. 3026). Trade rose from 2,449,957 in 1911 to 3,650,907 in 1914. Port Sudan exported Sudanese products (gum Arabic, grain, cotton, hides, etc.) and imported merchandise from Britain and India.

29.   In 1904, two names were considered, Port Cromer and Port Wingate; to avoid controversies, both were rejected for the more neutral name, Port Sudan (*Sudan Notes and Records* 17, 1 [1935]).

30.   Archives de la Marine, Vincennes, BB4 1507, Obock 1884–1891, no. 8.

31.   This question is the subject of the first chapter of my book, *Djibouti 1888–1967: Heritage et frustration* (Paris: L'Harmattan, 1997).

32.   Archives de la Marine, Vincennes, BB4 1507, Obock 1884–1891. Report of January 1884 of the frigate captain of the *Infernet* to the naval minister.

33.   H. Brunschwig, "Une Colonie inutile: Obock," *Cahiers d'Etudes Africaines* 8 (1968).

34.   Archives Nationales Paris, Fonds Marine, 3 JJ/360. Report of the captain commanding the *Primauguet*, 9 February 1889.

35.   Archives de la Marine, Vincennes, BB4 1507. Report of Lieutenant Guillo to the head of Indian Ocean Naval Division, 11 November 1891.

36.   Archives Nationales Paris, Fonds Marine, 3 JJ/360. Report of the commander of the *Météore* to the vice-admiral commanding the Levantine Naval Division, in the port of Obock, 13 April 1888.

4   Port Cities as Nodal Points of Change: The Indian Ocean, 1890s–1920s

Kenneth McPherson

During the late nineteenth and early twentieth centuries, the port cities around the Indian Ocean helped change the economic, political, and cultural activity of the people of the region in new directions. Port cities were where the people of the region met and interacted with one another and with people from the West.[1] These interactions were not simply a matter of European modernity confronting Eastern tradition, or of high culture confronting mass culture in the public sphere; they produced new sets of relationships in a new type of urban environment among the peoples of the region, between the coast and the hinterland, and between Europeans and indigenous peoples.

Port cities had been centers of cultural and economic interaction long before the arrival of Europeans. Port cities have always been agents of social, cultural, and economic interchange. There were, however, vital differences in function between precolonial and colonial ports. In the precolonial era, ports were generally politically subordinate to hinterland authority (although often having a considerable degree of local autonomy, given the lack of centralization in the government of many premodern states). In addition, they were frequently secondary players in processes of social, cultural, political, and economic evolution in the hinterland, unlike their colonial counterparts.[2] There were, of course, exceptions. In insular Southeast Asia and along the coast of East Africa, for example, some port cities functioned as independent sources of power and as potent agents for change, but in general hinterland cities were the dominant centers.[3]

Beginning in the eighteenth century, the relationship between port and hinterland in the Indian Ocean region changed rapidly. Ports became the bridgeheads for the establishment of European territorial empires. The greatest of the port towns emerged as nodal points of European power. Cape Town, Karachi, Bombay (Mumbai), Madras (Chennai), Calcutta, Rangoon, Singapore, and Jakarta (Batavia) became home to large European communities involved in commerce and government. They also attracted settlers from many ethnic groups who took advantage of the new economic order introduced by European rule.[4] Such ports, unlike their pre-European predecessors, controlled their hinterlands, creating a new political and economic order based on the subordination of the interior to the littoral.

Pre-European Indian Ocean Ports

Before the arrival of the Portuguese in the late fifteenth century, Middle Eastern and South and Southeast Asian ports were both market places and entry points for the land-based Muslim states of the Middle East and the Hindu, Muslim, and Buddhist states of South and Southeast Asia.[5] In contrast, ports in East Africa, from the Somali coast to the Mozambique Channel, were linked to a much more politically fragmented hinterland and remained exotic cultural and linguistic urban centers with only fragile and tenuous links to frequently turbulent and hostile hinterlands.[6]

Many Indian Ocean ports were undoubtedly cosmopolitan and complex urban structures. From Aden to Kilwa, from Hormuz to the ports of the Malabar coast and the Maldives, and from Surat to Malacca and Acheh, Muslims from as far afield as Morocco and Central Asia settled and visited as merchants, rulers, pilgrims, sailors, artisans, soldiers, scholars, and clerics.[7] In the process they interacted with co-religionists and Hindus from the Indian subcontinent who were forming trade diasporas in Middle Eastern ports. However, Muslims, in contrast to Hindus, tended to migrate permanently, settling among co-religionists in distant lands and intermarrying with them; Hindu merchants remained birds of passage in non-Hindu lands—in time they returned to South Asia.

Around the Arabian Sea, ports such as Hormuz, Aden, Jiddah, Mokha, and Surat formed a commercial network that fed goods such as spices and cotton textiles into the markets of the Middle East, and from there into the Mediterranean. They were also the distribution points for goods to myriad markets along the Indian Ocean littoral. Intra–Indian Ocean maritime trade was of far greater importance, both in terms of value and volume, than trade with Mediterranean markets. The ports of South Asia, eastern Africa, and Southeast Asia functioned both as transshipment centers for cargoes and as feeder points for goods into and out of the hinterland.

These ports and the sea routes linking them bound the Indian Ocean into a distinctive self-contained commercial world with important, but relatively minor, linkages to East and Central Asia and the Mediterranean. Although in strict geographic terms it was an easily defined world, in terms of trade and the movement of merchants, sailors, pilgrims, and immigrants, its boundaries were porous. Muslims from regions beyond the Indian Ocean were frequent travelers across the ocean by the fifteenth century. They settled in ports on the Arabian Sea, in South Asia, and to a lesser extent in insular Southeast Asia; many also moved on into the hinterland, where they acted as intermediaries between the great civilizations of classical Islam in the Middle Eastern heartland and in South and Southeast Asia.

Although South Asian centers of Islamic civilization were distant from the ocean and linked only by tenuous land routes to the Middle East, foreign Muslim maritime travelers were central to the conversion of many South Asians in port cities and in areas such as Gujarat, the Malabar and Coromandel coasts, and the Maldives and Lakshadweep Islands. The greatest ports in South Asia, whether dominated by Muslims or not, had a vibrant Muslim cultural and political life by the fifteenth century. The ethos of this life was not necessarily the "high" Persianized culture of the great Islamic courts in the Ganges Valley or the Deccan, but more often represented an amalgam of popular foreign and indigenous idioms, particularly in southern and eastern India.

It was from this environment that Islam moved eastward across the Bay of Bengal with South Asian Muslim travelers to Malayan and Indonesian ports such as Pasai, Malacca, and Acheh. Here, beginning in the thirteenth century, port cities were no longer simply gateways to rich agricultural hinterlands, but had become wealthy transshipment centers for cargoes from throughout Southeast Asia and East Asia. The rise in demand in both East Asia—particularly imperial China—and South Asia for the spice and tin exports of Southeast Asia, and the intrusion of Chinese traders into the Indian Ocean stimulated the development of a new type of port in Southeast Asia, an entrepôt where the transshipment of goods, rather than supplying the hinterland, generated a new form of wealth and power based on international trade. In the process they became diffusion points for Islam in the Malay Peninsula and insular Southeast Asia.[8] By the fifteenth century, many of these ports were independent states, and the Islam they received from South Asia blended with popular religious practices. This last great process of religious change in insular Southeast Asia echoed earlier adaptations of Hindu and Buddhist practice.

The partners of the Muslims in maritime enterprise were Hindus from South Asia. Gujarati merchants were preeminent, a powerful commercial force in Malacca in particular. But whereas foreign Muslims in Southeast Asia in time merged into the local Muslim population, the Hindu communities remained exotic. The result was that by the fifteenth century the Hindus had been replaced by South Asian and Middle Eastern Muslims as cultural and religious interlocutors in the port cities of Southeast Asia and along the coast of East Africa, where Asian Islamic idioms blended with the cultures of Africa to give shape to the coastal Swahili culture and language.

Many ports were remarkably short-lived: their prosperity was tied to that of their hinterlands over which they exerted limited political and economic influence. When they lost that influence, the ports were abandoned. This was particularly true along the coast of East Africa, but it was also not uncommon in the Middle East and South and Southeast Asia, where the utility of the marketplace to the hinterland determined the life of the port.

Europeans and Indian Ocean Ports: The First Phase

The impact of Europe upon this commercial world was initially muted. In the early sixteenth century, the Portuguese seized control of strategically located port cities such as Sofala, Mombasa, Muscat, Diu, Goa, Colombo, and Malacca in an attempt to destroy Muslim commercial domination and redirect maritime trade away from the Middle East and around the Cape of Good Hope.[9] The enterprise had mixed fortunes. The Portuguese obtained valuable cargo, which they carried directly to Europe, but in general they failed to displace traditional trading and seafaring groups or to trade in areas they did not control. There were many factors making their task impossible. The hinterlands on which these ports depended were controlled by powerful empires—the Ottomans, Safavids, and the Mughals. At sea, the Portuguese were capable of inflicting damage upon their rivals, but they had no influence on hinterland markets controlled by these imperial powers, and this undermined any utility their advantage in maritime power might otherwise have offered.

In the ports the Portuguese controlled, there was sometimes intolerance of indigenous commercial and religious practices and culture, but more frequently a truce allowed the coexistence of the local population and their Portuguese overlords. The Portuguese added Christianity to the cosmopolitan mix and encouraged South Asian converts to settle in their ports along the Mozambique coast, but overall their impact on port cities was minimal. In commercial terms, by the seventeenth century, the Portuguese had become simply another trade diaspora around the Indian Ocean reliant on good working relations with indigenous merchants.[10]

In the seventeenth century, the Dutch, English, and French joined the Portuguese in the area. Weaker in resources and manpower than their Portuguese rivals, these newcomers were forced into an early accommodation with local commercial groups and political powers. Initially, they established "factories" (trading posts) in ports stretching from the Gulf to Southeast Asia. However, by the middle of the seventeenth century, the Dutch had driven the Portuguese out of Malacca and Colombo and had established fortified ports in the Indonesian archipelago at Jakarta (Batavia) and on the Cape of Good Hope at Cape Town. Initially, the English lagged behind the Dutch in terms of naval power, but they too gained control of a port when they acquired Bombay from the Portuguese and established fortified bases at Madras on the Coromandel coast and at Calcutta on the Hooghly River in Bengal. The French established a colony on Mauritius with settlers from France and slaves from Africa, and a port at Pondicherry to challenge the English trading post at Madras. The Danes established a factory on the Coromandel coast at Tranquebar.

Until the eighteenth century, none of the European successors to the Portuguese drastically altered patterns of maritime trade across the Indian Ocean or seriously contested the power of the major indigenous states. Like the Portuguese, they diverted some cargoes to Europe around the Cape and, like the Portuguese, they had to find a niche in the trading network that already existed. Their ports remained exotic urban structures in which Europeans and indigenous peoples had little contact outside commerce. They rapidly expanded an old trade in slaves and bonded laborers and artisans across the region, however, which led to the emergence of new port societies in which there was significant cultural interaction. In the Indonesian archipelago, Jakarta became a major market for slaves from South Asia and other parts of the Indonesian archipelago, and was the departure point for prisoners sent as laborers to Colombo and Cape Town.[11] East African Portuguese and indigenous ports were the departure points for cargoes of slaves to the French Mascarenes and the slave markets of the Americas. The French on Mauritius also imported indentured artisans from India and China.

As a result of this movement of people, Cape Town and Port Louis (on Mauritius) soon had mixed Afro-Asian-European populations and popular cultures. For a time Jakarta, too, developed a hybrid popular culture, and until the nineteenth century, Portuguese (the language of maritime trade across the Indian Ocean and indigenous and Eurasian Roman Catholic slaves from Bengal) was the lingua franca of the city. Jakarta was also the first port in the Indian Ocean region where Chinese merchants and artisans formed a significant diaspora, presaging the nineteenth-century settlement of Chinese on the Malay Peninsula and in Singapore.[12]

Europeans and Indian Ocean Ports: The Second Phase

From the middle of the eighteenth century, European-controlled ports developed new functions as a result of the spread of the Anglo-French conflict from the Atlantic to the Indian Ocean and the Indian subcontinent, the decline of Mughal power, and shift in Europe-bound cargoes from luxury goods to products for mass consumption such as cotton textiles and tea.

South Asia and its adjacent seas became an arena of complex struggles among the British and the French, European and indigenous forces, and rival European armies backed by their local allies, in the shadow of the rapidly declining Mughal Empire. By the early 1800s, the British were the major power in South Asia and had gained large swaths of territory surrounding their ports of Calcutta, Madras, and Bombay. Within a generation, the British in South Asia had changed their role from merchant to ruler. This transition had a fundamental impact on the nature of the port cities, which were their bridgeheads into South Asia. Bombay, Madras, and Calcutta became seats of government, justice, and military power, as well as the gateways through which the British moved deeper into the South Asian interior and the exit points for exports from the large territories the British controlled.[13] By the first decade of the nineteenth century, the British had not only vanquished the French in India but had driven their Dutch allies out of Ceylon, the Malay Peninsula, and southernmost Africa, and had gained control of Cape Town, Colombo, Malacca, and Mauritius. Paralleling this increase in British territory, the Dutch extended their control over the islands of the Indonesian archipelago out of their ports on Sumatra, Java, and the Moluccas.

The third factor affecting the fortunes of the European-controlled ports was the change in Europe-bound cargoes from the mid eighteenth century associated with increasing prosperity in Western Europe, which created a huge demand for cheap textiles, sugar, tea, coffee, and indigo, and later led to an upsurge in demand for a range of raw materials to feed the factories of Europe.[14] Economic activity in European-controlled ports rapidly intensified during this period as the British and Dutch exploited their new territories by developing plantations to produce cash crops for export, as well as extracting minerals and cutting timber.

The first major commodities for European consumption were South Asian cotton textiles and Chinese tea. Control of the major South Asian cotton textile and opium-producing areas following the collapse of the Mughal Empire and the elimination of the French as rivals in South Asia gave the British a commercial advantage in the China trade. The politics of the China tea trade shaped British policy in Southeast Asia and led to the establishment of a port at Penang in 1788, and indirectly to the establishment of the port of Singapore in 1819, as British way stations and markets.[15] In time, both these ports came to rely more on their tin- and rubber-rich hinterlands than they did on the tea trade.

Paralleling the intrusion of the British into Southeast Asia, the Dutch moved out of their coastal enclaves in the Indonesian archipelago to create a territorial empire with the island of Java as its heartland.

In the nineteenth century, European demand for raw materials and foodstuffs led to increasing European penetration of the Indian Ocean littoral and a renewed rivalry among the European powers for access to cargoes and colonies to play as pawns in global power politics. Ports were central to this process. Renewed French interest in the Indian Ocean littoral prompted the British to annex the western coast of Australia and establish a port and fort at Fremantle, which in turn encouraged the French to take a more intense interest in the affairs of their island colony of La Réunion and the main ports on the neighboring island of Madagascar. To the north, the establishment of the British at Aden and the opening of the Suez Canal in 1869 were followed by the settlement of the French at the Red Sea port of Djibouti and later by the Italians on the Eritrean and Somali coasts. Not to be outdone, the Portuguese in their decayed colonies on the Mozambique coast began to modernize ports such as Lorenço Marques (Maputo) as bridgeheads for extensive expansion into the interior, and the Germans seized ports on the Tanganyika coast as a prelude to occupying the hinterland.

The ports were affected not only by changing economic and political circumstances, but by new technologies as well. The triumph of steam and steel in shipping and railroads was rapidly reflected in the major European-controlled ports where facilities were provided to cater to these new innovations. Cape Town, Durban, Mombasa, Karachi, Bombay, Colombo, Madras, Calcutta, Rangoon, Penang, Singapore, Jakarta, and Fremantle were the major junctions for sea and rail routes; neighboring ports either vanished or were reduced to feeder status. The arrival of the telegraph linked these major ports with one another and with Europe, and affected the nature of commercial decisions and transactions. Technology was power, and in the nineteenth century, technology was in the hands of Europeans and centered in their ports. Indigenous merchants, sailors, and ship owners were adversely affected by this technological revolution as they lost their place in the maritime trade. Some survived as mariners on feeder routes between lesser and greater ports or to areas such as East Africa and the Gulf, which until the last years of the nineteenth century were not of pressing interest to Europeans. Others settled in the European-controlled ports as part of the indigenous service community.[16]

Although peripheral to European commercial interests, both East Africa and the Gulf did produce limited cargoes of goods for markets around the western Indian Ocean. This trade was run by Middle Eastern Muslims and Jews, and by Hindu, Muslim, and Jewish merchants, sailors, and ship owners from British India, in European-controlled ports such as Mombasa, Dar es Salaam, Mogadishu, Aden, and Bombay. Many of these groups formed distinct communities in ports such as Muscat, Bahrain, Kuwait, and Basra, which were not under direct European control. Of all these ports, Bombay was the most cosmopolitan. It was a predominantly Hindu city, but its population also included Muslim, Parsi, and indigenous Christian communities from all parts of the subcontinent, as well as substantial European, Eurasian, Jewish, and Armenian communities.[17]

Such cosmopolitanism was also evident in ports such as Singapore and Rangoon by the late nineteenth century.[18] In part, this reflected the function both ports had as markets for cargoes carried in indigenous vessels, but it was also a result of a new influx of migrants from India and China into the European-controlled ports of Southeast Asia beginning with skilled workmen from China and merchants from China and India,[19] responding to the need for cheap labor to open up the hinterland to commercial exploitation by Europeans. Plantations, tin mining, the spread of intensive rice cultivation in areas such as lower Burma under British rule, clearing forests and building railways and modern harbors required large numbers of laborers, and they came in the hundreds of thousands from the villages of British India and South China, mainly as limited-term indentured laborers, though many ended up settling permanently in the British or Dutch-controlled ports of Southeast Asia. Subsequently, there was a smaller migration from these ports westward to the ports of British India and to the plantations of Mauritius.[20] Villagers from British India also moved as indentured laborers to Mauritius beginning in the 1830s to replace emancipated slaves, to Natal as sugar plantation labor, to Ceylon to work on tea plantations, and to Kenya as railroad labor. Some eventually returned to British India, but others remained to form large communities in Durban, Colombo, Port Louis, and Mombasa.[21]

To some extent one needs to be cautious when using the term "cosmopolitan" to describe these cities. In Alexandria, Beirut, and Haifa, people did frequently adopt and adapt cultural forms drawn from other confessional or national groups. But in the port cities of the Indian Ocean, cosmopolitanism affected only certain sectors of society in a limited number of ways. If, however, the word is used simply to denote the presence of a variety of confessional, cultural, and racial groups within a single urban setting, then it can readily be applied to the major ports of the Indian Ocean region.

Europeans also came to the Indian Ocean region as permanent settlers, as well as transient merchants, administrators, and soldiers. From the late seventeenth century on, Dutch and Huguenot colonists settled at the Cape and in time merged to form the distinct Afrikaans-speaking people. In the 1820s, British farmers, indentured laborers, convicts, and members of the petite bourgeoisie settled in Natal, and along the western coast of Australia, where they established ports such as East London, Port Elizabeth, Durban, Fremantle, Bunbury, and Albany to serve the agricultural hinterland. British retirees from service in India reinforced this migration. A smaller number of Portuguese settlers moved into the Portuguese enclaves along the Mozambique coast from the mid nineteenth century, helping to create modern ports such as Lourenço Marques.

African ports established by European settlers were much more cosmopolitan than their Australian equivalents. European settlers in southern Africa and along the Mozambique coast remained an elite minority group whose plantations, farms, businesses, administrative machinery, and police and military forces were supported by African laborers and conscripts, and South Asian petty merchants, artisans, and laborers. These ports were constructed with the most modern European technology and were the railheads for the penetration of the interior, but socially they remained bastions of racial segregation with minimal cultural interaction between the component cultural, linguistic, and racial groups. In contrast, the ports on the western coast of Australia were exclusively European. The small indigenous population was vigorously and often violently excluded from participation in settler life, except occasionally as laborers, and was driven from its lands by British farmers and pastoralists. With the exception of the small pearling port of Broome, where Asian pearlers formed a large mixed-race community, none of the west coast ports had a significant non-European population.

Late in the nineteenth century, both the African and Australian ports underwent very rapid growth after the discovery of mineral deposits in their hinterlands and the price of agricultural commodities rose. Gold, diamonds, wool, wheat, beef, mutton, dairy products, and fruit attracted Europeans into the hinterland, and railroads spread out from ports to service the mining and agriculture carried out there. These ports became major commercial centers, as well as centers of secondary processing and some manufacturing.[22]

In this same period there was a renewed European interest in the ancient Gulf ports. Ottoman Basra benefited from improved economic conditions in Mesopotamia; Kuwait and Bahrain became important to Europeans for strategic reasons relating to Great Power rivalry over the Middle East, particularly Mesopotamia and Iran. For much of the nineteenth century, British interests in the Gulf centered on the defense of India against French, German, and Russian ambitions, heightened in the first decades of the twentieth century by the allure of oil. The Persian oilfields attracted considerable British investment and boosted the fortunes of formerly minor Persian ports such as Abadan and Bushire. To keep a weather eye on Persia, and mindful of the possibility of oil finds along the Arabian shore of the Gulf, the British took a keener and more proprietary interest in the stability and security of the port sheikhdoms of Kuwait, Bahrain, and the Trucial Coast. Oman, too, was not immune from these heightened concerns, and the British established a virtual protectorate there. On the opposite side of the Arabian Peninsula, the port of Aden served as a base from which to control a turbulent hinterland, given the importance of the port as a staging post on the vital shipping lane from the Mediterranean to the Indian Ocean via the Suez

Canal. This upsurge in interest led to an increase in the British military presence, including indigenous soldiers from the British Indian army, as well as a larger number of European administrators and diplomatic officers, and merchants and artisans from British India who formed a distinct service class.

Port Hierarchies

Beginning in the eighteenth century, the power of European-controlled ports was divorced from the hinterland. In these ports, authority was wedded to new types of economic and cultural activity and interaction with indigenous peoples, precipitating changes that gathered momentum in the course of the nineteenth century. These changes were fed by new technologies in communications. Europeans commanded economic production, banking, and shipping. In tandem with their overwhelming naval and military power, these technologies made the bridgehead ports the dominant urban centers in the Indian Ocean region. In the process, particularly in South and Southeast Asia, as some ports became centers of European political, economic, and military power, others declined or vanished. The great European-controlled ports such as Karachi, Bombay, Madras, Calcutta, Rangoon, Penang, Singapore, and Jakarta grew at the expense of other ports in Gujarat, Bengal, southern India, the Malay Peninsula, and Java, which either declined or refocused their economies to become feeder points for these great ports or enclaves of local maritime activity.[23]

In the Middle East and eastern Mediterranean, there was a parallel decline. Apart from the brief dominance of Portuguese power in the Gulf and along the Oman coast, European intervention in the Middle East had been minimal. But economic changes in the Ottoman and Iranian empires and the diversion of much of the transit trade between the Indian Ocean and the eastern Mediterranean by the development of links between the Mediterranean and northern European markets via the Cape route and across the Pacific led to the decline of many ports in the Gulf, Red Sea, and the eastern Mediterranean.

The decline of Middle Eastern ports was exacerbated in the nineteenth century by the British occupation of Aden, the opening of the Suez Canal, the subsequent British occupation of Egypt, and the establishment of French and Italian colonies on the Red Sea. This late-nineteenth-century colonial expansion led to the rise of a number of European-dominated ports—Port

Sudan, Massawa, Djibouti, Aden—at the expense of indigenous-controlled ports in the Red Sea and southern Arabia. Following the British occupation of Egypt, the ancient port of Alexandria, where Muhammad 'Ali had initiated a revival in the 1830s and 1840s, grew rapidly to emerge as a great cosmopolitan port, home to Greeks, Maltese, Italians, French, Britons, Jews, and Egyptians serving the cotton-based economy of Egypt and the transit trade of the Suez Canal. At the same time, a new Mediterranean port was created at Port Said, with a twin at Port Suez on the Red Sea, and new feeder ports were developed along the Red Sea to serve the Sudan and the Italian and French colonies in Eritrea and Djibouti. The Suez Canal also breathed new life into Mediterranean ports outside Muslim control. For both Italy and France, the canal opened up new routes to the Indian Ocean region. Marseilles, Genoa, and Naples became focal points for trade with the Indian Ocean region, although it had little significant influence on the cultures of these cities.

The Middle Eastern and Red Sea ports performed functions remarkably similar to the European bridgehead ports in South and Southeast Asia. In general they overwhelmed lesser ports and were essential parts of the process whereby Europeans extended their power, although European exploitation of the hinterland was not as intensive as it was in South and Southeast Asia. Europeans had begun their territorial expansion in South and Southeast Asia in the eighteenth century, but they did not overwhelm the Middle East until the early twentieth century. In the years between, the fortunes of some locally controlled ports on the Red Sea and the Gulf revived. Jiddah, on the Red Sea, benefited from the increase in number of Muslims performing the hajj, thanks to the availability of better shipping and shipping connections with South and Southeast Asia.[24] Basra and Abadan, at the head of the Gulf, grew in importance as the agricultural economy of their hinterlands expanded in the last decades of Ottoman and Qajar rule. The growth of these ports was matched in the Mediterranean by the revival of Haifa as the main port for an increasingly prosperous and populous Palestine and the development of Beirut, as the Lebanese economy underwent major structural changes.

The renewed growth of port cities in the Middle East had two sources: European intervention and economic changes in their hinterland. All these ports became centers for interaction between indigenous peoples and the larger world—in some cases (e.g., Alexandria, Haifa, and Beirut) with Europeans; in others, between various peoples from around the Indian Ocean.

Jiddah, in addition to the seasonal flow of Muslim pilgrims, was home to a large community of merchants from South Asia; Basra was a center for Muslim, Jewish, and Hindu merchants involved in the South Asian and Middle Eastern trade.

Middle Eastern ports can be divided into four categories: (1) those that were integrated into a prosperous hinterland and were major economic and political centers in their own right, such as Alexandria and Haifa; (2) those that were essentially transshipment or transit points for vessels on long-haul voyages, such as Aden and Port Said; (3) those that served prosperous hinterlands but were neither major economic nor political centers in their own right, such as Jiddah, Basra, and Abadan; and (4) those that had functions described in (2) and (3) but were also centers of European political and military power, such as Aden, Massawa, and Djibouti.

These categories are not mutually exclusive, but do indicate the main functions of the ports under discussion and the importance and attraction of the various ports to non-indigenous settlers. For example, Alexandria and Haifa had large non-Arab populations, including merchants, artisans, and military and government personnel. In contrast, Jiddah, Basra, and Abadan, which were subordinated to indigenous inland centers, had smaller foreign populations involved in a more limited range of activities. In between were ports such as Aden, Massawa, and Djibouti, which were both centers of colonial administration and served a relatively impoverished hinterland. Port Said was almost in a category of its own, as it serviced both its Egyptian hinterland and vessels passing through the Suez Canal to the Indian Ocean and the Mediterranean. It was also a major tourist port. Its mixed foreign population ranged from canal personnel to service providers for the tourist industry. The size and nature of foreign settlements in these ports varied considerably, as did the degree of interaction among indigenous populations and foreign settlers.

This same model can be applied to ports elsewhere in the Indian Ocean region. For instance, in eastern and southern Africa, Cape Town, Port Elizabeth, Durban, Lorenço Marques, Dar es Salaam, and Mombasa were bases both for European penetration of the hinterland and for European political and economic control. Formerly flourishing ports such as Lamu, Zanzibar, and Kilwa were reduced to minor feeder points linked to the outside world through their larger neighbors. In South Asia, Karachi, Bombay, Madras, Colombo, and Calcutta were the behemoths in political and economic terms that overshadowed all other ports and inland centers until well into the twentieth century.[25] The same held true for Southeast Asia, where Rangoon, Singapore, and Jakarta were not only the greatest ports in the area but the centers of European economic and political control to which all other ports in the area were subordinated. Singapore overshadowed previously prosperous ports such as Penang and Malacca in dominating the maritime trade of the Malay Peninsula; it became the major international transit point for maritime trade among the Indian Ocean region, East Asia, and the Pacific.[26]

Along the western coast of Australia, by the end of the nineteenth century, Fremantle was the only major international port, although earlier in the century ports such as Albany, Busselton, Bunbury, Rockingham, Geraldton, and Broome were directly linked to the global maritime economy. Fremantle's triumph was largely due to its proximity to the center of political power, located in Perth, the colonial capital upstream on the Swan River, and the construction of a railway network, which focused on Perth and Fremantle to the exclusion of other ports along the coast.[27] The smaller ports became feeder ports for Fremantle and stagnated until new economic forces revived them much later in the twentieth century.

The opening of the Suez Canal was an event of far-reaching importance. It revived the Red Sea as a major international shipping artery. It cut shipping costs, reduced traveling time, and facilitated the passage of European commercial and military shipping into the Indian Ocean. People and cargoes could travel more rapidly and cheaply. European warships could now reach their Indian Ocean bases more rapidly. The opening of the canal created or breathed new life into ports such as Massawa, Djibouti, Aden, and Port Sudan, both as naval stations and as markets for shipping between Europe and Asia. Reduced shipping costs and sailing times had their impact on both the cost and variety of cargoes and on the number of passengers carried. Increased cargo and passenger capacity meant that new dockyards were built, great hotels were established to accommodate foreign visitors and transit passengers, and naval facilities multiplied. New warehousing, greater and more regular cargoes, and increasingly specific cargo handling skills changed the structure of ports and heralded the emergence of a permanent port laboring class.

Steamships, railroads, the telegraph, banks, modern business houses, new medical procedures, and the increasingly sophisticated educational and cultural services that growing European communities demanded were serviced by a steady stream of arrivals from Europe. Medical advances reduced the mortality rate among Europeans in the colonies and encouraged greater numbers of European settler families. Indigenous peoples were recruited into economic and technological services, as they were into the colonial police and military forces, but generally in menial positions. The majority of Europeans lived in the larger ports; the communities located inland were much smaller, although in southern Africa and Australia they were still numerous.[28]

European passenger traffic grew, though most seaborne passengers were still Asians. Asian merchants and ship owners no longer dominated the sea lanes, nor did large numbers of itinerant Muslims, other than pilgrims on the hajj or "smugglers,"[29] seek passage across the ocean to lands now with new boundaries and complex laws that declared them foreign and alien. Asians traveled mainly on European-owned ships as migrant labor, colonial military levies, seamen, and as petty merchants and artisans to service new communities of their compatriots and co-religionists.[30]

By the twentieth century, ports around the Indian Ocean were bastions of European commercial, economic, and technological power, and the major regional centers for Western education and culture. They were cosmopolitan, though interaction was frequently segregated along communal lines. There were various subtle but vital processes of interaction between Europeans and their indigenous subjects. As the machinery of European domination grew, Europeans became more dependent upon locals to man the colonial administrations, military forces and police, business, industry, communications, trades, medicine, and education. By the first decades of the twentieth century, European education had been extended to sections of the indigenous population. For some local communities European rule led to new opportunities. In many port cities, beneficiaries of colonial rule established their own schools, newspapers, associations, hospitals, businesses, and factories.

This process included, for many, the adoption of Western cultural practices, dress, and housing, and the belief that ideas central to Western civilizations, such as liberty, justice, and nationalism, also applied to them. Some locals worked within the colonial system to gain a more equal place in society; others adopted the ideas of the West to establish modern indigenous states free from foreign rule. Still others rejected Western ideas, but used its technology of communication—the printing press, the telegraph, the railroad and steamship—to champion nationalism based on religion, language, and shared historical experiences.

Port cities were vital to this process. For example, in British India until well into the twentieth century, the only English-language tertiary educational institutions and medical schools open to Indians were in Karachi, Bombay, Madras, and Calcutta. In addition, most of the leading Western-style secondary schools and government-sponsored technical training institutions were also in these same cities, which were the major manufacturing and business centers of the raj and home to the majority of Indians involved in the Western professions and Indian-owned business and industrial enterprises.[31] The major English-language and vernacular newspapers and printing presses in South Asia were also there. By the last decade of the nineteenth century, these ports were centers of intense literary activity in which Indians adapted Western literary models to develop an enormous range of publications in the vernacular languages and English.[32] Daily newspapers, literary magazines, novels, and political and religious tracts gave expression to a variety of local ideas. Old identities based on language and religion were reinvented to adjust to the new social and economic processes evolving under colonial rule.[33]

To some extent the same processes of cultural and technical adaptation were underway in European-controlled Rangoon, Singapore, and Jakarta, where locally run publications both in the language of the colonial ruler and in local languages provided an outlet to debate the ideas of the colonial rulers and older cultural idioms and forms. Later, local artists adopted gramophone records and the moving pictures to give expression to indigenous interpretations of the past and the present.

Above all else, port cities provided new subjects and new platforms for debate. Economically dominant indigenous groups, merchants, journalists, and lawyers, found new constituencies and new issues to address. The rhetoric may have been drawn from traditional cultures and languages, but the audiences were new, as were the subjects debated.

The role of the colonial port as an agent of change in the hinterland increased in the late nineteenth century, thanks to the rapid growth of port-based vernacular newspapers that circulated in the interior and the migration of peoples to ports from the interior. The great ports of British India were demographically extremely hybrid. They were home to people originating in all corners of the subcontinent who jealously guarded their cultural and linguistic heritages in the new urban environment even as they gained access to Western-style education and the economic and political life of the city. In the process they funneled new ideas and aspirations back into the hinterland.[34] Employment opportunities in colonial port cities frequently opened up new areas of economic activity for particular communities. In Calcutta and Bombay, for example, Hindu caste groups had a near monopoly on administrative and educational positions at the cost of the Muslims, who had wielded political power in much of precolonial India.[35]

Elsewhere in the Indian Ocean region, even in European settler societies in Africa and Australia, the port set the tone for elite economic, cultural, and political life in the hinterland. In western Australia, the pace setter was the port conglomeration of Fremantle and Perth. In southeastern Africa, Cape Town, Port Elizabeth, Durban, and Lourenço Marques played the same role. Ports to the north—Dar es Salaam, Mombasa, and Zanzibar—on the Swahili coast performed the same function with respect to the diffusion of Afro-Asian Swahili language and culture.[36] But this was the exception; indigenous cultures fared poorly in the ports of South Africa, Mozambique, and Australia. In none of these ports were indigenous cultures able to secure a place by adapting and using Western technology. Instead, they were subordinated to the culture of the European settlers. In South Africa and Mozambique, an early form of apartheid separated the races. The cultural forms of the indigenous majority in the port cities were completely subordinated. In Australia, indigenous people were almost exterminated. This stands in strong contrast to South Asian ports where vernacular forms and idioms of cultural, economic, and political expression were interwoven with Western adaptations.

In the late nineteenth century, Indians began to play an important role in municipal government, and in 1909, they gained some representation to provincial legislatures. The most important municipalities and legislatures were in Bombay, Madras, and Calcutta (which until 1911 was the capital of British India), and they were the first to adopt the legislative system of the British. Although the Indian experience had its own characteristics, the processes of exposure and reaction were common to all ports around the Indian Ocean, with the exception of Australia. In time and pace the South Asian port cities were ahead of other Indian Ocean ports with an indigenous majority, but many of the elements that molded the life of port cities in India were common throughout the region.

By the 1920s, the great port cities of the Indian Ocean region were for the most part cosmopolitan and complex social organisms, multicultural in composition, and bound into colonial political systems that encouraged racial and cultural segregation, but most were also linked to a much larger world of ideas that affected traditional cultural, religious, and social values. Even in ports where indigenous political authority was maintained, new economic processes and population movements interacted to make the port community different from the hinterland. But the port could not exist in isolation from its hinterland, and the process of interaction between port and hinterland was, by the 1920s, drawing the hinterland into a larger global community. In the eastern Mediterranean, Alexandria and Beirut became national centers that had a dramatic impact upon their hinterlands. Although there are obvious differences between Alexandria and Beirut and the great ports of British India, the processes of exposure and reaction were similar, as was the experience of foreign domination.

Notes

1. Kenneth McPherson et al., *Port Cities as Centres of Social Interaction in the Indian Ocean Region. A Preliminary Historical Bibliography* (Perth: Centre of South and Southeast Asian Studies for UNESCO, University of Western Australia, 1981).

2. M. P. Singh, *Town, Market and Mint in the Mughal Empire 1556–1707* (New Delhi, 1985).

3. Kenneth McPherson, *The Indian Ocean: A History of People and the Sea* (New Delhi, 1993), chaps. 1–2.

4. Ibid., and McPherson, "The History of the Indian Ocean Region: A Conceptual Framework," *The Great Circle* 3, no. 1 (1981): 10–20; "Processes of Cultural Interaction in the Indian Ocean: An Historical Perspective," *The Great Circle* 6, no. 2 (1984): 78–92; Philip D. Curtin, *Cross-Cultural Trade in World History* (Cambridge, 1984); K. N. Chaudhuri, *Trade and Civilisation in the Indian Ocean: An Economic History from the Rise of Islam to 1750* (Cambridge, 1985); and Chaudhuri, *Asia before Europe. Economy and Civilisation of the Indian Ocean from the Rise of Islam to 1750* (Cambridge, 1990).

5. A. Reid, "The Structure of Cities in Southeast Asia, Fifteenth to Seventeenth Centuries," *Journal of Southeast Asian Studies* 2 (1980): 235–50; Reid, *Southeast Asia in the Age of Commerce 1450–1680*, 2 vols. (New Haven: Yale University Press, 1988, 1993).

6. G. Connah, *African Civilisations* (Cambridge, 1987), chap. 7; J. Middleton, *The World of Swahili* (New Haven: Yale University Press, 1985); M. Newitt, *A History of Mozambique* (Bloomington: Indiana University Press, 1995).

7. K. S. Sandhu and P. Wheatley, *Melaka*, 2 vols. (Kuala Lumpur, 1983); R. E. Dunn, *The Adventures of Ibn Battuta: A Muslim Trader in the 14th Century* (Berkeley: University of California Press, 1989); P. Risso, *Merchants and Faith:*

Muslim Commerce and Culture in the Indian Ocean (Boulder: University of Colorado Press, 1995).

8. K. R. Hall, *Maritime Trade and State Development in Early Southeast Asia* (Sydney, 1985), chaps. 8–9; Ma Huan, *Ying-yai Sheng-lan* (The Overall Survey of the Ocean's Shores) (Bangkok, 1997), reprint of Hakluyt Society translation (1970) of the 1433 original.

9. S. Subrahmanyam, *The Portuguese Empire in Asia, 1500–1700* (London, 1993); and *The Career and Legend of Vasco da Gama* (Cambridge, 1997).

10. A. Das Gupta and M. N. Pearson, *India and the Indian Ocean 1500–1800* (Delhi, 1997); S. Subrahmanyam and C. Bayly, "Portfolio Capitalists and the Political Economy of Early Modern India," *Indian Economic and Social History Review* 25 (1988): 410–24; S. Subrahmanayam, *Improvising Empire: Portuguese Trade and Settlement in the Bay of Bengal, 1500–1700* (Delhi, 1990); A. Das Gupta, *Merchants of Maritime India, 1500–1800*, Variorum Reprints (Brookfield, Vt: Ashgate Pub., 1994).

11. I. D. Du Plessis, *The Cape Malays* (Cape Town, 1947).

12. J. G. Taylor, *The Social World of Batavia: European and Eurasian in Dutch Asia* (Madison: University of Wisconsin Press, 1983); S. Abeyasekera, *Jakarta. A History* (Singapore, 1987).

13. T. Albuquerque, *Urbs Prima in India: An Epoch in the History of Bombay 1840–1865* (New Delhi, 1985).

14. Chaudhuri, *Trade and Civilisation* and *Asia Before Europe*.

15. K. McPherson, "Penang 1786–1982: A Promise Unfulfilled," in *Gateways of Asia: Port Cities of Asia in the 13th–20th Centuries*, ed. F. Broeze (London, 1997), pp. 109–26.

16. F. Broeze, "The Muscles of Empire: Indian Seamen Under the Raj, 1919–1939," *Indian Economic and Social History Review* 18 (1981): 43–67; Broeze, "Underdevelopment and Dependency: Maritime India during the Raj," *Modern Asian Studies* 18 (1984): 432–41.

17. E. Kulke, *The Parsees in India* (Delhi, 1974); Kenneth McPherson, *The Muslim Microcosm: Calcutta, 1918 to 1935* (Weisbaden, 1974); B. Israel, *The Bene Israel of India: Some Studies* (Hyderabad, 1984); N. Katz, *Studies of Indian Jewish Identity* (New Delhi, 1995).

18. C. M. Turnbull, *A History of Singapore, 1819–1975* (Kuala Lumpur, 1977); J. F. Warren, *Ricksahaw Coolie: A People's History of Singapore (1880–1940)* (Singapore, 1986).

19. H. Tinker, *Separate and Unequal: India and Indians in the British Commonwealth, 1920–1950* (Singapore, 1986).

20. C. M. Turnbull, *A History of Singapore*; H. Ly-Tio-Fane Pineo, *Chinese Diaspora in the Western Indian Ocean* (Mauritius, 1985); Warren, *Rickshaw Coolie*; A. Reid, *Sojourners and Settlers: Histories of Southeast Asia and the Chinese* (Sydney, 1996).

21. H. S. Morris, *The Indians in Uganda: Caste and Sect in a Plural Society* (London, 1975); Tinker, *Separate and Unequal*; U. Bissoondayal, *Indians Overseas: The Mauritius Experience* (Port Louis, Mauritius, 1984); H. Ly-Tio-Fane Pineo, *Lured Away: The Life History of Indian Cane Workers in Mauritius* (Moka, Mauritius, 1984); G. Clarence Smith, "Indian Business Communities in the Western Indian Ocean," *Indian Ocean Review* 2 (4 December 1989); S. Bhana, *Indentured Indian Immigrants to Natal, 1860–1902* (New Delhi, 1991); M. Emrith, *History of Muslims in Mauritius* (Port Louis, Mauritius, 1994); M. Carter, *Lakshmi's Legacy: The Testimonies of Indian Women in Nineteenth-Century Mauritius* (Port Louis, Mauritius, 1994).

22. F. Broeze, *Island Nation: A History of Australians and the Sea* (Sydney, 1998).

23.. Kenneth McPherson, et al., "Imperial Ports in the Modern World Economy: The Case of the Indian Ocean," *Journal of Transport History*, 3rd ser., 7, no. 2 (1986): 1–20; McPherson, "Engineering and Empire: The Making of Modern Indian Ocean Ports," in *The Indian Ocean: Explorations in History, Commerce and Politics*, ed. Satish Chandra (New Delhi, 1987), pp. 254–301.

24. S. Faroqhi, *Herrscher über Mekka: Die Geschichte der Pilgerfahrt* (Munich, 1990); F. E. Peters, *The Hajj: The Muslim Pilgrimage to Mecca and the Holy Places* (Princeton, 1994).

25. K. Dharmasena, *The Port of Colombo, 1860–1939* (Colombo, 1980).

26. L. K. Wong, "The Trade of Singapore," *Journal of the Malay Branch of the Royal Asiatic Society* 23 (4 December 1960): 5–315; McPherson, "Engineering and Empire."

27. P. M. Brown, *The Merchant Princes of Fremantle: The Rise and Decline of a Colonial Elite 1970–1900* (Perth, 1996); M. Tull, *A Community Enterprise: The History of the Port of Fremantle, 1897–1997* (St. John's, Newfoundland, 1997); Broeze, *Island Nation*.

28. K. McPherson et al., "Maritime Passenger Traffic in the Indian Ocean Region, *The Great Circle* 10, no. 1 (1988): 49–61.

29. Broeze, *Island Nation*.

30. E. B. Martin, "The Geography of Present-day Smuggling in the Western Indian Ocean: The Case of the Dhow," First International Conference on Indian Ocean Studies, section III (Perth, 1979).

31. Broeze, "Underdevelopment and Dependency"; McPherson et al., "Maritime Peoples of the Indian Ocean: Changing Occupations and Industries since c. 1800," *Mariner's Mirror* 74, no. 3 (1988): 241–54; McPherson, "Studying the Asian Port City," in *Brides of the Sea: Port Cities of Asia from the 16th–20th Centuries*, ed. F. J. Broeze (Sydney, 1989), pp. 29–56; McPherson, "The Social Experience of the Maritime World of the Indian Ocean: Passenger Traffic and Community Building, c. 1815–1939," in *Maritime Aspects of Migration*, ed. Klaus Friedland (Cologne, 1994), pp. 427–40.

32. R. Chandavakar, *The Origins of Industrial Capitalism in India: Business Strategies and the Working Class in Bombay, 1900–1940* (Cambridge, 1994); Yasmeen Lari and M. S. Lari, *The Dual City: Karachi during the Raj* (Karachi, 1996).

33. For an early instance of this process, see Kenneth McPherson, "Paravas and Portuguese: A Study of Portuguese Strategy and Its Impact on an Indian Seafaring Community," *Mare Liberum* 13 (June 1997): 69–82.

34. McPherson, *The Muslim Microcosm*; G. Tindall, *The City of Gold:. The Biography of Bombay* (London, 1924); Chandavarkar, *The Origins of Industrial Capitalism.*

35. McPherson, *The Muslim Microcosm*; S. N. Mukherjee, *Calcutta: Essays in Urban History* (Calcutta, 1993).

36. H. Kindy, *Life and Politics in Mombasa* (Nairobi, 1972); Martin, "The Geography of Present-Day Smuggling"; A. Sherrif, *Slaves, Spices and Ivory in Zanzibar* (London, 1987).

5 Haifa at the Crossroads: An Outpost of the New World Order

May Seikaly

The port cities along the Mediterranean coast of the Ottoman Empire all underwent changes in the nineteenth century in commerce,
finance, and communication that, combined with Western colonial penetration, transformed their societies. Western ambitions intervened where the
ambiguities and dilemmas of imperial and local politics made a society
particularly vulnerable. Change was also fueled by forces unleashed by the
state in the long process of reform, the Tanzimat, that it hoped would ward
off Western encroachment, as well as by the forces of European penetration,
whether by the great powers or by Christian and Jewish religious groups and
later by Zionist political activists who aimed to erode the obstacles to inte-
grating the empire into the world capitalist economy. It was in the port city
that this integration was most effective, where it "captured and reflected in
concrete form the entire episode of incorporation. Its physical appearance,
spatial layout, economic mechanisms, population dynamics, class structure,
political aspirations and cultural life could only be understood through the
prism of the colonial intercourse."[1] It was also in the port cities that physical
and human ingredients combined to produce a more versatile mercantile
and less traditionally oriented society.

In the course of the nineteenth century, the foundations for these developments were duplicated in large measure in Salonica, Alexandria, Beirut,
and, later on, Haifa. Each one of these ports was blessed by a strategic geographic position that made it a node for continental transportation, a harbor
that could be made to accommodate deep-sea vessels, a productive hinter-

land that could be exploited for its cash crops and markets, and a political and economic potential that attracted capital, exploiters, and workers. The pattern of change was also similar: sharp population growth, the assembling of many religious and ethnic minorities employed in mercantile professions, and the emergence of new social groups empowered by wealth. The introduction of capital stimulated investment in commercial and industrial projects, attracting labor. Haifa was the last in the line of modern port cities on the Mediterranean to achieve the mature status of a bustling cosmopolitan port, reaching its zenith in the 1930s under the British Mandate.

During the first decades of the century, Alexandria and Beirut were the only two ports in the eastern Mediterranean endowed with sufficient natural protection to provide safe harbors. Among the ports closest to the northern agricultural regions of Hauran and Marj Ibn 'Amir, Acre provided a secure town; Haifa had the better natural harbor but lacked an urban extension. Neither port could accommodate heavy tonnage vessels or had docking facilities. By the end of the century, Acre's standing had declined to the advantage of Haifa, as the coast of Palestine became part of the regular route of the major European steamship companies.[2] Although all these Mediterranean ports developed in similar patterns, there were clear differences dictated by their particular histories and stages of development.

By the mid nineteenth century, Haifa was still undeveloped. Its port and town facilities were negligible compared to Acre and Jaffa, but it attracted some European steamships and English yachts (in 1850, 162 vessels docked at Haifa). The potential of Haifa rested in its physical setting, the ethnic and religious diversity of its population, and its attraction to European religious and commercial activities. Eventually it became the foremost Palestinian harbor, supplanting Acre, overshadowing Jaffa, competing with Beirut, and imitating the major Mediterranean port cities.

Under the leadership of Dhaher al-'Umar al-Zaidani (1730–75), a powerful and protective state was formed in northern Palestine that fostered development. Security was ensured for agricultural production, mainly wheat and cotton for export, particularly to France whose agents resided in the Zaidani capital and port of Acre. Peasants and religious minorities were protected and thus had a stake in the success of the state.[3] In 1764–65, al-'Umar established a new town and secured it with walls.[4] Under the rule of the Ottoman Ibrahim Pasha,[5] a centralized government administered the region and implemented economic and social reforms. The country, particularly the agricultural regions, was forcibly introduced to the benefits of security and an egalitarian social and economic system, which paved the way for contacts with Europeans. By the end of the nineteenth century, these efforts bore fruit.

In 1948, following the exodus of approximately 80 percent of Haifa's Arab population, the cosmopolitan character of the city abruptly ceased. Among the participants in this process were the Zionists, whose ambitious plans for the town had been unfolding since the last two decades of the nineteenth century, adding one more layer to the factors affecting the development of the port and the form it assumed.

More than the other Palestinian ports of Gaza, Jaffa, and Acre, or inland cities of Jerusalem, Nablus, and Hebron, Haifa was the product of the changing international scene. Although it shared most of the features of the other port cities that had been revived during that century, Haifa was a new town unhindered by tradition and open to innovation, and it provided an excellent example of how changes could be made to meet the challenges of the new world order. Under the influence of political events that defined its character, Haifa assumed and molded the conflicting orientations of its residents. This situation culminated in the Mandate era and the inter-communal turbulence of the 1930s.

Topography and Demography

Geographically, Haifa sits on a strategic site accessible to a fertile agricultural hinterland in the east and north, protected by the bay of Acre and the route to Lebanon, from the south to Jaffa and Jerusalem, and further east, by the way of the Jordan Valley, to the wheat-growing areas of Hauran in Syria. A protected natural harbor with sandy shores enhances its position.

In addition to native Arabs and to Jewish immigrants, Haifa had attracted European settlers, both Jewish and Christian. Because Acre was subject to official Turkish regulations and prohibitions in an attempt to curtail European influence there, many foreign nationals and consuls chose Haifa as an alternative where a more liberal atmosphere prevailed.[6] In 1910, the population was less than 10,000, but by 1914 it had grown to 20,000, and by the first British census in 1922 to 24,634. It is safe to assume that a large proportion of the increase among all communities, as in other Mediterranean port cities, particularly Beirut and Salonica, was due to migration, both internal and external.[7]

The number of religious communities is another indication of the town's pluralistic and cosmopolitan character. By the mid nineteenth century, the population was 51 percent Muslim, 36 percent Christian, 13 percent Jewish.[8] Although the sources do not give figures for the whole century, one can conclude that the Muslims lost their numerical supremacy to the Christians; the Jewish community was also steadily growing. The Christian community, which had been estimated at over 20 percent of the total in the 1830s, grew to 40 percent in the 1870s and to 45 percent at the end of the century; it decreased to less than 40 percent in 1915 and dropped again to 36 percent in 1922. The Jewish community increased from 3 percent in the 1830s, to 10 percent by the end of the century, to 15 percent in 1915, and to 25 percent in 1922. The Muslim population decreased from nearly 80 percent in the 1830s, to around 45 percent by the end of the century; it was 38 percent in 1922.[9] These numbers do not include foreign residents: religious, merchants, consuls and their agents, and the new European Jewish immigrants (although they are often included, adding to the confusion in providing accurate statistics). Another reason for the inaccuracies was the biased reporting in favor of one community or the other often given by members of these foreign settlements.[10] It is, however, clear that the body of European residents in Haifa grew steadily after the mid nineteenth century. The reasons for the rapid growth of the population were many: enhanced security and building activities attracted villagers from the hills and entrepreneurs from the adjacent towns and districts.

Until the early decades of the twentieth century, the town remained squeezed between the mountain and the sea, with the eastern quarter exclusively Muslim, aside from a small Sephardic settlement attached to its eastern borders, and the western quarter inhabited by various Christian denominations. As was traditional in Middle Eastern towns, economic and religious institutions in the center of the city and, in this case, on the northern periphery along the seashore, between the two quarters. The seafront housed the commercial and social institutions of the town: the old suq, the official government buildings, churches and mosques, and the facilities of public service, for transportation and law enforcement. Most of the consular agents resided in rented quarters in this section close to the commercial center. Further west, outside the town, the German colony[11] stretched from the flanks of the mountain down to the sea.

Within the town walls, Europeans (both Christian missionaries and Jewish groups) attracted Arab workers. Jobs increased as European steamers transported goods from the surrounding agricultural areas. Consulates, merchants, and their agents and related services were other sources for jobs. When the Russians obtained a firman in 1857 to build a jetty at Haifa for the benefit of pilgrims to the Holy Land and the regular weekly calling of Russian steamers to the port, other Europeans viewed this with suspicion and cynicism,[12] reflecting the competition among their home countries. It also resulted in renewed efforts by the Uniate churches to attract adherents and provide them with livelihoods.

The construction of the Hijaz Railway to Haifa, completed in 1905, was the largest single building project of the time. It attracted workers from Acre, Nazareth, Nablus, and the Carmel and Marj Ibn 'Amir villages, reviving the Muslim population; laborers from Syria, Lebanon, and Egypt also converged on Haifa.[13] Oriental Jews from Morocco and Turkey, as well as some Ashkenazi Jews, settled there as well. By 1905, a Baha'i Persian community had settled in Haifa on the slopes of Mt. Carmel,[14] and a small Armenian community established itself in the old town shortly before World War I. Haifa emerged as a crossroads and a refuge for a heterogeneous population.

In the late 1870s, construction moved outside the town walls. Europeans built settlements on Mt. Carmel and to the south of Haifa. By the turn of the century, local residents, at first tentatively, also started to settle outside the confines of the old town, though still close to the boundaries of their old quarters, following the example of the Europeans seeking a more hygienic setting and less crowded surroundings. This spread was symbolic of the changing character of the town, and a first step in the weakening of ethnic, religious, social, and physical boundaries among communities that encouraged the absorption of hitherto isolated groups.

Education and European Presence

Christian, predominantly French, educational influence was first introduced to Haifa by the Roman Catholics, who built an imposing monastery on Mt. Carmel in the 1830s. This establishment had a large number of schools and convents and an impressive amount of real estate, even though it had a very small following among the population. They built the first Catholic school especially for the Uniate churches (the Greek Catholics and the Maronites), though they also accepted children of the Orthodox Church and Muslims. There were 14 Catholic schools by 1914; they educated both boys and girls.[15]

The education of the Orthodox community was contested. The Greek and Russian Orthodox churches each tried to replace the other by providing educational institutions, teaching in their respective languages. They could not compete with the French, however; most Orthodox sent their children to French (and some to English) schools, and by 1914, around 80 percent of Haifa's Catholics spoke French, as did a large number of its Orthodox inhabitants.[16]

English education for the Protestant community was introduced by the Christian Missionary Society, which opened two schools in the 1880s for boys and girls. Their influence grew after the British occupation. The Templars ran a German language school that was initially open only to the settlers' children, but later accepted other students. German influence also came through the Jewish Technical Institute, which was sponsored by Ezra, a German Jewish organization.[17] After the 1880s, other Jewish educational institutes were set up to serve the growing, mainly Ashkenazi, community; they taught Hebrew in addition to other languages and subjects. The least fortunate community were the Muslims, who had only three government schools;[18] the better-off families sent their children to the mission schools instead. The strongest educational influence remained markedly Francophone.

The German Templar pietistic colony, established in 1869 on the western boundary of the town, served more as a model than a direct influence. In Haifa it began as an agricultural settlement but grew into an urban center, planned and developed on European lines and quite unlike anything the society in Haifa knew. It provided a new style of urban living and offered services to the natives in its machine factory, bakery, and shops, as well as a profitable carriage transportation service to and from Acre and Nazareth.

In Haifa, as in other areas where missionaries were active, this "peaceful crusade" included an expansionist spirit, and it was often difficult to separate the economic from the altruistic aspects of their endeavor.[19] The religious institutions were closely linked to the consuls, who, along with their agents, were parishioners. The consuls living in Haifa represented the major European powers and often appointed local francophone Arabs as their agents. Many of these consular agents were natives of Scio and the Dalmatian isles who had married into native Syrian and Greek families. Other resident Europeans who engaged in commerce and later on in entrepreneurial services were of French and Maltese extraction.[20] With time these francophone agents enjoyed the protection of the states they represented and were able to provide similar protection to their co-religionists. In a cooperative system, the alliance of religious orders and sympathizers made its members land-owners, traders, and representatives of European powers and interest.[21] As a result, the merchant class that developed was largely Christian; it acquired socioeconomic privileges through the patronage of foreign agents. Local contacts with the Europeans had picked up momentum since mid-century, but more limited and selective, exposing some sectors of the society to certain aspects of modern Western living and thinking. One result was an expressed need for change, for better education, and for a reformed political system.[22]

This trend was strongest in Beirut, Jerusalem, and Jaffa, but Haifa followed suit after the turn of the century,[23] especially after the British occupation.[24] At that time, each Christian denomination reflected the policy line of its European patron. This campaign of Western penetration was more obvious in Haifa (a new town with a mobile, largely immigrant population and unencumbered by deeply rooted traditions) than it was in most other Palestinian towns. It was favored by missionaries and European consuls because there they could avoid the watchful Ottoman eye of Acre, the center of Ottoman administration and Muslim tradition.

Ports, Roads, and Railways

Ottoman officials and British policymakers both recognized Haifa's potential for development, but actual change came slowly.[25] The Ottoman government planned a major harbor for Haifa, the only such initiative in the eastern Mediterranean,[26] as part of its policy to centralize control and limit European encroachment. It was a project aimed at overshadowing Beirut, which was a source of political irritation to Istanbul because of the nationalist activities and pro-European orientations that thrived there. Haifa was also commercially viable because of its proximity to the increasing commercial activities in the north. Finally, by building the harbor, the Ottoman government would have a purely Ottoman port.

By the late 1870s, Acre and Nazareth were connected by a carriage route to Haifa (Jaffa was linked only in 1900 and Jenin in 1912).[27] By the end of the century, the Ottoman administration had succeeded in extending the road system to the interior, linking the major towns of the northern agricultural plains to each other, and to Haifa and the coast.

Various plans for railroad connections to benefit trade were also proposed both by European governments and by entrepreneurs. However, a comprehensive plan to upgrade the communication system was impossible to undertake for many economic and political reasons. One exception was the Hijaz Railway and its connection between Haifa and Dera'a (in today's Syria), which was completed in late 1905. This line was needed to divert economic benefits away from Beirut to the southern shores of the Mediterranean, and to endorse a project that would enhance a pan-Islamic orientation among Ottoman subjects. Through the connection with Dera'a, Haifa retained its importance as a port of export for wheat and barley from the interior of Syria. A large new central railway station was built and the old Russian pier of 1857 was extended to handle this traffic.

The British, too, had designs on Haifa as the "most suitable landing site in Syria" to protect the Suez Canal and Britain's eastern dominions.[28] Railways, ports, and canals figured in the various projects proposed by their policymakers, who finally settled on developing a transportation network centered in coastal northern Palestine; its importance was strongly felt when Turkey attacked the Suez Canal in 1915 and 1916 and threatened Britain's lifeline to the east.[29]

As part of this network, railways were built prior to and during World War I mainly for strategic and military purposes. It was via a railway built by the Expeditionary Force that Britain entered Palestine from Egypt and occupied the country between 1917 and 1918. It became part of the Palestine railways system along with the Hijaz Railway, with its headquarters at Haifa, where the British administration enlarged the station and erected large workshops. The railways, along with the deep-sea harbor built in 1933, made Haifa a major transport center in the eastern Mediterranean.

Haifa's location was the obvious locus for British strategic interests in time of war and for its economic interests in time of peace. The inhabitants of Palestine were made aware of their role through the *Palestine News*, the official organ of the British occupation. The 30 March 1919 issue reported that Haifa was destined to become a center of "the highest degree of civilization," according to British government plans, with the building of a major harbor (both military and commercial) and enlargement of the railway system.[30] This announcement was published in Arabic so that local inhabitants could read it, and it was communicated to Dr. Chaim Weizmann, president of the Zionist Organization, in detail, explaining the role Haifa would play as a commercial frontier for a British territory extending to Egypt.[31]

Economy and Society in Haifa

In the last thirty years of the nineteenth century, commercial activity in Haifa expanded rapidly in conjunction with the development of Palestine's surplus and export-oriented agricultural economy. Europeans managed the bulk of this trade, and European interests were clearly the driving force behind both the expansion and the fluctuations in exported commodities. Wheat and cereals were always in demand in the neighboring regions and Europe; cotton, and sesame and olive oil production was stimulated or discouraged according to European market demands. When the French demand for sesame grew in the 1850s, the north produced large crops for that market. When it diminished, the north reverted to producing wheat and cotton. Cotton production tripled after the outbreak of the U.S. Civil War, when European demand for it rose, and almost disappeared again in the 1870s.[32] To control production, the coastal commercial community and the producers in the interior had to forge closer links until the countryside became dependent on the city's commercial movers, who provided financial backing and controlled the land.

The expansion of trade, initially of exports but later also imports and transit trade as well, and the diversification of services in Haifa gradually involved the local Arabs in all aspects of the business from production to handling and shipping. Whether as merchants or local agents for European firms and shipping companies, Arab traders acted as collectors of exportable commodities from the Palestinian producers or from the Haurani peasants. Links between these merchants and the peasants in the villages were important in order to build trust for the credit and loan operations conducted for preharvest financing and to assure production for European markets. Because many export agents were linked to France or Germany through origin, affiliation, or education, these two countries had the lion's share of exports until World War I. Knowledge of the language and family, religious, or cultural ties to the country of import were vital for success in handling transactions in the importing country.

Real estate, building, and retail markets developed along with external and trade-related finance. The legal framework for real estate to become a market in the Ottoman Empire were the laws promulgated to guarantee individual rights of disposal over land, which Europeans had been pressed for.[33] It also satisfied the official rapacity for revenue. Religious orders such as the Templars, Christian churches, and Jewish groups purchased land, as did Europeans, for settlement. A number of landowning families acquired their titles by virtue of their traditional notable roles in their home towns — the Madis in Ijzim, the Abdul-Hadis in Arraba, the al-Khamra and al-Khalil in and around Haifa town. This list also included families of the emerging commercial bourgeoisie, mostly Christian from the coastal towns and proteges of European consuls, such as the Sursuks of Beirut and their partners the Khuris in Haifa, as well as a number of Jewish buyers of the Marj villages such as the Halfons and Levis.

Expansion in the prewar years had helped Haifa's trading community to develop through export-import and transit trade and to reach a reasonable level of sophistication. Agricultural produce was the only commodity exported; manufactured exports were negligible, and imports from abroad increasing. These developments spelled disaster to the future of the peasant economy as it did to peasant societies the world over. For the peasantry of northern Palestine, the impact of the Zionist policy of land purchases and settlement on agricultural land compounded their problems and represented an additional threat to their future. The repercussions of that policy were to unfold in the 1930s, with a revolt by dispossessed peasants. Nevertheless, Haifa port fulfilled its role, becoming one outpost in the Mediterranean chain of ports supplying Europe with raw materials and creating a society demanding European manufactured goods. By 1918, Haifa exhibited a cosmopolitan, mercantile character that was outward oriented, and at the same time projected differentiating, sometimes narrowly introverted features accentuated by the new circumstances in the town, particularly altered cultural, economic, and political conditions.

Society in Haifa showed vertical and horizontal stratifications on the confessional and social levels.[34] The criteria for social differentiation between the religious communities and among members of the same community were wealth and education. Although segregated religious communities had had contacts for at least fifty years, wariness and suspicion remained features of their relationship. Members of these communities who were directly involved in the process of economic and social change in the city were the first to break the traditional mold as inter-communal boundaries gradually crumbled. Haifa began to resemble Beirut, where heterogeneity was pronounced and tolerance and change encouraged. However, in Haifa, differences that had governed relations among religious and social groups for a long time were close to the surface and flared up rapidly at the first signs of strife.

The European presence, the spread of education, economic expansion, and an improved communication network all worked toward eroding these walls of isolation. Change filtered in through families who had acquired a social base in Haifa: Europeans, representatives of coastal banking and merchant families (the Sursuks, Twaini, Salams, Khuris), and a long train of immigrants from within Palestine, and from Syria and Lebanon.[35] The influx of European Jews settling in the town was to have its major effects on local society and its sociopolitical orientation. All of these groups helped define social consciousness and identification among the local inhabitants.

A landed/commercial bourgeoisie emerged in all religious communities.[36] This new class of entrepreneurs was connected with the growing trade with Europe, patronage of foreign agents, and links to other Levantine communities in similar conditions.[37] Christian representation in this class was more pronounced than Muslim. The latter came by their status through wealth acquired in the Ottoman era, but their ranks were strengthened by an immigrant group of entrepreneurs, particularly more sophisticated, educated, and sometimes wealthy Damascenes and Beirutis. From this stratum, a middle class emerged, whose wealth was a result of the growing importance of the town and opportunities for employment. It included both Muslim and Christian land proprietors in the town and families holding official and professional positions. As for the large, poor, laboring class, made up of mainly of Muslim manual workers employed in the railways, the port, the building and commercial sectors, and including craftsmen, they were the most exposed to the detrimental effects of the colonial process affecting Palestine.

Identity and Politics

After the mid nineteenth century, Haifa's Arab intellectuals showed signs of developing a social, cultural, and political consciousness.[38] Cultural activities seem to have been sponsored at this early stage by European and religious groups, probably with political motives. Though recorded data are scarce on the particulars of social and cultural life, it seems that it developed in each group with minimal interaction. Until the war, Europeans in Haifa had their own cultural activities, which often included local Christians and Jews. Whether as spiritual guides, educators, employers, or partners, Europeans also exposed their beliefs and ways of life to the Arabs as the culture of modernization. By 1914, these influences and Arab interaction with them were expressed in the cultural and political identity of Haifa society. Although the Muslim community as a whole was only marginally affected by Europeans, aside from a small stratum of Western-educated wealthy families, European culture was more critically and selectively acquired.

Arab cultural activities in Haifa lagged behind the more animated life in Jerusalem and Jaffa, and was led exclusively through religious affiliations. Most literary and social clubs and committees were organized by and for the benefit of one or another religious sect and were pale replicas of their counterpart organizations in Jerusalem and Beirut. However, it was in these gatherings that social, economic, and political ideas circulating in the region were imparted and ties between participants were established. Here, too, books and newspapers, published locally or imported, were made available and discussed.

Political orientations, with definite aspirations for a democratic system with equal representation, be it pan-Ottoman or pan-Arab, were issues of general concern among the young literate members of these communities.[39] It is only in retrospect that these conditions can be gauged as a result of community developments after World War I. By then ideas that had been circulating since mid-century were popularized through their importation by settlers from Beirut, Damascus, Cairo, and the Palestinian inland towns, and they were propagated through education and the press. Although some adherents to these political ideas remained adamant supporters of the French, others progressed from pro-British to Arab nationalism to unification with Syria and finally to demanding an independent Palestine.[40]

The concerns of all communities were reflected in the Arab press. After 1908 various newspapers were published in Haifa by Christians: *al-Nafa'is* and *Jirab al-Kurdi*, owned by Khalil Baidas and Tawfiq Jana respectively, were established in 1908. *Al-Karmil*, which survived until the 1940s, was founded by Najib Nassar in 1909, and *al-Nafir*, owned by Elia Zakka, in 1911.[41] While most of these papers were short-lived, they represented an embryonic literary and cultural movement among the Arab community and were a potent vehicle for politicization. They also provided many services: they reprinted scientific and news items from well-known papers circulating in Egypt, Beirut, and Europe, and they exposed and analyzed local events as they unfolded in Palestine. The Haifa paper, *al-Karmil*, was a strong critic of the Zionists and reported their activities in the city and in northern Palestine.[42] This orientation was framed within the general thrust of nationalist ideologies that had become exclusive in each ethnoreligious group. By 1914, in conjunction with the strong nationalist currents reaching Haifa via Beirut and Jerusalem, the Arab nationalists in the town recorded some triumphs by starting a branch of al-Muntada al-Adabi[43] in 1911 calling for Ottomanism. Another endorsement of this nationalist stand was their participation in the 1913 Arab Congress in Paris.

Participation in nationalist movements was lukewarm in Haifa. The francophone influence combined with concerns about economic stability defined the political orientation of the Haifa Arabs, a mercantile society whose prosperity depended on a stable society and friendly trade relations that were incompatible with nationalist demands. The newly emerging merchant/entrepreneur class in all religious groups adhered, if only superficially, to the demands of nationalism, but their economic and cosmopolitan interests dictated their true allegiance. They sought political power for themselves. Muslim families like the al-Khamra, al-Khalil, Shukri, and Karaman, who had been powerful before the British occupation, continued to wield power afterwards. The ambitions of Christian families, particularly after 1918 (Bishop Hajjar, Tuma, Khayat, Khuris), found fulfillment under the British.

All through the period under study, the cosmopolitan character of the town remained, but societal tensions fed by divergent nationalist orientations threatened it. The Jewish community grew rapidly before and after the war, in tandem with the success of European penetration and its endorsement of the Zionist project. The tiny Sephardic community residing in Haifa since early in the century was flooded by young Ashkenazi Zionist settlers, driven by a nationalist commitment to build a state. By the 1920s, this orientation was the overriding feature of the Jewish community of Haifa. Similarly, Arab nationalism and its many variants affected both Muslims and Christians. Adherents to these ideological currents from all parties became more vocal by the 1920s; although economic competition had often been at the base of tension between religious groups, in the end it was ideology, not economics that undermined the stability of the town and led to communal splintering in the 1930s.

In 1918, a new administration launched Haifa into an era of modernization that attracted people with mercantile outlooks and tolerance of diversity. But these people soon clashed with the administrative centralizing policies and the plans of the Zionist movement, both of which spawned mounting oppositional reactions from the Arab society, even from those who were least inclined to change the status quo. The Arabs of Haifa were particularly sensitive to the Zionist project, because Haifa and the north experienced its impact earlier and more closely than other regions of Palestine. These developments worked against the aspirations of those strata of the population hoping to build a cosmopolitan port city. Furthermore, the fears of this stratum were realized when Haifa lost its heterogeneous, portlike features after 1948.

Notes

1. Cagler Keyder, Eyup Ozveren, and Donald Quartaert, "Port-Cities in the Ottoman Empire: Some Theoretical and Historical Perspectives," *Review* 16, no. 4 (Fall, 1993): 520.
2. Alexander Scholch, "European Penetration and Economic Development of Palestine, 1856–1882," in Roger Owen, ed., *Studies in the Economic and Social History of Palestine in the Nineteenth and Twentieth Centuries* (Chicago, 1982), p. 43; Ruth Kark, *The Land That Became Israel* (New Haven, 1990), p. 67.
3. For this period, see Amnon Cohen, *Palestine in the 18th Century* (Jerusalem, 1973), pp. 11–14; Emile Tuma, *Filastin fi-l ʿAhd al-ʿUthmani* (Amman, n.d), pp. 37–52.
4. Cohen, *Palestine in the 18th Century*, pp. 137–44; and Alex Carmel, *Tarikh Haifa fi ʿAhd al-Atrak al-ʿuthmaniyyin* (Haifa, 1979), pp. 77–96.
5. Tuma, *Filastin*, pp. 53–100; Charles Issawi, *Studies in the Economic and Social History of the Middle East and North Africa* (New York, 1982); Scholch, "European Penetration," pp. 10–87; Baruch Kimmerling and Joel Migdal, *Palestinians: The Making of a People* (New York, 1993), pp. 6–10; William Polk, *The Opening of South Lebanon* (Cambridge, 1963), pp. 90–94.
6. I. Schattner, "Haifa: A Study in the Relations of City and Coast," *Israel Exploration Journal*, 4 (1954): 43; also see Mary Eliza Rogers, *Domestic Life in Palestine* (London, 1863). Rogers, the sister of the British vice-consul Edward Rogers, lived in Haifa and had close contacts with the communities there between 1855 and 1857. She refers to the growing European community in Haifa and the choice by her brother Edward of Haifa as his base.
7. May Seikaly, "The Arab Society of Haifa: A Study in Transformation, 1918–1936," D. Phil. thesis, Oxford University, 1983, p. 20, table I.
8. Rogers, *Domestic Life*, p. 85.
9. Carmel, *Tarikh Haifa*, pp. 147, 209–10; Rafiq al-Tamimi and Bahjat Halabi, *Wilayat Beirut* (Beirut, 1335/1914), p. 232; Najib Qubʾain, *Taqrir Tarikhi lil-taiʾfa al-Injiliyya al-Usquftyya al-ʿArabiyya bi-Haifa* (Haifa, 1940); *Census of Palestine, 1922* (Jerusalem, 1922), p. 6.
10. May Seikaly, *Haifa: Transformation of an Arab Society, 1918–1930* (London, 1995), pp. 19–21.

11. The German colony was established in 1869 by the Templar Association, a German pietistic movement of puritanical social persuasion. Its members combined the zeal to live the true Christian life with productive endeavors. They supplied their colony and the local community with agricultural produce, European style goods, and machinery workshops. See Seikaly, *Haifa*, p. 23; Alex Carmel, "The German Settlers in Palestine and Their Relations with the Local Arab Population and the Jewish Community 1868–1918," in *Studies on Palestine during the Ottoman Period*, ed. Moshe Maoz (Jerusalem, 1975), pp. 442–65.

12. Rogers, *Domestic Life*, pp. 396, 411.

13. Carmel, *Tarikh Haifa*, p. 227.

14. Ebenezer Esselmont, *Baha'ullah and the New Era* (London, 1923), p. 5.

15. See Carmel, *Tarikh Haifa*, pp. 267–71; Zev Vilnay, *Khaifa Be'avar Ve Bahoveh* (Tel Aviv, 1936), pp. 146–50.

16. Tamimi and Halabi, *Wilayat Beirut*, p. 251.

17. Carmel, *Tarik Haifa*, p. 272.

18. Ibid., p. 267; Tamimi and Halabi, *Wilayat Beirut*, p. 237.

19. Scholch, "European Penetration," p. 11.

20. Ibid., pp. 87–90, 178–79, 86; also see Seikaly, *Haifa*, pp. 26–44.

21. Ibid., pp. 10–87; Rogers, *Domestic Life*, pp. 50–98, 104, 154, 309.

22. Ibid., pp. 178–80.

23. See Albert Hourani, "Ottoman Reform and the Politics of Notables," in *The Emergence of the Modern Middle East* (London, 1981); Leila Fawaz, *Merchants and Migrants in Nineteenth-Century Beirut* (Cambridge, 1983), pp. 85–89; Rogers, *Domestic Life*, pp. 376, 380, 391–92.

24. See Seikaly, *Haifa*, chapters 1–3.

25. Tamimi and Halabi, *Wilayat Beirut*, p. 230; Rashid Khalidi, *British Policy Towards Syria and Palestine, 1906–1914*, St. Antony's Middle East Monograph 11 (London 1980), pp. 62–66.

26. Kark, *The Land that Became Israel*, p. 69.

27. Ibid., p. 60.

28. Halford Lancaster Hoskins, *British Routes to India* (London, 1966), pp. 399–407.

29. Khalidi, *British Policy*, p. 367.

30. *Palestine News*, 30 March 1919, p. 1.

31. Public Records Office, FO 371/E3807/131/44. Memo, Dept of Overseas Trade to Dr. Weizmann, 26 April 1920.

32. Scholch, "European Penetration," pp. 13–17; 60–61.

33. Ibid., p. 21; also, Issawi, *Studies in the Middle East and North Africa*, pp. 62–76; Kimmerling and Migdal, *Palestinians*, pp. 11–12.

34. Ilbert, "Beyrouth," p. 20.

35. See Seikaly, *Haifa*, chapter 3.
36. The socioeconomic stratification of the Arab communities of Haifa has been inferred from a study of marriage registers for the period 1890–1920, Seikaly, *Haifa*, pp. 35, 43, n. 32.
37. Ibid., pp. 26–29.
38. Rogers, *Domestic Life*, esp. pp. 161–63, 361, 400, 407.
39. Yehoshua Porath, *The Emergence of the Palestinian Arab National Movement, 1918–1929* (London, 1974), pp. 26–28.
40. See Seikaly, *Haifa*, chapters 3 and 13.
41. Jamil Bahri, *Tarikh Haifa* (Haifa, 1922), pp. 29–34; also Ahmad al-Aqqad, *Tarikh al-Sahafa al-'Arabiyya fi-Filastin* (Damascus, 1967).
42. Seikaly, *Haifa*, chapters 3 and 13.
43. Izzat Darwaza, *Nasha't al-Haraka al-'Arabiyya al-Haditha* (Sidon, 1971), pp. 353–60. The Muntada was the platform of Arab nationalist students in Istanbul. Its aim was to revive Arab culture, irrespective of religious differences, within the framework of Ottomanism.

6 Islamic Universalism and the Construction of Regional Identity in Turn-of-the-Century Basra: Sheikh Ibrahim al-Haidari's Book Revisited

Hala Fattah

Like most port cities in the Indian Ocean, Basra was shaped by a number of diverse influences emanating from its peculiar position as a hub for regional trade and culture.[1] Strong commercial contacts in the Indian Ocean had a long history; traders from Iraq, Persia, the Gulf, and Arabia had been conducting business with the Indian ports of Gujarat, Konkan, and Malabar from the very beginning of the Islamic era.[2] Even though Basra province was part of the Ottoman Empire from at least the mid seventeenth century onwards, the overland and seaborne trade that was its *raison d'être* was, to a large extent, centered in India. Basra and other ports in the region shipped such goods as grain, wool, dates, and horses to India. Basra received textiles, sugar, rice, paper, glass, and iron in return, which were more often than not transshipped to Persia, Syria, and the Arabian Peninsula. More significantly, India continued to be the region's main commercial outlet until the early twentieth century.

Over time, the India-centered nature of regional trade tended to endow certain ports and market towns of Iraq, Arabia, and the Gulf with a distinctive character, a cultural specificity that was absent in other economic centers of the region. Traditionally both a market for overland trade, and a bustling international port, Basra had a heterogeneous and fluctuating clientele. By the nineteenth century, Persians, Afghans, Indians, and Arabs from the littoral as well as the interior made Basra their primary—or sometimes secondary—home.[3] Because trade necessitated the emergence of family firms overseas to link up with the parent company at home, many regional merchants set up shop in India.

Indian influence was particularly pervasive in Basra from the last quarter of the nineteenth century on. Although many of Basra's merchant families sent younger brothers or sons to Bombay in pursuit of business, many of these junior partners settled in western Indian towns and regions and founded families of their own. They contributed to the cultural life of their new home towns with great enthusiasm and formed family associations that tried to integrate their cultural traditions with those of their newly adopted home region. Under the influence of wealthy Arab patrons, Arab schools were opened in Bombay and Arabic-language presses were established to publish newspapers, books, and journals.

The city also became a magnet for Gulf businessmen seeking medical attention or political refuge; a number of Arab exiles temporarily out of favor with Ottoman or, much later, British authorities, were sent there to cool their political ardor.[4] It is also worth noting that the social, economic, political, and literary links between Iraq and India continued to be reaffirmed throughout the century. As late as 1907, high officials from Hyderabad were traveling to Basra and Baghdad on horse-buying expeditions.[5]

Of course, strong trading connections with Bombay and Calcutta only reinforced the Ottoman Empire's diverse economic base and its multiplicity of links with the outside world. But Basra also functioned as an Ottoman military base. From at least the middle of the seventeenth century on, it was the locus of a significant part of the imperial fleet and a base for seaborne operations against Portuguese, Dutch, British, and Gulf Arab navies and merchant shipping. In the last quarter of the nineteenth century, its fleet in shambles and its governors insolvent, the town still commanded a measure of respect, even among the Gulf sheikhdoms on the opposite side of the Shatt al-Arab. In 1871, in a move underpinning Basra's military role, the town became the base of operations for the Ottoman re-occupation of the Arabian Peninsula. The military expedition that set off to reconquer Najd by land and sea was, in large part, composed of Nizam troops and tribal armies led by the sheikh of the Muntafiq confederation of southern Iraq, the ruling sheikh of Kuwait, and other provincial notables.[6]

The point is that Basra had a double heritage: on the one hand, its strong trading links with India encouraged diverse peoples to settle in the area around the port on a temporary or permanent basis. The date trade, the largest seasonal fair in the Shatt al-Arab region, drew merchants, agriculturalists, shippers, and livestock traders from all over the Indian Ocean for three months a year.[7] The port of Basra itself was not only a conduit for foreign trade but a depot and market for a steady stream of tribal merchants from the Arabian Peninsula and the province's interior. In other words, the inhabitants of both the port town and its hinterland, although not socially or even religiously in harmony with one another, still found a rationale for mixing and socializing at Basra.

Because it was the economic hub of the Shatt al-Arab region, Basra became a zone of rapid cultural diffusion. A composite culture based on the transient lifestyle of merchants, shippers, sailors, traveling ulama, and journeying officials became the overriding feature that marked Basra off from inland towns or European-influenced enclaves. It was this dynamic that helped shape the ideological climate that spurred the competing cultural movements of the last quarter of the nineteenth century.

On the other hand, Basra was also home to a landholding and merchant elite of Arab lineage and Ottomanized culture; however, that culture was often a veneer. For instance, up to 1908, Turkish was hardly spoken in Basra except by the administrative class and was so little in demand that one clever Rushdiyya-educated lawyer, Suleiman Faidi, was able to monopolize the business of translation into Arabic of all of the Turkish-language documentation required by the Basra courts.[8]

Because of their short stays in office, the Ottoman walis at Basra were not of a mind to transform the social or economic climate of the place. Conditions remained primitive. At the turn of the century, there was only one doctor in Basra and two medium-sized hospitals. Even drinking water was circumscribed: the rich drank from the middle of the Shatt, the poor from the muddy Ashar River. And because there were no paved roads, in winter, the rich hired porters to carry them across the muddy streets.[9]

Basra's real government lay in the hands of a clique of powerful local families, of which the al-Naqib, the Salman, the Mandil, and the Sani' families were the most important. The Naqibs were easily the foremost merchant-ulema family of Basra. Their prosperity rose through *waqf* lands, date properties and mercantile activities with India. Before 1908, their most famous representative, Sayyid Talib, eldest son of the *naqib al-ashraf*, had established intra-regional connections with the sheikhs of Muhammara and Kuwait, playing the emerging power of the Saud family of Riyadh against the still-powerful Rashid amirs of Ha'il (northern Najd) and, even in the face of his many entanglements with several Ottoman walis of Basra, remained friendly with the Porte and its representatives.[10] Paying lip service to the Ottoman administration, Sayyid Talib's influence reached its apex when he was appointed *mutassarif* (district governor) of al-Ahsa.[11]

The overpowering dynamic running through Basra's history was therefore regional. Whether small trader or rich landholder, Basra looked to the Gulf for prosperity and profit. It is therefore all the more fascinating that the radical changes that shook Basra's moral-religious climate in the latter part of the nineteenth century came from the long-neglected interior.

Basra the Port and Basra the Hinterland

In 1907, a British report noted that, despite the importance of its transit trade, the port of Basra was still undeveloped.[12] Because it was "restricted by a bar where only at the full moon and new moon was there enough water to allow access to fully loaded vessels,"[13] the harbor was dotted with small native boats and lighters unloading the larger ships. In many ways, the report continued, Basra resembled the less significant Gulf anchorages of Bushire and Bandar Abbas in both the nature of its trade and its inefficient port administration.

Nonetheless, Basra served British interests well. By 1907, British merchants had capitalized on a century and a half of effort and made vast inroads in the regional markets of Iraq, the Mediterranean and the Indian Ocean. In Iraq alone, British ships captured 96 percent of the volume of Basra trade and gained unquestioned supremacy in the foreign trade of the Iraqi provinces.[14] In that respect, the British perception of Basra was indeed correct: it had proved to be a necessary point of entry for the control of Gulf markets, and beyond that, those of the Middle East. But the more pervasive notion that Basra was only the sum total of its harbor was completely off the mark. In fact, from the point of view of its different constituencies, Basra was many things. Far from it simply being a port for foreign trade, the province of Basra also had a large and diverse hinterland, embracing a swath of nomadic territory and a settled interior, riverine market towns, and shrine cities. Although the traditions of the port were often at odds with those of the hinterland, they were not completely distinct. British shippers and merchants, who rarely ventured inland, can be forgiven for thinking that Basra was nothing more than a shabby, nondescript harbor, an obligatory stage in the journey from British India. But the reality was that the port-province of Basra was host to a multiplicity of currents emanating from a scattered and disparate population with competing loci of authority. It was during the years

1876–1914 that those currents came to a head, ushering in a new religious-cultural momentum that was to grip Basra for decades to come.[15]

The Expansion of Shi'ism and the Resurgence of the Khilafa Idea

From about 1780 to 1908, the province of Basra witnessed a resurgence or revival of two overlapping cultural trends that contended for ideological space. One was the increasing conversion of southern tribesmen (many living within the reconfigured Basra vilayet) from imperfectly applied, little-assimilated Sunni tenets to more strictly held Shi'i principles. The second development dates from the accession of Abdülhamid II to the sultanate. It consisted of the Hamidian strategy of reinculcating a more rigorous Islam into "lapsed" Sunni communities everywhere in the empire, and popularizing that ethical commitment so that it reached a larger audience. These two contradictory impulses clashed, touching off a serious struggle for the hearts and minds of the ordinary town- or country-dweller. The permutations of the problem not only impinged directly on the nature of the Sunni-Shi'i relationship within the province of Basra (as well as Najaf and Karbala), but had a direct bearing on Sultan Abdülhamid's strategy of ideological legitimation.[16] Because the Sunni counter-offensive was part of an ideological campaign to win back the empire, Sultan Abdülhamid was actively concerned in its propagation in the particularly sensitive Arab province of Iraq.

The local historian who records these developments, Sheikh Ibrahim al-Haidari, even while devoting a large section of his history to the emergence of sectarian identity in "the south," also wrote detailed accounts of Basra's history and traditions that linked it to the Gulf region as a whole. His attention to and emphasis on the geographic and social boundaries of the province provides evidence of the political dimensions of space, especially as it pertained to the ever-shifting frontier in Iraq, Arabia, and the Gulf. It is here that the influences of regional trade are most clearly seen; Basra the province and Basra the port, although attached to different foci in reality, emerge as one and the same in the literary imagination of Sheikh Ibrahim Fasih ibn Sabghatullah al-Haidari.

A spate of new research on the dynamics of moral and religious authority in late-eighteenth- and early nineteenth-century Iraq has uncovered a wide-ranging and systematic movement of conversion from Sunni to Shi'i tenets.[17] Beginning in the late eighteenth century and continuing at an accelerated pace until at least the 1920s, this sectarian change transformed the moral-cultural climate of most of Iraq's tribes, whether sedentary or nomadic. Although conversion had been a feature of Islamic history from the inception of the first *fitna*, it intensified as a result of various historical circumstances. Conversion was a deliberate policy on the part of the leading ulama of Najaf to create a defensive cordon of Shi'i tribes against further Wahhabi incursions. It was also the byproduct of a sedentarization process in the nineteenth century, as formerly nomadic tribes settled on newly watered tracts of land as tillers of the soil. If it is true that, in Batatu's words, "Islam sat lightly on the bedouin,"[18] then perhaps settled tribesmen were more inclined to listen to the moral admonishments of the tribe's resident *sayyid*, a descendant of the Imam 'Ali through his wife Fatima al-Zahra'. The latter often functioned as a pole around which the tribe's sheikh and followers could reconcile their often fragmentary visions of the world.[19] As a result of this acculturation, tribesmen were also more eager to hear out Shi'i *ākhūnds* and *mu'mins*, missionaries who circulated among the tribes to preach and proselytize.

Although tribal settlement was actively encouraged by several Tanzimat-era walis in Iraq, who considered it the duty of the more urbane and benevolent of the padishah's men to "civilize" the rabble in the countryside,[20] the mass conversion to Shi'ism was a totally unexpected outcome. Even though many of the chiefs of the paramount tribes, with whom the Ottoman walis had been accustomed to meet, remained Sunni,[21] this was nonetheless viewed as a disturbing phenomenon by Ottoman observers, who took note of the development only after it had made vast inroads among the southern Iraqi tribes. In 1869–71, the rapid acculturation of Iraqi tribes had reached such proportions that it began to alarm the Porte. However, it was only in 1886 that Sultan-Caliph Abdülhamid II realized the extent of "the Shi'i threat."[22]

After many reports had filtered into the Yıldız palace from all corners of the empire, Sultan Abdülhamid decided to act. Couching his message in the vocabulary of pan-Islamic resurgence, he embarked on a full-scale re-education process in which Sunni "missionaries" and schools would act as the vanguard of an Ottoman-led Sunni counteroffensive in Iraq and other "wayward" provinces. Although the pan-Islamic message did not originate with the Shi'i problem in Iraq but may have had its roots in a genuinely

thought-out campaign of ideological resistance and legitimation devised by
the sultan-caliph himself, Iraq was an important part of the experiment.[23]

An example from Iraq may be sufficient to explain the effect of Hamidian
policy on the ground. The Baghdad-born *'alim* and judge, Sheikh Mustafa
Nur al-Din al-Wa'iz (1844–1912), who had been a member of the legal
establishment in both Baghdad and Basra, was transferred to the Shi'i district
of Hilla-Diwaniyya in 1882. Under the influence of Hamidian efforts to
revive Sunni *fiqh* and education, the wali of Baghdad, Hassan Rafiq Pasha
appointed five ulama as roving professors of law in the five districts judged
most in need of such attention. Significantly, these districts were populated
for the most part by Shi'i tribesmen and townsmen.[24] In his capacity as judge
and professor of law, al-Wa'iz was given the task of reforming education in
the district. He devised a curriculum that was reminiscent of classic Ottoman
principles of religious education. He began:

> The things that bring about eternal happiness and knowledge and
> result in succor and success [are] victory for the peasant, and [to that
> end] the highest posts of honor for the individual are the principles of
> religion, and its organization through knowledge; however, of late,
> ignorance has taken over with the appeal of fraudulent preachers
> (*du'at*) and has blanketed large areas of Iraq.[25]

Heaping praise on Sultan Abdülhamid for being "a renovator of mosques
and religion,"[26] he continues to list the characteristics of the ideal teacher.
He must be familiar with the religious principles he will be teaching, understand what the purpose of education is, be clear in class, courteous, gra-
cious, respectful, and dignified and never, ever be intolerant.[27] The true
teacher must explain the difference between a Prophet and a Messenger,
make students believe in all the Prophets and Messengers of God, elucidate
the virtues and moral excellence of the Ahl al-Bayt (the Prophet's House)
and "however much he can, elaborate upon the stories of the *sahāba* (Companions), and especially on the three *Rāshidūn* (Rightly-Guided Caliphs,
'Ali being conspicuously absent) and their right to the Caliphate."[28] Significantly, al-Wa'iz was one of the select Iraqi ulama who received decorations
and honors from the sultan in the early part of the twentieth century.

Because pan-Islamism was a universalist ideology that aimed at reinvig-
orating the Islamic *ummah* as a whole, it also influenced the Indian subcontinent, and found ready echoes in Basra. As a result of the Russo-Turkish

war (1877–79), after which the Ottoman Empire ceded more than one-third of its territory to foreign powers, as a matter of strategy, "the empire had no alternative but to rely on its Muslim elements for survival."[29] The increasing emphasis placed on the caliphate idea during the war instigated a strong response from Indian Muslims who donated large amounts of money to the Ottoman campaign, organized solidarity events, and wrote articles in the newly emergent local press in support of the padishah's troops.

There is also evidence that Iraqi Arab religious leaders from Baghdad and Basra made important connections with the Indian notability, particularly the nawabs of Hyderabad (in the Deccan) and forged a pan-Islamic bond that did not entirely originate with Sultan Abdülhamid's *khilafa* question. For instance, during the Russo-Turkish war of 1877–79, Sayyid Salman Efendi, *naqib al-ashraf* of Baghdad, involved himself in the campaign to aid the empire's wounded soldiers and the families of those killed in the war. To that end, he dispatched his brother Sayyid 'Abdul-Rahman Efendi to Bombay to collect funds for the war effort. While in India, Sayyid 'Abdul-Rahman wrote a pamphlet calling for Muslim solidarity with the empire (originally published in two languages, Arabic and Urdu), addressing it to all Indian Muslims. Sayyid 'Abdul-Rahman's mission was reportedly very successful, and a sum of 10,000 rupees was collected in a short period of time, but the story does not end there.[30]

While aboard ship, and especially during his stay in Hyderabad, Sayyid 'Abdul-Rahman also composed numerous verses that he collected in a *diwan* so that he could publish them in *Diyar al-Hindiyya* (The Lands of India).[31] Basically jottings "so that he could remember everything in place," they are also a subtle account of the links between Muslim intellectuals from Baghdad and Bombay, links that had survived the barrier of language and were translated in the warmest of welcomes from amir to court poet.

Sectarian Change, Regional Realities, and Political Centralization in the Narrative of Sheikh Ibrahim al-Haidari

Perhaps the one historian who captures the various trends best was Sheikh Ibrahim Fasih ibn Sabghatullah al-Haidari (1820–82). Descended from a long line of religious scholars, al-Haidari was one of the most eminent scholars of Baghdad. Up to 1830, the Haidari *sadah* held the position of *mufti* (jurisconsult) for both the Hanafi and Shafi'i schools of law;[32] then, for reasons that Sheikh Ibrahim does not make clear, they were stripped of the Hanafi post. The Haidaris were also entitled to collect the *jizya* tax from the Jewish, Christian, and Sabean communities in Basra; and some time afterwards (the information is sketchy), members of the Haidari family were granted salaries from the state. Finally, they were important landholders, possessing, by one count, thirty villages outside of Baghdad and in the north.[33]

Al-Haidari's history is significant, in part for the importance he places on sectarian identity. Whereas other historians mention Iraqi sects *en passant*, al-Haidari makes the examination of Shi'i tribes and merchants a major aspect of his work. Even though he gives short shrift to the Shi'i merchant families in his book (devoting one page to them, whereas Sunni families, his own included, consume 15), his attitude is not completely one of benign neglect. Although written in a sober and matter-of-fact tone, his point was to note which families (four out of 13) originally had been Sunnis and which had become Shi'i or, in his ideological terminology, *rafada* (rejecters).[34]

But his disquiet with the status quo is especially evident with the tribal confederations and families in Iraq. He notes, for instance, that the great tribal confederations of the Rabi'a, the Banu Tamim, the Khaza'il, part of the Zubaid, the Shammar Toqah, and the Banu Lam *tarāfādu* (had become Shi'i), and dated their conversion to the turn of the century. Of the Banu Tamim (one of the Arab confederations that settled in Iraq at the time of the Islamic conquest), al-Haidari states that "they became *rafada* in Iraq sixty years ago as a result of the efforts of the *rafada* devils [who settled amongst them]," obviously a reference to the Shi'i *mu'mins* or scholar-preachers who had a hand in spreading the Shi'i *da'wa*, message, in the south or east of the country.[35] Of the Shammar Toqah, he notes, "They claim that they are descended from the famous Shammar tribe (from Najd, one of the 'aristo-cratic' camel-breeding tribes) but the latter deny it."[36]

However, it is in his section on Basra that al-Haidari really betrays his bias against the Shi'a. He notes that, from a historic point of view, with the exception of Basra and the *ahl al-jūnūb* (the people of the south), the people of Shatt al-Arab are all Shi'a. Therefore,

> The *rafada* in Basra province are not from Basra itself but from the 'Ajam [Persians, sometimes foreigners] and al-Bahrain and some from the desert areas of Shatt al-Arab, for if [the individual] is from Basra, he would be Sunni and likewise for those from the south.[37]

Then, striking a blow for Sunni "orthodoxy" that Sultan Abdülhamid would have appreciated, he says, "And the people from the Shatt al-Arab and the districts surrounding Basra who became *rafaḍa* did so because of lack of ulama."[38] Warming to his theme, al-Haidari continues:

> If Basra's resplendent past as one of the great centers of Islamic learning remains only a memory, and has sunk into the abyss of ignorance, it is because there are no scholar-preachers or patrons of learning to teach or spread the message of Islam. Had it not been for the valiant efforts of the merchant houses of Zubair [a town near Basra] and Najd, especially those of the Zuhair family, the region would have long ago fallen into intellectual decline. . . . Basra needs education and religious teachers and the building of schools and the spread of industries and skills.[39]

Here was the crux of the problem: if the Ottoman Empire refused to intervene in Basra's educational system, then the townspeople would come under the combined influence of schismatics from both the Shatt al-Arab and the Shi'i shrine cities. The danger was great because, unlike Baghdad (and al-Haidari was fiercely proud of Baghdad), Basra was an alarmingly open town. In a key passage, he laments the fact that he had

> never seen a town or village comparable to Basra in the ruins of its mansions, the dominance of foreigners on the town and its inhabitants, and in the lack of education of its people and the destruction of its mosques and schools.[40]

These "foreigners" were, of course, all those traders and middlemen who ran the India trade: the horse suppliers, date growers, grain merchants, and ship captains that bought, sold, and transshipped goods from Aleppo, Ha'il (northern Najd), Muhammara, and Kuwait. Even though al-Haidari finds many of these people to be of dubious character, he spends a large section of his book detailing the port towns and market towns of the Gulf region, whence they came. In the process, he redraws the region, revealing the gradual erosion of the Porte's influence in southern Iraq and the Gulf and describing the reality of shrinking frontiers under the impact of European advances.

The book can be read on several levels. For although it is clear that his work was written partly to reassert the Ottoman state's hegemony over areas in dispute (such as Arabistan and Yemen), the author also manifests a secondary loyalty to local dynasts such as the Rashid family in northern Najd.[41] Although it is true that the Rashid amirs were on-and-off Ottoman allies, they too played the Porte off against other potentates, and at one point even asked the British for protection in their struggle to free themselves of Ottoman domination. Sometimes al-Haidari's divided allegiances conflict with each other on the same page, as for instance when his admiration for local rulers in the Gulf threatens to overwhelm his attachment to the Ottoman state. Yet it is all of a piece for al-Haidari; his fractured loyalties and shifting identities are well within the realm of modern sensibilities. At the same time, his ideological defense of both the Ottoman state and local powers in the Gulf and Arabian Peninsula must be perceived as being totally in keeping with his heightened pan-Islamic consciousness; from within that politicized worldview, his attack on British designs in the Gulf therefore comes as no surprise (of which more later).

Al-Haidari was writing in an era in which concerted international attempts were being made to mediate the tangled "border question" between Ottoman Iraq and Qajar Iran. To understand his attention, one has to be familiar with the frontier problem up to his time. The conferences at Erzerum (1844–47), held under the auspices of a four-nation frontier commission, had taken place some years before al-Haidari put pen to paper; however, the issues surrounding the demarcation of the Iraq-Iran frontier were still causing reverberations. For instance, one of the most perplexing issues that the commission had to face was the ownership of Muhammara and the adjoining districts on the Shatt al-'Arab. Because both Turkey and Persia claimed it, the commission resorted to a time-honored way of settling the question. It attempted to determine whether the Kaab tribe, the most important tribe in and around Muhammara and its neighboring districts, had paid taxes to either empire and if so, for how long. It also tried to determine the length of Kaab occupancy in the districts of Arabistan. In order to ascertain the historical background to these questions, Sheikh Thamir, the former chief of the Kaab tribe in Arabistan/Khuzistan, was asked to attend the proceedings of the border commission; and on the morning of 11 August 1843, the sheikh made his appearance at the conference.

In answer to the question of the commissioners, the sheikh stated his name and title but when asked to produce evidence of legal writ confirming his possession of the districts in question, he immediately replied, "I have no papers; we do not understand such things."[42] He then proceeded:

> Gobban [Qubban, the old administrative capital of Arabistan] is situated near the sea, and extends from the Karun River to the Shatt al-Arab. My ancestors have been in possession between one and two hundred years. I paid the *mīrī* tax to Bussorah [Basra] till last year, but not regularly since 1836–1837. We paid the *mīrī* tax for that part of the land that belongs to Turkey. Part belongs to Persia, and I have paid 1,200 *tomans* a year to the Persians for that part of it until thirty-three years ago when the sum was increased, last year's tribute is in the hands of a banker, but we do not know who to pay it to as Persia and Turkey both claim the land.[43]

Although the port of Muhammara and its adjoining districts were finally awarded to Persia in return for Ottoman control of the Kurdish principalities on the northern frontier, boundary questions continued to bedevil the region, as they do today. For al-Haidari, the commission's grant of Muhammara to Persia did not make the slightest difference; he continued to support Ottoman pretensions to a wider imperial frontier. Writing in 1869, he continued to claim that:

> On the eastern bank of Basra is 'Abadan and Qubban and they are inside the borders of Basra and part of *sāwād al-'Iraq*. Muhammara, Abadan, Qubban, Dawraqistan are all within the properties [*milk*] of the High Porte up to a district called Buniyya which is also part of the Porte's domains, and the island of 'Abadan [on the opposite side of Shatt al-Arab] is called the *minbar* [pulpit] of Iraq because it has so many scholars and saints.[44]

Al-Haidari's depiction of the territories on the Shatt is remarkable both for its all-inclusiveness and its specificity. Thus, on the one hand, 'Abadan, Muhammara, Qubban, and Dawraqistan were all included under Ottoman sovereignty because they were well within the borders of Ottoman Basra; on the other hand, 'Abadan is claimed as part of Iraq. The novelty is that although al-Haidari's Iraq is clearly within the Ottoman sphere, it is already delineated as a distinct territory. Thus, muffled as it is, the first indication of an emergent Iraqi identity appears almost incidentally in al-Haidari's work. The corollary is that it is attached to a resurgent Sunni awareness.

Al-Haidari also seems to be the first Iraqi historian who clearly perceives the seeds of conflict in the Ottoman policy of centralization in the mid nineteenth century. He traces the resurgence of Ottoman sovereignty in Bahrain and Yemen, but he also notes the British creeping annexation in the Gulf. His account of the situation in Bahrain deserves to be quoted in full:

> Al-Manama and al-Muharriq [two towns of Bahrain] are the property of the state but there is a strong rivalry between the English and the Ottomans over Bahrain. Although Bahrain's rulers continue to claim fealty to the Porte, and even though the state did not forget the people of Bahrain, it seems to have been concerned with other more important matters. Bahrain's people are facing a dilemma with the English. It is very surprising that the *walis* of Baghdad can continue to ignore the problems of this great region especially since it is part of the Arabian peninsula which itself is part of the Ottoman state. This is all the more astonishing since the state extinguished the power of Ibn Saud (who is a dependent of the state) so how can they allow the English to interfere in the affairs of Bahrain when it is openly part of the High Porte? As for the claims of the Iranian state on Bahrain, it is on the level of their claims that Mecca and Medina are also theirs, as is the whole of the Arabian peninsula! And as for the fealty (*intisab*) of some of the people of Bahrain at certain times to the Iranian state, because of the fear of English domination, it is like the drowning man who attaches himself to a few blades of grass [the logic being] that they can repulse Iranian troops but they cannot defeat the English navy. Because they have nothing to fear from the Iranians, they can swear allegiance to them. Their allegiance to the Iranians comes only after they swore in the loudest voices and from every corner [of Bahrain] that they were part of the Ottoman state. [They were forced to do this] because no one answered their pleas.[45]

Al-Haidari clearly puts the blame for the sorry state of affairs in Bahrain and later in Yemen as well, on the Ottoman state's inaction.[46] The empire's half-hearted centralizing policies were roundly castigated by the author because they failed to block British political and economic ascendancy or reassert Ottoman claims in the Gulf. Even though the reality was that most of the sheikhdoms on the littoral had already moved away from Ottoman rule in all but name, al-Haidari thought the empire should persevere in its efforts at foiling secessionist tendencies. Not realizing that it was too late and that regional autonomy had already won, Sheikh Ibrahim al-Haidari, the diehard Ottoman centralizer, continued to berate the walis of his time for not upholding the status quo ante in Iraq, Arabia and the Gulf.

Conclusion

By the beginning of the twentieth century, a major transformation had occurred in the moral-religious climate of southern Iraq. Led by the 'atabāt (Shi'i shrine cities), the Shi'i conversion movement made large inroads among Iraq's tribes, both semi-settled and settled. Over the decades, the 'atabāt themselves grew more powerful. Shi'i activism became more pronounced with "the emergence of the mujtahids as a major force in politics between 1908 and 1920, influenced by the revival of the Usuli legal school, the centralization of the Shi'i leadership, and the impact of the modernist Islamic thinkers."[47] Ironically, this set the tone for the greater participation of the Iraqi Shi'a in their country's politics and national rebirth in the era of independence.

The Sunni counteroffensive, by contrast, sputtered to a halt after the 1908 revolution because sectarian issues were not the overriding consideration that tied communities together in Iraq. In spite of a widespread tendency in the literature to view Iraqis in purely sectarian terms, there were other developments that counterbalanced growing confessional cleavages in the period 1876–1914. For one thing, the external threats posed by Russian or British designs on the Ottoman Empire and Iran made influential observers realize that the rapprochement of the Muslim peoples as a whole was imperative. It is therefore not completely correct to view sectarian issues as leading to separatist movements walling off religious groups from one another. Paradoxically, as the influence of the Shi'i shrine cities began to be felt in the countryside, attracting the attention of Sultan Abdülhamid and the Sunni hierarchy in Baghdad and Basra, opportunities were created for dialogue and debate between the two strains of Islam. Sultan Abdülhamid himself sought to bring Shi'is into his universalist Islamic ideology, a move welcomed by many Shi'i mujtahids in the empire.[48]

More significantly, the economic dynamic that had tied Basra the port and Basra the hinterland together, albeit unevenly, came apart at the turn of the century. The British penetration of regional trade networks shattered a cohesive economy sustained by local merchants and their counterparts in India. More than any other factor, the economic depression created by the loss of traditional occupations and vocations is what most troubled people in Basra. In February 1913, two years before the occupation of Basra by British troops, Sayyid Talib al-Naqib, de facto ruler of Basra, convened a meeting of all the principal notables of the town. A *mazbata* (petition) re-questing permission from the Porte to undertake a program of provincial reforms was circulated and signed by everybody present. According to the British official who drafted the dispatch to Baghdad, "It is proposed that the taxes of the Province be devoted to local needs and that only the balance, if any exists after the local requirements have been satisfied, be sent to Con-stantinople. A copy of the document is to be handed to the Vali and its contents are also to be telegraphed to the Grand Vizir and the Ministry of the Interior."[49] Reminiscent of al-Haidari's complaints 44 years earlier but couched in more novel terminology, the authors of the *mazbata* claimed that:

> Under the impact and the deepest sorrow and emotion, we beg to state that we have wept till we can weep no more over the present ruin of our beloved country, the coveted prey of our enemies who are forever endeavoring to wrest it from us. . . . Knowledge and learning in all their branches have perished, and are buried deep in the misfortunes of ignorance. Poverty and indigence have seized our whole community in their grasp and are dragging us to our destruction. Families, which once supported large numbers of the poor and needy, are today them-selves in poverty and distress. What is the sole reason for this abject humiliation? . . . We have pondered and found one basic source . . . and this is the fact that in our world, learning and education and all they mean are utterly obliterated.[50]

Even in his own day, Sayyid Talib's *mazbata* was viewed as a secessionist tactic.[51] Quite possibly it was. But the Basra notability's tactics also masked signs of desperation. The *mazbata* was the last-ditch stand of a regional elite in a world gone awry, where foreign challenges and the radical reorientation of trade were inexorably leading to a vacuum of power that could no longer be filled by the traditional power structure. In that sense, the period between 1876 and 1914 redefined Basra's role to such a great degree that its repercussions are still being felt today.

Notes

1. I wish to thank Professors Laila Fawaz, Sugata Bose, Steven Heydemann, Robin Ostle, Robert Ilbert, and Ms Juliana Deeks for their superb organization of, and participation in the two conferences on Ports in the Indian Ocean and Mediterranean held at Oxford and Aix-en-Provence. I also wish to thank the Social Science Research Council, St. John's College, Oxford, and the Maison Mediterraneenne des Sciences de l'Homme for a marvelous stay. It was a pleasure to meet with a number of distinguished colleagues at both conferences and I take this opportunity to thank them all for their inspiration and energy.

2. Omar Khalidi, "The Hadhrami Role in the Politics and Society of Colonial India, 1750s–1950s," in *Hadrami Traders, Scholars and Statesmen in the Indian Ocean, 1750s–1960s*, ed. U. Freitag and W. G. Clarence-Smith (Leiden: E. J. Brill, 1997), p. 67.

3. See my *The Politics of Regional Trade in Iraq, Arabia and the Gulf, 1745–1900* (Albany: State University of New York Press, 1997), pp. 77–83.

4. M. Morsy Abdullah, "Changes in the Economy and Political Attitudes and the Development of Culture on the Coast of Oman between 1900 and 1940," *Arabian Studies* 2 (1980): 171.

5. Kāzim Saʿd al-Dīn, trans., "Riḥla ilā Baghdād taʾlīf Nawwāb Ḥamid Jonek Bahadūr," *al-Mawrid*, 18, no. 4 (1989).

6. G. E. Lorimer, *A Gazeteer of the Persian Gulf, Oman and Central Arabia* (Calcutta: Government Press, 1908), p. 1130.

7. Fattah, *The Politics of Regional Trade*, pp. 69–70.

8. Suleīman Faīḍī, *Fī ghāmrāt al-nidāl mudhakīrrat Ṣuleīman fiāḍā* (Baghdad: Tijara and Tibaʿa Press, 1952), p. 44.

9. Ibid., p. 53.

10. Fattah, *The Politics of Regional Trade*, pp. 79–81.

11. Haifa Ahmed al-Nakib, "A Critical Study of Sayyid Talib Pasha al-Nakib," M.A thesis, University of Leeds, 1973, pp. 35–36.

12. Charles Issawi, *The Fertile Crescent, 1800–1914* (Oxford: Oxford University Press), pp. 261–62.

13. Ibid.

14. Fattah, *The Politics of Regional Trade*, p. 156.

15. Azmi Ozcan, *Pan-Islamism: Indian Muslims, the Ottomans and Britain (1877–1924)* (Leiden: E. J. Brill, 1997), p. 40.

16. Selim Deringil, *The Well-Protected Domains: Ideology and the Legitimation of Power in the Ottoman Empire, 1876–1909* (London: I.B Tauris, 1998), pp. 1–15.

17. Yitzhak Nakash, *The Shi'is of Iraq* (Princeton: Princeton University Press, 1994), pp. 25–48; Selim Deringil, "Legitimacy Structures in the Ottoman State: The Reign of Abdul-Hamid II (1876–1909), *International Journal of Middle East Studies*, 23, no. 3 (1991): 345–56; and by the same author, "The Struggle Against Shi'ism in Hamidian Iraq," *Das Welt des Islam* and *the Well-Protected Domains*, pp. 99–101, passim. See also Gokhan Cetinsaya, "The Ottoman Administration of Iraq, 1890–1908." Ph.D diss., University of Manchester, 1994, pp. 222–80.

18. Hanna Batatu, *The Old Social Classes and the New Revolutionary Movements of Iraq: A Study of Iraq's Old Landed and Commercial Classes and of Its Communists, Ba'thists and Free Officers* (Princeton: Princeton University Press, 1978), p. 39.

19. Ibid., pp 155–56; Nakash, *The Shi'is of Iraq*, pp. 37–41.

20. Deringil, *The Well-Protected Domains*, pp. 93–104.

21. Nakash, *The Shi'is of Iraq*, pp. 43–48.

22. Deringil, "Legitimacy Structures," pp. 346–49; Cetinsaya, "Ottoman Administration of Iraq," p. 229.

23. Deringil, "Legitimacy Structures," pp. 346–49; Deringil, *The Well-Protected Domains*, pp. 99–100.

24. Sayyid Mustafa Nūr al-Dīn Wa'iz, *Al-rāwḍ al-azhār fī tārājīm al-sayyīd ja'far*, ed. Ibrahīm al-Wa'iz (Mosul: Ittiḥād Press, 1948), p. 207.

25. Ibid., pp. 207–9.

26. Ibid., pp. 209.

27. Ibid.

28. Ibid., pp. 209–10.

29. Ozcan, *Pan-Islamism*, p. 44.

30. Cetinsaya, "Ottoman Administration of Iraq," pp. 53–55.

31. Sheikh Abdul-Raḥman ibn Abdullah al-Ḥasani, "Diwan," unpublished ms. Ar.1756, Or. 2398, Bibliotheek der Rijksuniversiteit, Leiden, folios 1–2.

32. Sheikh Ibrāhīm ibn Faṣīḥ ibn Sabghatullah al-Ḥaīdarī, *Kitāb unwān al-majd fī bayān aḥwāl Baghdād wa al-Baṣra wa Najd* (Basra: Basri Press, n.d), p. 87.

33. Al-Haidari, *Kitab 'unwan al-majd*, p. 87.

34. Ibid., p. 101.

35. Ibid., pp. 111–13.

36. Ibid., p. 113.

37. Ibid., p. 161.

38. Ibid.

39. Ibid.
40. Ibid., p. 126.
41. Ibid., p. 197.
42. Richard N. Schofield, *The Iraq-Iran Border, 1840–1958*, vol. 1 (Oxford: Archive Editions, 1989), 1: 108.
43. Ibid.
44. Al-Ḥaidari, *Kitāb 'unwān al-majd*, pp. 179–80.
45. Ibid., p. 190.
46. For Yemen, see al-Haidari, *Kitab 'unwan al-majd*, pp. 191–93.
47. Nakash, *The Shi'is of Iraq*, p. 49.
48. Cetinsaya, "Ottoman Administration of Iraq," pp. 246–62.
49. I.O.R L/P&S/10/212, From Scott to H.B.M's Consul, Baghdad, February 1913.
50. Ibid.
51. Ibid.

7 Damascus and the Pilgrim Caravan

Abdul-Karim Rafeq

Writing in the early 1870s, the Damascene author Nu'man al-Qasatli mentioned that the first calamity that befell Damascus in the nineteenth century was the shift from caravan to navigation by steamship (*sufun al-bukhar*), which affected the flow of trade among Damascus, Anatolia, and Rumelia. When the Suez Canal opened in 1869, the Damascus caravan trade declined further as Turkish and Balkan pilgrims began to favor travel to the Hijaz by sea; it was cheaper and more secure than going overland, both for themselves and their merchandise.

According to Qasatli, the abundant streams of gold ran dry that had once poured into Damascus with the pilgrims on their way to and from the Hijaz (*fa-imtana'a al-hujjaj 'an al-ityan ilayha fa-khasirat jadawil al-dhahab al-ghazira al-lati kanu yaskubunaha biha dhihaban wa-iyaban*).[1] Qasatli estimates the number of pilgrims that passed through Damascus every year at over eight thousand; they bought food supplies and sold merchandise they brought with them from their place of origin or from the Hijaz. If each pilgrim spent fifty lira (the type of lira is not specified), according to Qasatli, the total sum the pilgrims spent in Damascus every year would exceed four hundred thousand lira; this gives some indication of how much Damascus benefited from the pilgrim caravans.[2]

The Damascus economy depended almost entirely on the pilgrim trade. Damascus textiles were noted for their quality (hence the Western word damask for fine silk or linen fabric with the pattern woven into it), but it was Aleppo that had attracted European merchants and consuls since before the Ottoman conquest, with its flourishing local, regional, and international trade. The Silk Road passed through Aleppo, bringing silk, perfumes, and spices from the Far East. By comparison, no European merchant or consul was established in Damascus until Muhammad 'Ali (1831–40) opened up Syria as a whole to Western influence and allowed consuls and missionaries in Damascus. Even before that, however, European merchants had local agents in Damascus to buy products such as ash (*shnan* or *qila*) made by the Bedouins in the desert by burning an alkaline herb. It was much sought after by the French for making soap and glass.

Damascus's trade with Baghdad through the Syrian desert was always hazardous. Bedouin tribes were in control of the desert route and very often intercepted caravans and disrupted trade. Most of the trade between Damascus and Egypt was transported overland via Gaza and 'Arish and by the sea route that connected Sidon, Haifa, and Jaffa with Dumyat (Damietta). Damascus also traded with Anatolia, but the volume of this trade was far smaller than that with Aleppo.

The importance of the pilgrim caravan trade to Damascus was tremendous. The organization, provisioning, and transportation of pilgrims benefited a large sector of the population. A number of guilds provided products and services to the pilgrims, and goods bought by the pilgrims contributed to the flourishing commerce of Damascus and of Syria as a whole. Thus, the shift from caravan travel to steamships in the nineteenth century had drastic effects on the pilgrim caravan and on the Damascene economy.

Damascus and the Organization of the Pilgrim Caravan

For security, pilgrims always traveled in groups. Those from Anatolia and the Balkans joined forces and were referred to collectively by the Damascenes as the "Rumi" (plural Arwam) pilgrims (*al-hajj al-rumi*), a name used earlier by Syrian Muslims to refer to the Greek Byzantines. The Ottoman sultan himself was referred to in contemporary Syrian writings as the *sultan al-Rum*. Pilgrims coming from Aleppo and its countryside were known as *al-hajj al-halabi*, and those coming from Persia as *al-hajj al-'Ajami*. When possible, they all passed through Aleppo, where they joined up with the Aleppo pilgrims, but they sometimes accompanied the trade caravan from Baghdad to Damascus instead. Pilgrims from Iraq, especially Mosul, also usually joined up with the Aleppo pilgrims.

Persian pilgrims attracted the attention of the Damascenes because they were Shi'is, whereas the majority of Syrians and pilgrims were Sunnis.

Persian pilgrims often arrived in Damascus too late to join the caravan. Whether this was accidental or calculated is not known, but it is clear that many Persian pilgrims stayed on in Damascus, trading in diamonds and other gems and marrying into the local population.[3]

The Damascene ulama were displeased with these intermarriages between Shi'i Persians and Sunni Damascenes. The eighteenth-century Hanafi mufti of Damascus, 'Ali al-Muradi, at the request of the Ottoman chief judge in the city, issued a fatwa invalidating intermarriages between Sunnis and Shi'is.[4] The Ottoman sultan in his capacity as guardian/servitor of the Two Holy Sanctuaries of Mecca and Medina—sovereignty over the holy places of Islam belonging only to the Ottoman sultan—also denied the Shi'i rulers of Persia the honor of sending a separate pilgrim caravan to the Hijaz.

The sultan allowed only two pilgrim caravans to function in the Ottoman Empire, one from Damascus, the other from Cairo. For a few years after the Ottoman conquest of Yemen, a third caravan was organized there, but it was abolished long before Yemen separated from Ottoman rule in 1635. Individual pilgrims had to travel to the Hijaz on their own and at their own risk.

Between the sixteenth and the early nineteenth century, about 15,000–20,000 pilgrims assembled in Damascus every year to join the caravan to the Hijaz. The French traveler Volney, who visited Syria in the early 1780s, estimated the number of pilgrims who assembled in Damascus at 30,000–50,000.[5] A Jesuit missionary in Damascus gave the number in 1739 as 15,000–20,000.[6]

Because many pilgrims went on the pilgrimage for commercial purposes, the vicissitudes of trade with the Far East through Mecca affected their number.[7] On some occasions, however, some natural calamity or war caused an upsurge in religious devotion, and increased the number of pilgrims as well.[8]

Many pilgrims stayed on in Damascus, some permanently as residents and some temporarily as *nuzala'* (roughly, "nonresident aliens") or as *mujawirun* (people living next to religious shrines). Damascene biographical dictionaries abound in information about these *nuzala'* and *mujawirun*, giving their geographical origins, ethnic backgrounds, the school of Islamic law (*madhhab*) to which they belonged, their education, and profession. The pilgrim caravan thus served as a catalyst, bringing people of diverse origins and affiliations to the city. Damascus benefited from this mix of population and cultures, but paid for them in the plagues and other contagious diseases that pilgrims also imported.

Anxious to uphold his prestige as protector (*hami*) and servitor (*khadim*) of the Two Holy Sanctuaries, shortly after the conquest of Syria in 1516, the Ottoman sultan designated a powerful local chieftain to assume the command of the pilgrim caravan. In the sixteenth and seventeenth centuries, Bedouin chieftains from the southern regions of the province of Damascus, notably from Nablus, 'Ajlun, Lajjun, and Jerusalem, who were district governors (*sanjaq bey*) and ipso facto chief tax farmers of these regions, were appointed commanders of the caravan and entrusted with ensuring its security. If a chieftain was nominated commander without being a district governor, he would be made one upon assuming the command of the caravan. Being influential local rulers of Bedouin origin with tribal troops at their disposal, the chieftain commanders were able to control the tribes that threatened the caravan in the desert. They assumed their command of the caravan at Bab (or Bawwabat) Allah (the Gate of God, which leads to the Holy Cities), at the southern extremity of the neighborhood of Midan outside the city walls. Neither they nor their troops entered Damascus, thus sparing the city the chaos and depredation invariably associated with troop occupation.

When the chieftain commanders were weakened during the first half of the seventeenth century, partly by attacks directed against them by the paramount amir of Mt. Lebanon, Fakhr al-Din Ma'n II (1590–1635), who had expanded his rule into Palestine, and partly by disciplinary measures by the state, the Ottoman government appointed Janissary chiefs from Damascus in their place as commanders of the caravan. Some of these Janissaries were also appointed district governors at the same time to keep the troops assigned for the caravan with them and to collect taxes from their localities to finance the caravan. When the Janissaries of Damascus became rebellious after influential Damascene grain merchants joined their ranks to benefit from their privileges and began to challenge the authority of the Ottoman governor of the city, the authorities eliminated several of them. A fresh Janissary corps, known as the Kapi Kullari (slaves of the Sultan or Imperial Janissaries), was dispatched to Damascus in 1659 to balance the old Janissaries, who became known as *yerliyya* (locals). The annals of Damascus give details about the clashes between the two Janissary corps until they were abolished in 1826.

After the weakening of the Janissaries of Damascus, the sultan appointed officials as district governors and commanders of the pilgrim caravan. Some of the official commanders tried to keep for themselves part or all of the customary payment made to certain powerful tribes on the desert route to ensure the security of the caravan. The payment was known as *sarr* (bagged money) because it was put in a cloth bag and was given to the Bedouins in two installments, one on the way to the Hijaz and the other on the way back. Given the unreliability, lack of experience, and greed of most official commanders, they often tried to avoid paying the Bedouins the second installment, to which the latter reacted by attacking the caravan.

The Ottoman sultan's military reputation had been greatly diminished by the defeats he sustained in the Balkans: it had ended with the humiliating treaty of Carlowitz in 1699, which lost to the Austrians territories the sultans had controlled for three hundred years. In 1708, because he could no longer afford to risk his religious reputation and responsibility as protector of the Two Holy Sanctuaries, the sultan appointed the governor of Damascus as commander of the pilgrim caravan. This dual role of governor of Damascus and commander, which continued well into the nineteenth century, brought both great prestige and heavy responsibilities. The governors who ensured the security of the caravan had prolonged tenure. Members of the local 'Azm family ruled Damascus for long periods in the eighteenth century because they were successful in ensuring the safety of the pilgrims.

Damascus, however, suffered as a result of this appointment. Making the governor of Damascus commander of the pilgrim caravan meant that he was away from the city for three months every year, accompanying the pilgrims to the Hijaz. As the one responsible for financing the caravan, he was also absent for an additional month before the caravan departed on a tour (*dawra*) of his province to collect taxes in his capacity as chief tax farmer. Damascus was thus left in the hands of a deputy governor for four months a year, a situation taken advantage of by militant groups who threatened public security. The mercenary troops employed by the governor to accompany the caravan also stayed with him in Damascus, not in the provincial districts, as was the case with the earlier commanders. Soon these mercenaries, composed of Turkomans, Kurds, and Maghariba (from North Africa), refused to quit Damascus after the return of the caravan and the completion of their assignment. Instead they terrorized the inhabitants of the city and the countryside, adding to public insecurity.[9]

Transportation and Economics of the Caravan

The pilgrim caravan generated a variety of economic activities in Damascus and its surrounding countryside. For example, the pilgrims bought up large supplies of *buqsumad(t)*, dry cubes of rusk that lasted indefinitely and were eaten soaked in water or tea. The bakeries in Damascus produced huge quantities of *buqsumad*. A special guild known as *ta'ifat al-buqsuma-diyya* (guild of rusk makers) regulated this production and the profession.[10]

The 15,000–20,000 pilgrims, together with the troops and officials accompanying them, traveled on mules, donkeys, or camels, depending on the conditions of the terrain and its roads. The journey from Damascus through the desert to the Hijaz required camels that could endure the hardships of the road. A guild of "travel agents" called *ta'ifat al-muqawwimin*, oversaw the transportation. The guild had a head (*sheikh*), aides to the head, and a number of agents (*muqawwimin*). A code of ethics required the travel agents to honor their commitments to the pilgrims. To ensure this, the sheikh of the *muqawwimin* and the members of the guild appeared in court, where they swore before the judge to be collectively responsible for implementing in full the terms of the contracts for transporting the pilgrims. This was intended to prevent any *muqawwim* from leaving the passengers stranded en route. The contract between the agent and the passenger was registered in the law court to guarantee the rights of both parties.[11]

Transportation was highly organized. The pilgrim was seated in a wooden box on one side of the camel, balanced by another box on the other side carrying a second passenger. The box was known as *mahara* (less frequently as *shaqdufa*) and its maker was *maha'iri*, a surname carried today by many families in Syria, indicating the profession of their ancestors. The guild of *maha'iriyya* did a thriving business during the pilgrimage.[12]

Another group involved in the transportation of the pilgrims was the *'ak-kama*, who led the camels and served the pilgrims. They were organized in a guild of their own known as *ta'ifat al-'akkama*.[13] The torchbearers, organized in a guild known as *ta'ifat al-masha'iliyya*, provided light when the caravan traveled at night. Like the *'akkama*, the services of the *masha'iliyya* were not limited to the transportation of pilgrims; they also transported goods and animals.[13]

The fare paid by the pilgrim to the travel agent was agreed upon between the parties and duly registered in court, where it was usually referred to as the "price for Muslims" (*s'ir al-Muslimin*), which suggests that it was a special discounted fare for pilgrims. On 11 Shawwal 1158 (6 November 1745), for example, a *muqawwim* charged a pilgrim for the trip from Damascus to Mecca the sum of seventy piasters: forty for the camel, five for drinking water on the journey, fifteen for carrying fifteen *okkas* of baggage (one *okka* equals about 2.8 English pounds),[15] five for the wooden seat (*mahara*), and five piasters for the services of the '*akkam*.[16]

The cost of the pilgrimage was high by the standards of the time, and not many people could afford it. For the one-way fare of seventy piasters one could have bought a small house in Damascus.[17] For the round trip fare one could have bought an average-sized house (priced at 170 piasters in 1746).[18]

Camel rent was the most expensive item on the journey. Bedouin chieftains, especially in the region of Hawran, made a lot of money by renting out thousands of camels every year for the transport of pilgrims and merchants, troops, and officials accompanying them. Rental was organized through the intermediary of the guild of cameleers (*ta'ifat al-jammala*) in Damascus.[19] The court records of Damascus give the names of the Bedouin sheikhs and villages in the Hawran region who rented out thousands of camels for the transportation of the pilgrim caravan in 1762.[20] The location of these villages indicates the frontier of settlement and security in the Hawran at the time.[21]

Each year, there was a fair in Muzayrib, about 62 miles southwest of Damascus, where the pilgrims halted for about a week to wait for late arrivals. Those who wished could deposit their valuables in the town's fortress. Relatives and peddlers usually accompanied the pilgrims to Muzayrib. It was the last chance for the pilgrims to purchase supplies before the caravan proceeded through the desert to the Hijaz.[22]

In addition to the benefits that accrued to the Damascenes and the villagers from providing supplies and camels to the pilgrims, they could trade with the many pilgrims who brought rare, marketable items from their home countries to sell or exchange for goods either in Damascus or the Hijaz, an aspect of the hajj that continues to be important to this very day. Many go on the pilgrimage more than once for the commerce it involves. The probate inventories of Damascus give detailed information about the belongings of deceased pilgrims, establishing the types, and sometimes origins, of the goods they carried with them.

Security required that merchants accompanying the caravan pay large sums of money to the commander of the caravan to ensure the safety of their goods. They dealt in Indian textiles, spices and perfumes from the Far East, and Yemeni coffee (known in the West as mocca after the Yemeni seaport of Mokha where it was exported), which was distributed all over Syria and beyond. A letter from an English merchant in Aleppo dated 19 October 1726 mentions that "the Hagis [pilgrims] are arrived and have brought a great supply of coffee."[23] Despite the religious controversy surrounding drinking coffee, which had been introduced into Syria early in the sixteenth century, and the ban on it enforced by the Ottoman authorities time and again, the consumption of Yemeni coffee was widespread, and the pilgrim caravan was its major transporter to Syria, though some was also shipped to Syria via Egypt through the seaport of Dumyat. Yemeni coffee soon found a rival in the coffee produced by the French, the British, and the Dutch in the West and East Indies. Coffee beans from the Yemen were planted in these regions and soon produced abundant crops. French coffee from Martinique was first sold in Syria in the 1730s.[24] Colonial coffee beans, however, were considered by the Oriental connoisseurs as inferior to Yemeni coffee in size, color, and taste. The Syrians began to distinguish between Yemeni coffee, which they called *bunn hijazi* (Hijazi coffee), and imported non-Yemeni coffee, which they called *bunn afranji* (Frankish coffee).[25]

Not much was written about the goods carried by the pilgrims from Anatolia and the Balkans until the publication of Colette Establet and Jean-Paul Pascual's important book, *Ultime Voyage pour la Mecque.*[26] The book records the belongings and goods carried by pilgrims who died on the hajj as reported in the probate inventories of Damascus. In a rare court document from Damascus dated 3 Sha'ban 1119 (30 October 1707), a group of Rumi pilgrims, identified by the names of the cities from which they came, were robbed by highwaymen in the region of Suwaydiyya near Antioch. The stolen goods included several loads of shawls and saffron, in addition to pack animals. Because Suwaydiyya was administratively attached to Hama, the governor of Hamah was held responsible for retrieving the goods. All the owners of the stolen goods were referred to as *hajj,* and the document confirms that those hajjis were on their way to perform the pilgrimage, which means that they either had assumed the title of *hajj* in advance, or, more probably, they were professional merchants going on the pilgrimage for commercial purposes and not for the first time.[27]

A report by the French consul in Damascus, dated 30 March 1842, gives a detailed description of the goods carried by the pilgrim caravan that returned to Damascus on 28 March of the same year. The goods included 225 loads of henna (*"substance colorante dont se servent les femmes de l'Orient pour se teindre les cheveux et les ongles"*), weighing 2,250 *rotles* and valued at 120,000 piasters (30,000 francs); 40 loads of mocca coffee (originally 90 loads, but 50 were stolen en route), weighing 4000 *rotles* and worth 140,000 piasters (35,000 francs); and 20 loads of Indian cloth for turbans, each load consisting of 2 bales and each bale contained 100 lengths of cloth; the price of a length was 200 piasters (total value 800,000 piasters, or 200,000 francs). The caravan also carried jewels valued at 170,000 piasters (42,500 francs), ostrich plumes worth about 100,000 piasters (25,000 francs), perfumes, eau de toilette, and incense worth more than 160,000 piasters (40,000 francs), and miscellaneous merchandise valued at 60,000 piasters (15,000 francs). The total value of the merchandise carried by the caravan, according to the report, was 387,500 francs, or 1,550,000 piasters.[28]

Impact of Steamships and Railways on the Pilgrim Caravan

The impact of sea navigation on the pilgrim caravan first became noticeable in the early 1840s, shortly after Muhammad 'Ali Paşa's withdrawal from Syria and the deterioration of security along the land routes. In his report to his superiors in Paris, dated 30 March 1842, regarding the return of the pilgrim caravan to Damascus from the Hijaz on March 28 and the goods it carried, the French consul in Damascus remarked that the volume of the merchandise carried by this caravan, important as it was, was far less than in earlier times ("que l'on connait du grand commerce qui se faisait anciennement entre la Mecque et Damas"). The report lauds the security measures taken at the time in Egypt by Muhammad 'Ali Paşa that rendered the passage of pilgrims by sea through Suez much safer than the caravan route through Damascus, which the Ottoman government could no longer keep safe from Bedouin raids.[29]

The number of pilgrims joining the Damascus pilgrim caravan kept falling. The caravan that returned to Damascus on 21 April 1845, for example, numbered 6,000 pilgrims, 2,000 of whom were Persians, 2,000 Turks, and the rest Arabs. Despite their falling numbers, the pilgrims, according to the French consul in Damascus, bought large quantities of textiles and energized the city's commerce. The report estimates the value of the merchandise the pilgrims bought at about six million piasters,[30] which again shows the importance of the pilgrim caravan to the economy of Damascus.

When the majority of the Turkish pilgrims chose to go by sea after the early 1850s,[31] the caravan route through Damascus lost its importance. The ships of the French Méssageries Impériales and the Compagnie Russe transported the pilgrims to Port Said and Alexandria; from there they proceeded by rail to Suez, and then by sea to Jiddah.[32] Some pilgrims went one way by sea and the other by land; the pilgrim caravan that returned to Damascus on 14 August 1862, according to a French dispatch from Damascus, had fewer pilgrims than when it left for the Hijaz; the rest had returned by sea. Because of this change, the commercial fair at Muzayrib and the quantity of merchandise carried with the caravan became insignificant.[33] By 1863, the returning caravan had only 250 pilgrims; the rest had gone back by sea. The caravan, however, did bring 650 black slaves of both sexes; 200 of them were sent to Aleppo and the rest were sold publicly in the bazaar in Damascus. The French consul, who reported the arrival of the slaves, comments that despite promises by the Sublime Porte to prohibit the trade in slaves, its volume grew every year.[34]

In another dispatch, dated 22 July 1864, the French consul in Damascus stated that most of the pilgrims that year went back to their countries by sea.[35] The Persian pilgrims also preferred the sea route over the insecure caravan route through Damascus. In the early 1870s, Persian pilgrims went by sea from the Persian Gulf to Jiddah.[36]

The opening of the Suez Canal in 1869 further hurt the caravan economy. The caravan that returned from the Hijaz to Damascus in early March 1878 included only 218 Syrian pilgrims, most of whom were young men who, according to the French consul in Damascus, had tried to avoid conscription by going on the pilgrimage.[37] No wonder that Nu'man al-Qasatli, writing in the early 1870s, lamented the drying up of the streams of gold that once had poured into Damascus. This coincided with other strains on Syria's economy as local markets flooded with goods from Europe. Before the nineteenth century, the Syrian economy was based on an efficient, highly organized guild system that controlled production, marketing, and services. Given the religious and ethnic pluralism of Syrian society, the guild system accommodated the various communities by emphasizing expertise, not religious affiliation. Mercantilist Europe at the time coexisted with this system through commercial treaties, known as Capitulations, with the Ottoman Empire.

Improved transportation by steamship, the enlargement of the seaport of Beirut, the opening of a carriage road linking Beirut with Damascus in 1863, and the building of a railway between the two cities in the 1880s, combined to allow European goods, notably textiles, to flood the Syrian market. This influx of European goods into Syria was also encouraged by the treaty between Britain and the Ottoman Empire in 1838, by virtue of which the latter reduced customs duties on imported goods to a mere 3 percent. Other European states soon had similar treaties.

The guilds involved in the production of textiles were the first to suffer. A disparity in wealth grew between the impoverished craftsmen and the nouveaux riches entrepreneurs, many of whom were Christians acting as agents for European manufacturers. Socioeconomic riots, which turned into attacks on Christians, occurred in Aleppo in 1850 and in Damascus in 1860. In reaction to European influence and the riots, local manufacturers resorted to partnerships and mergers across religious boundaries. Under the guild system, partnerships had been discouraged to prevent monopolies and high prices; emphasis was on individual initiative. Local manufacturers were not reluctant to import European techniques and machinery. The French jacquard loom, for instance, was introduced into Syria in the 1850s, as its patterns appealed to the public. European fashions spread among the population, increasing demand for the European fabrics.[38]

While these economic, social, and cultural changes were occurring in Syria in the second half of the nineteenth century, the pilgrim caravan continued to shrink. An English consular dispatch mentions that in 1903, it had only between 90 and 100 pilgrims. The paucity of pilgrims was explained in part by the spread of cholera, but the dispatch also comments that because "the same object can be attained, with infinitely less suffering, by the simple expedient of going round to Jeddah by sea . . . the fact remains that the number of pilgrims who took this [land] route is yearly becoming less."[39]

A new project for building a railway linking Damascus with Medina in the Hijaz, ostensibly to facilitate pilgrimage travel and revive the caravan route to Damascus, was set in motion by the sultan, who issued the order on 1 May 1900 for railroad construction to begin.[40] The money was raised by voluntary contributions from the entire Muslim world. German engineers were also involved in its construction.[41] Sultan Abdülhamid II (1876–1909), who had proclaimed himself caliph and advocated pan-Islamism, used the railway to enhance his prestige among the Muslims. Germany, which was involved in building the Berlin-Istanbul-Baghdad railway, supported the Islamic policy of the Ottoman sultan and welcomed the idea of the Hijaz Railway to extend its influence to the Arabian Peninsula and threaten British interests in the Red Sea.

The Hijaz Railway promoted the Islamic image of Damascus and also benefited the villagers in the Hawran who transported their goods on it. The beautiful terminal building in Damascus still stands as a historical monument, giving its name to the whole district. The railway, completed in 1908, did not, however, bring all the Muslim pilgrims back to Damascus; many of them continued to go to the Hijaz by sea. The railway also infuriated the Bedouin tribes who could no longer rent out their camels for the transport of pilgrims. Combined with the centralizing policy of the Ottoman state and its attempts to control the tribes, it led to a Bedouin revolt in 1909 between Amman and Ma'an, when the Ottomans denied them their traditional subsidies for the protection of the pilgrims. The government severely punished the Bedouin,[42] making them all too ready to support the Arab revolt of Sharif Husayn against the Ottomans on 10 June 1916. The tribes rallied behind Amir Faisal, Sharif Husayn's son and commander of the Arab forces, who, in collaboration with the British liaison officer, T. E. Lawrence (Lawrence of Arabia), blew up the Hijaz Railway. The aim was to interrupt the transport of troops and materiel to the Turkish and German troops amassed in the Arabian Peninsula.

The demise of the Ottoman Empire in the wake of World War I and the division of geographical Syria into a number of states under French and British mandates introduced drastic changes in the economic, social, and political orientation of Syria as a whole. Aleppo was cut off from its traditional markets in Anatolia and Iraq and lost its role as center of international transit trade. Damascus became the center of government, but the pilgrim caravan was a thing of the past, the lost golden age of its economy.

Notes

1. Nu'man al-Qasatli, *al-Rawda al-ghanna' fi Dimashq al-Fayha'* (Beirut, 1879; rpt., Dar al-Ra'id al-'Arabi, 1982), pp. 124–25.
2. Ibid.
3. Abdul-Karim Rafeq, *The Province of Damascus, 1723–1783*, 2nd ed. (Beirut: Khayats, 1970), pp. 59–62.
4. 'Ali al-Muradi's fatwa is entitled, *"al-Rawd al-ra'id fi 'adam sihhat nikah ahl al-sunna li'l-rawafid,"* 2 ms., copies are in the Asad Library, *'am* 6817 and *'am* 9674.
5. C. F. Chasseboeuf, Comte de Volney, *Voyage en Egypte et en Syrie*, ed. Jean Gaulmier (Paris–The Hague, 1959), p. 323.
6. *Lettres édifiantes et curieuses, écrites des Mission étrangères par quelque missionnaires de la Compagnie de Jésus*, ed. C. Le Gobien, J. B. Du Halde, and L. Patouillet, 34 vols. (Paris: Chez Nicholas le Clerc, et. al., 1707–73), 26:444 (letter from Damascus dated 4 November 1939).
7. Alexander Russell, *The Natural History of Aleppo*, 2 vols., 2nd ed. (London, 1734), 1:199.

8. For more information, see Rafeq, *Province of Damascus*, p. 61.

9. Ibid., pp. 52–58.

10. Law Court Registers (LCR), *Damascus*, 45:149, case dated 20 Rabi' I 1140 (5 November 1727).

11. LCR, Damascus, 174:50, case dated 19 Sha'ban 1175 (15 March 1762).

12. LCR, Damascus, 121:63, case dated 11 Shawwal 1158 (6 November 1745); Aleppo, 15:781, case dated 16 Sha'ban 1045 (25 January 1636).

13. LCR, Damascus, 121:63, case dated 11 Shawwal 1158 (6 November 1745).

14. LCR, Damascus, 33:96, case dated 13 Shawwal 1119 (7 January 1708).

15. John Bowring, *Report on the Commercial Statistics of Syria* (London: William Clowes and Sons, 1840; rpt., New York: Arno Press, 1973), p. 96; R. Dozy, *Supplement aux Dictionnaires arabes*, 2 vols. (Leiden: E. J. Brill, 1881; rpt., Beirut: Librairie du Liban, 1981), 1:44, mentions that the Okke is "poids turc de deux livres."

16. LCR, Damascus, 121:63, case dated 11 Shawwal 1158 (6 November 1745).

17. LCR, Damascus, 118:125, case dated 5 Rabi' I 1160 (17 March 1747).

18. LCR, Damascus, 115:86, case dated 8 Rabi' I 1159 (31 March 1746).

19. LCR, Damascus, 33:96, case dated 13 Shawwal 1119 (7 January 1708).

20. See, for example, LCR, Damascus, 168:61,172; 170:12 (and appendices, 1, 2).

21. For other details about transportation for pilgrims from Syria to the Hijaz, see Abdul-Karim Rafeq, "New Light on the Transportation of the Damascene Pilgrimage during the Ottoman Period," in *Islamic and Middle Eastern Societies*, ed. R. Olson (Battleboro, Vt: Amana Press, 1987), pp. 127–36.

22. See Rafeq, *Province of Damascus*, pp. 63, 67.

23. Public Record Office (London), State Papers, 110/25, pt. 2, letter dated 19 October 1726 (appendix 3).

24. Abdul-Karim Rafeq, "The Socioeconomic and Political Implications of the Introduction of Coffee into Syria. 16th–18th Centuries," in *Le commerce du café avant l'ère des plantations coloniales: espaces, réseaux, sociétés (XVe–XIXe siècle)*, ed. Michel Tuchscherer (Cairo: Institut Français d'Archéologie Orientale), *Cahier des Annals Islamologique* 20 [2001]: 127–42).

25. See, for example, LCR, Damascus (*Qassam Baladi* register), 409:51, case dated 29 Ramadan 1264 (29 August 1848).

26. Colette Establet and Jean-Paul Pascual, *Ultime Voyage pour la Mecque: Les Inventaires aprés décés de Pèlerins morts à Damas vers 1700* (Damascus: Institut Francais de Damas, 1998).

27. LCR, Damascus, 33:82, case dated 3 Sha'ban 1119 (30 October 1707).

28. Affaires étrangères (AE), Paris, Correspondance commerciale (CC), Damas, vol. 1, 30 March 1842.

29. Ibid.

30. AE, CC, Damas, vol. 2, 16 March 1847.

31. AE, CC, Damas, vol. 3, 25 October 1862.

32. AE, CC, Damas, vol. 4, 19 January 1870.

33. AE, CC, Damas, vol. 4, 21 August 1862, cf. 5 June 1856.

34. AE, CC, Damas, vol. 4, 21 August 1863, Damas, vol. 5, 1 May 1872.

35. AE, CC, Damas, vol. 4, 22 July 1864.

36. AE, CC, Damas, vol. 5, 19 January 1870.

37. AE, CC, Damas, vol. 6, 10 March 1878.

38. Abdul-Karim Rafeq, "Craft Organization, Work Ethics, and the Strains of Change in Ottoman Syria," *Journal of the American Oriental Society* 111, no. 3 (1991): 495–511.

39. Charles Issawi, *The Fertile Crescent, 1800–1914: A Documentary Economic History* (New York: Oxford University Press, 1988), p. 236.

40. Ibid., pp. 242–46.

41. For the Hijaz Railway, see William Ochsenwald, *The Hijaz Railroad* (Charlottesville: University of Virginia Press, 1980); Hasan Kayali, *Arabs and Young Turks: Ottomanism, Arabism and Islamism in the Ottoman Empire, 1908–1918* (Berkeley: University of California Press, 1997), pp. 146–47, 156ff.

42. Kayali, *Arabs and Young Turks*, pp. 109–10.

8 Aspects of Economy and Society in the Syrian Provinces: Aleppo in Transition, 1880–1925

Peter Sluglett

In the last few decades of the Ottoman Empire, particularly after the 1860s, the economy of the eastern Mediterranean underwent a series of momentous changes that resulted in transformations probably more complex and convulsive than had been seen over any comparable period of Ottoman rule. Economic historians[1] have shown how these changes were related to much wider trends, demonstrating the region's increasingly accelerating integration into the international market. Coastal towns boomed; harbors, roads, and railways were built to facilitate the import and export of goods more efficiently from the coast to the interior and vice versa, and an increasingly unfavorable balance of trade with Europe (and with the Far East for yarn, thread, and textiles) mounted year by year. Many traditional artisan activities declined, and there was a wave of migration, both from the rural parts of the region to the cities, and from the region to other parts of the Middle East—especially Egypt—and to the Americas.[2]

This much is undeniable. What is less clear is how what used to be represented as a rather doom-laden and negative scenario[3] functioned at the local level of city or province. In recent years a number of historians have shown that, rather than being swamped by the pressures of the European metropoles or being forced to be entirely subservient to them, the economy of the eastern Mediterranean generally exhibited a remarkable degree of adaptation and resistance, especially at the turn of the century, between the 1880s and World War I. To give some random examples, more than three times the number of looms in Aleppo were active in 1909 than had been the case in 1897;[4] new products, especially new textiles, were developed for local markets;[5] and owners of textile factories were energetic in discovering new markets for their products in the immediate hinterland of the cities in which many of the goods were produced. In addition, in spite of emigration and other demographic movements, the population of the eastern Mediterranean Ottoman provinces actually rose at the end of the century—albeit more rapidly in some places than in others.[6] Finally, the great notables of the inland cities evidently thought it worth their while to buy up great quantities of new, that is previously uncultivated, land to put under the plough.[7]

Aleppo at the End of the Nineteenth Century

In trying to map out the broad parameters of economic, social, and political change in Aleppo between the 1880s and the 1920s, it is more useful to use terms like "change" and "adaptation" than to try to counter, or indeed accept, notions of decline—or of "the decline of decline." For much of its heyday between the Ottoman conquest in 1516 and about 1800, Aleppo was the third most populous city in the empire after Istanbul and Cairo, and probably ranked third in overall economic importance as well. By 1900, it had been overtaken demographically by Alexandria, İzmir, Tunis, Damascus, Algiers, and Beirut, although remaining fairly close in size to the three latter cities.[8]

This fall in Aleppo's demographic ranking was at least partly due to two interrelated factors that also affected its economic status: the opening of the Suez Canal in 1869, and the very long time taken to construct the carriage road from Aleppo to the port of Alexandretta, a distance of some 200 kilometers, or 120 miles.[9] The opening of the canal and the simultaneous development of steam navigation meant that much of the overland trade from Iran and northern and southern Iraq to the Mediterranean that formerly passed through Aleppo now went by sea, so that the large camel caravans that used to traverse the Syrian desert no longer came to Aleppo.

Although Aleppo did show some economic stagnation in the late nineteenth century,[10] it is important not to overstate the case. In the first place, both imports and exports through Alexandretta rose between the early 1870s and 1902.[11] However, such external indices tell us little about agricultural and industrial production as a whole, which, as is becoming increasingly clear, remained directed principally toward satisfying the needs of the local market. The most cursory examination of the accounts and commercial correspondence of the two leading European merchant houses in Aleppo at the end of the nineteenth century[12] makes it clear that trade with the city's hinterland (in the broadest sense) constituted a vital component of their activities.

Another factor to take into account in any attempt to gauge the prosperity or otherwise of Aleppo in the late Ottoman period is that the city was expanding, particularly to the west and northwest. Six modern quarters were constructed, all with a combination of large single-family houses and apartment buildings: al-'Aziziyya in 1868, al-Niyyal in 1878, al-Saliba al-Saghir in 1882, al-Jamiliyya in 1883, al-Hamidiyya in 1888, and al-Sulaimaniyya in 1895. By 1900, these new quarters accommodated 10,584 people, some 10 percent of the city's population.[13]

The rest of this chapter will examine some of the principal features of the economic activity of Aleppo and the groups involved in it from the turn of the century to the early years of the mandate. What groups were most active in agriculture and commerce during this period? Was there in fact a major division of economic functions among Christians, Jews, and Muslims, or is this simply the reflection of a stereotype? In some ways a description of Aleppo between 1890 and 1925 exhibits a good deal of continuity with accounts of earlier periods—especially those by Masters for the mid nineteenth century, and even by Marcus for the late eighteenth century.[14] But there were some significant differences, as we shall see.

The Urban Political Elite before 1918

The composition of the city's urban elite (the "leading families") changed fairly substantially over the period under examination, incorporating a number of new families and individuals. As Ruth Roded suggests, this was largely a consequence of the changes introduced by the Tanzimat reforms. The new judicial, fiscal, and bureaucratic structures that evolved came to require more and more men with a modern, that is secular, education.[15] A register of civil officials for Aleppo in 1858 lists only 20 individuals, including the governor-general, the treasurer, and the qadi, while the provincial *salnames* of the late nineteenth and early twentieth centuries contain lists of employees spreading over several pages.

The older elite families who grasped what was now required in order to take advantage of the new bureaucratic opportunities (and the new economic opportunities that went along with them) generally managed to maintain their status, but the considerable expansion in the number of civil servants also facilitated the relatively rapid promotion of individuals of less venerable social origins. The rise to prominence of these individuals did not create an elite with different goals or values; rather, the new circumstances surrounding the expansion of the state apparatus allowed new members to join and merge into the old elite. According to Roded, the infusion of "new blood . . . contributed to a great extent to the survival of traditional notable power through the Ottoman period and into the twentieth century."[16]

Philip Khoury's study of Damascus politics between 1860 and 1920 describes a process unfolding roughly as follows. The Tanzimat reforms had the effect of bolstering (and also of helping to expand) a group with strong ties to Istanbul.[17] Abdülhamid's social and religious conservatism, together with the very real advantages that the urban notables derived from supporting him, meant that opposition in Syria (excluding Beirut) was largely confined to a few radicals and those Salafi ulama for whom the sultan's pan-Islamism was an inadequate substitute for more thorough-going Islamic reforms.[18] Thus when the Committee of Union and Progress (CUP) came to power in 1908, there was initially some, but not much, support for the coup. None of the Damascus deputies elected in 1908 had been very closely associated with the committee beforehand, and after the counter-coup and the subsequent ousting of Abdülhamid, the CUP's "centralizing" policies gradually lost it much of whatever respect its earlier anti-absolutist ethos had attracted.

In the years between 1909 and 1914, the CUP's growing tactlessness and apparently headlong rush towards Turkish nationalism meant that the government in Istanbul became increasingly at odds with public opinion in Syria. The principal goal of the leaders of the Syrian opposition was to restore a form of reconstructed Ottomanism; they do not seem to have had any clearly defined aspirations for Arabism as such, and were more inclined to favor a form of government involving a degree of administrative decentralization. With the defeat of the empire in 1918, of course, the Ottomanist option was no longer available. In his highly nuanced study of the years immediately after the end of the war, Gelvin describes the choices confronting politically conscious Damascenes, first under Faisal, and then under the French.[19]

Although no equivalent of Khoury's Damascus nationalist prosopography yet exists for Aleppo, there is some evidence to suggest that, as in Damascus, the anti-Hamidian faction was either pro-Ottomanist or vaguely pro-Unionist, rather than Arabist. In addition, some four years after the 1909 revolution, the British consul in Aleppo recorded that "there is an openly expressed and general desire among high and low, both among the Arabs throughout this district and Christians of all sects and races, that the present government should be done away with and that England should take over and govern the country." That this was something more than wishful thinking on Consul Fontana's part was confirmed in a simultaneous report by the French consul that such approaches had indeed been made to his British colleague, and by requests to Fontana for a "British government of the country" some three months later.[20]

After the end of the Ottoman period, as in Iraq and in a rather different way in Palestine, some Aleppine notables came to side with the mandatory regime, some became pillars of the opposition, and some managed to walk a fine line between the two, producing ambiguities that can seem quite baffling. Because of the city's proximity to Turkey (and the former *Halab vilayeti*'s connections with Antakya and Iskenderun), a degree of reverse irredentism existed well into the 1920s. In November 1919, after Britain had declared its intention to withdraw its troops from Syria and it was clear that there were, at least for the time being, insufficient French troops to replace them, Ibrahim Hananu returned to Aleppo not simply to organize resistance to the French, but to do so in cooperation with the Kemalists, in spite of the fact that he had been one of the relatively few Aleppines to have fought with Faisal in the Arab revolt. This cooperation survived the fall of Aleppo to the French under General Trenga in July 1920 and only ceased with Hananu's arrest in July 1921 and the signing of the Franco-Turkish (Franklin-Bouillon) border agreement later in the same year.

This combination of uncertainty, resistance to the imposition of European rule, and generally pro-Turkish sentiments was replicated in northern Iraq and Kurdistan during the same period; the inhabitants of this region had no particular desire to be dominated either by a British or, rather later, by an Arab government. Here, too, they also rebelled against the imposition of local administrative authority and received logistical and military support from Kemalist forces in the process. Such apparently anomalous behavior can probably be explained by the extreme uncertainty of the situation both in northern Syria and northern Iraq; until well into the 1920s it was by no

means clear how long the British and French would be able to go on imposing effective authority in the area, and how far the Turks would be able
or willing to resist them.

It goes almost without saying that the political elite of Ottoman Aleppo
was entirely Muslim, although the province had sent two Christian Armenians to the Ottoman parliament in the elections of 1908, 1911, and 1914,
and Christians and Jews had been members of the administrative council
(*majlis idara*) since the early days of the Tanzimat. In 1908, along with the
appointed officials, the Christians Arghaki Ilyan (Elian) and Jurji 'Abdini,
together with the Muslims 'Abd al-Rahman Zaki Paşa (al-Mudarris) and
Muhammad As'ad Paşa (al-Jabiri) were members of the *majlis*.

Under the mandate several members of old established wealthy Christian
families (Aswad, Balit, Hindiyya, Homsi, Ilyan, Jinanji) were coopted into
the elite under the new political circumstances.[21] Socially, too, families of
foreign origin (Corneille, Girardi, Marcopoli, Poche, Sola, and Villecroze),
and to a lesser extent, some of the longer established Jewish families originally from Italy (Picciotto, Silvera, Kabbaya), retained or achieved a certain
amount of social (and political) prominence in the inter-war period, although the wealth and standing of the Poches and the Marcopolis probably
put them in a class above the rest.[22]

Merchants, Manufacturers, and Agricultural Wholesalers
1880–1925: Some General Characteristics

The composition of Aleppo's trade underwent considerable change during the late Ottoman period. Some traditional local products could no
longer compete with mass-produced European imitations; tastes changed,
and certain long-established markets simply disappeared. According to Quataert, "Ottoman manufacturers confronted an opportunity of sorts with the
price depression of 1873–96. As agricultural prices fell and local peasants
reduced their purchases of imported goods, domestic manufacturers found
new internal markets for their goods if they were able sufficiently to reduce
costs."[23]

However, although the empire's share of world trade contracted, the internal Ottoman market grew. In the process the area of land under cultivation expanded considerably, specifically, for our purposes, to the north and
northeast of Aleppo, where the land had never previously been cultivated,

or at least not for many generations.[24] In the last decades of Ottoman rule, members of the Jabiri, Kayyali, Mudarris, Ibrahim Paşa, Qudsi, and Rifa'i families bought substantial plots of land in 'Azaz, Bab, Jarablus, and Manbij.[25] These purchases took place on a large scale, 'Abd al-Rahman Zaki Pasha al-Mudarris, Muhammad Nafi' al-Jabiri, and Muhammad As'ad al-Jabiri in particular became very substantial landlords during the period between about 1890 and 1914. An interesting feature of many of these transactions is that several parcels of land were bought by named individuals on a certain day and then purchased from those individuals by one of the notables several days later, suggesting that the great landowners assured themselves security of tenure by buying from a "previous owner." There are some, though not many, records of Christians purchasing land.[26] The end product of this process, noted by 'Abdullah Hanna in the 1970s, was that by the time of the Land Reform, in the governorate of Aleppo alone the Mudarris family had 69 substantial holdings, the Jabiris 22, the Rifa'is 21, and the Qudsis 15. In addition, the Rifa'is had three holdings in Raqqa governorate, and the Jabiris owned 12 plots in Idlib.[27]

Naturally there were good years and bad years, the results of good and bad harvests, and other constraints. There were poor harvests in 1909, which pushed up cereal prices; in 1910, crop production was also down, and a plague of locusts consumed much of what was produced. The severe winter of 1911 caused the death of two-thirds of the flocks of goats and camels between February and April, but in 1913, there was abundant rain and a good cereal and silk harvest. According to Andrea Marcopoli, "Local producers of cotton cloth, silk and cotton-silk have found it easy to sell their produce both locally and on the European and Turkish markets" and workers' wages rose about 20 percent in the space of a year. Two new ice factories and three steam-powered mills were constructed in that year.[28]

In the early twentieth century, as is still the case, textile manufacture constituted the main industrial activity of Aleppo.[29] In a list of commercial establishments published in 1908,[30] there were:

27 merchants in yarn (*tujjar ghazl*)

72 merchants in and/or owners of establishments making silk cloth (*aqmisha haririyya*)

42 merchants in and/or owners of establishments making cotton cloth (*aqmisha ghazliyya*)

  6 merchants in indigo and other dyes

10 merchants selling "Syrian cloth" (*al-aqmisha al-shamiyya*)

32 merchants in "textiles" (*manifatura*)

14 merchants in broadcloth (*jawkh*)

 8 merchants in various kinds of cloth and novelties (*khirdawat*)

10 merchants in various kinds of cloth and various European goods

 5 carpet merchants

 4 (raw) wool merchants

Unfortunately, the list gives no indication of the size of the various establishments. Many individual names appear several times in these and other categories, and many of those listed under one heading appear in several other lists as well. Thus Elias Faris, Elias Qushaqji, and Hajj Ibrahim Halwani (?/Halwati) were merchants, owners of silk-weaving establishments, and proprietors of (presumably small) banks. Although I have not carried out a complete statistical survey—and the names are sometimes ambiguous—it is clear both from first and last names that at least three-quarters of those listed in the various categories above were non-Muslims in a city where, according to al-Ghazzi's figures for 1900, 65.5 percent of the population were Muslims, 26.4 percent Christians, and 7.9 percent Jews.[31]

The *Dalil* provides an interesting summary of commercial and politico-administrative activity in the years immediately before World War I. It also contains the names of the principal government officials and directors of government organizations—the Régie des Tabacs, the Ottoman Bank—alas often simply in the form of "Tawfiq Efendi" or "Farid Beg"—the members of the administrative council of the vilayet, the European consuls and their dragomans, the heads of the religious communities, the ulama and *ashraf* (*ashab al-rutab al-sharifiyya*), and the "notables" (*wujaha'*) of the city, a category that includes a number of prominent Christians and Jews.[32]

Among other occupations listed are lawyers (nine; six of them Christians), doctors (18: two Jews, 15 Christians, one unidentifiable), dentists (five: two Christians, three Muslims), pharmacists (17: 11 Christians, two Jews, two Muslims, two unidentifiable), and 22 individuals who were "bank[er]s" (*ashab muhallat al-baniqa*—the word *sarraf* is not used in this document) and commission agents. There are no Muslims in the latter category, which includes the Marcopoli brothers, Joseph Andrea, and Ibrahim Hayyim Shibta'i, and several members of prominent Christian families: Homsy (Albert, Na'um, Désiré, Nasrallah), Kalandani (Iskandar, Rashid, Salim), and Aswad (Yusuf, Elias).

There are two other categories that are of interest in showing the direction of commercial activity, although, again, the *Dalil* makes no attempt to rank according to the volume of trade. These are "Establishments of merchants and commission agents importing European goods" and "Establishments of domestic merchants and commission agents trading internally (*al-dhakhiliy-ya*) and with [other parts of] the Ottoman Empire (*bilad barr al-Turk*)." The 29 importers of goods from Europe include the city's prominent European merchants, many of whom still lived in the great khans in the center of the city:[33] August Félix, Alfred Girardi, Poche Frères, Joseph Sola, J. T. Peristiany, Molinari, Corneille, Eugène Catoni, Joseph Marcopoli, as well as members of the (Christian) Aswad, Balit, Khabbaz, Kusa, Naquz, Hindiyya, and Najjar families and the (Jewish) Khawwam, Shawb, and Kabbaya (Gabbay) families. There do not appear to be any Muslims on this list, and there are only four Muslims (Ahmad Maskana, Mahmud Dabbagh, 'Abd al-Rahman 'Awf and Mahmud Zaki) out of the 39 on the list of traders with the Ottoman interior, which is composed largely of Armenian Christians and Jews.

Hence, according to this list, there are few areas where Muslims clearly predominate. Even among the 25 grain wholesalers, there are only seven unmistakably Muslim names, the rest being, again, mostly Armenian Christians and Jews. However, all eight sheep traders are Muslims, as are the owners of the two flour mills, 'Abd al-Rahman Sumaqiyya, 'Ali Sumaqiyya and Fu'ad Mudarris, two families that often inter-married and continue to do so. The only area or listing of any size that is almost exclusively Muslim is that of the 18 weigh-masters or metal stockholders, *tujjar mal al-qubban*.

It is difficult to know precisely what conclusions to draw from the *Dalil*, which is not an official document; there is no indication of how the information it contains was collected or of how comprehensive it claims to be. Some corroboration can be found by comparing it with the list of members of the Chamber of Commerce in 1921, where very many of the same names appear. Class I includes three banks (Ottoman Bank, Banco di Roma, and Banque de France), two international companies (Singer, Forbes Mac-Andrew), Andréa Frères, Orosdi Bek, Poche Frères, Joseph Aswad et Frères, Carlos Balit and Company, Albert, Nasri, and Désiré Homsy, Rizqallah Ghazzala, Mikhail and Mansur Jinanji, Corneille and Company, Vincenzo Marcopoli and Company (all Christians); Binyamin Frères, Hillel Picciotto and Company, Jadda' and Sons, Yacqub 'Anzaruth, Kuzam and Sha'yyu (Jews) and only five Muslim names, Fu'ad Mudarris, 'Ali Sumaqiyya and 'Abd al-Rahman Sumaqiyya, and Muhammad and Muhammad Sa'id Hinaidi 'Atalla.

Again, this is very preliminary, and the two listings are not compiled in the same fashion; the 1908 *Dalil* is a survey with no ranking, whereas the Chamber of Commerce lists firms in order of their economic importance. Banking and bill discounting were important activities in both documents, and trade with Aleppo's hinterland rather than trade with Europe seems to have dominated the city's commerce. Many of the same Christian, "European," and Jewish names that occur in the 1908 document figure prominently in categories I and II of the 1921 document; similarly, there are only six unequivocally Muslim names out of the 54 names listed in class II in 1921 (and four in class I), showing the continuation of a relatively low rate of Muslim participation in trade and commerce from the prewar into the early inter-war period. In this limited sense, therefore, the ferment that took place in the Arab provinces of the Ottoman Empire between the 1890s and the 1920s—the reign of Abdülhamid II, the Young Turk revolution of 1908–9, World War I, the Arab government and the French Mandate—seems to have had remarkably little effect on this aspect of the economy of Aleppo. Although Muslims dominated politics, landowning, and large parts of the wholesale grain trade, Christians and Jews continued to control banking, finance, and textiles in northern Syria, until, and well after, the world depression of the late 1920s and 1930s.

Notes

1. Reşat Kasaba, *The Ottoman Empire and the World Economy: The Nineteenth Century* (Albany: State University of New York Press, 1988); Şevket Pamuk, *The Ottoman Empire and European Capitalism, 1820–1913: Trade, Investment and Production* (Cambridge: Cambridge University Press, 1987).

2. This is a constant motif of the consular reports, especially from Damascus, e.g., in 1903: "[Emigration from this region to America is increasing] to the detriment of the agricultural and economic interests of whole districts such as the Bikaa where in some villages 80% [sic] of the young males have left the country" (F0 618/3, Damascus Consulate, Quarterly report, 1903). In 1911, Andrea Marcopoli, consul of Portugal in Aleppo, wrote to Lisbon:
"L'état économique du pays, le service militaire appliqué aux non-Musulmanes et l'insuffisance des salaires sont les motives d'une constante migration pour l'Amérique et l'Egypte" (Fonds Marcopoli, Correspondence Consulaire, Nov. 1910–Sept. 1915, Report on Commerce, Agriculture and Industry for 1910, 27 February 1911).

3. For a convincing challenge to the notion of decline in an earlier period, see two articles by André Raymond, "Signes urbains et études de la population des grandes villes arabes à l'époque ottomane," *Bulletin des Etudes orientales* 27 (1974): 183–93, and "La conquête ottomane et le développment des grandes villes arabes: Le cas du Caire, de Damas et d'Alep," *Revue de l'Occident Musulman et de la Méditerranée* 27 (1979): 115–34. For a more recent analysis, see Cemal Kafadar, "The Question of Ottoman Decline," *Harvard Middle East and Islamic Review* 4, no. 1–2 (1997–98): 30–75.

4. Charles Issawi, *The Economic History of the Fertile Crescent 1800–1914: A Documentary Economic History* (subsequently Issawi, *EHFC*) (Oxford: Oxford University Press, 1986), pp. 374–75.

5. Donald Quataert, *Ottoman Manufacturing in the Age of the Industrial Revolution* (Cambridge: Cambridge University Press, 1993).

6. Justin McCarthy, "The Population of Ottoman Syria and Iraq, 1878–1914," *Asian and African Studies* 15, 1 (1981): 3–44.

7. In spite of "the paucity of tillers when compared with the extent of land they try to cultivate" (Consul Jago's Report on the Vilayet of Aleppo, June 1890, FO 861/22), a state of affairs that still existed in the 1930s and 1940s. Personal communication, Ismet Mudarris, Aleppo, February 1988.

8. Although, to keep things in perspective, it should be remembered that in 1800, when Aleppo was a city of 100,000 inhabitants, Alexandria and Beirut were still villages, with populations of 10,000 and 6,000, respectively. For the population of Aleppo in 1800, see Abraham Marcus, *The Middle East on the Eve of Modernity: Aleppo in the Eighteenth Century* (New York: Columbia University Press, 1989), "Appendix: A Note on Population," pp. 337–41. There is a more recent study by Thomas Riis, "Observations sur la population d'Alep au XIXe siècle," *Bulletin d'Etudes Orientales* 51 (1999): 279–98, based (*inter alia*) on the baptismal records of various Christian parishes. For the other cities, see Bernard Hourcade, "The Demography of Cities and the Expansion of Urban Space," in *The Social History of Cities in the Middle East*, ed. Peter Sluglett (Boulder: Harper Collins, forthcoming), tables 5.2 and 5.6.

9. For the slow progress of this venture, see Issawi, *EHFC*, pp. 231–34, 239–40. The road was completed in 1885, and reconstructed in 1903.

10. McCarthy, "The Population of Ottoman Syria," p. 34, says rather cryptically, "[The city of Aleppo's] population only increased at the same rate as the surrounding province (about 1 percent per year)."

11. Issawi, *EHFC*, pp. 129–30.

12. The Marcopolis and the Poches; see the forthcoming work of Rudiger Klein.

13. See Heinz Gaube and Eugen Wirth, *Aleppo: Historische und geographische Beiträge zur baulichen Gestaltung, zur sozialen Organisation und zur wirtschaftlichen Dynamik einer vorderasiatischen Fernhandelsmetropole* (Wiesbaden: Dr

Ludwig Reichert Verlag, 1984), p. 454, table 17. At first these quarters were inhabited almost entirely by Christians (and Jews in Jamiliyya), but by the late 1930s there had been a substantial migration of more affluent Muslims, "quittant la ville ancienne pour chercher dans la ville nouvelle un confort plus moderne. Les quartiers de Djamilia et Azizia virent la construction de nombreuses maisons neuves." Some 14,000 building permits were granted between 1922 and 1937. C. Godard, *Alep: Essai de géographie urbaine et d'économie politique et sociale* (Aleppo, 1938), pp. 10–11.

14.   Marcus, *Middle East on the Eve of Modernity*; Bruce Masters, "The 1850 Events in Aleppo: An Aftershock of Syria's Incorporation into the World Capitalist System," *International Journal of Middle East Studies* 22 (1990): 3–20. One significant difference was that modern methods of communication, such as the telegraph and the railways along which the troops summoned by telegraph could be transported, meant that outbreaks of violent disorder, a fairly common feature of earlier periods, could be more easily suppressed and were thus much rarer.

15.   Ruth Roded, "Ottoman Service as a Vehicle for the Rise of New Upstarts among the Urban Elite Families of Syria in the Last Decades of Ottoman Rule," *Asian and African Studies* 17 (1983): 63–94; "Social Patterns among the Urban Elite of Syria during the Late Ottoman Period (1876–1918)" in *Palestine in the Late Ottoman Period: Political, Social and Economic Transformation*, ed. David Kushner (Jerusalem, 1986), pp. 146–71; "The Waqf and the Social Elite of Aleppo in the 18th and 19th Centuries," *Turcica* 20 (1988): 71–91.

16.   Roded, "Social Patterns," p. 161.

17.   "The notables were content to accept directives from the imperial capital and did their utmost to harmonize their aims with those of the dominant power group in Istanbul, which now included members of the Damascus elite" (Philip Khoury, *Urban Notables and Arab Nationalism; The Politics of Damascus 1860–1920* [Cambridge: Cambridge University Press, 1983], p. 53). This group also included Abu'l-Huda al-Sayyadi from Aleppo, who exerted a particularly strong influence over Abdülhamid.

18.   See David Dean Commins, *Islamic Reform: Politics and Social Change in Late Ottoman Syria* (New York: Oxford University Press, 1990). It is interesting that this book contains only two references to 'Abd al-Rahman al-Kawakibi. The subjects of Commins's study were generally sympathetic to the ideas of Muhammad 'Abduh; some had links to the Wahhabis of Najd.

19.   James L. Gelvin, *Divided Loyalties: Nationalism and Mass Politics in Syria at the Close of Empire* (Berkeley: University of California Press, 1998).

20.   Reports of consuls Fontana and Laporte quoted in Rashid Khalidi, *British Policy towards Syria and Palestine 1906–1914* (London: Ithaca Press, 1980), pp. 284–85, 298.

21. A status that had often derived from their having been dragomans at various European consulates. Thus, in Aleppo in 1908, members of the Balit family were dragomans at the French and Austrian consulates, the Homsy family at the Belgian, Italian, and American consulates, and Elias Hindiyya at the Austrian consulate.

22. Jean-Claude David and Thierry Grandin, "L'habitat permanent des grands commerçants dans les khans à Alep à l'époque ottomane," in Les villes dans l'Empire ottoman; activités et sociétés, ed. Daniel Panzac 2 vols, (Paris: CNRS, 1994), 2: 85–124.

23. See Quataert, Ottoman Manufacturing, p. 15.

24. For an account of this process see Norman N. Lewis, Nomads and Settlers in Syria and Jordan, 1800–1900 (Cambridge: Cambridge University Press, 1987), esp. chap. 3, "Settlement in the Province of Aleppo, 1831–1914," pp. 38–57. "[W]hen the new Lands Department—the tapu—was established in Aleppo in 1866, it was a Jabiri who headed it (and held the post until his death)" (p. 49).

25. This paragraph is based on many discussions of the process with members of the Jabiri, Mudarris, and Qudsi families and on a survey of the Ottoman land registers for the qadha of Bab in the Aleppo Land Registry in April–May 1988 covering the (Rumi) years 1306–16 (1890–1900). The information in these volumes was copied into the present land register at various times during the cadastral survey conducted in the 1920s and 1930s.

26. Among transactions involving Christians are the purchase of 300 donums in Ghuz village (Bab) by the heirs of Antun Qushaqji in August 1315, and of about 70 donums in the same village by Nicos Walad Badros a month later. In a letter to his aunt in 1925, Rodolphe Poche (1889–1967) mentions his property in Braij, some 50 kilometers east of Aleppo, apparently bought by his father Frederick in 1891. See Fonds Poche, Correspondence Administrative, 1890–1902, letter of 15 July 1891 from Frederick Poche (Consul of Belgium and the United States of America) to the Tapu Department of Bab and Jabbul.

27. 'Abdullah Hanna, Tarikh al-Fallahin fi'l-Watan al-'Arabi, 5 vols. (Damascus, 1987), 3:506–91.

28. Fonds Marcopoli, dispatches from Consul Andrea Marcopoli, Aleppo, to Ministry of Foreign Affairs, Lisbon, dated 20 May 1909, 27 February 1911, 5 March 1911, 28 February 1912, 14 June 1913, 20 February 1914. Marcopoli had become vice-consul of Portugal in 1866.

29. See Jocelyne Cornand, "L'Artisanat du Textile à Alep: Survie ou Dynamisme?" Bulletin des Etudes Orientales 36 (1984): 79–126; "Toutefois, le textile reste encore le principal secteur de production de la ville," p. 81.

30. Dalil Suriya wa Misr al-Tujjari (1324/1908), pp. 72–98. I learned of the existence of this publication from an article by Boutros Labaki, "The Commercial

Network of Beirut in the Last Twenty-five Years of Ottoman Rule," in *Decision-Making and Change in the Ottoman Empire*, ed. C. E. Farah (Kirksville, Mo.: Thomas Jefferson University Press, 1994), pp. 243–62. I am most grateful to Roger Owen and Michael Hopper of Harvard University for making a copy of the *Dalil* available to me.

31. Gaube and Wirth, *Aleppo*, p. 434.

32. E.g., Gurgi Khayyat, Fathalla Riyyal, Yurghaki Efendi Elian, Salim Efendi Zallum, Karnik (?) Efendi Koymakjian, Gurgi Efendi Achikbashi, Musa Efendi Munshi, Elias Effendi ʿAbdini, Simyantob Munshi Efendi, Kostaki Efendi Homsi, Yusuf Efendi Mosuli, Mikhail Efendi Mahmalji, Bashir Efendi Balit.

33. See David and Grandin, "L'habitat permanent des grands commerçants." Two other articles by J-C. David offer penetrating insights into both the mindset of the Christians of Aleppo and the perception of them by other groups: "L'espace des Chrétiens à Alep. Ségrégation et mixité; stratégies communautaires (1750–1950)," *Revue de l'Occident Musulman et de la Méditerranée*, 55–56 (1990): 152–70; and "Les territoires des groupes à Alep à l'époque ottomane. Cohésion urbaine et formes d'exclusion," *Revue des Etudes du Monde Musulman et de la Méditerranée* 79–80 (1996): 225–54.

9   Representing Copts and Muhammadans: Empire, Nation, and Community in Egypt and India, 1880–1914

C. A. Bayly

In the autumn of 1909, Lord Morley, secretary of state for India, rose in the British Parliament to announce the creation of separate electorates for Indian Muslims under the Indian reforms scheme of the Liberal government, usually called the Morley-Minto Reforms.[1] Three years earlier, Lord Minto, viceroy of India (1905–10), had made a vague promise to a number of self-styled leaders of India's diverse Muslim inhabitants to respect their political importance in view of the nearly 20 percent of the Indian population they represented. He also acknowledged their vaunted status as a "ruling race."

By the end of 1909, however, Muslim leaders and their British supporters had ensured that these vague obligations were regarded by the British government as a debt to be paid with interest. In that year, Muslims were given direct electorates to the enlarged legislative councils in provinces where they formed a substantial segment of the population, despite widespread official dislike of any form of direct popular representation. This arrangement contrasted with the "collegiate" and indirect electoral bodies that were conceded to the remainder of the small Indian voting population. Indirect electoral colleges were all that was deemed appropriate for contemporary Egypt under the Liberal government's parallel scheme of local self-government there.[2]

In marked contrast to the case of Indian Muslims was the response of Morley's counterpart at the Foreign Office, Sir Edward Grey, to the demand for separate electoral arrangements made by Coptic Christians in Egypt some eighteen months later.[3] Following a formidable campaign of telegrams to the foreign secretary, a section of the Coptic leadership had gathered in a congress at Asyut in Upper Egypt and requested separate representation in the Egyptian local legislative bodies whose powers were being expanded.[4] They wanted part of the money they remitted as taxpayers to these local bodies to be applied to the mandatory teaching of Coptic Christianity in local elementary schools (*kutabs*). Like the Indian Muslims, they claimed a larger portion of government positions than the generous 45 percent of (mainly inferior) positions they already held. They particularly sought access to the senior office of provincial governor (*mudir*) from which they claimed they had been excluded since the British occupation of 1882. Finally, they demanded that the government allow a Sunday holiday to all Christians in government service to match the Friday holiday enjoyed by Muslims.

With the firm support of the British consul general in Egypt Sir Eldon Gorst (1861–1911) and most other British officials in Egypt, Grey rejected all these demands. He also refused to meet M.S.W. Fanous, the main Coptic representative in London. In his annual report on Egypt for 1911, Gorst stated that the Copts were already over-represented in government service. He asserted that the demand for special representation would backfire on them at a time when tensions between Copts and Muslims had only just begun to subside. These tensions had been inflamed following the assassination by a Muslim nationalist of the Coptic prime minister, Boutros Ghali Pasha, in February 1910.[5] Gorst disregarded the parallel that Coptic and British publicists drew between the Copts' position in Egypt and the Muslims' position in India. He also ignored the view that the Copts were a "race" naturally favorable to British rule and one that had begun the upward march of European civilization at the time of the pharaohs. Grey's rejection also came despite the powerful lobbying of Anglican Christian and American Presbyterian friends of the Copts and Coptic representatives in the British press.

On the face of it, the Coptic separatists' failure was as predictable as the success of the Indian Muslim League. Copts represented only about 7 percent of the Egyptian population, and in no province, even Asyut in Upper Egypt or the cities of Cairo and Alexandria where they were strong, did they amount to more than 20 percent.[6] This contrasted with the numerical preponderance of Indian Muslims in the Punjab, North-West Frontier Province, and eastern Bengal.[7] The Copts, who were mainly moneylenders, professional people, and shopkeepers, with a few landowners in poorer Upper Egypt, could not compare in status and prominence with the Muslims in the Indian army or as a landed class in North India. The Copts evidently could not, or would not, afford the British strong political support against Egyptian nationalism and a pan-Islamic movement invigorated by the Young Turks, support of the kind that their Indian Muslim contemporaries were expected to lend against the militant and predominantly Hindu nationalists of Bengal and Bombay.

This chapter seeks to provide a connective and comparative history of these events. It suggests that the Muslim "victory" needs to be examined in greater depth. Indian Muslims were by no means united behind the demand for separate representation. Many were in favor of moving toward the inclusive nationalism of the Indian National Congress. Why were these voices not registered? Even when the importance of British policies of "divide and rule" are given full weight, the British could have secured continued cooperation from many Muslims without the concession of direct electorates. In fact, neither Morley nor Minto was entirely happy with the new constitutional arrangements. Domestic political opinion was still broadly hostile to "Mohamedanism." Why, then, were such large concessions made?

Equally, the "failure" of the Copts was more complete than it might have been. In his final years as Britain's first consul-general in Egypt under the occupation from 1883 to 1907, Lord Cromer (1841–1917) had favored recruiting the Copts to the British cause. In the later 1920s and 1930s, the British government returned to the idea of supporting Egyptian minorities as a way of buttressing its influence in the country.

Even if the political outcome was broadly predictable, however, an examination of the controversies illuminates the way in which indigenous publicists and European lobbyists tried to take advantage both of old social connections and of new discourses in race and religion to generate agitation in Britain. If there was a "new imperialism" emerging at the beginning of the twentieth century, it was assuredly one of publicity and propaganda. At the same time, spokesmen of the colonized peoples also began to present their case more vigorously in metropolitan circles with the aid of telegrams, newspapers, and high-profile publicists.

The Eastern Mediterranean and the Indian World

In the 1990s, historians of the Middle East and India continued to write about the dire consequences of colonial policies of divide and rule for the twentieth century,[8] but most often they wrote studies of the voices of the victims. We need to return to an earlier literature in order to reconstruct the ideas and policies that led to these social ruptures.

In the 1960s, Roger Owen and Robert Tignor showed how intimately connected British administration in Egypt was with its Indian forebear, particularly in the realms of policing, irrigation, and political management.[9] The collisions and convergences among "Islamic modernists" in the two regions—Jamaluddin al-Afghani, Sheikh Muhammad Abduh, and Sir Syed Ahmed Khan—have also been addressed in a number of more recent works.[10] John Gallagher and John Darwin dealt with the Indian Khilafat movement of 1919–24 and the intimate link between British policies toward the Wafd, the Indian National Congress, and Muslim League in the aftermath of World War I.[11] Well-researched studies have been written about Coptic reform[12] and the emergence of a separatist Muslim leadership. Apart from a few short paragraphs, however, no one has made a direct comparison between the electoral fate of the Copts and Indian Muslims.[13]

The proposal for the Aix conference was informed by a vision of the Indian Ocean and the Mediterranean Sea on the threshold of modernity at the end of the nineteenth century. In it, Fernand Braudel's notion of the history of the *longue durée* was inflected with the structuralist concerns of K. N. Chaudhuri, whose work on the Indian Ocean made of it a mental as much as a material realm. The conference rubric was also influenced by postmodern concerns with "decentered discourses" and the critique of grand narrative. How do the interests of this chapter in broad comparisons between imperial governance and nationalist movements fit with these methodologies?

Imperialism and nationalism should not, of course, be depicted as monolithic abstractions working outside particular economic, cultural, or political structures. In our period there are many examples of inter-regional networks of influence, news-gathering, trade, pilgrimage, and migration that played an important role in the detailed workings of empire and nationalist self-assertion. Indian students at the al-Azhar seminary in Cairo, for instance, formed a network through which the ideas of Mahomed Abduh were brought into the same public arena as those of Syed Ahmed Khan and the Ali brothers, and other major reformers in India.[14] Merchant communities continued to link India, the Red Sea, and Egypt as they had done since the writing of the medieval Geniza documents. Sindhi merchants, Bohras, and Memons from northern and western India appeared regularly in the Egyptian mixed courts.[15] The roll call of European firms, from Thomas Cook and Peninsular and Oriental Steamships on, looks very similar in Alexandria, Port Said, and Bombay.[16] European-domiciled and mixed-race communities, including Maltese, Jews, and southern Italians, spread out from the Mediterranean ports into the Red Sea and Indian Ocean. Russell Pasha, the British police chief of Cairo and Alexandria in the later days of the occupation, even claimed to have discovered an eastering network of prostitutes recruited from the Cote d'Azur. These women, he reported, passed first to Alexandria, then to Cairo, and on to Bombay and Far Eastern markets as they became older and less saleable.[17]

Such small-scale networks supported the structures of empire and the politics of nation. As Roger Owen has pointed out, in the early days of the occupation, large numbers of British officers moved from India to Egypt and tried to establish a kind of Indian princely state writ large.[18] In 1882, Coles Pasha, who had begun his career as a policeman among the Bhil "tribals" of western India, tried to apply his workmanlike racial stereotypes in Egypt, recruiting Sudanese into the force. He saw them as African embodiments of the simple virtues of his earlier Bhil subordinates.[19] The British brought in their train many Muslim soldiers and junior administrators from India who returned home from Egypt with a new understanding of the universal struggles of empire and Islam.[20]

These networks worked for nationalists, too. Wilfrid Scawen Blunt, scourge of empire in Egypt and India, was one beneficiary. In 1880, prophesying the emergence of a liberal Islam, he lived at Jiddah, learning of the wide connections of Islam from Indian, Syrian, and Egyptian pilgrims.[21] Later, during the Urabi revolt, he sat at the feet of Muhammad Abduh at al-Azhar. A few months later, when he required introductions to Indian Islam, he set these contacts to work. With recommendations from Jamaluddin al-Afghani's pupils, he was passed along the ancient trade route to al-Hind, which traveled through southern Arabia to Ceylon and on to the south Indian Marakyyar and Lebbai trading communities. Susan Bayly delineated these speakers of Tamil-Arabic in 1989.[22] From there, Blunt moved inland up into the Deccan, where the old Arabic-Indian connections merged with the Iranian-Mughal ones in Hyderabad.[23] In this city he hoped to found an Islamic university. When Blunt wanted to publish an Arabic version of his *Future of Islam*, he went back to al-Azhar to have it translated, secure in the knowledge that the "English-knowing Muhammadans of India" had already received and used it in their own internal polemics. In these ways, empire, nation, and community were constructed along the existing networks of trade and culture.

However, between 1880 and 1920, these links were bound more tightly
and subjected to new stresses. In the context of international economic and
political conflict, imperial rule in both regions became more purposive and
centrally directed. Apologists for empire opened a broader ideological offensive in the public media. Nationalist leaderships also began to learn from
each other in metropolitan centers and project mutually reinforcing ideas.
Historical change itself became more centralized. It was precisely in this
period that the history of events began to take primacy in causation and to
rupture the social and cultural circuits of the *longue durée*. The historiography of the "fragment" and the "decentered discourse," on its own, is insufficient to construct a meaningful narrative, even of the fragments themselves. Metropolitan politics, economics, and culture needs to be brought
back decisively into the picture.

New Imperialism, New Nationalism, and New Communities

That the British formal and informal empire in the Middle East and in
India was in crisis between 1880 and 1914 is a truism, as crisis was both the
cause and consequence of imperial expansion. Of course, political, economic, and social conflicts were becoming more severe over this whole area.
Since the 1882 occupation, revived French pressure on the British in North
Africa had coincided with the German "drive to the east" and tension with
Russia on the borderlands of India. Imperial crises were intertwined with
internal ones for British cabinets. Gladstone's government, which decided
on the occupation of Egypt in order to make safe the route to India, was the
same one that suppressed the Irish Catholic peasantry. The later Liberal
government of 1905–16 was grappling with an Irish Protestant backlash at
the same time as it faced an upsurge of revolutionary terrorism in both India
and Egypt.

Islamic reaction, millenarian and modernist, dogged the heels of all British governments of the period. Nightmares about Wahhabi holy war in India
had hardly faded when the imperial government was faced with the Arabist
movement in Egypt, the rise of Mahdism in the Sudan, and fear of a hostile
Muslim response to the British occupation of northern Nigeria. Most dangerously for European empires, the Young Turk movement and revolution
of 1907–8 seemed to presage a new, more vigorous Islamic reaction that was
believed to combine modern military organization and traditional zealotry.
The ripples were soon felt in Egypt and India.

The British could always outface direct threats to their rule, as Kitchener did in the Sudan and Curzon in India. More insidious was the sense of crisis that derived from new methods of publicity and criticism directed against bureaucratic rule throughout the colonial world. The Indian National Congress (1885), the Urabist Constitutional Council (1881–82), and the Indian Muslim League (1906) quickly picked up techniques of propaganda and public meeting that they had seen used by European and European-expatriate newspapers. The Irish Home Rule agitation provided a model in India and in Egypt.

In the early stages of these colonial wars of publicity, European radicals played a leading role. A. O. Hume, a dissident Indian Civil Service officer much taken with the power of the press, moved from a kind of popular empire loyalism to outspoken criticism of the Anglo-Indian beureaucracy.[24] In 1885, he founded the Indian National Congress. William Wedderburn and Annie Besant[25] helped raise the stakes on imperial issues for domestic politicians through their mastery of metropolitan propaganda and pamphlet warfare.

Wilfrid Scawen Blunt, however, was the most dogged of all these figures.[26] He was a powerful symbol to non-European nationalists and emboldened their attempts at publicity. Dissident English Catholic gentleman and Byronic champion of the oppressed, Blunt moved in the inner circles of the establishment at the same time as he excoriated the Egyptian bondholders war[27] and the Anglo-Irish Protestant Ascendancy.[28] He took time off to lambaste the government of India, whose economic policy, he asserted, was rapidly pushing the Indian people toward "cannibalism."[29] Egyptian nationalists adapted Blunt's methods of publicity with alacrity. He encouraged them in defending Arabi, the nationalist insurgent of 1881–82, from the charge of fanaticism and kept Egyptian autonomy under discussion in European capitals.[30]

From the early 1880s, imperial issues were broadcast and magnified in a public arena expanded by electoral reform, which made all politicians sit up and take notice. The imperial view had to be refined and projected back to the metropolitan public in a more favorable light. Auckland Colvin and Edward Malet, chief defenders of the occupation, released a continuous press bombardment in its favor. Lord Dufferin, an Anglo-Irish landlord, having laid out a moralizing blueprint for British government in Egypt in 1882,[31] instituted as viceroy (1883–87) a survey of rural India that tried to prove that the poor had not been impoverished by British rule.[32] Lord Curzon (viceroy,

1898–1905) later battled with Indian publicists, especially Dadhabhai Naoroji, MP, on the issue of Indian famine.[33] Alfred Milner was another high-level publicist for imperial policy in Egypt and South Africa.[34] Most tenacious of all was Lord Cromer himself, first in his annual reports as British consul-general in Egypt and then in a series of volumes on Egyptian government and white rule over natives. His books went into many editions and were distributed through a newly centralized book trade.[35]

Newspapers and high-profile books waged wars of imperial propaganda. From 1882, *The Times* of London had had an influential correspondent in Egypt.[36] Egypt was an international issue in a way India could never be. The political importance of events there was increased by the constant sniping of the French press against British authority and French patronage of several Arabic newspapers. Their editors escaped prosecution for sedition under the adapted British India press legislation applied in Egypt because they could find a safe haven under the terms of the Capitulation system.[37] But even in India, the indigenous press had learned how to survive prosecution. It knew how to play on Liberal sentiments at home and had begun, in the early 1900s, to consolidate itself and to produce syndicated national news.[38]

A defining moment in these wars of publicity and representation was the Imperial Press Conference of 1909. There the now retired Lord Cromer began to bait the Egyptian and Indian newspapers for "sedition." He was sharply contradicted by the Indian nationalist and editor Surendranath Banerjea, who impressed the Canadian, Australian, and South African editors present by claiming that this was only fair criticism of unpopular bureaucracy.[39] Banerjea also apparently earned the admiration of W. T. Stead, the first of Britain's populist press barons, who had organized the conference.

Two final points must be made about the new imperialism of the public sphere. First, the rise of Labour provided important internal allies for colonial nationalists. Keir Hardie, leader of the British Labour Party, wrote extensively on Indian issues and made common cause with Egyptians.[40] Secondly, London as a city began quite suddenly, in the 1890s, to play the role of metropolitan imperial center that Paris had long played for the French empire. In part this arose from greater opportunities for travel among the English-speaking colonial intelligentsia and also from the expansion of the British and colonial universities. In part, it reflected the emergence of a radical Anglo-Irish literary and political culture in the capital associated with Oscar Wilde and Bernard Shaw. These circles played host to young nationalists as various as M. K. Gandhi; the Coptic nationalist Salama Musa; the

Indian economic thinker Dadhabhai Naoroji; and the Chinese leader Sun Yat-sen.[41]

Contemporary historians have spent years searching out the most minor of anticolonial movements in the Indian or Egyptian countryside. Resistance to colonial rule in both dependencies was doubtless widespread, even before 1919. But to be effective in modifying British policy and attitudes it needed to be combined with powerful advocacy in the imperial center. It was the new capacity of nationalist publicists to bring miscarriages of British rule to the attention of metropolitan audiences as much as local resistance in itself that marked their critical breakthrough. The same was true for sectional leaderships such as those purportedly representing the Copts or the Indian Muslims.

Two other sorts of imperial tensions become more pressing in the years after 1900 and provide the background for the attitudes of the Liberal government (1905–16) toward community and nation. One was the economic dilemma facing the British empire. The attempt from the 1860s on to push forward the production of cash crops, especially cotton, in western India and later in Egypt had created patchy wealth in both societies, but had significantly raised the level of social and economic conflict.[42] Agrarian economies largely dependent on a single cash crop were extremely volatile. India had passed through serious trade depressions in the 1870s and 1890s that provided a background to political discontent. The massive spread of irrigation had also led to an expansion of malaria.[43] In 1908–9, Egypt faced a serious slowdown arising from the spread of the boll weevil and a plunge in world demand for cotton.[44] In Lower Egypt, the rapid expansion of irrigation had put a larger population at risk from bilharzia.[45]

The governments in Calcutta, Cairo, and London therefore found themselves facing indigenous dissidence alongside strong countervailing pressures to suppress nationalist agitation from European business lobbies who argued that political unrest was damaging trade.[46] Worker militancy spread among the large European population of Cairo, Port Said, and Alexandria.[47] At much the same time, western Indian nationalists attempted to gain support from striking Indian workers in Bombay's undercapitalized and underprotected cotton-weaving mills.[48]

The sense of global economic danger was strengthened by the palpable competition that British goods now faced, especially from Germany, in both its Middle Eastern and Indian markets. Britain still benefited from the inward flows of investment income and salaries of lawyers, soldiers, and civil servants remitted from Egypt and India,[49] but sales of manufactured and semi-manufactured goods to these markets were now becoming critical to economic welfare.[50] Manufacturing companies selling to Middle Eastern and Asian markets established a glossy new trade journal, *The Near East*, which began publishing in 1909. The interests represented formed a powerful lobby both in Cairo and in London, and one also determined to suppress political agitation and denounce the weakness of the British government.[51]

As the Liberal government faced these challenges and the increasing likelihood of global war, it was hamstrung by the imperial problems and assumptions that it had inherited from its Gladstonian predecessor of the 1880s. These aristocratic Liberals were not democrats. For them "local self-government" both in the United Kingdom and the colonies meant the downward delegation of parochial and local matters. High politics was still to be determined by the educated super-elite. In India and Egypt, where less than 10 percent of the population could read and write (partly as a consequence of British education policy), they believed that no real democratic advance could be contemplated. But these men also realized that the days of Cromer and Curzon had gone as surely as those of Abdülhamid II and the Empress Dowager. Local opinion would have to be accommodated within legislative bodies. For a government, moreover, whose politicians had cut their youthful electoral teeth calling for the protection of "minorities" of Christians and Jews in the Ottoman Empire, issues of the fate of minority communities remained sensitive. Lord Morley was a journalist himself and Sir Edward Grey had become interested in Christian issues in the Ottoman lands. Yet how and when did Copts and Indian Muslims come to be defined as minorities in need of protection?

The British and the Copts: Pure Texts and Patriarchial Churches

Images of the Egyptian Copt had been projected to the British elite in the two generations before Grey's decision of 1911, thanks to the rise of mass literacy in Britain and the expansion of the habit of book-reading among the voting public. American Presbyterian missionary activity among Copts had already brought them to the attention of imaginative travel writers. The theme of "lost" ancient Christians was a return to one of the founding myths

of European global expansion. But in the romantic imagination of the late
nineteenth century, this theme intersected with the more exotic, almost
necrophiliac trope of disinterring the ancient Egyptians. As early as 1870,
Edwin de Leon, a former United States consul general for Egypt, published
Askaros Kassis, the Copt: A Romance of Modern Egypt (1870). In this bizarre
work, with chapter titles such as "New Love at Old Luxor," de Leon depicted
a romantic triangle between the swarthy, magnetic Copt, the American girl
Edith, and Sir Charles, an English "bounder." The exoticism of the text jars
with such dialogue as "By jingo! It must be my old chum at Eton, Askaros
Kassis."[52]

A more scholarly version of this sensibility had arisen even earlier from
the foreign-policy strategies of the Anglican Church, which was to remain
a key player on the Coptic issue. In the eighteenth century, the established
church (and its Scottish equivalent) had generally disavowed missionary
work among the "pagans," concentrating instead on "degenerate" Christian
communities and Jews. Following the evangelical revival toward the end of
the eighteenth century, British Protestants set in train plans to encircle Roman Catholic and Muslim societies by infiltrating and reforming the Greek
Orthodox Church and the Monophysite Christians of the Eastern rite in
Egypt, Mesopotamia, Kurdistan, and India.

Very early in the nineteenth century, British missionaries and evangelical
officials in southwestern India had established links to the Syrian Christians
of the Malabar coast and had attempted to recapture indigenous Christians
who had been brought over to the Nestorian rite.[53] Tensions arose between
high church protagonists who tried simply to influence indigenous hierarchies (these were often associated with the venerable Society for the Propagation of Christian Knowledge) and the evangelicals of the Church Missionary Society who resorted to more confrontational proselytization.

After 1815, and in spite of French objections, the Mediterranean also
became a British sea, with large British and British-protected communities
established at all major port cities from Nice to Alexandria. Levant merchants, returned India hands, vacationing consumptives, and royal relatives
swelled these populations. Egypt came into view when Muhammad 'Ali's
regime was forced to allow the British a wider commercial and political role
there after 1838. Both missionary branches of the Anglican church now
became more active on the Mediterranean littoral.

Before 1880, the critical interest for Anglicans was the discovery of pure
Coptic biblical texts at a time when scientific textual criticism was coming

into its own.[54] Copts were regarded with anything from mild disdain to outright hostility as heretics. This, rather than innate secretiveness, helps to explain the suspicion with which Anglicans were hereafter always viewed by the Copts themselves. In Alexandria, Port Said, Ramleh, and later, Cairo, Anglicans competed with French Catholic missionaries and kept relatively apart from the Greek Church. Anglicans remained divided in their views of Egyptian Christians, but disapproved of the strenuous educational activities among Copts set in train by American Presbyterians after 1840.[55]

The occupation of 1882 initiated a new phase of British interest in Coptic Christianity. Most educated Coptic Christians had supported Urabi's movement of "Egypt for the Egyptians," but they appear to have been alarmed by the rhetoric of holy war against the infidel that the nationalists adopted after the British bombardment of Alexandria that year. For its part, the British political establishment represented the occupation as a blow against Muslim tyranny and a reinforcement of security for India. The powerful church lobby argued that the occupation should also be seen as providential intervention to protect minorities, particularly Copts, against misgovernment and to end North African slavery.[56] Quite apart from reasons of state, the established church needed to take the domestic initiative back from Anglo-Catholics and Dissenters by proclaiming its international mission. The Coptic church itself, rather than simply Coptic texts, had now become the object of attention.

The influx of Anglicans into Egypt after 1882 increased knowledge about the Coptic church, but stirred sharp debate. Some churchmen continued to regard Monophysite doctrine as "soul-destroying heresy." Others believed that reformed and educated Coptic Christian priests could bring the East into the Anglican fold and signal the final collapse of Islam. Some commentators even saw parallels between Coptic and Anglican Christianity. In 1883, the Reverend W. H. Oxley, for instance, sought out Copts in Cairo and interviewed a deacon named Joseph Hannah at length; Oxley wanted "to discover the points of similarity with ourselves; and their [the Copts'] customs that have never changed, shed so much light upon our own, and confirm me more than ever in the belief that our branch of the Church Catholic has preserved the essentials and is in the right against Rome."[57]

Most Copts did not regard themselves as living under appalling Muslim oppression, as the more ardent of their Anglican admirers, such as Mrs. E. L. Butcher,[58] claimed. The Coptic patriarch was, however, prepared to ascribe the purity of Coptic liturgical practice to what he described as "the

Mohammedan persecutions in past times."[59] Subsequently, Britons and some Coptic separatists were themselves only too ready to broaden this analysis into one of racial difference between Copts and Muslim Egyptians.

After 1882, Anglicans tried to obtain influence by cultivating Coptic elites, especially landowners and rich shopkeepers in the big towns. In the early 1890s, they were sucked into the violent controversies that broke out between members of the reforming Coptic Tewfik (Pioneer) Society and Patriarch Cyril.[60] After that, relations improved markedly. Bishop Blyth, the Anglican bishop of Jerusalem and the East, developed new links to the Eastern Christian churches.[61] Many new Coptic churches were built and some repaired, activities that had been discouraged under the independent government of the khedives. Some tensions remained, though, and these combined with the dislike that many young Copts felt for foreign rule. Those educated by American Presbyterians were averse to the episcopal order of the Anglican Church. Others steered clear of Anglicans in order not to give the Muslim political authorities the sense that the Copts were "conspiring with the English."[62]

The Coptic hierarchy's own tentative opening to the Anglicans gave Coptic Christians a small number of influential proponents in England among bishops and fellows of Oxbridge colleges. These men discreetly argued that, though Christian and pro-British, the Copts were oppressed in their homeland. This was because the Egyptian government discriminated against them in employment, and they were not even able to take advantage of the legal opportunities of the Capitulation system, as were the Greek and many Catholic Christians. The domestic public was alerted to a "Coptic problem." This meant that the authorities in Egypt were obliged at least to keep the matter under review.

In contrast to Anglican churchmen, British officials in Egypt were often ambivalent and even hostile to their co-religionists. One author noted that the English mistrust of Copts was akin to their disdain for Jews. In this view, Copts were a race of venal shopkeepers, cruel usurers, and low clerks who tried to gain jobs from the British by craven appeals "in the name of that Saviour who died for both of them."[63] They were a weak and sickly race compared with the stolid Egyptian Muslim peasant. The *fellah*, indeed, was beginning to acquire some of the characteristics of the "sturdy peasant" of the Punjab in the eyes of officials influenced by earlier Indian experience. Lord Cromer himself initially gave little credence to Coptic claims to superiority or difference. He remarked, to the irritation of some Copts and their Anglican supporters, that Copts were simply Egyptians who went to church.[64] Later his opinions changed. In the early 1900s, Egyptian national opinion was galvanized by concessions the British secured from the Ottomans and the French that perpetuated their control over the Suez Canal and the Sudan. Boutros Ghali Pasha, the Copt who later became prime minister, was one of the few Egyptians politicians who was prepared to support the British. In order to stymie the opposition, Cromer began to contemplate a subtly divisive, pro-Coptic policy in his last few years.

Constructing the Copts as a Separate Race (1890–1914)

Despite their high representation in the lower levels of the Egyptian administration, some Coptic leaders came to argue that their "community" was disadvantaged in employment at the higher levels and excluded altogether from many other positions of power. Copts had lost the monopoly they had held before Muhammad 'Ali as collectors of land tax, though they had expanded their numbers in other areas of the administration. Copts were still blocked not only by the predominance of the old Turkish elite, but by the influx of Syrians (mainly Lebanese), many of whom were also Christians, and by Europeans.[65] After 1882, the British were blamed for further damaging Coptic interests by favoring Muslims in order to buy political credit with the khedive and the Ottomans.

Although the Coptic elite's disadvantages were measured in terms of education and employment, as with Indian Muslims the sense of grievance could be deepened by a historical myth of decline projected in newspapers designed for the community. At that time, Indian Muslims were arguing that they should be protected as the ancient ruling race of the country. Some Egyptian Muslim spokesmen also asserted that they were descendants of the conquering Arab race and should be liberated from Turks and Christians. Almost as an aside, Copts were stigmatized as "sons of Pharaoh."

For their part, a section of the Coptic intelligentsia reacted to this by claiming that they were the only true descendants of the ancient Egyptians. They were, therefore, not only the most ancient and authentic Christian community on earth, but also the originators of Western civilization, having passed on their lore to the Greeks in ancient and Hellenistic times. They created the myth of the Coptic Athena, as it were, and there were many European observers prepared to encourage them in this endeavor. Of course, this pharaonic ideology was not restricted to the Copts. It became an important element in the Egyptian—as opposed to the pan-Islamic—version of regional nationalism. Secularist and nationalist Copts such as Salama Musa also used it to argue for unity against the British on the grounds of common Egyptian descent.[66] All the same, the pharaonic myth was a particularly powerful weapon in the armory of those, both European and Coptic, who argued for special protection for their community.

On the British side, John Ward, fellow of the Society of Antiquaries, made the idea explicit in his *Pyramids and Progress* (1890). He said that under the benign eye of "a splendid selection of Indian officers,"[67] Britain would inaugurate a new era of progress in the country. Its engineers would launch Egypt once again on a program of great public works; meanwhile, the Egypt Exploration Fund would reveal the secrets of mankind's past. Central to this mission were the Christian Copts, "whose blood is uncontaminated by intermarriage with Arabs and negroes."[68] Here the British reformer had to aid him: "a race which inherits all the ability and quickness of its Egyptian forefathers and can be trained to carry out the English ideas of justice and morality."

This idea was not limited to English-language writing. In 1882, H. de Vaujay described the "melancholy, taciturn and sombre" Copts[69] as "the real representatives of the ancient Egyptians,"[70] citing their resemblance to the figures of the ancient monuments in Upper Egypt as proof. De Vaujay pictured a history of racial and religious persecution. The Coptic custom of circumcision was taken to be an inheritance from the ancient Egyptians. This practice summoned up the idea of racial purity in the minds of Europeans influenced by contemporary eugenicist ideas.[71]

The racial interpretation of Coptic difference was based on the identification of Copts as the true ancient Egyptians. The first such assertion had apparently been made by French scholars during the Napoleonic invasion, and after 1870, gained wide currency in both European and Coptic circles. In the 1870s and 1880s, Gaston Maspero, French director of the Cairo Department of Antiquities, and Flinders Petrie, his British rival, dispatched to London and Paris quantities of material relating to the "races" conquered by the pharaohs that fed the new fashion for anthropometric racial analysis. In 1880, the Reverend H. G. Tomkins addressed the Anthropological Institute of Great Britain on "Flinders Petrie's collection of ethnographic types from the monuments of Egypt."[72] In Tomkins's vision of ancient history, the Egyptians battled against "Negritic" races; they were infiltrated by "Hebraic" types and suffered the attacks of barbarous plunderers from across Sinai, who were identified with the ancestors of the modern Arabs. A kind of ancient race war was postulated from the evidence of the pharaonic stelae, and this was deemed to foreshadow the race war of the modern era.

The interests of Anglicanism, eugenics, and Coptic reclamation surfaced in a more subtle form in the writing of Miss Agnes Lewis of Cambridge University, who claimed to be one of the two first women to visit the Coptic monasteries of Egypt and Nitria. She asserted that the degenerate state of the Coptic church was a result of dietary and marriage customs that debased the Coptic "race." Enjoined to fast for 170 days every year, Copts were chronically undernourished.[73] Rural Copts secluded their women and denied them education, she asserted. The dissolution of the church was hastened by the custom of selecting bishops from ignorant and isolated monks. Here Miss Lewis's experience as one of the first women at Cambridge must surely have shaped her views.

Formerly a journalist for the Coptic community newspaper, Kyriakos Mikhail had come to London to argue for the freedom of the Egyptian press as the controversy over Coptic representation came to a head in 1909–11.[74] He became the major Coptic proponent of racial difference. "The genuine Egyptians," Mikhail proclaimed, "are the Christian Copts. They alone trace an unadulterated descent from the race to whom the civilization and culture of the ancients were so largely due."[75] Because of their practice of Christian endogamy, "they have kept their blood pure from admixture with semi-barbarous Arabs and savage Kurds, or other foreign elements whom the licentiousness of Mohammedan family life has introduced into the country."[76]

Medieval and early modern Coptic literature makes it clear that the Coptic elites did indeed maintain a tradition that they had suffered sporadic persecution over the centuries of Muslim rule.[77] Even after Muhammad 'Ali had opened government positions to them in the nineteenth century, Egyptian Muslims regarded them with some suspicion as usurers and clerkly fraudsters.[78] Coptic Christian families generally continued the practice of monogamy and accorded women a relatively high status within the family.[79] Nevertheless, the ideology of eugenics and family purity deployed after 1900 by Anglicans and a number of Coptic separatists, such as Mikhail, was well calculated to appeal to northern European, and specifically British, opinion. Kyriakos Mikhail painted a picture of Coptic life where, as in Britain, the wife and daughters sat at the table. Because "the family concept" was

Western European, "the Copts should take again the high place in the civ-ilized world [occupied by] their pharaonic ancestors."[80]

Mikhail's letter campaign in the British newspapers during 1910 and 1911 focused the attention of influential people in Britain on the issue, though Coptic claims were ultimately rebuffed. Constitutionally and electorally this was a sensitive time in Britain, with conservative opinion ranged against a government that was believed to be overthrowing ancient rights, notably those of the House of the Lords. Most British newspapers and periodicals supported the Coptic position against that of Sir Eldon Gorst. The *Spectator*, for instance, made explicit the comparison developed here: "Just as in India, we must stand by the Mohammedan minority and see they suffer no op-pression at the hands of the Hindoos, who outnumber them so greatly, so in Egypt, we must stand by the Copts and Christians and safeguard them from Mohammedan oppression or neglect."[81] The *Daily Mail* urged that the Copts be treated as "a separate community,"[82] whereas the *Evening Times* referred to them as "the oldest body of the Cross in the world and descen-dants of the Pharaohs."[83] Most significantly, the venerable *Church Times*, organ of the Anglican Church and newsletter of its priests, wrote passionately in favor of Coptic claims to special representation.[84] This periodical gener-ally had little to say on foreign affairs, but it kept up a constant barrage about the supposed decline of Christian morality in Britain, which was implicitly blamed on the permissiveness of the Liberal government.

What is striking is how closely connected were the press campaigns in Britain and its empire. Nationalists in both India and Egypt had learned rapidly to use the press, pamphlet, and telegram after the 1880s. But in Egypt, the British authorities found it particularly difficult to clamp down. The French deliberately frustrated British attempts to prosecute and silence dissident newspaper editors, being quite happy to see their old rivals coming under assault. The tenor of the newspaper war had already been raised by ex-president Theodore Roosevelt of the United States, who had recently visited the country and the United Kingdom.[85] Roosevelt denounced the British authorities as weak—not sufficiently imperialist—and accused them of abandoning the Egyptian Christians. The British suspected that American Presbyterian missionaries had put him up to it.

The influential clerics and academics who had interested themselves in the Eastern churches redoubled their efforts when Indian Muslims secured special representation. A. J. Butler, of Brasenose College, Oxford, and author of *The Ancient Coptic Churches of Egypt*, wrote in the *Nineteenth Century* to lay the blame on Lord Cromer, with whom he had had an early falling-out in Egypt. In India, Butler argued, the British had held the line between Hindus and Muslims. In Egypt, the administration had consistently pandered to the Muslims and treated them as "a kind of superior caste."[86] This had led to a growth of Muslim fanaticism that was now the greatest danger to British administration in Egypt. Even in India, the even-handed approach was now under pressure as a result of the constitutional reforms: "It was avowed and believed that British action was dictated by fear of the Muslim community in India—the most loyal subjects of the Crown in that country."[87] But Butler also believed that the new Oriental fanaticism was political and not truly religious. Muslims in Egypt were now more lax than ever. What was happening was that Hindu extremists in India and Muslim extremists in Egypt were using religion as a cover for disloyalty. Indeed, they were in secret league. He claimed that Ibrahim Nasif al-Wardani, assassin of Boutros Pasha, was associated with both Irish and Indian terrorists.[88]

Butler was joined in this chorus by Mrs. Butcher, author of *The Story of the Church in Egypt*. The sensibility to the Coptic problem was increased by its linkage with the broader issue of ancient Egyptian origins. Mikhail, for his part, invoked the authority of Flinders Petrie, who was at this time at the height of his influence as a cultural champion in the eyes of the British public. Petrie had himself earlier described the Copts with approval. In 1893, he asserted complacently that the "perceptions" of the ordinary Egyptian peasant "are far less keen then ours. The feeling of pain is hardly comparable with our own." By contrast, "the only class yet appreciably affected for the better by foreign influence is the Coptic community."[89] The link with the romance of Egyptology persisted. The *Church Times* carried regular articles on the way that the truth of the Bible story was being confirmed by the discoveries of Petrie and Maspero in ancient Egypt. More broadly, a kind of millenarian unease gripped much of the discussion of the Egyptian and Coptic questions.[90] Britain was in Egypt, it was often implied, to begin again the tradition of great engineering and irrigation works that had been the outward evidence of the perfection of ancient pharaonic civilization. Petrie's own cyclical understanding of the rise and fall of civilizations argued as much. How could it be, then, that the British should discriminate against their ancient Christian brothers, the begetters of their own civilization?

This debate was reminiscent of the millenarian ideas associated with the discovery of Indian "Aryanism" and its justification for the British presence in India a century earlier. Here, too, the triangular spiritual relationship among Britain, India, and Egypt had been invoked by men such as Francis Wilford, who had claimed that Hindus had formed the Pharaonic civilization and, through it, the modern West.[91]

Muslim Egyptians moved rapidly to counter the press barrage in Egypt and in Britain, already secure in the knowledge that neither Gorst nor Grey was likely to risk offending Muslim opinion at so critical a time. The use of the language of race by some Egyptian or Indian spokesmen in Europe was a strategic adjustment to the prevailing climate. In the dependencies themselves, more established schools of political thought remained dominant. For instance, Lutfi al-Sayyid, leader of the Egyptian wing of the national movement, developed his critique of Coptic claims by deriving his objections to Coptic separate electorates from Islamic law, not race theory. He denounced Mikhail for conflating the idea of Copts as a sect (tai'fat) with that of a Coptic nation (al-ummah). Copts did not enjoy "an independent communal existence within a specified homeland" any more than did Egyptian Muslims.[92]

Meanwhile, Egyptian nationalists in Europe also entered the fray. Duse Mohamed, a long-term resident of England, was a fierce critic of British rule in Egypt. He anticipated many of Edward Said's motifs, arguing that Western writers homogenized Egyptians, Indian maharajas, and Hindu priests into one passive Oriental Essence.[93] He reiterated Blunt's charges against the occupation and idolized Arabi as a true son of the soil.

Duse Mohamed was particularly skilled at turning British racial and eugenic arguments on their heads. Though there is some doubt about his facts, he asserted that the manumission of slaves at the time of the occupation had been unwisely applied to Egyptian domestic servants, especially female companions of older women. These women had turned to vice with European foreigners, leading to "an increase of half castes," drinking, debauchery, and a general decline in the racial health of Egyptians.[94] As for the Copts, they were no more the true descendants of ancient Egyptians than any other Egyptian: to say so is as absurd as to argue "that there are no real Britons than the Welsh."[95] Besides, he added, such racial arguments came ill from a ruling class of English aristocrats who had so recently served under Disraeli, who had been born a Jew.

Copts and Muslims in Egyptian Society and Politics

Did these wars of publicity reflect or bring about any significant social changes? The Copts were deeply but ambiguously integrated into Egyptian society. Though marked off as different, they had never been recognized as a wholly separate community, as Lutfi al-Sayyid noted. Many Coptic life-cycle rites were essentially the same as those of their Muslim neighbors. Their dress was similar, though color coding was different (Copts tended to wear black and blue). Copts attended local Muslim *kuttab* schools and learned the Arabic of the Qur'an;[96] some schools since the time of Muhammad 'Ali's reforms had taught Christian doctrine in Arabic where, as in the Asyut region, there were substantial numbers of Coptic pupils. Copts used the offices of the local qadi, though appeals involving two Copts might be taken to their own patriarch.[97] Copts were believed to have access to certain forms of spiritual benefit. An observer of village life in the 1920s wrote that if a Muslim woman had several miscarriages, she would ask for a newborn baby's dress from a Coptic woman so that the *barakat* (charisma) would be transferred to her. This was because Copts were "good people."[98]

At the same time, Copts were not equal to Muslims. Until 1802, they had been subject to legal inequities, including levy of the *jizya* tax on non-Muslims, and prohibitions against riding on horseback and appointment to many public offices. Opprobrium flowed from their role as moneylenders and local tax collectors.

Relations between some Copts and Muslim communities do appear to have deteriorated from the 1870s. As the foreign Christian powers infringed on the sovereignty of Egypt, Christians of all denominations became the target of greater suspicion as prospective fifth-columnists. Although almost all Egyptians outside the Turkish ruling class supported Urabi's resistance to the British in 1881–82, themes of holy war against the infidel inevitably surfaced. European observers sedulously cultivated the fears aroused. Flinders Petrie, for instance, claimed that the Copts had expected to be massacred if Arabi had driven out the British.[99]

Initially, British rule united the entire younger generation of Egyptians against it. Yet there appears to have been another marked deterioration of religious coexistence in the early years of the twentieth century. As late as 1903, Copts and Muslims had still been entering each others' places of worship. By 1910 that was no longer so in many centers. Formerly integrated young men's clubs in major towns had split.[100] Pro-Coptic British critics tended to blame the Egyptian administration for "pandering" to the Muslims.[101] Yet the virulent denunciation of Copts in the Muslim newspapers in 1909–11 does suggest that Islamic sentiment had tipped into a more intransigent phase. Salama Musa noted that Mustafa Kamil's pro-Turkish nationalist rhetoric and his newspaper *Liwa* was anti-Coptic, playing into the hands of the British who wished, in his words, to "indicise" the conflict. The Egyptian wing of nationalism led by Lutfi al-Sayyid tended to be more conciliatory to Copts, Musa thought.[102]

As in India, so in Egypt the Liberal government's declared policy of expanding local self-government took the steam out of the nationalist surge, which had been building up since the British atrocities at Dinshaway in 1907. Cromer's retirement in that year and Eldon Gorst's appointment as high commissioner and consul-general seemed to signal a more conciliatory phase and a retreat from what was seen as Cromer's policy of divide and rule in favoring Copts and Europeans. But the November 1910 assassination of Boutros Pasha, the Coptic prime minister, inflamed the situation again. Boutros's murderer, the young nationalist al-Wardani, appears to have acted mainly from political motives. Boutros was accused of selling out Egyptian national interests in the Sudan and the Suez Canal. But al-Wardani was said privately to have denounced Coptic "trickery" (comparing it to the actions of Muslims in India, ironically).[103] After his execution, amidst hysterical mutual abuse in Coptic and Muslim newspapers, he was popularly revered as a martyr for having slain a "Nazarene."[104]

This was the background for the Coptic congress that a group of landowners and lawyers from the province of Asyut convened in the spring of 1911. Significantly, the Copts of Asyut seem to have felt themselves more embattled than those of Cairo and Alexandria. The city lay at the head of the Sudan caravan, and commercial relations between Arab buyers and sellers and the Coptic and Jewish trading communities were not always good. In the 1860s, an Indian Sufi teacher, in flight from the British after the 1857 rebellion, had inaugurated a purification movement in the city's conservative hinterland. This soon developed rebellious and anti-Christian sentiments.[105] After 1900, new stresses arose. American Presbyterian missionaries increased their activities among both Copts and Muslims. Economic conflicts arising from the spread of commercial farming after the building of the Asyut barrage sometimes set the Christian tradesmen against Muslim farmer. Here Asyut differed from other regions. Young Copts in the delta had better relations with Muslims, because both groups resented strong European influence. Men such as Salama Musa consequently argued for a unified national movement. In Cairo, the strong links of patronage between the Coptic elites and hierarchy and the khedival court also eased friction.

Despite official apprehension, Coptic leaders at the Asyut congress leaned over backwards to conciliate the Muslims, arguing that their protest was really against the British government.[106] It was only outside the congress, and especially in Britain, that the exclusive rhetoric of Coptic purity and authenticity was heard. Nevertheless, the response from all quarters was sharp. The Coptic patriarch, under pressure from the British and khedival party, voiced opposition to the congress.[107] Gorst worked hard to have the meeting abandoned and publicly denounced it in a series of statements culminating in his annual administration report for 1911.

By far the strongest reaction came, naturally, from Egyptian Muslims. An Egyptian (i.e., Muslim) conference was convened at Cairo in the April 1911. Though careful control by the ministerial party and the British blunted its political edge, attacks on self-appointed Coptic leaders were venomous. They were denounced as traitors, enemies of Islam, and degenerates.[108] The popular reaction was even more violent. Coptic funerals and processions were attacked by mobs in major cities. In Cairo, people dressed up as Coptic priests were pelted and jeered at in staged public demonstrations.[109]

In Asyut, a Canadian missionary was assaulted and local Christians predicted an imminent massacre along the lines of the Armenian atrocities.[110] This was an insistent theme of this period and one fed by the indigenous and European press.[111] In one village a stand-off developed between a Coptic landlord and his Muslim *fellahin*.[112] In these cases, the immediate political conflict seems to have converged with a longer history of resentment of Copts as moneylenders and bazaar merchants in the towns and as wealthy magnates in some parts of the countryside. In other words, Coptic-Muslim relations came briefly and sporadically to resemble the sort of conditions that were becoming more characteristic of Indian "communalism."

In the medium term, the Coptic-Muslim issue in Egypt died down again and was overwhelmed by more pressing concerns. Agricultural and commercial prosperity returned in 1911 after two poor years. The dying Gorst, subjected to bitter attacks from all sides, resigned and was replaced by Kitchener, who was thought to be a "safe pair of hands." He was strongly pro-Muslim in consequence of his Indian and Sudanese experience. Most important, the Italian invasion of Tripoli, which Egyptians thought to have been connived at by the British, re-ignited an inclusive struggle for independence that overwhelmed the differences between the Copt and Muslim, pan-Islamic Ottomanism and Egyptian nationalism.[113] Later, during the anti-colonial movement of 1917–23, most younger Copts again sided with their Muslim neighbors. Serious communal conflict of the sort seen between 1903 and 1911 did not resume again until the rise of the aggressive Muslim Brotherhood in the late 1920s and early 1930s.

Some general features of the events of 1910–11 should now be mentioned, as they bear comparison with the contemporary Indian situation. Both in Egypt and in Britain, the debate about Coptic special representation was very much a war of the telegram, press, pamphlet, and public meeting. As we have seen, the most radical Coptic intellectual, Kyriakos Mikhail, was essentially a publicist who argued as much for the freedom of Coptic newspapers as he did for special Coptic representation. The eugenicist tinge of Kyriakos Mikhail's intervention in Britain was well adjusted to the form of contemporary debate. The Coptic separatists also secured strong support from the Anglican and academic lobby. Personal and public factors intertwined. Anglican newspapers denounced Gorst as anti-Christian, and used his unorthodox private life as evidence against him.

In these political controversies, racial and historical stereotypes played a mediating and not simply a coincidental role. Mikhail, Butcher, and others needed to appeal to the British public's Egyptological fantasies and racial perceptions if they were to gain any degree of political leverage. But the Anglo-Egyptian official mind was equally inclined to represent political conflicts in racial terms. In a letter to Grey that was not included in his published official report, Gorst stated that Copts in the countryside "played towards the [Muslim] peasant, the same part as does the Jew in Russia."[114] Jews were, indeed, a point of reference for practically every discussion of race and politics during this period. It was this, rather than any Islamic ceremonies that the office might demand, that disqualified Copts from the office of *mudir*. The official report conveyed the more acceptable view that the Copt was not by race or upbringing fit for executive action, a stereotype traditionally applied to "effeminate" Bengalis in the supposedly masculine Indian administration.[115]

This longer-term predisposition to deny Copts a major political role became irresistible in the light of the economic and political problems of the immediate pre-war period. With German diplomatic advances in the Middle East and gathering trouble with the Italians in Tripoli, the British government could not afford to alienate Muslim opinion, which was beginning to turn against it in Egypt and India. The government was in the process of moving against radical spokesmen such as Sheikh Shawish, and it badly needed support of the khedival party, the French, and the moderate nationalists. This point was driven home by the British Chamber of Commerce in Egypt and the trade press. Smarting from the trade depression of 1909–10, their representatives accused Gorst of vacillating, departing from the firm ways of Cromer and the Tories. Further political conflict over Coptic aspirations had to be avoided. A correspondent to the Near East argued that the Copts in Egypt, like domiciled Europeans and Eurasians in India, had been allowed to make too much trouble.[116]

Representing the Muhammadan in India

British stereotypes and literary constructions of the "Indian Mussulman" mediated the politics of Muslim political representation on the subcontinent in much the same way as visions of Egyptian antiquity did for the Copts. These stereotypes also influenced Muslim understanding of themselves at a time when modernist, purist, and pan-Islamic ideas were in sharp contention. British images of Indian Islam were, however, more complex, contradictory, and mutable than much postcolonial analysis has allowed.

British scholar-officials and missionaries had built up a complex sociology of Indian Muslims in the course of the nineteenth century. Working with Indian Muslim subordinate officials, policing sectarian conflicts and religious endowments, officials could not afford to deploy simplistic stereotypes at the level of local governance. An appreciation of the variety of Indian Islam, rather than an attempt to homogenize it, was a feature of this deeper archive. Periodicals such as the *Bombay Literary Society*, founded in 1804, had made officials well aware of the interpenetrating communities of trading Muslim Khojas, Bohras, Memons—and of the Ismaʻili heritage of the west coast that linked the Arabian Sea to the Ottoman and Mediterranean worlds. Meanwhile, the *Friend of India*, mouthpiece of the Serampore Baptist mission, revealed an understanding of the varieties of Bengali Islam. It drew attention, for instance, to the Baul sect, which found its members among both Hindus and Muslims. In the south, again, the distinctive features of its Tamil-Arabic society were well known in the early nineteenth century. Jafar Sharif's *Kanun-i Islam*, on Muslim popular culture in central India,[117] and

Mrs. Meer Hasan Ali's *Observations on the Mussulmans of India*[118] were both highly sympathetic accounts that were widely available and quoted. Officials were well aware of the way in which Hindu and Muslim society shaded into one another through saint cults and local cultures.

Beyond local knowledge drawn from the writings and testimony of Muslim informants, there existed another level of discourse that inflected the broader politics of the Indian and British empires. Although Muslim fanaticism was an insistent theme, these broader narratives of Indian Islam changed over time in ways that are reminiscent of the changing views of Copts and Egyptian Muslims.

The deism of the later eighteenth century and the dependence of the East India Company's officials on Indian Muslim administrators inclined the British in India to take a favorable view of Islam. The deists and free thinkers of the early East India Company government were aware of Edward Gibbon's preference for Islam over Christianity. It was India's People of the Book who had, at their most liberal, created the Mughal Emperor Akbar's Indian "constitution," a mythical starting point for equitable government in India, which the British themselves sometimes claimed to be emulating.[119] Modern Muslims may, in this view, have fallen away from the high standards of the past, but the institutes of Akbar, and behind them the medieval ethical (*akhlaq*) literature and the legal norms of Hedaya, had preserved proper standards.

By the late 1830s, this framing narrative was beginning to disintegrate. Evangelical Christians denounced the "false Prophet" of Islam. So-called Wahhabism was implicated in a series of anti-British outbreaks. In fact, the Wahhabi tendency in India was only indirectly linked to the following of Abdul Wahhab in the Arabian Peninsula. The Indian reformers were purist but orthodox Sunnis who used the Urdu version of the Qur'an and Muhammad Isma'ils *Taqwiyat-i Iman* (Refuge of the Faith) as their agents of regeneration.[120] They were as likely to be in British government service as they were to be secretly plotting *hijrat* and *jihad*. The events of the 1857 rebellion powerfully reinforced these emerging prejudices. Muslims were widely regarded as prime movers in the outbreak. Subsequently, Dr. W. W. Hunter, a Bengal civil servant, publicly asserted that Indian Muslims could never be loyal subjects of the British Crown.[121]

Some Muslim leaders now began to argue that a rapprochement between Muslims and the British government was vital if what they began to regard as their community was to survive. Even before 1857, Syed Ahmed Khan

(1817–98) had proposed an "opening of the doors of interpretation" to Western learning. After the rebellion, he propagated the idea of a modernizing liberal Islam through his foundations, the Ghazipur Scientific Society and the Aligarh Mohamedan Anglo-Oriental College.[122] Despite differences over the role of the Khilafat, in their emphasis on the utility of modern knowledge for Islam, Syed Ahmed's views had much in common with those of Jamaluddin al-Afghani and Sheikh Mahomed Abduh in Cairo.[123]

After 1857, Syed Ahmed Khan pleaded for the special treatment of Indian Muslims, who were now reviled as instigators of the insurrection. His advocacy encouraged a group of Muslim notables and professional people to work closely with the British government. It was their political descendants who, in 1906, led the Simla deputation to request separate electoral representation for the community. How were Muslims able to achieve a reevaluation of their faith and political reliability in the eyes of British political elites sufficient to achieve this turnabout?

Syed Ahmed's own personality and connections were as important as British desires and prejudices in the rehabilitation of the Muslim image. He managed to promote his ideas through a combination of private friendships and effective public advertisement. This was something to which the Egyptian Coptic separatists could never aspire. The mid nineteenth century was a time when personality and personal presence remained vital. Syed Ahmed's status as an aristocrat connected to the old royal court, a Muslim cosmopolitan, and a scientist appealed to the class-conscious British officials with whom he worked as a subordinate judge before 1857. On his side, Syed Ahmed laid much stress on the need for Anglo-Indian friendship. The Islamic ethical tradition derived from Aristotle lauded the virtues of friendship, but on the need for Anglo-Muslim sympathy Syed Ahmed also quoted St. Paul.[124] His brief military role during the rebellion helped foster a reputation for manliness, a virtue that he constantly emphasized in his later educational projects. The importance of Syed Ahmed's large size and powerful physique should not be underestimated in these relationships with the British. It contrasted with the imputed effeminacy of Bengali nationalist politicians, the "deviousness" of the Maratha Brahmins, and what were seen as the sharp, "Levantine" characteristics of Egyptian Coptic lawyers.

Syed Ahmed's critical social breakthrough in India was brought about by his friend, Col. G.F.I. Graham, who became superintendent of police in a district near the one where he was posted as subordinate judge. Graham arranged for two of the duke of Argyle's pamphlets on Indian government to be translated and published by Syed Ahmed's printing press. Graham then secured the duke's patronage for Syed Ahmed's Muhammadan Literary Society.[125] The connection prospered. The duke, as secretary of state for India, personally invested Sir Syed with the Order of the Star of India when he later visited England in 1869.

In his 1862 pamphlet on the *Causes of the Indian Rebellion*[126] and his controversy with W. W. Hunter over the supposed Muslim proclivity to "holy war,"[127] Syed Ahmed provided a moderate indigenous voice in the vigorous debates about responsibility for the Mutiny. The viceroy's circle and the India Office took note. In London, his reputation was consolidated. He became an honorary member of the Athenaeum club; he was entertained by Lord Lawrence,[128] former viceroy; he met with the Mutiny historian, Sir J. W. Kaye; and he attended Charles Dickens's last public reading.

By no means were all British commentators impressed. The British evangelical disdain for Muslims had not altogether abated after 1870. It was zealously perpetuated by Bible societies and continued as a subplot in the anti-slavery movement, the partition of Africa, and the Eastern Question. Some retired Indian officials, such as R. N. Cust and Sir William Muir, played an important role in keeping antagonism alive. Muir's researches as a scholar and as an intelligence official during the rebellion reveal a nuanced understanding of Muslim complexity. Back in Scotland, however, he wrote A *Life of Muhammad*, which recycled the usual charges of tyranny against the Prophet and claimed that Islam was incapable of change.[129]

Syed Ahmed rode to the defense of the Prophet and summoned up Edward Gibbon in his defense. His Muslim biographer, Altaf Hussain Hali, even states that the main purpose of the Syed's visit to England was to find material in the British Museum with which to refute Muir.[130] If so, it is a striking testimony to the political importance of contemporary metropolitan polemics about religion. The mid-Victorian interest in moral and political heroes, stimulated by Carlyle's recent endorsement of Muhammad, also helped the cause. Syed Ahmed's pamphlet about the Prophet was published by the bookseller Trubner, whose editions of Oriental texts and works on both India and Egypt gradually spread a more sophisticated knowledge of Islam among the British educated classes. Complimentary editions of the book were sent to the khedive and the sultan. Meanwhile, Syed Ahmed also employed his observations of Europe to denounce his Indian co-religionists for ignorance, maintaining his reputation as a reformer.[131] By first fostering manly friendships with the British rulers and then beginning to exploit the domestic British print media, this school of Indian Muslim politicians was beginning to make its voice heard.

More influential yet in building up a Muslim lobby in London was Syed Amir Ali (1849–1928), who was to play a critical role in the 1900s, alongside Sir Syed's political descendants. Like Syed Ahmed, Amir Ali was the descendant of Muslim aristocrats and governors who had firsthand experience of the world outside India, in Persia and Afghanistan.[132] Like Syed Ahmed, Amir Ali had learned English and avidly read Gibbon, the Bible and Western classics. He was later to write English works on the Saracens and Moorish history and *The Critical Examination of the Life and Teachings of Mohammed* (1873). It is revealing that Amir Ali's *Short History of the Saracens* (1889) was reprinted during World War I for British officers working in the newly conquered Arab countries of the Middle East.[133]

Amir Ali's intimacy with the British ruling class was even closer than Sir Syed's. Early on he had attracted the attention of his English schoolmasters at the Hooghly College and was later introduced to the viceroy Sir John Lawrence. When he went to England in 1869–73, he carried with him three letters from the viceroy Lord Mayo, and made a full round of the Anglo-Irish connection in London. Returning to India, he served on the Bengal Legislative Council and the bench of the Bengal High Court. When he retired from the Calcutta judgeship in 1904, he and his English wife returned to England and resumed their connections with British high society.[134]

Amir Ali was one of the founders of the London mosque, but more important were his acquaintances in the Reform Club,[135] where he met and lobbied major Liberal politicians and journalists. On his Swiss holidays he socialized with diplomats and nationalists from Egypt and the Ottoman Empire.[136] In 1909, at the pinnacle of his career, Amir Ali was appointed to the Judicial Committee of the Privy Council. It was by means of these links that he was able in 1909–10 to lobby for Muslim special representation, a cause that had taken root in his mind since he first complained of Hindu dominance of government employment to the National Mohammedan Association in the Bengal of the 1870s.

Official patronage in India, then, was critical in propelling a handful of the Indian Muslim elite into the consciousness of domestic political elites. By contrast, Egyptian Copts could gain little by way of advocacy from the feeble British educational establishment in Egypt and their special pleading was openly opposed by most retired officials. Yet issues of patronage apart,

the Indian Muslim spokesmen seem also to have been able to present themselves more effectively than the Copts, despite the apparent advantage of the
Christian faith enjoyed by the latter. The Indian Muslims were gentlemen,
cosmopolitans, and soldiers who were relatively at ease in domestic English
social circles and could eat with and, at least in the case of Amir Ali, marry
Europeans. These aristocrats and landowners stressed the themes of friendship and manliness that appealed to the first generation of British men coming out of Arnold's revivified public schools.

The favorable view of Islam that such men tried to promulgate in the
face of the Islamophobia of the Eastern Question was reinforced by changing
political, literary, and academic sensibilities. In literature, the noble Arab
chieftain, a latter-day reinvention of the noble savage, was given stronger
form by the writings of Blunt's wife Anne, William Doughty, and, more
distantly, by Lady Hester Stanhope. The *fin-de-siècle* delight in exotic wisdom raised to prominence the figure of the Sufi mystic, virtual antithesis of
the Muslim holy fanatic or Malay running amok. A generation after *Askaros
the Copt* came to the bookstalls, fictional Arab sheikhs of great chivalry gave
him bibliographic battle. The theme of the relaxed and wise Sufi was widely
spread by the popularity of translations of Omar Khayyam, the classical Persian poet.[137]

Muslims never had the powerful group of Anglican academics and missionaries to speak in their favor that the Copts enjoyed, but scholars such as
the Cambridge Islamist E. G. Browne strove to lighten the image of Islam
and Muslim states in the eyes of metropolitan audiences, easing the birth of
the "loyal Mussalman of India."[138] Two retired principals of Syed Ahmed's
Aligarh Anglo-Mohommedan College, Theodore Beck and Theodore Mor-
rison, also acted as strong advocates of Muslim interests in Britain in the
early years of the century.[139] Aligarh's status as a kind of Indian Oxbridge
contrasted with the low reputation of the Egyptian educational service. T. W.
Arnold, a major Oriental scholar, had taught at Aligarh and had conducted
research in Islamic history along with the learned Maulana Shibli Nu-
mani.[140] He seeded Oxbridge and London colleges with British disciples
who had a closer and much more sympathetic understanding of the varieties
of Islamic faith and experience. Scientific biblical criticism made it easier
for educated people to understand the origin of the Qur'an. As Andrew Porter
points out,[141] later nineteenth-century missionary discourse was by no means
as hostile to Islam as it had been earlier in the century. The emphasis was
more likely to fall on teaching and debate than aggressive proselytism. This

change of mood was reflected in a number of missionary conferences held in India and London in the 1900s that attempted to understand the Islamic faith.[142]

An important turn in the arrival of favorable conjuncture for the triumph of Muslim separate representation was the change of official sensibilities in India itself. Despite the assassination of the viceroy Lord Mayo by a Muslim zealot in 1872, the Indian empire began to warm to the idea of the Muslims as a bulwark. When political leaders claiming to represent Indian Muslims came forward in the wake of Syed Ahmed Khan, they were increasingly to have an attentive, if not always a positive, response. Fear of the Muslims as external enemies and internal seditionists was tempered by respect for them as conservative landlords and breedstock for the Indian army. Whereas the Copts were degraded in the official mind by their association with Jews and moneylenders, the bugbears of the era, Indian Muslims had exactly the opposite experience. Measures such as the Punjab Land Alienation Act of 1900 were designed to protect "agricultural races" from despoliation at the hands of usurers. The agricultural races included, preeminently, India's Muslims, whereas the usurers were believed to be Hindus.[143]

Two more openly political trends reinforced this re-evaluation. The founding of the Indian National Congress at Bombay in 1885, and Syed Ahmed's group's conspicuous denunciation of it as an enemy of Muslim interests, alerted officials to the possibility of divide and rule. Syed Ahmed was never a "communalist," as some Indian historians claim.[144] His hostility seems to have been directed more against overweening Bengalis than against Hindus as such. His was a Muslim version of Hindustani patriotism. But the colonial government wished well any movement of opinion that offered a counterweight to their Calcutta critics. The Muhammadan Educational Conference and Muslim representatives before the Education and Public Service Commissions (1883 and 1887, respectively) had woven a powerful rhetoric of community decline, which, as with the Copts, was increasingly represented as racial decline. Its corollary was that Muslims needed special treatment in schools, government service, and in local elected bodies. Officials encouraged this position and began to argue that British rule was designed to protect Indian minorities, particularly Muslims.[145]

Indian Muslims, though allegedly backward in the race to Westernize, took increasing advantage after 1890 of modern means of communication and of opportunities for movement across the empire to capitalize on these earlier political openings. In India, publications such as the *Aligarh Institute*

Gazette and the *Oudh Akhbar* sometimes flattered official sensibilities. Muslims began further to expand their connections in London around the turn of the century. Despite their ambivalence about Western education, substantial numbers of Muslims had gone to the Inns of Court in London and several of them had spent long periods in the capital. This was a time when Hindus were much less in evidence because of continuing ritual restrictions on sea travel. The London branch of the Muslim League, founded in 1906, fronted publications that were reviewed in the British press. Even a trade journal such as the *Near East* covered the sage sayings of Indian Muslim leaders on the future of Islam, implicitly contrasting them with the sedition of the Egyptian nationalists.[146] Professions of loyalty by Indian Muslim leaders inevitably contrasted with contemporary Hindu agitators and seditionists.

A final important figure in the metropolitan projection of the Indian Muslim around the turn of the century was the Aga Khan. This prince's role in politics in India was somewhat convoluted.[147] As a leader of the Isma'ilis, North Indian Sunnis regarded him with some suspicion. He also retained close connections with major Congress leaders through his Bombay interests. While in Britain, though, the Aga Khan's role was to represent the acceptable face of Islam and stand as the staunch defender of a special status for Indian Muslims. He was already a close friend and informant of Valentine Chirol of *The Times*. In 1898, he met the future King Edward VII at the Epsom races. Edward and the prince had common interests in racehorses and beautiful women. The Aga Khan later wrote, "Throughout the Reforms scheme of 1908 [in India], when the Turkish revolution broke out, and at other times, I had the great honour of being consulted for a long time by his Imperial Majesty in great confidence."[148] The king was much more politically active than Queen Victoria had been and seems to have intervened privately with his ministers to favor Indian Muslims and the Khedival party in Egypt. The Aga Khan acted as advocate for both dependencies. He traced his descent from the Arab world and held much property in Cairo and Upper Egypt. He claimed to believe that the Egyptian court needed help, being in a state of "political helplessness" in comparison with Indian princes and even the inhabitants of British India.[149]

As Francis Robinson argues, the London branch of the Muslim League, which included a small but growing number of Indian Muslim barristers and students, was much more politically influential and well directed than its vacillating Indian branches. To a very large extent it was able not only to persuade the Liberal government to make concrete Lord Minto's vague promise to help Indian Muslims in 1906, but in concert with retired ICS men, it was also responsible for securing for Indian Muslims in several provinces a number of seats on the new legislative councils well in excess of their proportion of the population.

The distance of Muslims from the predominantly Hindu extremist movement and its associated terrorism between 1905 and 1910 made a favorable impression on powerful British publicists such as Valentine Chirol. His *Indian Unrest* displayed much greater warmth toward Indian Muslim aspirations[150] than his later *Egyptian Question* did toward their Arab co-religionists. As the man on the India desk of *The Times*, he was able to take much of the British press with him and severely embarrass the British government on the Muslim issue.[151] The *Church Times*, friend of the Copts, was unable to match the weight of the "Thunderer." Chirol himself regarded the Copts as a small minority,[152] much more frightened of the nationalists and inclined to link up with them, than India's sturdy Muslims ever were likely to do.

As the controversy over the nature and extent of Muslim separate representation came to a head in the years after 1906, a final group of incontrovertible weight took to the field in their interest. These were officials on the spot and in Britain. A key figure in the reform scheme was Minto's secretary C. Dunlop Smith. Dunlop Smith's views mirrored those of the age. He feared Muslims both as militant enemies and as a well-organized political lobby. Comparing the moderate Congress leader G. D. Gokhale with Mohsin-ul Mulk, a leading Muslim Leaguer, he characterized the former as "weak and not of that stock that breeds leaders of men" and the latter as "a strong wise man."[153] Dunlop Smith's views were shared by Hare, the governor of East Bengal and hater of high-caste Hindu seditionists, and by the young Harcourt Butler, proponent of a conservative and pro-Muslim agrarian policy of "men with broad acres" within the ICS.

Most of the retired officials in London surrounding the India Council were also, to one degree or another, supporters of Muslim claims. Two Tory former viceroys, Lord Lansdowne and Lord Curzon, lined up behind the league to embarrass the Liberal government. The former lieutenant governor of the United Provinces, Sir James la Touche, was also an outspoken advocate of theirs. Only his Catholic Irish successor, Lord (formerly Sir Antony) Macdonnell, warned against policies favoring the Muslims.[154]

Why was it predominantly those Muslims who sought special political status in India for their community who were able to use personal connections and metropolitan public controversies to their advantage? Why did

Muslims who supported the Congress and feared the consequence of separate electorates not have their opinions heard? Lack of official patronage in India and England is one reason, but also, nationalist Muslims were not well enough positioned culturally and politically to project their case publicly. In this they resembled the Coptic separatists. Not all members of the Young Party of Aligarh who staged a rapprochement with the Congress after 1913 opposed separate representation for their community, of course. But Muslim nationalists did tend to be much younger men brought up in the colleges of Calcutta, Allahabad, or Lahore alongside their Hindu coevals. They had neither the strong connections to the great Muslim magnates, princes, and nawabs of their separatist elders nor to British officials who distrusted their radicalism. Other opponents of Muslim separate representation, such as the literary men Akbar Allahabadi and Nazir Ahmed, were figures in the Urdu and Bengali cultural worlds of the small towns and villages who lacked access to other English media, let alone to London clubs, quarterlies, and reviews.[155]

Finally, alongside politics and connections, issues of literary and polemical representation played some part in making antagonism between Hindus and Muslims an easier concept to grasp. By their very nature, the lay figures of the new metropolitan media tended to categorize and exaggerate difference. Muslims might be either fanatics or loyal warriors and gentlemen, but they were definitely Muslims and could not be confused with Hindus, Christians, or others. The more distant from the tactile, syncretic culture of rural India were those making these representations, the more hard-edged the distinctions. In the small towns of the United Provinces, Sir Syed could speak of Hindustani patriotism as often as he wrote of Hindus and Muslims. In London, the language of public representation required a sharper dichotomy between Islam and Hinduism. A similar abstraction from a more complex reality can be traced, as we have seen, in the work of officials such as Sir William Muir.

Conclusion: Representing Communities

When the Liberal government came to debate the issue of Muslim separate representation in the aftermath of the Muslim League delegation of 1906, it was faced with an alliance of official and non-official sentiment in its favor much greater than that which could be counted on by the Copts. Neither Viceroy Minto nor Secretary of State Morley was a strong advocate of Muslim special representation. The Liberal cabinet, whose weighty figures included anti-Ottoman and covertly Islamophobic members such as David Lloyd-George and Sir Edward Grey, were doubtful about creating direct special electorates for Muslims with representation beyond their weight in the population. Instead, to push it through, official interests combined with coordinated lobbying in the metropole by privileged colonial subjects. They used the contemporary language of race and eugenics and the possibilities offered by mass journalism and publishing to great effect.

Muslims were in a much stronger position in India than Copts were in Egypt. They held a large, though dwindling, proportion of subordinate administrative offices. They dominated the post-Mutiny Indian Army. Above all, they had a numerical predominance in Bengal, the Punjab, and in North Indian towns, which the Copts were unable to match even in provinces such as Asyut. This made it possible for the British to contemplate special electoral arrangements that would be more transparent than the complicated Belgian system advocated by Coptic leaders.[156]

Beyond this, however, it must be said that the elaboration of a micro-history of separation and communal conflict by the colonial power and by local leaders in India over several generations had given Muslim claims a plausibility that the Copts lacked in Egypt. Gyanendra Pandey's[157] view that the British created and privileged a "communal narrative" in India from the beginning of the nineteenth century is correct, though partial. The categories of Hindu and Muslim had been consolidated in the field of urban policing and justice, census-taking, and revenue assessment since the 1830s. Directly and indirectly Indian Muslims had a long history of representing themselves to authority in India and, indeed, in London. By contrast, the anti-Coptic riots of 1882 and 1911 could not plausibly be teased into a coherent history of institutionalized difference. Communalism was not part of the vocabulary of colonial policing in Egypt to the extent that it was in India from as early as the 1830s.

At the same time there was more at issue than the longevity and interests of the colonial power itself. An indigenous narrative of Hindu victimhood had also emerged very early in the nineteenth century in India. Rather than dwindling as the Coptic narrative of victimhood had, powerful forces of religious purification in both major Indian religious communities carried it forward. It was reinforced by perceived differences of language, bodily purity, dress, and intellectual culture. It is true that conflicts and differences between Hindus and Muslims were not necessarily the only, or even the

dominant, features of social tension at the beginning of the twentieth century. The Bombay newspapers of 1911 were resounding with the controversy
that had arisen over the policing of a Sunni-Shi'a riot during Mohurrum in
the city.[158] Caste and sectarian conflict among Hindus was also well known.
Large numbers of Indian Muslims, possibly a majority, thought of themselves
as integrally Indian. Yet in North India particularly, an indissoluble core of
institutions had been established that insisted on difference and this set apart
the Indian Muslim and Coptic cases.

Copts learned the Arabic language and were taught the Qur'an. Demands
were heard for a revival of secular old Egyptian among Copts, but with little
result.[159] Despite continued interpretation of cultures, much of the North
Indian Muslim and Hindu leaderships had, since the early nineteenth century, espoused different versions of the Hindustani vernacular.[160] Residential
populations in cities and even the countryside were more sharply separated.
Copts generally lived adjoining their Muslim neighbors.[161] Copts harbored
their Christian heritage, but, with the partial exception of the American
Presbyterian section of the community, they did not have powerful external
links of sentiment, as did the Indian Muslims who went on the hajj. In
general, Copts were said to prefer Egyptian Muslim to Christian rule. Copts,
of course, were treated with some disdain by many Egyptian Muslims,[162]
especially if they were attempting to assert themselves. But they were still
perceived to be part of the body politic, however inferior. In some ways,
Copts held a position in Egyptian society analogous to that of the small,
advanced trading communities such as the Parsis of western India or the
Jains. By contrast, Indian Muslims may have been treated as outcaste by
orthodox Hindus, but they were also respected as rulers and feared as de-
spoilers. Amongst Hindus there were already extreme nationalists such as
V. D. Savarkar, who treated Muslims as foreign invaders, and other moderate
ones such as G. D. Gokhale, the senior Congress leader, who respected their
claim to separate representation.[163]

All these variables—colonial policy, the public representation of difference, and the microsociology of separatism—determined the course of relations between these respective minorities and the majority population during the later phases of British dominion. After 1911, the British government
began again to lose control of the political situation. In Egypt, the Italian
invasion of Tripoli and the excitement generated by the struggle of the Young
Turks against Christian encirclement encouraged the rise of a new wave of
nationalist militancy. In general, the differences between Copts and Mus-

lims and the pro-Turkish and Egyptian patriotic traditions that had emerged after 1882 were overwhelmed. During World War I and its aftermath, there were sporadic anti-Coptic outbreaks, but more representative were cases where mullahs and Coptic priests paraded arm-in-arm with demonstrators against British rule. All had suffered from "war imperialism."

In India, British relief that they had encouraged respectable Muslims to become loyal subjects of the empire was soon dampened by a rapprochement between Young Party Muslims and the Congress nationalists. Local issues such as the status of Aligarh Muslim University came together with a burst of sympathy with the Turks and Libyans to push younger Muslims into alliance against the British government. Men such as M. A. Ansari took part in the Indian Muslim Medical Mission to Turkey during the Balkan War of 1913.[164] Many retained their connections with the Congress after 1922, when communal politics resumed in earnest. For them association with pan-Islamic modernizers in Turkey and Egyptian nationalists confirmed their Indian nationalism.

In India, however, the issue of separate minority representation remained at the center of the political stage. It was only because in 1916 the Congress agreed that Muslims should continue to have special representation beyond their proportion of the population that the anticolonial alliance of Gandhi and the Khilafatists could take shape. The Congress-Khilafat alliance of 1919–24 did not prove that Indian nationalism was ultimately homogeneous or that the events of 1909 were nothing more than a colonial ploy, as some have argued. What it did show was that a substantial section of the Muslim leadership was prepared to draw strength from a tactical alliance with the Congress. Most of that leadership nevertheless continued to insist that Muslims were different and needed special political arrangements to preserve those differences.

This sense of separate identity was a consequence of the power and physical concentration of the Muslim community in India. It also reflected the resolute projection of the idea of the Indian Mussalman as both a potential danger and potential savior, in metropolitan and colonial politics, by British and Indian agencies. The now fashionable study of racial and religious representations cannot explain historical change unless it is grounded in a study of the political institutions and connections that make those representations possible. Equally though, mere assertions of the primacy of politics and economic interest make little sense unless one pays attention to the mode in which those interests are projected and perceived.

Author's note: Venturing in part into a new field, I have been indebted to others in writing this essay. I would like to mention particularly Juan Cole, Ronald Hyam, John Iliffe, Sugata Bose, David Arnold, Leila Fawaz, Roger Owen, Kathy Prior, Avril Powell, Carey Watt, Susan Bayly, Eugene Rogan, and members of the meeting at Aix-en-Provence.

Notes

1. The outstanding studies of Muslim separatism and politics in India are Francis Robinson, *Separatism among Indian Muslims: The Politics of the United Provinces' Muslims 1860–1923* (Cambridge, 1974), esp. pp. 133–74; and Mushirul Hasan, *Nationalism and Communal Politics in India 1911–28* (Delhi, 1979); see also Hasan, *Communal and Pan-Islamic Trends in Colonial India* (Delhi, 1981); M. N. Das, *India Under Morley and Minto: Politics behind Revolution, Repression and Reforms* (London, 1964); M. Rahman, *From Consultation to Confrontation: A Study of the Muslim League in British Indian Politics, 1906–12* (London, 1970).

2. The quite explicit parallel between the post-1906 constitutions in Egypt and India made by British politicians and officials is brought out in Coles Pasha, *Recollections and Reflections* (London 1919), pp. 173–83 (chap. 24, "Constitutions in the Making"). The best and shortest modern study of the Egyptian reforms, which also makes the parallel, is Ronald Hyam, *Britain's Imperial Century 1815–1914* (London, 1976), pp. 259–63.

3. Peter Mellini, *Sir Eldon Gorst: The Overshadowed Proconsul* (Stanford, 1977), pp. 211–13; the Coptic campaign in Egypt and London and its rejection can be followed in FO 371/vols. 1111, 1112, 1113, Public Record Office, London, especially Kyriakos Mikhail to H. Monson and enclosures in Monson to Foreign Office, 2 April 1911, 3371/1113; Copts to Grey and to House of Lords, 15, 16 February 1911, ibid., 111; Grey to Gorst, 10 March 1911, ibid.

4. Gorst to Grey, 18 March 1911, Gorst's annual report, Foreign Office Confidential Print [FFOCP] 9986, p. 33.

5. Ibid., p. 32.

6. The best analysis of the distribution of Copts, with maps, is in E. J. Chitham, *Coptic Community in Egypt: Spatial and Social Change* (Durham, 1986).

7. The best analyses of Muslim distribution in India remain Anil Seal, *The Emergence of Indian Nationalism* (Cambridge 1968); Robinson, *Separatism*; see also Peter Hardy, *The Muslims of British India* (Cambridge, 1972).

8. See, e.g., G. Pandey, *The Construction of Communalism in Colonial North India* (Delhi, 1989); Veena Das, *Mirrors of Violence: Communities, Riots and Survivors in South Asia* (Delhi, 1990) Michael Gilsenan, *Lords of the Lebanese Marches* (London, 1996).

9. Robert L. Tignor, "The 'Indianization' of the Egyptian Administration under British Rule," *American Historical Review* 68 (1963): 636–61; Roger Owen, "The Influence of Lord Cromer's Indian Experience on British Policy in Egypt, 1883–1907," *St. Antony's Papers* 17 (1965).

10. Jamal Mohammed Ahmed, *The Intellectual Origins of Egyptian Nationalism* (Oxford, 1960); Albert Hourani, *Arabic Thought in the Liberal Age, 1798–1939* (London, 1962); Christian Troll, *Sayyid Ahmad Khan, A Reinterpretation of Muslim Theology* (London, 1978); more recently, J.R.I. Cole, *Colonialism and Revolution in the Middle East: Social and Cultural Origins of Egypt's 'Urabi' Movement* (Princeton, 1993); Javed Majeed, "Nature, Hyperbole and the Colonial State: Some Muslim Appropriations of European Modernity in Late 19th Century Urdu Literature," in *Muslim Thinkers Confront the Modern*, ed. John Cooper et al. (London, 1998).

11. John Gallagher, *The Decline, Rise and Fall of the British Empire* (Cambridge, 1981); John Darwin, *Britain, Egypt and the Middle East* (London, 1982).

12. Samir Saikaly, "Prime Minister and Assassin: Butrus Ghali and Wardani," *Middle East Studies* 13 (1977): 112–23.

13. The comparison is mentioned in the excellent work by B. L. Carter, *The Copts in Egyptian Politics, 1918–52* (London, 1986), pp. 70–71.

14. Especially Troll, *Sayyid Ahmad*, conclusion.

15. See, e.g., the forthcoming work of Dr. Claude Markovits of the CNRS, Paris, on the Sindhi trading communities across the world, including Egypt.

16. Advertisements in Near East (London, 1910–14); cf. "Bombay City," *Thacker's Indian Directory* (Calcutta, 1910–14).

17. Sir Thomas Wentworth Russell, *Egyptian Service 1902–46* (London 1949), p. 179; cf. Ronald Hyam, *Empire and Sexuality* (London, 1990), p. 144.

18. Owen, "Influence of Indian Experience."

19. Coles Pasha, *Recollections and Reflections*, pp. 1–4, cf. 21; the Sudanese had "the same mixture of courage and childishness and, alas, addiction to strong drinks [sic]" as the Bhils, ibid., p. 36.

20. E.g., Haji Maulavi Sheikh Mahommed Samiullah, former subordinate judge who accompanied Lord Northbrook's staff to Egypt in 1888, obituary, *Pioneer* (Allahabad), 23 April 1908; cf. *Allahabad Review* 5 (1893): 144.

21. W. S. Blunt, *The Future of Islam* (London, 1882; first published in the *Fortnightly Review*, 1881), p. 10; cf. p. 136.

22. W. S. Blunt, *India under Ripon* (London, 1909), pp. 12–62; Susan Bayly, *Saints, Goddesses and Kings: Hindus and Muslims in South Indian Society 1600–1900* (Cambridge, 1989).

23. Blunt, *India under Ripon*, pp. 59–63. The fractures in these connections were also clear. Blunt was careful not to dwell on the Egyptian desire for the return of the Khilafat among Indian Muslims.

24. William Wedderburn, *Allan Octavian Hume* (London, 1913); for Hume's early attempts to propagandize for popular imperialism as a district magistrate, Hume to Secretary Government, North-Western Provinces, 10 January 1861, NWP General Proceedings, 26 Jan 1861, 55 and 56, Range 216/4, India Office Records, British Library.

25. Besant propagated the Theosophical movement throughout India and helped found the Benares Hindu University; in 1916, she founded the Indian Home Rule Leagues. Wedderburn was an active congressman throughout its first twenty-five years.

26. Elizabeth Longford, *A Pilgrimage of Passion: The Life of Wilfrid Scawen Blunt* (London, 1979).

27. W. S. Blunt, *The Secret History of the English Occupation of Egypt* (London, 1907).

28. W. S. Blunt, *The Land War in Ireland, Being a Personal Narrative of Events* (London, 1912).

29. W. S. Blunt, *Ideas About India* (London, 1884); Longford, *Blunt*, p. 154.

30. Theodore Rothenstein and others kept up a constant barrage against the government and its supporters, ibid, 172–78, passim. They maintained contact with al-Afghani and Abduh. The occupation, meanwhile, saw the rapid expansion of the Egyptian press, strengthened by Syrian Christian immigrants; Martin Hartmann, *The Arabic Press of Egypt* (London: Luzac and Co., 1899), pp. 4–6, 30–32.

31. Lord Dufferin, "Correspondence Regarding the Reorganization of Egypt," *Parliamentary Papers*, 1883, lxxxiv, c. 3468.

32. *Government of India Revenue and Agricultural Proceedings*, 1886, IOR.

33. Bipan Chandra, *The Rise and Growth of Economic Nationalism in India* (Delhi, 1966), pp. 17–18, passim; D. Naoroji, *Poverty and Un-British Rule in India* (London, 1901).

34. Alfred Milner, *England and Egypt* (1892; 9th ed., London, 1902, with a summary of events to 1898). Milner was acutely conscious of French opposition to British influence in Egypt, pp. 337, 346.

35. *Modern Egypt* sold 9,000 copies in the United Kingdom and 4,000 in the United States in its first two years; it then went into cheap editions. The Marquess of Zetland, *Lord Cromer, Being the Authorized Life of Evelyn Baring, First Earl of Cromer* (London 1932), pp. 305–6; see Cromer, *Modern Egypt* (London, 1908); Cromer, *Abbas II* (London, 1915); Cromer, "The Government of Subject Races," *Political and Literary Essays, 1908–13* (London, 1913), and numerous magazine articles and reviews; Afaf Lutfi al-Sayyid, *Egypt and Cromer: A Study in Anglo-Egyptian Relations* (London, 1968).

36. Moberley Bell, manager of *The Times* in the 1910s, had been special correspondent in Egypt in the 1880s, Coles Pasha, *Recollections*, pp. 24–25; Val-

entine Chirol, the powerful India correspondent had also been in Egypt in the last days of Khedive Isma'il.

37. For this problem for the British authorities, see, e.g., Gorst to Grey, 8 January 1910, enc. *Letters re Negotiations with the French*, FOCP 9909, pp. 12–25.

38. See Margarita Barns, *The Indian Press: A History of the Growth of Public Opinion in India* (London, 1940), pp. 317–22.

39. S. N. Banerjea, "Mr. Banerjea wiped the floor with Lord Cromer," in *A Nation in Making* (1925: repr. Bombay, 1963), p. 243.

40. J. Keir Hardie, *India, Impressions and Suggestions* (London, 1909). Keir Hardie, however, took the Hindu side in the contemporary communal controversy, ibid., p. 25, a point noted by *Revue du Monde Musalman*, nos. 11–12 (Nov.–Dec. 1907): 582–85. I am indebted to Dr. S. Bayly for this reference.

41. See Salama Musa, *The Education of Salama Musa*, trans. L. O. Shuman (Leiden, 1961), pp. 63–70, on his connection with the circles of Shaw and the Fabians, De Valera, H. G. Wells, and awareness of the Indian question; ibid., p. 135, for Keir Hardie. The authorities were aware of Musa's attempts to found a "socialistic, rationalistic newspaper in Egypt," J. Robertson, MP, to Grey, 3 April 1911, FO 371/1113, PRO; cf. J. Y. Wong, *The Origins of an Heroic Image: Sun Yatsen in London 1896–97* (Hong Kong, 1986).

42. Roger Owen, *Cotton and the Egyptian Economy* (Oxford, 1970); cf. Elizabeth Whitcombe, *Agrarian Conditions in Northern India* (Berkeley, 1972); C. J. Baker, *An Indian Rural Economy, 1880–1955: The Tamilnad Countryside* (Delhi, 1984); Sumit Guha, *The Bombay Deccan 1800–1939* (Delhi, 1986), which all deal with consequences, malign and benevolent, of interrelated cotton booms.

43. Ira Klein, "Population and Agriculture in North India, 1872–1971," *Modern Asian Studies* 8, no. 2 (1947): 191–216.

44. *The Near East* 3 (December, 1909): 138, 145.

45. Musa, *Education*, p. 14.

46. E.g., *The Near East* 3 (July 1910): 61.

47. Ibid. (October 1910), p. 122, on the Cairo railway strike which was blamed on the "rabble of the Boulac quarter" stirred up by nationalists apeing French syndicalism; Gorst to Grey, 28 May 1910, on "the numerous population of low-class Europeans who are a constant element of disorder," FCOP, 9909, p. 1407; for the social background and controversies, see Yacoub Artin, "Essai sur les causes du rencherissment de la vie materielle au Caire dans le courant du XIXe siècle (1800 à 1907)," *Mémoires de l'Institut Egyptien* 2 (1889): 57–114.

48. Rajnarayan S. Chandavarkar, *The Origins of Industrial Capitalism in India* (Cambridge, 1995).

49. P. J. Cain and A. G. Hopkins, *British Imperialism*, 2 vols. (London, 1993); Milner, *Egypt*, has the best analysis of the drain of wealth from Egypt through debt repayments, canal bonds, salaries, etc.

50. See trade returns in *Annual Report* 1911, FOCP, lxxiii, annex 1, pp. 99 ff.

51. *The Near East with which Is Incorporated the Anglo-Egyptian Mail* had titles in English, Greek, and Arabic and displayed an acute interest in investments and markets in the Balkans, the Ottoman Empire, and India, as well as Egypt.

52. Edwin DeLeon, *Askaros Kassis, The Copt: A Romance of Modern Egypt* (Philadelphia, 1870).

53. S. Bayly, *Saints, Goddesses and Kings*, passim.

54. *Association for the Furtherance of Christianity in Egypt. Letters and Papers* [concerning relations between the Church of England and the Copts, 1836–48] (London, 1883), esp. pp. 13–14.

55. For Coptic church history, see, e.g., S. H. Leader, *Modern Sons of the Pharaohs: A Study of the Manners and Customs of the Copts of Egypt* (London, 1919), pp. 239–60; E. L. Butcher, *The Story of the Church of Egypt*, 2 vols. (London, 1897), 2:379–402.

56. *Christianity in Egypt. Proceedings at Jerusalem Chamber, Westminster, 22 February 1883* (London, 1883), p. 3.

57. W. H. Oxley, *The Copts: Some Particulars Concerning the Ancient National Church of Egypt* (London, 1883), p. 7.

58. Butcher, *Church of Egypt* 2:380–82.

59. Oxley, *The Copts*, p. 9.

60. Butcher, *Church of Egypt*, 2:381–85.

61. Reverend Montague Fowler, *Christian Egypt, Past, Present and Future* (London, 1901), pp. 220–23.

62. Ibid., p. 139.

63. 'W,' "Copts and Moslems in Egypt," *Blackwood's Magazine* 1150 (August 1911): 205.

64. Leader, *Modern Sons*, p. 322.

65. Hartmann, *Press*, pp. 15–17, 48: "The Christian Syrian woman . . . is fearless, enterprising, energetic"; Milne Cheetham believed that Copts were restive because of increasing pressure from educated Muslims, Cheetham to Grey, 1 August 1911, FO 371/1113, PRO (this, of course, bears comparison with Indian Muslims' fear of Hindu competition).

66. Musa, *Education*, pp. 50, 177; this author wrote *Egypt: Cradle of Civilisation.*

67. John Ward, FSA, *Pyramids and Progress* (London, 1890), p. vii.

68. Ibid., p. xx.

69. H. de Vaujay, *Description de l'Egypte, le Caire et ses environs* (Paris, 1883), p. 30.

70. Ibid., p. 28.

71. A. P. de Sande et Castro, *Juge aux Tribunaux Internationaux de l'Egypte, L'Egypte* (Paris, 1901), p. 481.

72. H. G. Tomkins, "Flinders Petrie's Collection of Ethnographic Evidence from the Monuments of Egypt," *Journal of the Anthropological Institute of Great*

Britain 18 (1889–90): 206–39; cf. "Les races connus des Egyptiens," *Annales du Musée Guimet* 1 (1880): 62.

73. Agnes Smith Lewis, "Hidden Egypt: The First Visit by Women to the Coptic Monasteries of Egypt and Nitria," *Century Illustrated Magazine*, 1904, p. 757; cf. Billie Melman, *Women's Orients: English Women in the Middle East 1718–1918* (Basingstoke, 1995).

74. Kyriakos Mikhail, *The Freedom of the Press in Egypt: An Appeal to the Friends of Liberty by Kyriakos Mikhail*, 3rd ed. (London, 1914).

75. Kyriakos Mikhail, *Copts and Muslims under British Control* (London, 1911), p. viii.

76. Ibid.

77. E.g., E. Amelineau, "Un Evêque de Keft au VIIe siècle," *Mémoires de l'Institut Egyptien* 11 (Cairo, 1889): 261–423, on hero bishops.

78. Artin Paşa's memoir on inflation in ibid., p. 59, quotes al-Jabarti to the effect that Copts stationed outside the city were the first to levy the widely hated octroi tax on the citizens of Cairo under Mehmet 'Ali.

79. But see the ambivalent discussion of this in Musa, *Education*, pp. 15, 20–21.

80. Mikhail, *Copts*, p. x.

81. *Spectator*, 22 April 1911, cited in ibid., p. 114.

82. *Daily Mail*, 17 Feb. 1911, cited in ibid., p. 107.

83. *Evening Times*, 23 September 1911, in ibid., p. 121.

84. *Church Times*, 24 February, 1911.

85. *Near East*, 3, July 1910, p. 61.

86. A. J. B[utler], "The Misgovernment of Egypt," *The Nineteenth Century and After*, Oct. 1910, p. 590; cf. "Copts and Muslims in Egypt," ibid., Sept. 1911, pp. 588–94.

87. Ibid., p. 593.

88. Ibid.

89. Flinders Petrie, *Ten Years' Digging in Egypt, 1881–1891* (London, 1893), pp. 184, 186. This was published by the Religious Tract Society.

90. E.g., *Church Times*, 17 March 1911, review of Adolf Dissmann, *Light from the Ancient East*, 31 March 1911, "Egyptology."

91. C. A. Bayly, "Orientalists and Informants in Banaras, 1780–1860," presented at conference on "Reciprocal Perceptions of Different Cultures in South Asia," Bonn, December 1996.

92. Charles Wendell, *The Evolution of the Egyptian National Image from Its Origins to Lutfi al-Sayyid* (Berkeley, 1972), pp. 240–41.

93. Duse Mohamed, *In the Land of the Pharaohs: A Short History of Egypt from the Fall of Ismail to the Assassination of Boutros Pasha* (London, 1911), p. 4.

94. Ibid., p. 264.

95. Ibid., p. 275.

96. Musa, *Education*, p. 22; Gorst, *1911 Report*, pp. 45–46.

97. Barbara Watterson, *Coptic Egypt* (Edinburgh, 1988), p. 167.

98. Winifred S. Blackman, *The Fellahin of Upper Egypt: Their Religious, Social and Industrial Life Today with Special Reference to Survivals from Ancient Times* (London, 1927), p. 65.

99. Flinders Petrie, *Ten Years' Digging*, p. 174; cf. J. R. I. Cole, *Colonialism and Revolution in the Middle East* (Princeton, 1991), p. 247.

100. "Misgovernment in Egypt," *Nineteenth Century and After*, October 1910, p. 589.

101. Ibid., p. 590.

102. Musa, *Education*, pp. 48–49.

103. "Report of an Enquiry into the Society of Mutual Brotherhood, submitted by the Procureur General to the Ministry of Justice," enclosed in Gorst to Grey, 17 April 1919, FOCP 9909, p. 136; Samir Seikaly, "Prime Minister and Assassin: Butrus Ghali and Wardani," *Middle Eastern Studies* 13, no. 1 (1997): 112–23.

104. Gorst to Grey, 6 May 1910, FOCP, 9909, pp. 139–42; al-Liwa, which exculpated Wardani, had previously praised the Indian terrorist Dhingra, hanged for the assassination of a leading British official.

105. Cole, *Colonialism and Revolution*, p. 196.

106. *Coptic Congress Held at Assiout on March, 6, 7, 8, 1911* (Assiout, 1911) FO 371/1111 PRO; this publication had emblazoned on its cover the ancient sign of the God Horus.

107. The Asyut Copts had another version: see *The Copts and Sir Eldon Gorst's Report* (Assiout, May 1911), p. 12, FO 371/1113.

108. See the enclosures from the Muslim press, especially *al-Liwa* and *al-Anali*, in the various letters from Fanous to Grey and Mackinnon Wood, 4, 7, 12 and 20 April 1911, FO 371/1111 PRO.

109. Mikhail, *Copts and Muslims*, p. 94; cf. Seikaly, "Prime Minister and Assassin," p. 116.

110. Ibid.; Milne Cheetham to Sir Arthur Bigge, 9 April 1911, FO 371/1113, PRO.

111. This was not simply a European or Christian panic; Egyptian Muslim agitators specifically used this as a threat: see Ali Fahmy Mohamed's [a writer for *Kotr-al-Misr*] massive unfinished manuscript, "The Future Egypt," p. 67, which predicted an "Armenian massacre of the Copts," FO 317/111, PRO.

112. Cheetham to Grey, 18 June 1911, 9986, FOCP, pp. 172–73.

113. See the correspondence in FOCP, 10091.

114. Gorst to Grey, 18 March 1911, FOCP 9986, p. 35.

115. Gorst's annual report for 1911, 9986, ibid., p. 45.

116. *The Near East* 4 (17 May 1911), p. 25.

117. Jafar Sharif, *Islam in India or the Qanun-i Islam: The Customs of the Musalmans of India*, trans. G. A. Herklots (1832, rpt. London, 1921).

118. Mrs. Meer Hasan Ali, *Observations on the Mussalmans of India* (London, 1830).

119. Abul Fazl, *Ayeen Akbery or the Institutes of the Emperor Akber*, trans. T. Gladwin (London, 1800), vol 1, Warren Hasting's minute and translator's introduction.

120. Q. Ahmad, *The Wahabi Movement in India* (Calcutta, 1966); Peter Robb, "The Impact of British Rule on Religious Community," in *Society and Ideology*, ed. Peter Robb (London, 1994), pp. 142–76; "Memorandum on the Wahhabis," Mayo Papers, Add. 7490/29, Cambridge University Library.

121. W. W. Hunter, *The Indian Mussalmans: Are They Bound in Conscience to Rebel against the Queen?* (London, 1871).

122. Troll, *Sayyid Ahmad Khan*; cf. Mushirul Hasan, "Resistance and Acquiescence in North India: Muslim Responses to the West," in *India's Colonial Encounter*, ed. M. Hasan and N. Gupta (Delhi, 1993), pp. 39–63.

123. Troll, *Sayyid Ahmad*; Jamal Ahmed, *Egyptian Nationalism*.

124. G.F.I. Graham, *The Life and Work of Sir Syed Ahmed Khan*, ed. Zaituna Umer (1885: rpt., Karachi, 1974), pp. 34–35.

125. Graham, *Sir Syed*, pp. 54–55.

126. Extensive excerpts in ibid., pp. 27–35.

127. Syed Ahmed Khan, *Review of Dr. Hunter's "The Indian Mussalmans"* (Benares, 1871).

128. A. H. Hali, *Hayat-i Javed: A Biographical Account of Sir Sayyid by Altaf Hussain Hali*, trans. K. H. Qadiri and David Matthews (Delhi, 1979), pp. 112–17.

129. C. A. Bayly, *Empire and Information: Intelligence Gathering and Social Communication in India 1780–1870* (Cambridge, 1997), pp. 325–26; Hardy, *Muslims*, pp. 62–63.

130. Hali, *Hayat-i Javed*, p. 107.

131. Syed Ahmed Khan, *A Speech in Persian with a Translation in English on Patriotism and the Necessity of Promoting Knowledge in India, Delivered by Syud Ahmud [sic] at a Meeting of the Mahomedan Literary Society at Calcutta* (Ghazipur, 1863).

132. K. K. Aziz, *Ameer Ali: His Life and Work* (Lahore, 1968), p. 2.

133. Ibid., p. 11.

134. Ibid., pp. 11–15.

135. "Memoir," in ibid., p. 571.

136. Ibid., pp. 11–15.

137. Omar Khayyam, *The Rubaiyat of Omar Khayyam*, trans. by Edward FitzGerald, ed. with an introduction and notes by R. A. Nicholson (London, 1909); M. Adams, *Omar's Interpreter: A New Life of Edward FitzGerald* (London, 1989).

138. David McLean, "A Professor Extraordinary: E. G. Browne and His Persian Campaign," *English Historical Review* 96 (1978): 117–29.

139. Robinson, *Separatism*, pp. 111, 117, 118, 122, 137, 165, 168–69, 199, 207.

140. David Lelyveld, *Aligarh's First Generation: Muslim Solidarity in British India* (Princeton, 1978), pp. 196–97, 243–48, passim.

141. Andrew Porter, "Evangelicalism, Islam and Millennial Expectation in the Nineteenth Century," unpub. paper in author's possession.

142. See, e.g., *The Mohammedan World of Today: Being Papers Read at the First Missionary Conference on Behalf of the Mohammedan World Held at Cairo April 4–9th 1906*, 2nd ed. (New York: Fleming H. Revell and Co., 1906). I thank Dr. Avril Powell for this reference.

143. N. G. Barrier, *The Punjab Land Alienation Bill of 1900* (Durham: Duke University Press, 1966); The Aligarh Institute Gazette was full of racial typecasting, e.g., the trustee's address to Roos Keppel, ibid., 17 February 1909, spoke of the "welfare of our race," speaking of Muslims, noting that the frontier peoples were characterized by "intelligence, manliness and physical strength, though backward in education"; cf. Susan Bayly, "Caste and Race in the Colonial Ethnology of India," in *The Concept of Race in South Asia*, ed. Peter Robb (Delhi, 1995), pp. 165–218; Carey A. Watt, "Education for National Efficiency: Constitutional Nationalism in Northern India, 1909–16, "*Modern Asian Studies* 31, no. 2 (1997): 339–74.

144. Ayesha Jalal, "Exploding Communalism: The Politics of Muslim Identity in South Asia," in *Nationalism, Democracy and Development, State and Politics in India*, ed. A. Jalal and S. Bose (Delhi, 1997), pp. 76–103.

145. Robinson, *Separatism*, chap. 3.

146. *The Near East* 3 (Dec. 1909): 143 (Syed Amir Ali on "The Life and Teachings of the Prophet Muhammad" at Caxton Hall); ibid., (Aug. 1910): 146 (Syed Abdul Majid on Ottoman constitutional reform at Caxton Hall, London).

147. Robinson, *Separatism*, pp. 226–27, passim.

148. N. M. Dumasia, *The Aga Khan and His Ancestry: A Biography and Historical Sketch* (Bombay, 1939), p. 88.

149. Ibid., p. 304.

150. V. Chirol, *Indian Unrest* (London, 1909), pp. 5–6, passim.

151. Robinson, *Separatism*, p. 169.

152. V. Chirol, *The Egyptian Question* (London, 1919), pp. 157–58.

153. Dunlop Smith in Morley to Minto, 29 Oct. 1911, Minto Papers, India Office Collections, cited in Robinson, *Separatism*, p. 166, n. 4.

154. For Macdonnell's attitudes, see his minute for his successor, 1901, Macdonnell Papers c355, Mss. Eng. Hist., Bodleian Library, Oxford.

155. For nationalist strains of Muslim thought parallel to Salama Musa's among Copts, see Mushirul Hasan, *Nationalism and Communal Politics*, esp., pp. 42–58.

156. On the Belgian system of special electoral representation, see speech of Maitre Marcos Hannah, *Coptic Congress*, pp. 36–37.

157. G. Pandey, *The Construction of Communalism in Colonial North India* (Delhi, 1989); my views here are based on petitions from Hindus and Muslims and reports on riots in British and Indian archives from 1809 onward; Indian newspapers including the *Hindi Pradip* (Allahabad) and the *Bharat Jivan* (Benares); reports on the Indian vernacular press, etc., see my published works.

158. See, e.g., *Gujarati*, 15 Jan. 1911, Vernacular Press Reports, Bombay, IOR; in ibid., see extensive polemic between Hindu and Muslim newspapers about the history of communal conflict, e.g., *Mumbai Vaibhav*, 4 Feb. 1911, on the cult of Shivaji.

159. Sahirin Mohammad, *Copts and Muslims: A Study on Harmony and Hostility* (Leicester: Islamic Foundation, 1991), pp. 11–12.

160. Christopher King, *One Language, Two Scripts: The Hindi Movement in North India* (Bombay, 1994).

161. Gabriel Baer, "Social Change in Egypt, 1800–1914," in *Political and Social Change in Modern Egypt*, ed. P. M. Holt (London, 1968), p. 146, for the growing residential homogenization of better-off Copts and Muslims.

162. "98.4% of the population consider the Copt to be vermin of the lowest type," Ali Fahmy Mohamed, "The Future Egypt," FO 371/1111, PRO.

163. Hasan, *Nationalism*, p. 87.

164. Mushirul Hasan, *A Nationalist Conscience: M. A. Ansari, The Congress and the Raj* (Delhi, 1987), pp. 22–37.

10   İzmir 1922: A Port City Unravels

Reşat Kasaba

On 9 September 1922, the people of İzmir woke to an eerie silence. The last of the Greek army that had occupied the city since 14 May 1919 had withdrawn in the early hours and the Turkish army was expected to arrive at any moment. Tens of thousands of Greeks and Armenians who had been pushed toward the city from the interior had been massing on the waterfront for several days; they were desperate to leave before the arrival of the nationalist troops. The Turkish army entered İzmir later that morning, capturing the most valuable prize of their difficult campaign against the Greeks.

Nobody knew what to expect from these poorly trained, poorly fed, but fiercely determined fighters. The scorched-earth tactic the Greek army had used in its retreat from the interior made the Christians fearful that the Turks would now retaliate by destroying İzmir and persecuting its inhabitants. By the end of the day there were already rumors of attacks on the Greek and Armenian properties, sporadic looting, robberies, rapes, and murders. This apparent deterioration of public security led to panic, especially among the non-Muslim and foreign residents of İzmir. Some among them tried to hide; others attempted to flee, and the mass of people on the waterfront continued to grow. Ernest Hemingway, who was traveling in the Balkans as a war correspondent for the *Toronto Star*, wrote a short story called "On the Quai at Smyrna," describing the horror on the İzmir pier:

> The strange thing was . . . how they screamed every night at midnight.
> I do not know why they screamed at that time. We were in the harbor

and they were all on the pier and at midnight they started screaming.
. . . The worst . . . were the women with dead babies. You couldn't
get the women to give up their dead babies. They'd have babies dead
for six days. Wouldn't give them up. Nothing you could do about it.[1]

Unbearable as these conditions were, they would get even worse on 13
September, when a fire started in the Armenian district and quickly spread,
consuming large parts of İzmir. Now, squeezed between the fire and the sea,
the refugees literally had no place to flee. British journalist Price Ward described the scene this way:

> What I see as I stand on the deck of the *Iron Duke* is an unbroken
> wall of fire, two miles long, in which twenty distinct volcanoes of
> raging flames are throwing up jagged, writhing tongues to a height of
> a hundred feet. Against this curtain of fire, which blocks out the sky,
> are silhouetted the towers of the Greek churches, the domes of the
> mosques, and the flat square roofs of the houses. From this intensely
> glowing mass of yellow, orange, and crimson fire pour up thick clotted
> coils of oily black smoke that hide the moon at its zenith. The sea
> glows a deep copper-red and, worst of all, from the densely packed
> mob of many thousands of refugees huddled on the narrow quay,
> between the advancing fiery death behind and the deep water in front,
> comes continuously such frantic screaming of sheer terror as can be
> heard miles away.[2]

Many people who were trapped on the quay got into boats or jumped
into the water, trying to reach one of the 21 allied warships docked in the
harbor.[3] Others sought safe haven in one of the consulates, foreign schools,
or other public buildings that were associated with İzmir's expatriate community. One of the survivors who took refuge in the Smyrna theater that
had become the U.S. headquarters would later remember the "grim humor
in the sign over the arched door in black letters two feet high. It was the
name of the last movie shown: *Le Tango de la Mort*."[4] None of these places
were particularly welcoming, especially toward those whose citizenship
status were not clear—which, unfortunately, was the case for many of the
city's residents. They were turned away, sometimes by force. The Allied states
whose ships were in the harbor and whose representatives were in town had
not yet articulated a clear policy regarding the new developments in Asia
Minor.

On 16 September, the nationalist forces arrested most of the male refugees between the ages of 18 and 45 who were on the pier and issued an ultimatum that unless the foreign ships evacuated the people on the quay by the end of the month, they too would be arrested, forced back into Anatolia, and put to work in clearing the debris and rebuilding the towns and cities in the interior.[5] The dismal state of relations among the communities and the apparent determination of the Turkish government to make good on its threat accelerated the armistice negotiations. On 24 July 1923, the new Turkish regime signed a peace settlement with the European powers in Lausanne, Switzerland, ending one of the most ruinous chapters in the history of the eastern Mediterranean.

In one of its most controversial clauses, the Lausanne treaty barred the return of the refugees who had left Anatolia during the war and stipulated the exchange of the remaining Greek Orthodox residents of Turkey for the Muslims of Macedonia and western Thrace.[6] The implementation of this measure caused considerable confusion and pain on both sides of the Turco-Greek divide. For one thing, it was by no means clear as to who would be included in this compulsory exchange. For example, both the Turkish-speaking Anatolian Greeks (*Karamanlis*) and ethnic Arabs whose religion was Greek Orthodox were deemed "deportable," even though none of them spoke Greek and they had little knowledge of and no affinity with the kingdom of Greece. So ambiguous was the status of the *Karamanlis* that, although the Greek delegate at the Lausanne negotiations referred to them as the "Turkish speaking persons of the Orthodox faith," his Turkish counterpart described them as "Orthodox Turks."[8] In the end, almost all the *Karamanlis* were resettled in Greece, where they initially suffered discrimination and harassment on the grounds that their Greekness and Christianity were suspect and that they were "baptized in yogurt."[9] Most of the Greek Orthodox Arabs, by contrast, moved to the areas under Syrian mandate to avoid deportation.[10] In Greece, too, this stipulation was initially interpreted in a very broad and confusing way to include not only Turkish-speaking Muslims of Thrace and Macedonia but also Albanians, on the grounds that they were Muslims.[11]

Along with about 190,000 refugees who fell under this treaty, more than 1.2 million Greeks left Asia Minor between 1912 and 1923. About 400,000 Muslim Turks were forced to make the opposite journey during these years and settle in the lands and homes left behind by departing Greeks.[12] The relative importance of these numbers can be appreciated if we remember that in 1922 the population of Greece was only about 4.8 million and that of the Ottoman Empire had declined from 20 million in 1906 to 18.5 million in 1914. In other words, through the wars and the exchange, Turkey lost 6 to 7 percent of its population; Greece was faced with a flood of refugees that equaled over a quarter of its population.[13]

The impact of this ethnic engineering on İzmir was particularly far reaching. According to a census conducted by the Ottoman government, the population of the city in the 1880s was about 208,000: 80,000 Muslims, 54,000 Greeks, 15,000 Jews, 7,000 Armenians, and 52,000 foreigners. In other words, at that time, roughly 60 percent of the city's residents were non-Muslims and foreigners.[14] Between the early 1880s and 1914, İzmir absorbed a large number of migrants and refugees. European sources put the city's population at 300,000 on the eve of World War I, whereas the Ottoman sources estimated it to be 211,000, with an ethnoreligious breakdown that continued to give non-Muslims a plurality.[15] In 1927, the first census of the new republic found that there were 184,254 people living in İzmir, 88 percent of whom were classified as Muslims.[16] Based on these numbers, and by taking into consideration the immigrations to İzmir during the war and the resettlements under the terms of the Lausanne treaty, we can assume that between 1914 and 1927, İzmir lost close to half of its population and an overwhelming majority of its non-Muslim residents.

The violent separation of the Greeks and Muslims of Asia Minor from each other in these years represents one of the most important turning points in the region's history, second, perhaps, only to the capture of Constantinople by the Turks four and a half centuries earlier. Yet despite the very large number of people involved and the huge disruptions it caused in the region, we seldom think about the radical shift that must have taken place in the minds of the people as they planned, instigated, and participated in this momentous shuffle. We forget that the communities that were separated in 1923 had been living together for centuries and that even those people boarding ships in İzmir and elsewhere would not have dreamed that their departure would be permanent. Rather than exploring these topics, what passes as analysis of these events is usually limited to justifying the tragedy from the Turkish side or lamenting it from the Greek or Armenian perspective.

To the Turks, 9 September 1922 was liberation day for İzmir, the crowning event in their successful war of deliverance from the occupying Greek and Allied Forces. School children in Turkey learn nothing of the forced migration of millions of people; instead they read the celebratory accounts of how "the enemy" was "dumped into the sea."[17] Official versions of history insist that there was no deliberate persecution of Greeks and Armenians under Ottoman rule and that the difficulties these communities faced during the war were unavoidable because of the chaotic circumstances of those years. Some on the Turkish side even suggest that Greeks and Armenians were partly to blame for some of their misfortune because of their equivocal stand toward foreign invasion at the end of World War I and the outright treachery of some of the Greeks during the occupation years.

What Turkish nationalists see as a triumph was, of course, a catastrophe for the Greeks. In 1922, the Greeks were forced to abandon one of oldest centers of Hellenic civilization in Asia Minor and leave a city and a region that had become a site of great commercial prosperity. The waves of refugees from Anatolia presented a heavy burden on the small state of Greece and the problems associated with settling these families remained unresolved for most of the 1920s.

In the grecophile accounts of these disasters, part of the blame goes to the misguided policies of the Greek government and part of it to the wavering policies of the Great Powers. There is no doubt, however, who was responsible for the material, physical, and spiritual losses and pain the Greeks and Armenians of western Anatolia suffered: "The destruction of Smyrna happened, however, in 1922, and no act ever perpetrated by the Turkish race in all its bloodstained history, has been characterized by more brutal and lustful features, nor more productive of worst forms of human sufferings inflicted on the defenseless and unarmed,"[18] wrote George Horton, the American consul general in İzmir and a man known for his deep Greek sympathies.

The two sides have such diametrically opposed perceptions of those fateful years that even the accounts of well-known events for which there is ample eyewitness testimony do not agree with each other. For example, in describing the fire that left İzmir in ruins, the Greek and Armenian survivors report having seen "Turks taking bombs, gunpowder, kerosene and everything necessary to start fires, in wagon-fulls . . . through the streets" in the Armenian district.[19] Pro-Turkish accounts, by contrast, either ignore the whole episode or claim that the Greeks had severed "all the rubber pipes of the fire brigade"[20] or that "actual culpability has never been proved,"[21] or that "there was in fact not one fire, but many," some of them set by Christians, some by Turks,[22] or that "any description of uniformed Turkish soldiers lighting fires in the city . . . may be assumed to be part of the fire-fightings rather than incendiary attempts."[23]

Before the Fire: The Myth of the Millets

Whatever the sympathies of their authors, most explanations of ethnic conflict in the Middle East start with the millet system, that is, with the notion that Ottoman society had consisted of neatly demarcated communities (called millets), each with a distinct language, culture, and religion, and living and working in separate neighborhoods or villages. Even though histories sympathetic to the Greek or the Turkish perspectives use the notion of the millet as representing a prototype for a primordial understanding of nations, they differ in their perceptions of the relationship between the Ottoman state and these communities.[24] The Turkish versions project a benevolent image of the Ottoman administration as a system of rule that gave its subject people considerable autonomy to practice their religion and maintain their cultural habits and characteristics.[25] In this perspective, through the institution of millets, the Ottoman state becomes responsible for protecting and preserving non-Muslim religions and cultures in their domains. For Balkan historians, by contrast, millets were the depositories not only of the essential characteristics of each community, but also of the tremendous resentment these communities felt for their suffering under the "Turkish/ Muslim yoke" that had oppressed them for centuries.[26] Although they stand at opposite ends of an interpretive spectrum, both of these versions seem to suggest that centuries of cross-community relations had not affected the essential characteristics of these millets in any significant way.

What gets lost in these competing explanations and claims is the fact that as an administrative category the millet dated back only to the middle of the nineteenth century.[27] Before that Ottoman society had resembled a kaleidoscope of numerous, overlapping, and cross-cutting relations and categories more than it did a neatly arranged pattern of distinct elements.[28] In addition to the *Karamanlis*, in Anatolia there were Armenian-speaking Greeks who used Greek letters to write Armenian; in Istanbul, there were Greek-speaking Jews who used the Hebrew alphabet to write Greek and Greeks who spoke Ladino.[29] Turkish novelist Halit Ziya attended a Catholic school that was established by Spanish priests, where he was assigned a geography book written in Turkish with Armenian letters.[30] The idea that these communities could be easily identified, separated from each other, moved, and relocated across long distances contradicted both the actual conditions and the world-views and expectations of the people who became the subjects of these policies.

Most of the Greeks expected their departure to be temporary, both in 1914, when they were relocated by the Young Turks, and in 1923, when they were exchanged. In September 1922, in the days, if not the hours, before they left the pier in İzmir, some were still negotiating to buy property in the interior,[31] and some of the ailing refugees were seeking reassurance that their bones would be sent back to be interred in Anatolia should they die abroad.[32]

To be sure, whether somebody was Muslim or not was a very important criterion in the stratification of Ottoman society and, when all is said and done, non-Muslims were considered the second-class citizens of the state. But religion was only one of the markers Ottomans used to categorize their subjects. They also referred to ethnicity, tribal ties, Sufi affiliations, occupation, and nomadism when identifying their subjects. These categories changed, overlapped, or cut across each other, and the Ottomans did not consistently favor any one of them over the rest. Their approach was much more flexible. For example, in earlier centuries, nomadism was central to the achievements of the state, and hence nomadic tribes were at the center of the empire's initial organization. But after the sixteenth century, as the establishment of a bureaucratic administration became the central concern of the state, nomadic tribes found themselves at the receiving end of some very harsh treatment, especially if they resisted settlement.[33] Underlying this administrative flux was a social fluidity that allowed people to convert, settle down, join or quit Sufi orders, move in and out of cities (with the exception of Istanbul), and combine nomadic and sedentary forms of agriculture. To make matters more complicated, some of the converts, such as the *dönmes* (from Judaism) and "crypto-Christians," were never completely accepted by the Muslim community as genuine believers. Some of these communities led a dual life well into the 1930s, fulfilling all the requirements of their former religion in addition to the new one.[34] In cities like İzmir, walls did not separate neighborhoods, and there was nothing in either the daily lives of the people or the administrative codes of the empire that required, en-forced, or reinforced residential segregation.

In the second half of the nineteenth century, the changing conditions in the eastern Mediterranean made the straightforward application of ethnic and national categories even more difficult. Starting in the 1830s, the region's trade grew several times over, and İzmir became firmly established as a major Mediterranean port placed at the center of a vast commercial network that extended outward to other sites in Europe and inward toward the sites of cultivation and production in its hinterland. These conditions of economic expansion entailed the even closer interaction of people of different ethnic and religious backgrounds. From rural farms to European ships, at every stage of the activity that prepared İzmir's exports, any one of the region's many ethnic religious groups or foreigners was equally likely. A similar chain that included an equally diverse and increasingly wealthy group of participants conveyed the region's imports into the interior.

İzmir benefited from the expanding economy of western Anatolia to a much larger extent than did the other cities of the interior. The city's wealth helped support a robust cultural life where "it was always possible to catch an Italian opera or a French operetta, or comedy or tragedy troops performing on the waterfront in these languages."[35] In 1852, İzmir had six newspapers in five different languages. By the last quarter of the nineteenth century, the city supported 17 printing houses and one of the earliest public theaters in the Ottoman Empire.[36] In addition to its economic good fortune, İzmir also benefited from being far from Istanbul and hence relatively free of direct government control, especially of the stifling censorship that characterized Sultan Abdülhamid's reign.[37]

On all levels and in all occupational groups, western Anatolian society was diverse. It became even more so in the course of the nineteenth century. There were Greek and Turkish peasants, non-Muslim and Muslim merchants, Muslims who worked for foreign banks and for the Public Debt Administration,[38] Greek bandits who kidnapped Muslim notables, Muslim notables who supported Muslim bandits, Muslim bandits who kidnapped Muslim notables, and Muslim bandits who sought the mediation of Levantine residents when they got into trouble with the state.[39]

The municipal council of İzmir, created in 1868, provides a good example of the degree to which the various ethnic and religious communities had become intertwined in the nineteenth century. The council had 24 members: six Muslims, five Greeks, three Armenians, one Jew, and nine foreigners. Even the executive council that was to oversee the day-to-day affairs of the city had two Muslim and two non-Muslim Ottoman members, and four foreigners.[40] Associations such as the *Hilal-i Ahmer Cemiyeti* (Red Crescent Society), Sporting Club, and the Association of Turkish and Greek

Journalists maintained an ethnically mixed membership throughout the period of the Greek occupation.[41] Even some of the bands of brigands were
multiethnic in composition. One such band captured in 1919 had 21 members: nine Greeks (five Ottoman, four from Greece), six Turks, and two
Armenians.[42] At the end of May 1919, the commander of the Greek army
was met on the outskirts of the town of Ödemiş by a joint Muslim-Christian
delegation pleading with him not to enter the city.[43]

İzmir's fire brigade was underwritten by the London Insurance Company
and included both non-Muslim and Muslim firefighters. During the great
fire, some from this brigade confronted the Turkish troops and accused them
of torching the buildings while the firefighters were trying to put out the
flames—to which a soldier responded, "You have your orders and I have
mine"[44] According to one contemporary account, on 10 September, "the
Turkish Military Governor, learning that there were still twelve Greeks in
the fire department, ordered their immediate expulsion and arrest."[45]

Professor Konstantinos Karatheodeoris from Göttingen University constitutes another example of the enduring complexities of loyalties and their
incompatibility with rigid categories. He was hired by the Greek government
to establish the "Hellen University of Smyrna" in 1919. Karatheodoris's father, Kara Todori Paşa, had been a high-ranking employee of the Ottoman
Foreign Ministry and played a prominent role in the delegation that represented the Ottoman Empire at the Berlin Conference in 1878.[46] During his
travels in western Anatolia in 1921, Arnold Toynbee met a Greek doctor
who was born in a village near Konya in central Anatolia. He was educated
at the American College at Beirut, conscripted into the Turkish army during
World War I, captured by the British in Palestine, and released after being
interned, only to be conscripted again by the nationalists.[47] Finally there is
"Dimos," who had served as the "doorman and messenger of the Greek
Consulate for twenty years" and chose to stay behind "as the only employee
of the consulate" when the rest of the personnel evacuated the city on 7
September 1922.[48]

We can multiply the examples of the fluidity of the social, economic, and
ethnic categories in the Ottoman Empire, but this still leaves unanswered
the question of why these conditions could not be maintained, and why the
conflict in Asia Minor deteriorated so quickly into an ethnic conflict with
Greeks and Armenians on one side and Muslim Turks on the other. The
scale of killing, destruction, and the numbers who were made homeless and
exiled are too large and the eyewitness accounts are too detailed and numerous to ignore as the biased observations of one group or the other. A

French officer described the scene in İzmir on 13 September as follows:
"The Armenian quarter is a charnel house. . . . In three days this rich quarter
is entirely ravaged. The streets are heaped with mattresses, broken furniture,
glass, torn paintings. . . . One sees cadavers in front of the houses. They are
swollen and some have exposed entrails. The smell is unbearable and swarms
of flies cover them"[49] On the other side, Halide Edip, who accompanied
the Turkish troops in western Anatolia, recounts how the "Turkish army
reached one city after another, only to find it a heap of ashes; its population
scattered, women half mad with grief, digging at the stone heaps with their
nails. . . . Hell seemed to be on an earth in which two peoples struggled,
one for deliverance, another for destruction. There was no quarter given on
either side."[50]

Causes of the Collapse

What made the people of western Anatolia rape, mutilate, and kill their
neighbors with such impunity? Can there ever be a sufficient explanation
for the wanton destruction of lives and property that took place in this region
during the first two decades of the twentieth century? Part of the answer to
this question has to come from within the region where the killings and
deportations took place. In many instances people harassed, beat, forced out,
and even shot their neighbors precisely because they knew them. In doing
so, they were acting not on behalf of some grandiose plan or under the
impetus of a deep hatred toward a specific ethnic or religious group, but to
redress an insult or a slight committed by a specific individual or family. For
example, Horton tells the story of a "powerful Turk who had made with
several Christian girls" who was "seized and hanged" by the fathers and
brothers of the girls soon after the Greek army landed.[51] Such acts of revenge
played a big part in the rapid deterioration of the relations between these
communities, first under the Greek occupation and then after the reestab-
lishment of Turkish rule. But this can only be a part of the explanation,
because we can also point to many instances of Turkish villagers looking
after the property of their Greek neighbors when the latter were driven away
to the islands in 1914, or Greek peasants protecting their Turkish neighbors
from the excesses of the regular and irregular forces of the Greek army.[52]

In any case, if all that took place were petty acts of revenge, the destruction
in western Anatolia would never have reached the level it did after World
War I. For the civic and economic networks in the region to fall apart with

the speed that they did, there had to have been a much more forceful and sustained attack, and such an attack could have come only from sources that were not integral to these networks. To put it another way, the cosmopolitan and prosperous networks that sustained İzmir were destroyed not as a result of the natural evolution and eventual clash of separate and inherently antagonistic communities, but through the decisive intervention of forces whose origins lay elsewhere.[53]

The external intervention that was responsible for the destruction of İzmir and its surrounding areas had three components. The first two consisted of the competing ideologies of Greek and Turkish nationalisms, and the third, the substantial number of fighters who were either external or at best marginal to the civic networks of western Anatolia.

Two Nationalisms in Conflict

Mutually exclusive and antagonistic as they were, the nationalist ideologies of the Greeks and Turks were similar in one important respect: they were both products of post-Enlightenment Europe and were shaped by the same internally conflicting trends of thought concerning the history and the desired orientation of their respective communities. In the case of Greek nationalism, there was the Hellenistic thesis that emphasized the importance of reconnecting the Greeks with their history, which was the source of classical Western civilization.[54] Many distinguished Greek and grecophile scholars became ardent followers of this line of thinking, contributing to the creation of neo-Hellenic enlightenment that was influential not only among the Greeks, but also in Western Europe in the late eighteenth and early nineteenth century. This line of thinking was very critical of the Orthodox Church. Adamantios Koraes, a leading thinker of this school, wrote: "If the Graeco-Roman Emperors had given to the education of the race a small part of that attention which they gave to the multiplication of churches and monasteries, they would not have betrayed the race to the rulers more benighted than themselves."[55]

No Greek nationalist could afford to turn his back on the East completely, however. It was there that the Byzantine history was centered, the seat of the Orthodox Church was located, and most importantly, an overwhelming majority of ethnic Greeks continued to live until the first decades of the twentieth century. The "Romeoic" thesis, which put more emphasis on this East ern heritage, saw the history of the Greeks as deeply intertwined with the history of the Eastern Church and regarded some aspects of Hellenistic enlightenment with suspicion because of its pagan undertones.[56] Both the Romeoic and Hellenic prescriptions for the future of the Greek nation had the same goal of creating a unified state that would include most or all of the ethnic Greeks of the region. But their understanding of who the Greeks were and what the character of the Greek state should be varied widely. For example, some of the more secular advocates of Greek nationalism had a much more grandiose vision of a Hellas "stretching from the river Pruth to the Nile," and they regarded the church hierarchy as being too conservative and too wedded to the Ottoman state to be trustworthy.[57] These conflicting lines of thinking pulled the Greek nationalism in opposite directions with equal force, ultimately causing it to become immobile and inflexible.

Most ethnic Greeks, especially those in the diaspora (in relationship to the new country), had at best an ambivalent attitude toward both strands of Greek nationalism. By using family networks, ethnic ties, and other historical links that dated back many centuries and extended far into Europe, the Greeks of the Ottoman Empire had played a key role in bringing about the commercial boom of the nineteenth century in the eastern Mediterranean. What put them in such an advantageous position in these networks were their multifarious links with other groups, their mobility, and the expansive nature of their activities. From their perspective, confining or focusing these activities within the boundaries of a small state was neither practical nor desirable, especially if it had to happen at the expense of other centers such as İzmir or Alexandria.

Even though the initial excitement of independence had attracted some migration to the kingdom of Greece, this did not last long and most of these families returned to their homes after having been disappointed in their prospects in the new country.[58] For example, "the town of Ayvalık, which was devastated and depopulated in 1821 had by 1896 re-acquired an almost exclusively Greek population of thirty-five thousand"[59] In İzmir, the Greek population increased from thirty thousand to seventy-five thousand between the 1830s and 1860s.[60] The wealth of Asia Minor continued to attract a steady stream of Greek nationals to the region throughout the rest of the nineteenth century. The partisans of the new state were unhappy with the cosmopolitanism of the Greek communities of Anatolia; they appeared to be so removed from their heritage that some of them did not even speak Greek. The nationalists saw the wealthy families of İzmir and Istanbul as helping not the Greek cause, but their own interests and the interests of the Ottoman state. To correct this situation, some of them organized campaigns to "Hellenize" the lost communities, efforts that were not greeted with any enthusiasm by the locals and for the most part failed.[61]

These feelings of resentment and suspicion played a large role in pushing Greece into the two Balkan wars in 1912 and 1913, and then into the occupation of western Anatolia in 1919. Although some in Greece believed that only by uniting the wealthiest and the most successful parts of the Greek diaspora with the new homeland could Greek nationalism succeed, others did not trust the highly cosmopolitan and liberal nature of the networks abroad, and they sought to harness these to serve the interests of the new state.

As soon as the Greek army landed in western Anatolia, the whole region fell into chaos and became the site of an extremely destructive conflict that lasted for three years. There were close to 400,000 refugees from the Balkans who had been settled in western and southern Anatolia between 1912 and 1919.[62] These people were naturally apprehensive about the prospects of living under the Greek rule and resisted it as much as they could. Their uncertainty was matched by the status of Anatolian Greeks who had been expelled to the islands and to Greece by the Young Turk governments before and during the Balkan wars. By the end of 1920, 126,000 of these refugees were returned and settled in western Anatolia by the Greek administration.[63] According to some estimates, at least 150,000 Muslims were left homeless as a result of the resettlement of the Greek refugees.[64]

In addition to these massive movements that shuffled and reshuffled the region's population several times over, the Greek invasion also forced the much more difficult and painful process of untangling the intricate local relations that had connected various ethnic and religious groups together. Greek youth who had been recruited into the Ottoman army during World War I, primarily to work in labor battalions, were "liberated," only to be drafted into the Greek army to fight their erstwhile friends and neighbors. As the Greek army spread into the interior, the occupying forces removed the Ottoman administrators from the upper echelons of the civil administration and put Greeks in charge of the area. However, because these officials were brought from Greece, most of them did not speak any Turkish, which made it impossible for them to establish even the semblance of authority in the first months of the occupation.[65] In 1922, when the Greek army was roundly defeated and forced to flee, they "carried the Christian population with them, often by force."[66] They burned most of the villages and cities in the interior, which in turn created the pretext for revenge among the Turkish troops and Muslim residents in İzmir.[67] In retrospect, it would not be an exaggeration to claim that the only accomplishment of this profoundly misguided policy was to galvanize the sentiments of exclusion within Turkish nationalism and plant the very seeds of enmity that are often mentioned as the cause of this conflict.

In ways that were no different from its Greek counterpart, Turkish nationalism also contained some deep ambiguities at its core affecting not only how the Turks thought of themselves and their history, but also the policies they implemented in the late nineteenth and early twentieth century. The first and the most critical among these had to do with the ethnic definition of Turks as a community and a nation. Through the writings and activities of intellectuals from Azerbaijan, Crimea, and the Volga region of Russia such as İsmail Bey Gasprinski, Ağaoğlu Ahmet, and Akçuraoğlu Yusuf, Ottomans became aware of a community of ethnic Turks who were spread across a large territory extending from the Mediterranean basin into Central Asia. This conception of Central Asia as the font of Turkish civilization was reinforced by the influence of some of the Sufi orders who had moved westward from Central Asia over many centuries.[68]

Another important tie to the East was established more circuitously, by way of Europe, where exiled Ottoman intellectuals read the works of early Orientalists who were interested in Central Asian cultures, Turkic tribes, and languages.[69] The translations of the works of these European scholars would be used in the debates about the history and nature of Turkish identity, especially in the early decades of the twentieth century. There was, however, the obvious but awkward reality that this wide and broad community of Turks who were supposed to constitute a community had no real experience that linked them with each other. The Muslim Turks in places like İzmir clearly had much more in common with their Greek or Armenian neighbors than they did with their cousins in the Caucusus, along the Volga, and in Central Asia. Nevertheless, the idea of a distinct Turkish race found its way into new Turkish nationalist thought and was melded into a historical narrative that took some liberties with facts but served the requirements of the time very well.[70]

Like its Greek counterpart, Turkish nationalism also had a somewhat uncertain and wavering relationship with religion. In the course of the Greek-Turkish war, Mustafa Kemal deliberately appealed to Muslims in Anatolia. He particularly benefited from the help of the Sufi *tarikat*s during the war and accepted and used until his death the honorific title *ghazi*

(holy warrior), which was given to him by the Nationalist Assembly. However, in the years that followed the end of the war, Mustafa Kemal became
increasingly firm in his belief that the difficulties the Ottoman Empire suffered in the eighteenth and nineteenth centuries were caused by its failure
to take part in the scientific and industrial development of the West. He
placed the blame for this squarely on Islam. In the 1920s, he turned vehe-
mently against all religion, orchestrated an all-out effort to eradicate the
impact of Islam and Islamic institutions in the new state, and made sure that
secularism was enshrined as a founding principle of the republic. The radicalism of this new orientation ushered in a thorough soul-searching and a
persistent debate about the place of religion in modern Turkey, which continues to occupy a central place in the politics of Turkey today.

Countering the pull of Asia and Islam on Turkish nationalism was the
attraction of the West, whose ideals and institutions had become lodestars
for the nationalist leaders. In the minds of Atatürk and his colleagues, there
was no doubt that Western civilization provided the only acceptable model
of progress, and the positive sciences the only means of getting there. Ironically, this new orientation implied that in order to move forward, the new
nation would have to turn its back not only on religion, but also on its newly
discovered history in Central Asia. For a while, in order to justify such a
complete turn away from the east, some writers put forth and defended, at
considerable cost to historical and archeological accuracy, the idea that Anatolia had always been the cradle not only of Turkish but all civilizations.[71]

Over the years, nationalist leaders on both sides have compensated for
the ambiguities that marred the foundations of their respective ideologies by
assuming a particularly rigid and intolerant stand on all issues that involved
their history and their relationship to each other. They feared that any compromise would expose the weakness that lies at the core of both Greek and
Turkish nationalism and prevent the two nations from fulfilling their "historical destinies." It is not a long road from this uncompromising rigidity to
the justification of violence and destruction that was carried out in the name
of these ideologies in and around İzmir.

Intruders

No analysis of the western Anatolian catastrophe would be complete without referring to the outsiders who carried out most of the killings and the

destruction of property in the region. On the Greek side, the troops who occupied, attempted to govern, and, in their retreat, destroyed many of the towns in the interior came for the most part from Greece.[72] The bands of local Greeks who joined the Greek army were on the margins of the social and economic networks in Anatolia and were attracted by the messianic-nationalist rhetoric of the Greek army. Toynbee lists the names of some of these brigands as Yokatos Yoryi (Loaded George), Hajji Topuz Oğlu (Palmer Club's Son) Panayoti, and Kumarcı Oğlu (Gambler's Son) Poti, and comments that they were "not all so very respectable . . . if their family professions were accurately recorded in their surnames."[73]

Until a properly disciplined Turkish army was put together in 1921, armed irregulars (*efes, çetes, zeybeks*) served as the backbone of the resistance against the Greeks in western Anatolia. As was the case with their Greek counterparts, the names of the Muslim *çetes* do not suggest that these groups had deep roots in the area or belonged to reputable professions. The better known among them were Yürük (Nomad) Osman, Deli (Mad) Osman, Koca Arap (Big Arab), Parmaksız Arap (Thumbless Arab), Kürt (Kurd) Mustafa, Harput'lu (from Harput) Ömer, Piç (Bastard) Osman.[74] Kara Ali, the right-hand man of the famous bandit, Çakırcalı had deserted his army post in Yemen and found his way to western Anatolia.[75] Even after the centrally organized army seized control of operations, these bands continued to operate as an auxiliary force, and they played a key role in retaking İzmir. For both sides, then, victory was contingent on the performance of large numbers of groups who had no interest in the civic and economic networks in the region. Here I will touch on only those who helped the Turkish side, because they ended up playing the decisive role in how the history of İzmir and western Anatolia unfolded in these crucial years.

The origins of the armed irregulars who joined the nationalist forces were diverse. There were draft dodgers, tax evaders, and petty criminals among them. But a great many of them originated from among the tribal communities who had been moved from the eastern provinces of the Ottoman Empire as part of the state's recurrent campaigns of settling nomadic groups. The first of these campaigns was organized at the end of the seventeenth century, and they became increasingly more comprehensive as the imperial administration acquired the features of a modern state in the following centuries. But moving these groups and even granting them land did not always ensure that they would abandon their old ways and settle. Most of them continued their pastoral and nomadic lives in their new environment, combining them with some farming that they usually incorporated into their annual cycles of migration.

In the second half of the nineteenth century, as the Ottoman state pressed them for more taxes and for military service, these tribes became even more rebellious. In addition to various forms of passive resistance that they had always utilized, they started to organize and support armed units to rob merchants, kidnap wealthy individuals for ransom, and collect protection fees from caravans.[76] The banditry spread to such an extent that "in 1883 the entire mountainous region in the interior of western Anatolia was under their control." It is estimated that at the end of the nineteenth century there were at least 4,000 bandits organized in tens of different groups in western Anatolia; against them the state could field no more than 125 policemen and 2,035 gendarme forces in the region.[78] The Ottoman army organized a number of campaigns in the late nineteenth and early twentieth century to punish these çetes and restore the authority of the central administration in the countryside, but the advantage in these encounters lay with the brigands who were organized in smaller units dispersed in the terrain, and had created a network of support for themselves. On those rare occasions when the Ottoman army captured a famous bandit, he was punished in the most emphatic way so that others would desist from following or helping such individuals and their followers. For example, when Çakırcalı Mehmet Efe was caught after fifteen years of banditry, he was killed, skinned, torn to pieces, and his decapitated body was hanged from his foot to destroy all myths and rumors about his invincibility.[79]

As an alternative measure, the government relocated Kurds and Circassians in an attempt to use them in suppressing these groups in western Anatolia. But it soon became apparent that these new arrivals were no more willing to go along with the directives of the state than the previous tribes who had been settled there.

After the Balkan wars, as the Ottoman Empire drifted into World War I, the government abandoned all pretense of seeking to impose order in the hinterland of İzmir. The anarchy that ensued enticed even more people to take to the mountains in order to pursue a life of banditry. In addition to the Muslim outsiders such as the Circassians, Tatars, and Kurds, there were also a large a number of Greek bandits partaking in the fruits of the general lawlessness in Anatolia. During these early years, none of the bandit groups paid much attention to questions of national or religious affiliation in choosing either their friends or their prey.

As they drew the Greek army across western Anatolia, Mustafa Kemal's forces made extensive use of these bandit groups. This was perhaps inevitable. The Ottoman army had been fighting on many fronts continuously since 1911; it had suffered a series of defeats and had officially been demobilized by the armistice in 1919. By the time the nationalist effort was getting organized, there was but a skeleton left of this once formidable fighting force. When the Greek army entered Aydın in 1919, all that remained to defend that city were 10 officers, 43 soldiers, 46 pack animals, and two cannon batteries.[80] The resources of the irregular troops, by contrast, were formidable. Most of them had stayed out of the war and had used the years of turmoil and conflict to enrich and arm themselves and their followers. By force, intimidation, and offering protection, they had built for themselves a network of support among the villagers and nomadic tribes. The nationalist leaders were aware of the risks involved in relying too heavily on these groups.[81] In addition to being poorly trained and lacking discipline, they had resisted all efforts at being incorporated into the regular army, which began to be rebuilt after 1920. The fears of the nationalist lawmakers proved to be justified in that several of the bandits rebelled openly against the nationalists, and one even went over to the Greek side with his three thousand men, four cannons, and four hundred machine guns.[82] In many cases, however, in return for their support, the nationalists gave the bandit leaders a free hand in expanding their activities, raiding the cities, robbing the urban population, and especially in confiscating the properties of the fleeing Christians.

Needless to say, their service during the war improved the image of the *çetes* significantly in Turkey. For example, Mustafa Kemal invited four hundred followers of one of the more notorious bandits, Demirci Mehmet Efe, to Ankara during the war and gave him the rank of colonel in the Turkish army.[83] In some of the propaganda material, Mustafa Kemal himself was referred to and idealized as *Sarı* (Blond) *Zeybek*.[84] In the years that followed the final victory of the nationalist forces, *çetes* would be celebrated as romantic heroes and the veteran *zeybeks* would become permanent fixtures in parades and ceremonies marking national holidays.

The Responsibility of the State

The overwhelming presence of these *çetes* in some of the more violent crimes that were committed, especially in İzmir, is sometimes used as a way of clearing the regular nationalist army and the Ottoman and Turkish governments from any responsibility in the events surrounding the İzmir fire. There is no doubt that without the presence of these outsiders, neither İzmir nor its interior would have been destroyed, at least not to the extent that they were. Yet the fact remains that no matter how weak they might have been, neither the nationalist government nor its army was very effective or interested in preventing the persecution of Greeks and Armenians or protecting these communities at a moment when such protection was sorely needed. After all, Mustafa Kemal himself was in İzmir while the city was burning, and he even had to move from his headquarters on the waterfront to the home of his future wife in Göztepe when the fire came too close. On the journey, he had to pass through the entire city, and it was feared that "the waves of panic-stricken people would overwhelm the Ghazi and smother him."[85]

Why, then, did the late-Ottoman and the early nationalist regime lose interest in the terrible fate of the Greeks and Armenians? Was there a preconceived plan of mass murder directed at Armenians and Greeks? Was what happened in western Anatolia a part of this master plan, or, alternatively, did the Ottoman and Turkish officials seize on these events that were beyond their control and use them to realize their ultimate goal of ridding Anatolia of Armenians and Greeks? If so, why? Was a racist ideology or sentiment behind the commitment of these crimes or the failure to prevent them? These key questions lie at the heart of the Ottoman Empire's fateful years. It is unlikely that a reasonable conversation will take place among historians or that anything resembling a consensus will emerge unless these questions are addressed in a way that is perceived as fair by all parties to the discussion. The following points, however, may provide a reasonable place to start such a conversation, especially in relation to the Greeks and Armenians of İzmir.

It is quite clear that starting from the final decades of the nineteenth century, the Ottoman, the Young Turk, and the nationalist administrations became increasingly suspicious of the position and the aspirations of the Greek and Armenian residents of the empire. The persecution of Muslims in the Balkans after the Ottoman-Russian War of 1877–78, the shifting policies of the great powers, and the uncertainties inherent in Turkish nationalism are some of the factors that brought about this general mistrust. By the early decades of the twentieth century, the Greeks and Armenians had become the "others" of Turkish nationalism. The rhetoric the nationalist representatives used in some of their deliberations in the Ankara Assembly leaves no doubt as to how they had come to perceive these communities.[86] In addition to this ideology, which now advocated the creation of a homogeneous nation, the Young Turks and their nationalist descendants also possessed a fledgling communication network and a new secret police organization, the *Teşkilat-ı Mahsusa*, both of which they used very effectively in remaking Anatolian society.[88] Needless to say, little room was left in this environment for those who believed that some reconciliation might still be possible. For example, Mehmet Refet, the editor of the İzmir newspaper *Köylü*, was first imprisoned by the Greeks and then sent into exile by the Turks because his liberal views clashed with both of the competing nationalisms in the region.[88] It would still be wrong, however, to assume that these hardening political attitudes accurately reflected the sentiments of the population at large. One way of demonstrating the growing disjunction between late-Ottoman and Turkish politics and society would be to point out the popularity of the *Köylü* itself, which, with its liberal editorial policy, had attained a very wide circulation in the early years of the Young Turk period.[89]

Identifying the culprits and specifying the circumstances of the destruction of İzmir will undoubtedly take much more research and conversation among researchers. In the meantime, it serves no historical purpose to impute collective guilt or ascribe indiscriminate victimhood for an entire people forever. When history is presented from a perspective that seeks to justify either one of these points of view, it produces a distorted picture that cannot do justice to the actual record of events.

After the illustrious historian Arnold Toynbee toured Greece and western Anatolia in 1921, he wrote a book that makes it very difficult to put all the blame or the pity on one or the other side. In fact, his *Western Question in Greece and Turkey* included so many descriptions of killings and destruction inflicted by the Greek army that it was found to be unduly harsh in its criticism of Greece, and he was forced to resign from the coveted Koraes Chair of Modern Greek and Byzantine History at the University of London in 1924.[90] It was the fact that they witnessed the destruction in western Anatolia that prompted authors like Toynbee and Halide Edip to warn their readers about the pitfalls of exalting the glories or idealizing the sufferings of national communities, as well as justifying the crimes committed against them. It is with their words that I conclude this essay. Toynbee wrote:

> The politicians and chettes are unlikely to be found among those homeless and starving masses, and we cannot harden our hearts against

their misery in the comfortable belief that they are suffering for their own crimes. Neither did they sin nor their fathers, that the tower has fallen upon them.[91]

Halide Edip echoes him:

There is no such thing as a guilty nation. One of the obstacles to peace is the hysterical and exaggerated propagating of people's sufferings for political purposes. It burdens the younger generations of each nation with the crimes or the martyrdom of their fathers in which they have had no share. The consequence is either a destructive and pathological feeling of revenge or shame in the generation which is not responsible for the past. And the political gambler takes advantage of this passion and uses it to the detriment of one nation or another.[92]

Notes

Author's Note: Elena Frangakis-Syrett read and commented on a draft of this essay. I am grateful to her for her many useful comments.

1. Ernest Hemingway, "On the Quai at Smyrna," *The Short Stories* (New York, 1995), pp. 87–88.
2. Michael Llewellyn Smith, *Ionian Vision: Greece in Asia Minor* (London, 1973), p. 310.
3. Marjorie Housepian, *The Smyrna Affair* (New York, 1966), p. 86.
4. Ibid., p. 161.
5. Bilge Umar, *İzmir'de Yunanlıların Son Günleri* (Ankara, 1974) p. 333.
6. For a full text of the Lausanne treaty, see Great Britain, *Parliamentary Papers, Turkey*, no. 1, 1923, *Lausanne Conference* (London, 1923), pp. 817–28.
7. On the *Karamanlis*, see Richard Clogg, "Anadolu Hristiyan Karındaşlarımız: The Turkish-Speaking Greeks of Asia Minor," in *Neohellenism*, ed. John Burke and Stahis Gauntlett (Canberra, 1992), pp. 65–91; Stephen Ladas, *The Exchange of Minorities: Bulgaria, Greece and Turkey* (New York, 1932), p. 378. On Orthodox Arabs, see ibid., 383.
8. Clogg, "Anadolu Hristiyan Karındaşlarımız," p. 65.
9. Ibid., pp. 66, 83.
10. Arnold Toynbee, *The Western Question in Greece and Turkey*, 2nd ed.(London, 1923), p. 242.
11. Ladas, *Exchange of Minorities*, pp. 377–78.
12. Ibid., pp. 437–42. This period as a whole was one of considerable mobility for the population of western Anatolia. Following the establishment of their special surveillance organization, Teşkilat-ı Mahsusa, in 1914, the Young Turk

governments expelled over 98,000 Greeks from western Anatolia, but not from İzmir and other large cities. Most of these people returned during the Greek occupation to be deported again under the terms of the Lausanne Treaty. Engin Berber, *Sancılı Yıllar: İzmir, 1918–1922* (Ankara, 1997), pp. 58–61.

13. Kemal Karpat, *Ottoman Population, 1830–1914* (Madison: University of Wisconsin Press, 1985), p. 190; George Th. Mavrogordatos, *Stillborn Republic: Social Coalitions and Party Strategies in Greece, 1922–1936* (Berkeley: University of California Press, 1983), pp. 186–87.

14. Karpat, *Ottoman Population*, pp. 122–23.

15. Çınar Atay, *İzmir'in İzmir'i* (İzmir,1993), p. 213; Karpat, *Ottoman Population*, p. 174.

16. *Umumi Nüfus Tahriri* (Ankara, 1929), pp. ix, 36.

17. For a preliminary comparison of school books in Turkey and Greece, see Herkül Milas, "İlkokul Kitapları" in *Türk Yunan İlişkilerine Bir Önsöz: Tencere Dibin Kara* (Istanbul, 1989), pp. 34–48. See also the essays in *Tarih Eğitimi ve Tarihte Öteki Sorunu*, ed. Türk Tarih Vakfı (Istanbul, 1998).

18. George Horton, *The Blight of Asia* (Indianapolis, 1926), p. 112.

19. Housepian, *The Smyrna Affair*, p. 141.

20. Halide Edip, *The Turkish Ordeal* (New York, 1928), p. 386.

21. Stanford Shaw and Ezel Kural Shaw, *History of the Ottoman Empire and Modern Turkey*, 2 vols (Cambridge, 1977), p. 363.

22. Justin McCarthy, *Death and Exile: The Ethnic Cleansing of Ottoman Muslims, 1821–92*, (Princeton, 1995), pp. 291–92.

23. Heath Lowry, "Turkish History: On Whose Sources Will It Be Based? A Case Study on the Burning of İzmir," *Osmanlı Araştırmaları* 9 (1988): 13.

24. Pandey argues that in Indian historiography the notion of "community" is reified in a similar way and used misleadingly as a precursor of the "nation." See Gyanendra Pandey, *The Construction of Communalism in Colonial North India* (Delhi, 1992), pp. 1–22.

25. See for example, Benjamin Braude and Bernard Lewis, Introduction, in their edited volume, *Christians and Jews in the Ottoman Empire: The Functioning of a Plural Society: The Central Lands* (New York, 1982), p. 1.

26. See for example, L. S. Stavrianos, *The Balkans since 1453* (New York, 1961), pp. 96–115.

27. For a background and discussion of the implications of the millet institution, see Benjamin Braude, "Foundation Myths of the Millet System," in *Christians and Jews in the Ottoman Empire*, ed. Braude and Lewis, pp. 69–88; Daniel Goffman, "Ottoman Millets in the Early Seventeenth Century," *New Perspectives on Turkey*, 11 (Fall, 1994): 135–58.

28. See Halil İnalcık, "The Meaning of Legacy: The Ottoman Case," *Imperial Legacy: The Ottoman Imprint on the Balkans and the Middle East*, ed. Carl Brown (New York, 1996), p. 24.

29. Clogg, "Anadolu Hristiyan Karındaşlarımız," pp. 67–68.
30. Halit Ziya, Uşaklıgil Kırk Yıl (Istanbul, 1987), p. 119.
31. Dido Sotiriyu, Benden Selam Söyle Anadolu'ya, (Istanbul, 1989), p. 205.
32. Berber, Sancılı Yıllar, p. 72.
33. See Cengiz Orhonlu, Osmanlı İmparatorluğunda Aşiretlerin İskânı (Istanbul, 1987); Xavier de Planhol, "Geography, Politics, and Nomadism in Anatolia," International Social Science Journal 11, no. 4 (1959): 525–31.
34. On "Crypto-Christians," see, R. M. Dawkins, "The Crypto-Christians of Turkey," Byzantion 8 (1933): 247–75.
35. Ibid., pp. 136–37, 238, 239.
36. M. A. Ubicini, Letters on Turkey, pt. 1: Turkey and the Turks (New York, 1973), pp. 249–50; Tuncer Baykara, İzmir Şehri ve Tarihi (İzmir).
37. Housepian, The Smyrna Affair, p. 91.
38. For example, for a while the only Muslim employees of the İzmir branch of the Ottoman Bank were the distinguished novelist Uscedilligil and Atatürk's future father-in-law Muammer Bey. (Uşaklıgil, Kırk Yıl, pp. 320–23). Among the employees of the İzmir branch of the PDA was Abdulhalim Bey, who served briefly as acting governor when the Turkish army took the city in 1922 (Umar, İzmir'de Yunanlıların Son Günleri, p. 280).
39. For extensive descriptions of banditry and relations between bandits, local notables, and the state, see Sabri Yetkin, Ege'de Eşkiyalar (Istanbul, 1996); and Ersal Yavi, Efeler, (Aydın, 1991).
40. Gerasimos Augustinos, The Greeks of Asia Minor (Kent, 1992), p. 93.
41. Berber, Sancılı Yıllar, pp. 133, 163, 191. For example, Adnan Menderes, who would later become the prime minister of Turkey, played in a mixed football team in the fall of 1919. Umar, İzmir'de Yunanlıların Son Günleri, p. 238.
42. Berber, Sancılı Yıllar, p. 91.
43. Ibid., p. 229.
44. Housepian, The Smyrna Affair, pp. 142–43.
45. Cited in Lowry, "Turkish History," p. 14.
46. Berber, Sancılı Yıllar, p. 441; Toynbee, Western Question, p. 166.
47. Toynbee, Western Question, p. 256.
48. Berber, Sancılı Yıllar, p. 465.
49. Housepian, Smyrna Affair, p. 136.
50. Halide Edip, Turkish Ordeal, p. 367.
51. Horton, Blight of Asia, p. 79.
52. Toynbee, Western Question, pp. 294, 389.
53. In recent years a number of studies have approached communalism and communal violence in North India from a similar perspective, which highlights the role of "external forces and agencies." Ian Copland, "The Further Shores of Partition: Ethnic Cleansing in Rajasthan 1947," Past and Present 160 (August

1998): 203–39. See also Sandra Freitag, *Collective Action and Community*, (Berkeley, 1989), especially part III; Gyanendra Pandey, *Construction of Communalism*.

54. Michael Herzfeld, *Ours Once More* (New York, 1986), pp. 18–21.

55. Quoted from Toynbee, *Western Question*, p. 337.

56. Herzfeld, *Ours Once More*, p. 20; Richard Clogg, "*I kath'imas Anatoli*: The Greek East in the Eighteenth and Nineteenth Centuries," in *Anatolica: Studies in the Greek East in the Eighteenth and Nineteenth Centuries* (Aldershot, 1996), p. 5.

57. Clogg, "*I kath'imas Anatoli*," p. 1.

58. The establishment of independent Greece did not affect the movement of people between the islands and the Anatolian mainland. See Tuncer Baykara, "XIX. Yüzyılda Urla Yarımadasında Nüfus Hareketleri," in *Social and Economic History of Turkey*, ed. Osman Okyar and Halil İnalcık (Ankara, 1980), pp. 279–86. Even during the Balkan wars, one of Dido Sotiriyu's brothers returned from Greece complaining that "land in Greece is very hard to work; it is full of stones and swamps." His plan was to work in İzmir or sell his land there and use the money to start a small business in Greece (Sotiriyu, *Benden Selam Söyle*, p. 50).

59. Clogg, "The Greek Millet" p. 195.

60. Ibid.

61. Clogg, "Anadolu Hristiyan Karındaşlarımız," pp. 80–81.

62. McCarthy, *Death and Exile*, p. 161.

63. Berber, *Sancılı Yıllar*, p. 322.

64. Ibid., p. 247.

65. Ibid., pp. 299–317.

66. Halide Edip, *The Turkish Ordeal*, p. 363.

67. The extent of destruction that was carried out in the Balkans and western Anatolia between the Balkan wars and the end of the Greek occupation is well documented. It is obvious that each of the sides in these conflicts carry a part of the blame in that they all contributed to this carnage. For documentation, see Carnegie Endowment, *The Other Balkan Wars* (Washington, D.C., 1993); Toynbee, *Western Question*; McCarthy, *Death and Exile*; Housepian, *Smyrna Affair*. Unfortunately, most of the writing about this period seeks to vindicate one side or the other. It is, of course, futile to try to draw up balance sheets and compare the sufferings of different groups. Overall, if we look at the period between World War I and the exchange, the Greeks and Armenians appear as the biggest losers in the conflict. In much larger numbers than the Muslim Turks, they ended up being ejected from the only place they had known as home for generations. But if we broaden our time frame and include the emigration of more than one million Muslims from the Balkan states after

1878, we find that the latter group also suffered deeply in these tumultuous years. (See Karpat, *Ottoman Population*, p. 75; Nedim İpek, *Rumeli'den Anadolu'ya Türk Göçleri* [Ankara, 1994], p. 41.)

68. See Raymond Lifchez, ed., *Dervish Lodge* (Berkeley, 1992); Richard Tapper, ed., *Islam in Modern Turkey* (New York, 1991); Ahmet Yaşar Ocak, *Türk Sufiliğine Bakışlar* (Istanbul, 1996); Fuad Köprülü, *Islam in Anatolia after the Turkish Invasion* (Salt Lake City, 1993).

69. Kushner, *The Rise of Turkish Nationalism*, p. 10.

70. Various arguments supporting this thesis were articulated and presented at a congress that was convened in Ankara in 1932 (see *Birinci Türk Tarihi Kongresi*, Istanbul, 1932).

71. Bernard Lewis, *The Emergence of Modern Turkey* (New York, 1961), pp. 3–7.

72. Toynbee, *Western Question*, pp. 166–67.

73. Ibid., p. 282. Toynbee writes that eventually many local Christians formerly engaged in peaceful occupations joined these bandits.

74. Yetkin, *Ege'de Eşkiyalar*, p. 31.

75. Ibid.

76. Armed resistance by the tribes against the centralizing drive of the state go back to the seventeenth century. See Çağatay Uluçay, *18 ve 19. Yüzyıllarda Saruhan'da Eşkiyalık ve Halk Hareketleri*, (Istanbul, 1955), pp. 80–81.

77. Ibid., p. 31.

78. Ibid., pp. 70–73.

79. Yetkin, *Ege'de Eşkiyalar*, p. 172–73.

80. Ibid., p. 112.

81. *TBMM [Türkiye Büyük Millet Meclisi] Gizli Celse Zabıtları, I*, (Ankara, 1980), pp. 264–65. The Greek state had a similar relationship with the brigands that roamed the countryside in Thrace, Macedonia, and Thessaly. It was only in 1912 that the Greek army became a professional, regular fighting force. Up to that point, the Greek state relied on brigands to protect its interests and take advantage of the incursions these fiercely independent elements organized into the Ottoman territories. See John Koliopoluos, *Brigands with a Cause* (Oxford, 1987).

82. Halide Edip, *Turkish Ordeal*, p. 231.

83. Yavi, *Efeler*, pp. 124–25. Greeks never abandoned their brigands either, even after the establishment of the central army. Right before the Balkan wars, Eleutherios Venizelos is reported to have said that "whereas the regular army fought for the state, the irregulars, as true descendants of the pre-Independence armatoles, fought for the freedom of the unredeemed Greeks" (Koliopoulos, *Brigands with a Cause*, p. 296).

84. Ibid., p. 1.

85. Falih Rıfkı Atay, *Çankaya* (Istanbul, 1969), p. 324.

86. *TBMM, Gizli Celse Zabıtları*, p. 322.
87. The 1927 census shows how effective and efficient this campaign was. According to its findings, only between 11 and 38 Greek-speaking individuals were left in places like Ödemiş, Seferihisar, Tire, all old centers of Greek life (*Umumi Nüfus Tahriri*, p. 23).
88. Berber, *Sancılı Yıllar*, pp. 192–93, 270.
89. Zeki Arıkan, "Tanzimat ve Meşrutiyet Dönemlerinde İzmir Basını," *Tanzimat'tan Cumhuriyet'e Türkiye Ansiklopedisi* 1: 109.
90. See Richard Clogg, *Politics and the Academy: Arnold Toynbee and the Koraes Chair* (London, 1986).
91. Toynbee, *Western Question*, p. xv.
92. Halide Edip, *The Turkish Ordeal*, p. 307.

11 Negotiating Colonial Modernity and Cultural Difference: Indian Muslim Conceptions of Community and Nation, 1878–1914

Ayesha Jalal

The vexed question of Muslim loyalty to India, given their affiliation with the worldwide community of Islam, or *ummah*, has generated an intricate web of narratives on the *qaum*, the loosely defined community-turned-nation, and the *watan*, or the territorial homeland. Rather than being mutually exclusive, territorial nationalism and Islamic universalism were the two main strands informing discourse on Muslim identity after India's formal loss of sovereignty in 1857. Elsewhere in this volume, C. A. Bayly highlights the importance of the multiple voices and cultural concerns that informed the narratives of empire and nationalism. In keeping with that concern, this essay aims at reevaluating the competing communitarian versions of nationalism in India in order to broaden the enterprise of assessing the historical significance of European modernity in contexts where the politics of cultural difference held sway.

The loyalties and disloyalties of Muslims, not just to the Indian "nation" but also to the British raj, has led to two general misconceptions among historians of nationalism and imperialism in South Asia. Assertion of a religiously informed cultural identity by an articulate group of *ashraf*, "respectable" Muslims, is seen to have encouraged the separatist politics that eventually culminated in the partition of India in 1947. By the same token, the British decision to concede separate representation under the Morley-Minto reforms of 1909, irrespective of whether or not it was inspired by an invidious policy of divide and rule, is interpreted as signaling the success of the "Muslim community" in registering its distinctive identity in the formal arena of Indian politics. Both viewpoints are echoed in Bayly's otherwise engaging comparative analysis of the nexus among empire, nation, and community in Egypt and India, resulting in the failure of the Copts and the success of the Muslims in securing separate representation from the imperial rulers in the early twentieth century. This chapter therefore takes a somewhat different angle of vision and calls into question the very notion of a Muslim separatism at a time when the idea of an Indian nation was itself in the process of being forged, negotiated, and contested. It turns the spotlight on the interplay among class, region, and community in exploring the territorial and extra-territorial allegiances of India's Muslims in both their restrictive and expansive dimensions.

An individual Muslim's first point of reference was undoubtedly the community. This community could just as well be that of the family, the local kinship network, or of language, region, or religion. Capping the relationship between the individual and community with a religious category did not mean that other associations fell by the wayside. Whether in conformity with or in resistance to the dominant discourse that privileged religion, these relationships continued to influence an individual's attitudes and choices in life. The community of the individual was more variegated and creatively experienced than the forced homogeneities of a religiously defined category in census enumeration suggest. That is why it is necessary to expose communitarian discourses on identity to a more rigorous test than colonial epistemology permits.

The City as Identifier in Pre-Colonial India

The city[1] and the ummah formed the two poles in the space of Indian Muslim belonging. Like a Persian or an early Mughal miniature, where the division of space invokes multiple levels of consciousness, interpreting the territorial aspects of Muslim identity is like contemplating a two-dimensional landscape without allowing the roving eye to fall into a purely three-dimensional perspective. The spiritual bond with the ummah meshes with associations to family and the larger kinship group. A Muslim's identification with a nonterritorial community of Islam and the sense of belonging to a territorially located community means that space is both infinite and finite at the same time. It is this dialectic inherent in their religiously informed cultural identity that has lent historical complexity and depth to a Muslim's relationship with the *watan*, the homeland.

An affinity to territory is typically decried in normative Muslim thought as distracting from identification with the nonterritorially defined ummah. Yet a nonterritorial conception of the community of Muslims has never meant the complete absence of territorial identification on the part of the faithful. Mecca and Medina occupy a special place in Muslim consciousness the world over. A specific geographical location like Arabia has been a powerful religious symbol for Muslims over the centuries. But the sense of belonging to a given territory provides a more immediate point of reference for their sense of identity. Mir Taqi Mir (1722–1810) took the point to mystical heights when he declared:

Why talk of Mecca or Kaaba, who cares for pilgrimage?
Dwellers of the street of love, greet these places from afar.[2]

This is an allusion to a Muslim's spiritual relationship with the *ka'ba*, the center, or the *qibla*, the direction toward which prayers are said, which is everywhere and yet a specific space sanctified by the Holy Prophet's prostration before Allah. Praying in the direction of the *ka'ba*, the material and spiritual center of Islam, represent the spatialization of Muslim belief in one God as well as membership in the ummah.[3] The architectural geometry and sacred space of the *ka'ba* has been reproduced by Muslims everywhere in the world, from the mosque as the place of collective worship to the home as private abode.

This idea of space as both universal and specific has allowed the articulation of territorial identity to take a variety of forms in the Muslim psyche. In India it found its expression in a genre of Urdu poetry known as *shahir-i-ashoob* or *ashoobia shairi* (lament for the city), which encapsulates the sociocultural turbulence of cities in the late Mughal period. Unlike the love poetry, where the individual yearns for the beloved whether human or divine, in the *shahir-i-ashoob* the poet locates his existential self through an attachment to a *watan*. Yet it would be erroneous to regard this genre of poetry as proto-nationalist, pure and simple. There are certainly references to *qaum*, which is used loosely to refer to a clan, religious community, or sect that does not fit easily into the English term "nation," whose connotations in popular discourse militate against its straightforward equation. Unless one contextualizes the use of words like *qaum* and *watan*, Urdu poetry can become a hunting ground for many imagined "nations" and "nationalisms" that thwart any effort at disentangling the individual identity of the Muslim from the discourse on the Muslim community and nation.

Until 1857 there was no obvious invocation of the national idea in the form it has come to assume in the postcolonial Indian state's secular nationalism and Pakistan's two-nation theory. The city, or place of abode, appears central to the sentiments of the poet as part of a given social setting. Mirza Asadullah Khan Ghalib (1797–1869), the preeminent Urdu poet of the nineteenth century, felt passionately about the city of his birth, Agra, and considered living in Delhi an exile. For him Agra was the "playground" for his "love-distracted heart," where the "drunken breeze of morning ranged through her gardens to lift up and to bear away men's hearts so that the drunkard longed no longer for his morning draught, so that the pious heart bent his mind no more to prayer." He longed for the "grain of dust of that land," for "every leaf in those fair gardens," and for the ripples in its rivers.[4]

Even as early as the late seventeenth century, Wali Muhammad Wali (1667–1707) of the Deccan, considered by many to be the father of Urdu poetry, had evoked the notion of the Muslim *qaum* and the *watan* while celebrating his attachment to a city like Surat, on the one hand, and Hindustan, on the other.

The themes of the *shahir-i-ashoob* comprise a rich social commentary on the vibrancy of life, as well as on the historical causes of degeneration and civil strife in various urban centers of the subcontinent. Mir Taqi Mir, who was among those excelling in this genre, noted that the wilds of today had been the bustling towns of yesterday and spoke patriotically of the spirit of martyrdom stirring his heart to put the oppressor's might to the test.[5] There was also an element of satire and humor in this poetry before 1857. After the suppression of the revolt, the *shahir-i-ashoob* began taking the form of *marsiyas*, or dirges, drenched in blood and tragedy.

Much the same sort of trend had attended Aurangzeb's overrunning of the city states of Bijapur and Golconda. The Bijapuri poet Ansari likened the situation in his conquered homeland to the advent of *kufar* and found little pleasing about the new circumstances. A Muslim conqueror being billed a *kafir* in a poetic lament about the destruction of a style of life is a warning against any facile equation of an individual's religiously informed identity with an undifferentiated community of Islam. In this instance, Ansari's identity, Muslim and Bijapuri, leads him to dub the new political dispensation *kufar*, an allusion to the loss of spirituality resulting from conquest and a remapping of physical space, a sentiment shared by other poets of Bijapur. Many wrote long *masnavis* on the devastation of their beloved city and the ensuing displacement. The common bond of Islam did not deter the Muslim poets of Bijapur from perceiving the Mughals as marauders who had destroyed the peace of the city and snuffed out its cultural efflorescence under the Adil Shahis. The local poets of Golconda felt much the same when Aurangzeb's troops marched victoriously into their city. Writing *ashoobia shairi*, they carped and complained about the sins of omission and commission of the new administration while invoking the lost historical glory of Golconda.[6]

In the heartland of Muslim power in northern India, Mirza Rafi Sauda in his *Qasida Shahir-i-Ashoob* wrote movingly about the anarchy, unemployment, corruption, and incompetence of the nobility and the service gentry, and the hunger of the poor that accompanied the collapse of the Mughals. There was no respectable profession left to pursue. In a potent comment on the invasion of sacred space, Sauda noted that the mosques were desolate with only donkeys roped up there.[7] Khwajah Mir Dard (1720–84), otherwise given to mystical contemplation, also rued the dismal state of politics at the twilight of Mughal supremacy. In a poem suffused with nostalgia for the past glory of the Mughals, he compared the changed circumstances to a storm preceding death and yearned to return to his original home, which for him could no longer be Hindustan:

Do you know, O Dard, all these folks,
Whence they came, whither they go?[8]

The themes of uprootedness and lack of direction among Muslims following the attenuation of centralized Mughal power pervades the *ashoobia* poetry of this period. But it is by no means restricted to this genre. It is communitarian to the extent that it bemoans the fate of the Muslims as a whole, but the expression remains that of the individual poet paying homage to the city of his birth or subsequent abode.

The importance of territorial location as a signifier of identity is further underscored by the linking of city names to the surnames of key figures like Akbar Allahabadi, Nazir Akbarabadi, and Mirza Khan Dagh Dehlavi, to name a few. Clearly then, the religious identity of individual Muslims was meshed with the territorial contours of the cities in which they lived. So great was the attachment that many resisted taking up jobs that entailed moving to another city. Altaf Husain Hali (1837–1914) complained bitterly of his brief stint in Lahore, where he was bereft of friends, physically unwell, and utterly miserable. Later, another import from the North West Provinces in the Punjab, Muhammad Husain Azad (1830–1910), castigated Muslim youth for their unenterprising resistance to mobility and extolled the virtues of *hubb-i-watani*, or patriotism. Passion for one's city, encompassing as it did a range of cultural experiences and social relationships, was rarely submerged in the largely imagined identifications of Muslims with India and Islam, despite the fact that the extraterritorial loyalties of Muslims, especially those belonging to the *ashraf*, professional classes, often led them to identify with places and countries of their ancestral origin.

The city's role as one of the primary signifiers of identity confounds any notion that territorial loyalties were absent from the consciousness of India's Muslims. Not only was territorial attachment a common feature of the Muslim psyche, irrespective of class, but together with language, it paved the way for an expansion in the spatial scales of loyalty, be it to a region or India as a whole.

Colonial Subjecthood and Cultural Difference

Despite strong attachments to city, region, and language, a communitarian Muslim identity came to acquire some of its main idioms during the transition from company to crown raj. There had been a sense of religiously informed cultural differences in the subcontinent long before the encounter with Western colonialism, yet even in their social and political performances, religiously informed cultural differences were negotiable and amenable to accommodations. In his pioneering study on colonial adaptations of the communication networks of late-eighteenth- and nineteenth-century northern India, C. A. Bayly notes that precolonial "social enquiry and representation were never communal in the sense that they saw India as a field of conflict of two irreconcilable faiths." Indo-Muslim "governing principles were not 'secular' in the sense that religion was seen as a matter of political indifference,"[9] and the colonial state's avowed policy of neutrality based on political indifference toward religion was easier to proclaim than translate into practice. As a moral stance, it clashed with the imperatives of ruling a culturally alien society. The British needed to appropriate existing symbols of cultural legitimacy, so for them religion could never be a matter of

political indifference. Intrinsic to the search for collaborators and the organization of social control, religion was in the service of the colonial state's
political purposes and thus had qualitatively different consequences from
the political treatment of religion in the preceding centuries.

British perceptions of Indian society as an aggregation of religious communities gave impetus to representations of identity in idioms that emphasized differences, not commonalities, among those who, among other things,
happened to be Muslim, Hindu, or Sikh. However, British social engineering on its own cannot explain the intensity of the process marking Indian
attempts to deploy the colonial state's categories to their own social and
political advantage. Indian subjectivity, whether interpreted in its individual
or communitarian colors, constituted an important, perhaps the most important, dimension in the discourse on identity in the late nineteenth
century.

Frequently accorded the pejorative label of "communalism" in an attempt to distinguish it from the lauded sentiment of "nationalism," this was
a subjectivity that drew upon religion as a major signifier of cultural difference. Still, if religion as faith was a matter of individual disposition, religion
in the service of communitarian culture was as yet a stretch removed from
its subsequent uses as political ideology. The erroneous conflation of the
two in most nationalist Indian and Pakistani reconstructions has obfuscated
the distinction between identity as culture and identity as politics in the
history of Muslims in the subcontinent. It is significant that the politically
loaded term "communalism" did not command the center stage of the public discourse on Muslim identity until after the 1909 formal introduction of
separate electorates at all levels of representation. So it seems appropriate to
probe the narrative inflections and substantive meanings of this discourse
without the teleological and essentializing tendencies retrospectively con-
ferred upon them.

Muslim as Rebel, Muslim as Category

The broad contours of the dialogue between the North Indian Muslim
elite and the colonial state on the one hand and the Hindu press on the
other were outlined soon after the suppression of the revolt of 1857. Colonial
depictions of Muslims as the instigators of the rebellion and the special
targeting of those living in Delhi created a powerful impression of the uneasy

coexistence of Indian Islam with British colonialism. Altaf Hussain Hali, who was to become the leading poet of a Muslim communitarian identity, spoke more as a patriot of Delhi than as a member of a religious community when he lamented the destruction of his beloved city by yet another set of invaders:

Sometimes Turanis looted homes
At others Duranis stole the wealth
Sometimes Nadar slaughtered the people
At others Mahmud made them slaves
Finally the game was won
By a refined nation of the west.[10]

Muhammad Hussain Azad, who like Hali went on to find employment in the colonial administration, contrasted the darkness of an enslaved Hindustan with the refulgence of a victorious England.

Such sentimentality was in contrast to the vitriolic writings of the Anglo-Indian press, determined to show up the Muslims as irremediably disloyal to the crown. This prompted Governor-General Mayo to depute W.W. Hunter to investigate whether Indian Muslims were bound by their religion to rebel against the queen. Published in 1871, Hunter's The Indian Musalmans, using Bengal as the point of reference, examined evidence used by the courts to try some of the principal actors in the so-called Wahhabi insurgency. Although denying that Islamic doctrine propelled all Muslims to rebel against a non-Muslim ruler, Hunter had no doubt that the community in India contained "fanatical" elements, which, unless checked, could stoke the fires of discontent among their ignorant co-religionists and launch a religious crusade. More important for future colonial policy was Hunter's opinion that Muslims, a "race ruined under British rule," harbored "intense feelings of nationality" and were prone to giving periodic expression of this in "warlike enterprise."[11]

External depictions of Muslims as a community united by religion offered an opening to those hoping to represent the special interests that the British believed existed, and sections of the Hindu press, for reasons of their own, saw no reason to deny. That this produced an internally discordant discourse on Muslim identity underscores the gap between epistemological certitudes and the existential fluidities relating to the community of Islam in India.

Among the many claimants to the leadership of India's heterogeneous

Muslim population was Sayyid Ahmad Khan, who took it upon himself to shepherd a straying flock of co-religionists into greener pastures within the colonial system. Although education absorbed most of his energies, he also manipulated the press to project a conception of Muslimness consistent with the colonial state's epistemology of communitarianism. The *Aligarh Institute Gazette*, which he launched in 1866, disseminated ideas about a Muslim community that was both Islamic and Indian. By 1876, the paper was jubilantly reporting the changing spirit of the times. Prejudices and superstitions were giving way to "national patriotism and friendly feelings." Sunnis and Shi'as had buried their differences and were at one in their support for Turkey. Muslims had every reason to "congratulate themselves" as the "feeling of unity of nation and religion now animates the two great divisions of Islam in matters which concern their common interests."[12]

It was simpler for Muslims to rise above their internal differences on matters concerning co-religionists in Turkey or Persia than to practice unity in religion within India. Remarking on the likely effects of the declaration of jihad by the Sheikh al-Islam of Constantinople a few months later, the *Aligarh Institute Gazette* thought it unlikely that Indian Muslims would rush to do battle with infidels. At most they would spread their prayer mats and earnestly urge Allah to come to the assistance of Islam. After all, even the most bigoted Muslim could not deny that "peace and security . . . under British rule," though not "free from faults," was "not to be found in any Muhammadan kingdom on earth."[13]

Although Indian Muslims identified with their co-religionists the world over, they were firmly situated in India where it was British rule—not the temporal and spiritual authority of the Ottoman caliphate—that was the salient reality. Sayyid Ahmad Khan, along with poets like Hali and Azad, repeatedly had to take up a cudgel against any attempt to confuse the identity of religion with the identity of country. The two ideas were different but not irreconcilable.

In 1874, in his poem *Hubb-i-Watan* (Love of the Motherland), Hali wrote feelingly about the need for a patriotism that was more substantive than mere self-interested attachment to one's country. A true patriot was one who regarded all the inhabitants of India, whether Muslim, Hindu, Buddhist, Brahmo Samaj, Shi'a, Sunni, or any other interdenominational sect as one:

If you want your country's well being
Don't look upon any compatriot as a stranger[14]

Hali regretted that in India there were rifts in the ranks of scholars, conflicts among Hindu pandits, and bickering among the doctors of medicine. Each and every one had a separate agenda.[15]

In 1878, Sayyid Ahmad Khan objected strongly to a speech made by Lord Northbrook that implied Muslims were "disloyal subjects of the Crown." It was true that Muslims were concerned with the fate of Turkey as "one nation sees another nation of the same creed drifting towards ruin and destruction." However, if Indian Muslims disliked British rule, they did not like the rule of other Western powers, any Muslim country, or even of their erstwhile sovereigns any better. "The Musalmans of India may wish to have national rule in India," but this was "a feeling which they share in common with all noble races" and could not be classified as disloyalty.[16]

The appearance of Hali's magnum opus *Musaddas-i-Hali* in 1879, was on the face of it a crowning achievement of Sayyid Ahmad Khan's school in deploying the poetic medium to proclaim a distinctive Muslim cultural identity. Yet although making much of the past cultural and scientific achievements of Islam, the poem was a stinging criticism of an Indian Muslim community that had lost its moorings due to educational backwardness, internal jealousies, religious bigotry, aristocratic avarice, and cultural decadence. Having lost sovereignty, wealth, intellect, and self-respect, Muslims existed by virtue of their religion alone.[17] Like many among the North Indian *ashraf* classes, Hali considered Muslims to be the descendants of foreign conquerors. But his solution for the Muslims did not lie in severing all ties with India. As he made clear in the majestically crafted *Shikwah-i-Hind* (Complaint to India), composed in 1888, the dilemma facing Muslims was the loss of the distinctiveness that had once given them a measure of dignity and humanity. "We were fire, O Hind," he exclaimed, "you've turned us into ash."[18] None of this was the fault of India, which had not only welcomed the Muslims, but also bestowed dominion and a plethora of gifts upon them. Hali instead blamed *qismat* (fate), which had brought Islam to the subcontinent and made certain that, unlike the Greeks, the Muslim armies did not turn away from its frontiers in defeat.[19]

Challenging Hali's questionable reading of the history of Islam in India or his spurious representations of Muslims as scions of foreign immigrants is to miss out on the richness of the poetic nuances. As the fire to ashes metaphor indicates, Hali recognized the indelible imprint of India on the Muslims. He could use his poetic imagination to evoke the past but not re-enact history. Simply intended to invigorate his dejected co-religionists, not erect walls of antipathy against non-Muslims, these self-projections of a member of the North Indian *ashraf* class were susceptible to serious misinterpretation by those who questioned Muslim loyalty to their adopted homeland.

Britain's repeated alarms and excursions in the Islamic world were invariably reflected in an ongoing and bitter public debate about the exact significance of a nonterritorially based religious bond for the Indian Muslims. The reactions of Muslims to accusations that they lacked attachment to India were predictable, though seldom uniform. Few were ready to disavow an affinity with co-religionists in other parts of the world. Incapable of winning the numbers game in India, the sense of belonging to a larger community of Islam was more in the way of a defensive reaction than a display of religious zeal. With the loss of political sovereignty and the emphasis on communities of religion, these Muslim populations outside India provided a psychological reinforcement for those consigned to the category of a minority. This, rather than any alleged religiously determined disloyalty to India or the British raj, explains the attitudes of the Muslim *ashraf* toward co-religionists beyond the territorial confines of the subcontinent.

Yet care was taken to stress the difference between an attachment to Ottoman Turkey and other Muslim countries such as Afghanistan. Support for Turkey emanated from a sense of religious duty toward the sultan, who was regarded by some, but not all, as the spiritual and temporal symbol of authority for all Muslims. The same could not be said of Muslim sentiments toward Afghanistan. In late 1878, worsening relations between the government of India and the amir of Afghanistan prompted a Muslim to argue in the *Delhi Gazette* that his co-religionists were secretly hoping for an Afghan victory as a first step toward establishing Islamic supremacy in India. This was promptly refuted by the *Awadh Akhbar*, published by Munshi Nawal Kishore, which asked whether the writer had expressed his own opinion or that of the Muslim community. Indian Muslims were "loyal and faithful subjects," preferring the "just and peaceful British rule to a barbarous and tyrannical Muhammadan government."[20] Two years later another paper asserted that, although Indian Muslims looked upon "Afghans as robbers . . . and treacherous people," they had the greatest respect for the Turkish sultan. A declaration of war by Britain on Ottoman Turkey would not incite Muslims to revolt, but it would be inadvisable for the government to ignore their feelings on the matter.[21] The *Aligarh Institute Gazette* thought it was a pure anachronism for Indian Muslims to consider the Turkish sultan as their caliph, even in the religious sense. Shi'as did not recognize any caliphs and regarded the twelve imams as their religious leaders. Sunnis only acknowledged the five successors to the Prophet as caliphs. All claims to the caliphate were false, and it was absurd to recite the name of any Muslim sovereign in the Friday *khutba*.[22]

For the most part, subtlety and pragmatism marked Muslim attitudes toward co-religionists in the Islamic world. Seeing extra-territorial loyalties as proof of the "pan-Islamic" sentiments of Muslims ignores the myriad other connections that intersected with their religiously informed cultural identity. Insofar as the term "pan-Islamism" refers to the idea of Islamic universalism, there can be no denying its significance in Muslim consciousness. But like the term "Wahhabi" and the more recent construction, "fundamentalism," the term "pan-Islamism" was deployed primarily to underscore the inherently fanatical and disloyal nature of Britain's Muslim subjects. It cannot be used uncritically. The *Mihiri Darkhshan* reacted ferociously to an article by Sayyid Ahmad Khan attacking the khedive of Egypt, in which he had said that Muslims could make for rebellious subjects and were generally oppressive as rulers. But the piece demonstrated the ability to distinguish between the convictions of a community and the views of an individual by rejecting the pronouncements as no more than a hypocritical attempt to win favor with the British. If Sayyid Ahmad had been "poor and expressed such sentiments," his loyalty might be "free from suspicion."[23]

The meshing of religion and culture with politics did not mean that all Indians were inherently bigoted in varying measures. Religiously informed cultural identities emphasized a sense of difference without foreclosing the possibility of Indians sharing common sentiments and coming together when circumstances were propitious for united action. There were, to be sure, disagreements on when unity outweighed all other considerations, but these were not simply because of the inexorable nature of religious distinctions in Indian society. Hindus were pitted against Hindus no less than Muslims against Muslims on how and when to bury their internal differences and forge a common front against the raj. Individual preferences derived from class and regional location. Membership in a religious community alone did not determine the responses of Indians in their infinite varieties and combinations. It is for all these reasons that the pejorative term "communalism" cannot explain the attitudes of Indian Muslims who, taking their cues from a Sayyid Ahmad Khan or an Ameer Ali, opted to stay away from the Indian National Congress founded in 1885.

Representing Communities and Nations

Despite his resolute stand against the Congress, Sayyid Ahmad consistently exhorted Muslims against cultural exclusivism and the curse of religious bigotry. Being Hindu or Muslim was a matter of "internal faith" and had "nothing to do with mutual friendship and external conditions." Quite as much as the Hindus, Muslims too "consider[ed] India as [their] homeland." For a man who did so much in shaping the notion of a distinctive Muslim cultural identity, Sayyid Ahmad confessed that by living together with Hindus in India, "the blood of both have changed, the colour of both have become similar. . . . We mixed with each other so much that we produced a new language—Urdu, which was neither our language nor theirs."[24]

Sayyid Ahmad's opposition to the Congress had less to do with the threats it might come to pose to the religious identity of Muslims than with the cultural pretensions and different claims of the North Indian *ashraf* class that he represented. He saw the Congress as a creation of the more advanced Bengali "nation" and not of Hindus as such. Ignoring the uneven impact of colonial economic and educational policies in the different regions of India, "the Bengalis [had] made a most unfair and unwarrantable interference with my nation." He called upon Hindus of the North West Provinces to "cultivate friendship" with upper class Muslims and "let those who live in Bengal eat up their own heads." Speaking first as a regionalist, he stressed the temperamental and material differences between Bengalis and the "people of *this country*." Shifting gears to show his religious biases, he warned that even in Bengal the tactics of the Congress would result in enmity between the Hindus and Muslims who constituted half the population of the province.[25]

Any concessions to the demands put forward by the Bengalis, who were unfamiliar with the methods of government, would destroy the peace of India. Giving full play to his aristocratic airs, Sayyid Ahmad thought members of the viceroy's council should be drawn from those of "high social position" and "good breeding," as no one wanted to be placed under the authority of a man of lesser origin, even if he possessed the requisite educational credentials. The Congress's demand for competitive examinations for the civil service would prove disastrous for Muslims, who were educationally handicapped. It was a sure recipe for placing the whole of India under the rule of Bengalis, "who at the sight of a table knife would crawl under . . . [a] chair"; the Rajputs and the "brave Pathans" would have none of this.[26]

The long and short of all this was that Sayyid Ahmad believed Muslims should refrain from all politics and concentrate their energies on education. But Sayyid Ahmad was not above voicing his opinions on political matters. He considered Ripon's introduction of the elective principle to local and municipal bodies in 1882 inimical to "Muslim interests." Equating Muslim with *ashraf* interests, he argued that this would be "like a game of dice, in which one man had four dice and the other only one." No Muslim would get elected and the "whole Council will consist of Babu So-and-So Chuckerbutty." The same would be true of Hindus in "our Province," even though they were relatively better off than the Muslims.[27]

In urging Muslims to reject politics and make humble submissions to the colonial authorities, Sayyid Ahmad's main objective was to ensure continued government support for the Muhammadan Anglo-Oriental College. This was the line of an educationist rather than a wily political operator with a hidden agenda for a religiously informed cultural nationalism. Frequent references to the Muslim *qaum* in his speeches have given rise to the notion that it was Sayyid Ahmad Khan who fathered the "two nation" theory, yet a careful reading of his speeches makes it plain that he used the term interchangeably to refer to the Indian "nation," as well as the Muslim "community." On one occasion, Sayyid Ahmad explained that in using the term *qaum*, he meant the inhabitants of a country, even though they might have distinctive characteristics. Just a year before the formation of the Congress, he had stated unequivocally that "Hindus and Mussalmans are words of religious significance, otherwise Hindus, Mussalmans and Christians who live in this country constitute one nation." In his "opinion all men are one"; he did "not like religion, community or group to be identified with a nation."[28] That a call for Muslim nonparticipation in the early Congress should have qualified Sayyid Ahmad as a separatist and anti-nationalist underscores the political nature of the distinction between a communalist and noncommunalist in retrospectively constructed nationalist pasts.

Sayyid Ahmad Khan may have been the most prominent spokesman of a regionally based North Indian Muslim elite, but his leadership had never gone unchallenged by the very Muslim *ashraf* classes on whose behalf he made his loudest appeals. By the late 1880s, Britain's imperial policies in India and new colonial conquests in the Islamic world were leading more and more Muslims to eschew Sayyid Ahmad's policy of nonparticipation in the Congress and stolid loyalty to the raj. This was evident in the increasing attendance of Muslims from the North West Provinces at the annual sessions of the Congress.[29] Encouraged by the trend, Badruddin Tyabji, a Bombay-based lawyer from the Bohra community who in 1887 became the first Muslim president of the Congress, tried parrying Sayyid Ahmad's objections to the "national" claims of the Congress. Tyabji was "not aware of any one regarding the whole of India as one Nation." India consisted of "numerous communities or nationals" that had "peculiar problems" of their own. The Congress had been established to discuss only those issues that affected all communities.[30] Far more significant was Tyabji's readiness to accept that if Muslims were indeed opposed to the Congress then it could not be regarded as "a general or a National Congress," and should suspend its annual meetings until the matter was resolved.[31]

Muslims like Mahboob Alam, the owner of the influential Lahore paper *Paisa Akhbar*, whose circulation in 1896 stood at a booming 10,000, agreed that Sayyid Ahmad's policy of nonparticipation in the Congress was designed to win favors from the colonial state. Many educated Muslims supported the Congress in principle but were unable to express this openly because they were in government service. Syed Ameer Ali was an employee of the colonial state, and Sayyid Mahmud, who privately sympathized with the aims and objects of the Congress, did not publicly oppose his father from a sense of filial duty. Their lack of autonomy from the colonial state explained Muslim attitudes.

The *Akhbar-i-Am* tried putting spanners in the wheels of both the Aligarh and the Arya Samaj bandwagons by asserting that the former was "no more represent[ative of] the social and political views of the Indian Muhammadans than the Diyanand Anglo-Vedic College . . . [was] of the Hindus [sic]." It was ironic that Sayyid Ahmad Khan, pronounced by the ulama to be an infidel, should have the audacity to declare Muslims who joined the Congress to be traitors to Islam. Seizing upon the principal contradiction in the contending strands of the narrative of Muslim identity, it maintained that if Muslims of the "old school" were the "true followers of Islam and those of the new school the reverse," then "the first sect that deserves to be excluded from the pale of that religion are the followers of Sir Sayyid Ahmad Khan."[32] Defining the rules of inclusion and exclusion in the community of Islam was not an appropriate vocation for a paper closely associated with the opinion of urban Punjabi Hindus. But by then Muharram Ali Chishti, the disputatious editor of the *Rafiq-i-Hind*, had ditched Sayyid Ahmad and hitched his wagons to the Congress instead. In Chishti's opinion, Muslims of the Aligarh school "did not represent the Indian Muhammadans" who regarded them as heretics. The sudden volte face of so vocal a defender of Sayyid Ahmad was attributed to Chishti's success in wangling his way to an important position in the pro-Congress Anjuman-i-Numaniya of Lahore.[33]

Changing personal circumstances made it relatively easier for upper-class Muslims to break ranks with Sayyid Ahmad Khan. Since 1895, Shibli Nu-mani (1857–1914) had been publicly opposing his old patron's policy of Muslim nonparticipation in the Congress. Differences with his colleagues at Aligarh led Shibli to help found the Nadwat-ul-Ulama in 1898, an insti-tution that he believed would give a boost to his personal aspirations of greater status as an intellectual leader of India's Muslims.[34] These hopes were belied by the stiff opposition his variant of modernist theology elicited among the ulama. At odds with the Western-educated Muslims of Aligarh for whom Islam was a matter more of culture than of religious doctrine, Shibli was institutionally and intellectually isolated enough to take an in-dependent line in political matters. In his post-Aligarh phase, Shibli was a frequent visitor at the Bombay residence of Begum Attiya Faizi, a woman whose superior intellect was later to charm no less a person than Muham-mad Iqbal. Here Shibli befriended Badruddin Tyabji, the first Muslim pres-ident of the Congress and a close relative of Attiya Faizi.[35] Shibli's exposure to the Tyabji family undoubtedly contributed to his political thinking at a time when events overshadowed Sayyid Ahmad Khan's intellectual influ-ence, if not legacy.

Compartmentalizing the Muslim: Politics as Identity

By the turn of the century, the idea of a distinct Indian Muslim interest that needed representing was regularly proclaimed in petitions aimed at winning an audience with colonial authorities. As yet there was no concerted move afoot to organize the faithful politically outside a select group con-sisting primarily of Urdu-knowing, if not Urdu-speaking, Muslims. Even as far afield as Bengal, it was Muslims with knowledge of Urdu and Persian who seemed most eager to find common cause with their co-religionists in northern India and the Punjab. However, class remained a formidable bar-rier. For the vast majority of Indian Muslims outside the realm of privilege bestowed by the colonial state, the concerns and activities of Muslim *ashraf* classes were for the most part distant, if not altogether irrelevant.

Ideological and class differences among Muslims meant that opposition to the Congress did not immediately result in a positive political alliance of their own. The Lahore-based newspaper *Sada-i-Hind* asserted in 1901 that the opinions of the "English-speaking Muhammadans" were not the "united voice of the country," and giving the Aligarh party the lead in political matters was thoroughly "undesirable."[36] Here was a powerfully enunciated challenge against Western educated Muslims as a whole, and the North Indian–based spokesmen of the community in particular.

Delighted with the turn of events, the *Tribune* dubbed the trend a "Revolt against Aligarh." Muslims were no longer prepared to heed the advice of Aligarh in political matters, which was "no small gain."[37] Unfortunately, the "new school of Muslims" neither wanted to work in "partnership" nor for a "common purpose." This was what distinguished them from the Congress, an organization "open to all and for the benefit of all who [called] India their home." There was no basis to the Muslim fear that as a minority they would be out-voted in the Congress. Care had been taken to insert a clause in the constitution to throw out any motion opposed by the members of any community. Still, it was Muslim loyalty that was the biggest barrier to their participation in the nationalist organization. The "loyal and brave descendants of the Pathan and Moghul rulers of India," instead of "joining the chattering 'Babus' in their disloyal agitation," preferred to "strengthen the hands of the authorities." Muslims would be more in "consonance with their own traditions" if they were "the guiding power in all political movements" and did not separate themselves in the interests of their own community. It was heartening that in the "general body" of Muslims there was "an awakening to a sense of national, as distinguished from sectional duty."[38]

Yet as the reaction to the partition of Bengal and the Swadeshi (own country) movement after 1905 made all too apparent, the "national" and "sectional" dimensions of Muslim concerns were closely interwoven with individual choices. The nawab of Dacca's brother, Khwajah Atiqulla, submitted a petition signed by 25,000 people to the government, arguing that as a community Muslims were opposed to the partition of the province. Atiqulla's relations with the nawab were less than cordial, and he was promptly charged with "selfish motives."[39] In a significant demonstration of their position, the Muslim-managed press in Bengal for the most part chose not to join the agitation to unsettle the settled fact of partition. The posture owed a great deal to their misgivings about the methods and aims of the Swadeshi nationalists. Even in the Punjab there was consternation about the spirit of the Swadeshi movement—it seemed to suggest that Hindus did "not wish Mussalmans well."[40]

At a time when many Hindu newspapers were inveighing against the meeting of the Simla deputation of Muslim notables with Lord Minto, this was tactical politics. Less tactful was the "discovery that Hindus [were] striving to trample [Muslims] under foot."[41] In December 1906, the formation of the All-India Muslim League to safeguard "Muslim interests" widened the breach between the supporters and detractors of Congress's conception of the Indian "nation." With constitutional reforms on the anvil, these contests, instead of encouraging a modification of the Western construct of the "nation," worked to cast Indian differences into the mold of exclusionary communitarianism and inclusionary nationalism. As the debate in the vernacular press indicates, the communitarian appeal to the minority was stripped of the inclusionary ideal largely as a reaction to the exclusionary implications in nationalist self-projections of the majority.

Adding its bit to the political lexicon on majority and minority interests, the *Vakil* argued that if self-government was granted "Hindus would be certain to drive the Muhammadan *malechhas* out of the country." This may have been putting the cart before the horse, but there was no getting away from the fact that "religious bigotry and racial hatred" had "found their way even into the public offices in India."[42] Under ordinary circumstances, such an alarming discovery might have had a sobering effect, but with the British about to initiate a fresh round of constitutional proposals, it was used to justify the demand that Muslims be given separate and adequate representation in the provincial and local councils under the new reforms.

Instead of drawing upon normative Islamic political theory, the Muslim upper classes took refuge in memories of a lost sovereignty. Assertions of a Muslim political identity were based on arguments that, although fewer in number than the Hindus, they derived their special importance from having been the "rulers of India for seven hundred years" and continued to contribute a great deal towards the defense of the country. It followed that Muslims in the provincial legislative councils should be "placed on a footing of equality with their Hindu fellow-countrymen."[43]

Race, Nation, and Nationality

In 1909, the Morley-Minto reforms conceded the principle of separate electorates to Muslims at all levels of representation. First instituted in 1880 in elections to municipal committees, the reforms were initially confined to the United Provinces and Bengal, becoming the norm in the Punjab only after 1919. From the point of view of competing communitarian discourses, the colonial willingness to grant separate electorates proved to be more important than its actual extension in different regions of India. Separate electorates institutionalized the split between the majority and minority components of the nation, which had been a recurring motif in the narratives on communitarian identities since the late nineteenth century. The compartmentalization of Muslims into an all-India political category was a watershed event with disastrous implications for Congress's variety of inclusionary nationalism. In a measure insisted upon by the All-India Muslim League and conceded by the British, separate electorates assigned Muslims the status of a constitutional minority. Yet here was a minority differentiated along regional, economic, and ideological lines, with no history of organized political activity. It was expected to reap benefits from separate electorates in an imperial system of collaboration and control geared to localizing and provincializing political horizons. Until such time as the British were inclined to concede power at the all-India center, being a protected minority was an uncertain resource at best. Although local men of power were spared the trouble of competing with non-Muslims for positions on the reformed councils, separate electorates within an arena of formal politics based on a restricted franchise offered nothing to the vast majority of disenfranchised Muslims. For all practical purposes, separate electorates were a class concession advanced in the name of a religious community.

Because Muslims were in a majority in the northwestern and the northeastern extremities of the subcontinent, recognizing them as an all-India minority was fraught with consequences for regionally specific discourse on communitarian interests and, by extension, on the politics of identity. For instance, in the Punjab, where separate electorates in 1909 affected only one or two municipalities, Muslim- and Hindu-owned newspapers doctored the debate on majority and minority rights to suit their own class and provincial purposes. By the time the dust had settled, Punjabis had fine tuned the competing narratives on race,[44] nation, and nationality that were communitarian in the regional rather than the supra-regional sense.

At the subcontinental level, the politics of Muslims continued to be informed by local and regional requirements rather than by the unities provided by affiliation with a common religion. Muslims could evolve a common sense of nationality only through a conscious reconfiguring of their individual self-identification with the religious community. Until the turn of the century, the narratives on communitarian identity projected by the press and publications emphasized culture as difference without elucidating a distinctively Indian Muslim conception of "nation" and "nationalism." Even those subscribing to the ideal of a universal Muslim ummah for political reasons, and scorned by Western observers as pan-Islamicists, were more anti-colonial than anti-national in orientation. For most Muslims, belonging to a larger community of Islam was a source of strength for their position in India. They most frequently countered the charge of extra-territorial loyalties by confirming Muslim allegiance to the British raj or contesting the exclusionary tendencies in the Hindu majoritarian discourse on the Indian "nation." Although rejecting the Congress, Western-educated Muslim opinion did not consider their extra-territorial loyalty to be an insurmountable barrier to forging a common Indian nationality. It was location in this nationality, not the concept itself, which most exercised the minds of Muslims who took it upon themselves either to question or accept Congress's claims to represent all of India.

Muslim ideas on "nation" and "nationality" emerged out of a searing criticism of Western nationalism inspired by Muhammad Iqbal (1873–1938), a middle-class poet and philosopher of the Punjab of Kashmiri ancestry. Despite the overwhelming emphasis on the Islamic ummah in Iqbal's mature philosophy and poetry, the entire corpus of his work is a celebration of individual freedom as much as it is of the Muslim community. In a poem written in 1903 entitled Zuhd aur Rindi (Continence and Debauchery), Iqbal, in a critically self-analytical mood, recounts an exchange with his neighbor, a maulana, who berated him for deviating from the Islamic path. How could he be a paragon of Muslimness if in his eyes a Hindu was not an infidel? Iqbal admitted his heterodoxies and departures from social conventions. He confessed a liking for music and the company of prostitutes even while being absorbed by the Qur'an and other tenets of the faith. Iqbal's Islam was not the same as anyone else's.[45] As a man of God, he was neither of the East nor the West; his home was neither Delhi, nor Isfahan, nor Samarqand:

> I always say what I deem to be the truth
> I'm neither the mosque's supplicant nor culture's slave.[46]

Iqbal ridiculed the Muslim religious leadership, the mullah in particular, whose misrepresentations of Islam crushed individual initiative and stunted the community's potential. Because he was at the root of religious discord, the mullah had no place in paradise, where there was neither mosque, nor temple, nor church.[47] Instead of heeding the mullah or even the ascetic mystics of Islam, Iqbal urged Muslims to follow the promptings of their own hearts in search of *iman* (faith). The liberating thrust of his poetic vision of the ideal relationship between the individual and the community was a source of inspiration for those seeking to fashion a Muslim response to the twin challenges of colonial modernity and Western nationalism.

Although he started his poetic career lauding the idea of *wataniyat* (love of the homeland), after visiting Europe in the first decade of the twentieth century, Iqbal became a hardened opponent of not only territorial nationalism, but also Western materialism and excessive rationalism. Echoing the thoughts of the great Bengali poet and philosopher Rabindranath Tagore, Iqbal considered aggressive territorial nationalism, and not religion per se, to be the source of all modern conflicts. In the *Milli Tarana*, or the anthem of the Muslim community, Iqbal invoked the ideal of Islamic universalism when he wrote:

> *China and Arabia are ours, India is ours*
> *We are Muslim, the whole world is our homeland*[48]

Unencumbered by territory, race, caste, color, or nationality, the *millat* for Iqbal was the ideal community with antecedents going as far back as the Prophet of Islam.

As he explained to a student audience at Aligarh University in 1910, the Muslim community had its own "peculiar conception of nationality," or *asabiyyat*, which was limited neither by territorial space nor by linguistic or economic interest. Based wholly on a subjective feeling of belonging to the community of the Prophet Muhammad, the Muslim sense of self did "not necessarily imply any feeling of hatred against other nationalities." The Muslim community was structured by the religious ideal, though not by its "theological centralisation" that would "unnecessarily limit the liberty of the individual."[49] An affective community like the Muslim one, far from being an irrational or abstract entity, was a product of a social synthesis flowing from shared spiritual and cultural values. To become a "member of the Muslim community," an individual had not only to profess an "unconditional belief in the religious principle," but also "thoroughly assimilate the culture of Islam." This alone would create the uniformity of outlook and values that "sharply defines our community and transforms it into a corporate individual [with] a definite purpose and ideal of its own." What Muslim society needed were individuals who, while holding fast to their own and resisting all that was inimical to its values, selectively assimilated the good features found in other communities.[50]

The core of Iqbal's message to the Muslims of India, then, was individual self-affirmation (*khudi*) leading to purposeful collective action. This was the natural progression for a people whose religion demanded submission to no other than Allah and identification with the *millat* or the supra-territorial community of the faithful bound by the teachings of the Prophet Muhammad. Yet although Iqbal's poetic vision undoubtedly inspired many of his co-religionists, its transformation into a dynamic principle of Indian Muslim identity laid it open to multiple interpretations and appropriations.

Iqbal wrote some of his most powerful poetry on Islamic universalism at a time when the reversal of the partition of Bengal, Italy's invasion of Tripoli, the war in the Balkans and the loss of many Muslim lives in a dispute over a mosque in Kanpur had riveted the attention of his co-religionists. His anguish at the impotence of Muslims, demonstrated by the European pincer movement against Ottoman Turkey, was shared by Shibli Numani, Mohamed Ali (1878–1931), the editor of the *Comrade* and the *Hamdard*, Ab'ul-Kalam Azad (1888–1958), whose *al-Hilal* appeared in 1912 from Calcutta, and Maulana Zafar Ali Khan (1873–1956), who gave a new lease on life to Punjabi Muslim journalism through his organ the *Zamindar*, and many others. But there were also significant differences in the way each proposed to handle the practical issue of organizing and directing the Muslim community's response to the changing context of politics in India and the Islamic world at large.

Shibli was not nearly as gifted a poet as Iqbal, but his firm grounding in Islamic history gave him a better sense of the problems posed by the discrepancy between the normative ideals and social practices of Muslims. Although he too looked beyond the frontiers of the subcontinent for ideational and spiritual nourishment, Shibli set his sights squarely on the predicament of Muslims within the spatial context of India. He rejected religion as the code for Muslim participation in politics, and in a series of polemical poems he berated the All-India Muslim League for its servile posture toward the British raj, which contradicted the very spirit of self-government instituted by the colonial rulers. Subjects had every right to express their opinions and criticize their rulers. Politics by definition meant balancing the "mutual demands of the government and the subjects." It was definitely not about the internal quarrels of the ruled.[51] According to Shibli, forging a joint front with Hindus was a better bet for Indian Muslims than futile hopes of uniting the ummah.

He blamed Sayyid Ahmad for stunting the growth of political consciousness among Muslims and turning them into a nation of cowards. By contrast, Hindus were making strides in the political field and extracting concessions from the colonial government. Shibli deplored the league's mendicancy; it was an upper class tamasha, a circus sanctioned by the government and paid for by wealthy benefactors like the Aga Khan and a pack of groveling Muslim landlords of northern India.[52] Although accepting the Muslim League as an established fact, Shibli wanted to see it thoroughly reformed and taking bolder political stands. It could do so only by shedding its "minority complex" and allying with the Congress to strike for substantive self-government.

Mohamed Ali was of a decidedly different opinion. One of the founding fathers of the All-India Muslim League, he chastised the "nationalists" of the Congress for refusing to accept that the only sort of patriotism "in vogue in this country [was] exclusively Hindu or Muslim." The educated Hindu "communal patriot" had no qualms about using the symbols of Hinduism for political mobilization and the construction of Indian "nationality," ignoring the presence of seventy million Muslims in the country. Using *swaraj* as the "war cry," the Hindu "communal patriot" simply "[refused] to give quarter to the Muslims unless the latter quietly [shuffled] off his individuality and [became] completely Hinduised." For all the talk of nationhood and unity, the "organs of Hindu 'nationalism' regarded Muslims as "a troublesome irrelevance," as if there was "no vital differences of feeling, temper, ideals and standpoints." Muslims were deemed to be a trifle "too clannish," and were rapped on the knuckles for being lost in "a world of unsubstantial shadows" and reprimanded for being only "dimly aware" of "such great secular causes as self-government and nationality." The goal of the Hindu patriot, Mohamed Ali charged, was nothing short of building a "modern shrine" in India exclusively for his own purposes.[53]

Implicit in Mohamed Ali's flaming rhetoric was a view of Indian nationality that genuinely sought to accommodate cultural differences. An ardent admirer of Iqbal's poetry and a believer of Islamic universalism by political choice, Mohamed Ali challenged the "secular nationalist" agenda that surreptitiously, if selectively, absorbed the Hindu ethos while squeezing out the Muslim dimensions. Urdu was a case in point. In their desire for a common language for India, the Hindus were demanding the replacement of Urdu with the Nagari script. This was tantamount to depriving future generations of Muslims of the capacity to study their own religious and literary heritage and to insulate India from other Asian countries. To make language the litmus test of patriotism was "sheer imbecility." "Islam was neither insular nor peninsular," Mohamed Ali declared. If it was true that "Muslims lacked something in their love for the land they lived in," then it was truer still that they had been "charged with a little too much of it for the lands of others." In adopting Urdu as their vernacular, a language that was not Islam's gift to India but vice versa, Muslims had shown sufficient evidence of affection for the cultural mores of their adopted homeland. They would not give up the language or the script merely to assuage the forces of "narrow and exclusive 'Nationalism' which [was] growing more and more militant every day."[54]

Citing instances of Hindu exclusivity was a strong rallying point for countering the charge of Muslim exclusivity in the debate over the future of Urdu. Even those given to less impassioned statements about their distinctively Muslim cultural identity resented the stigmatizing of Urdu as an alien implant on Indian soil. The issue of Urdu demonstrated just how well culture as difference could serve the sense of Muslimness and Indianness at one and the same time. Abdul Halim Sharar (1860–1920), who began his career as a journalist and went on to establish himself as one of the foremost Urdu literary figures of the early twentieth century, defended the language of his identity as he claimed a share of Indian nationality. On 30 September 1916, speaking at an Urdu conference in Lucknow, Sharar likened the development of the language to the life history of the *qaum's* greatness, whose "branches came out, blossomed, separated, met, moved, grew, fought, collided and then again became one." Deploying the Aryan race theory, he maintained that the coming of the Muslims to India had reunited the two branches of the Arya *qaum*. He objected to the efforts underway to establish that the people of Hindustan were the lost brethren of Europeans and to present the Muslims as an alien *qaum*. More influenced by the Persians than the Arabs, Indian Muslims did not trace their genealogy to the Semites, and were part and parcel of the Arya *qaum*. Even the Arabs who made India their home adopted local languages and blended into local society.

Urdu was a symbol of centuries of interaction between Hindus and Muslims. The role of Persian and Arabic in the development of Urdu was that of the father, although the linguistic antecedents of Hindi had mothered the child. To erase this fact was to forget the era when friendship and close relations existed between the two religious faiths. Sharar conceded that in retaliation for the promotion of Hindi, Muslims had begun claiming Urdu as their language. But Hindus had better claims to Urdu than Muslims did because more of them had written in the language. Instead of destroying a common asset in pursuit of petty jealousies, Hindus and Muslims should together rear their magnificent progeny.[55]

Sharar's pleadings underline the continuing attempts by some Muslims to situate themselves within the mainstream of Indian nationalism. One solitary individual who deserves a special mention in this respect is Mohammad Ali Jinnah (1876–1948), a Bombay-based lawyer with an uncommon aversion to all forms of Islamic orthodoxy. Firmly on the side of moderate nationalists in the Congress, Jinnah was the only Muslim of repute who had opposed separate electorates. More cosmopolitan than communitarian in outlook, Jinnah's career exemplifies the constant reconfiguring of the balance between the individual and the community in Islam. Starting off on the outer margins of the Muslim community, Jinnah negotiated his space in all-India politics by becoming the "ambassador of Hindu-Muslim unity" and then gradually reconstituting himself as the foremost individual protagonist of the Muslim League's "two nation" theory. It is a telling example of how the individual Muslim made or unmade his community of association in practice without explicitly denying the ideal of the Islamic ummah.

The life and times of Abu'l-Kalam Azad (1888–1958) provide another extraordinary tale of the infinite permutations of the relations of an individual to the Muslim community. Regarded by many as the most important of Muslim "traditionalists," the shifting sands of Azad's religious and political beliefs demonstrate the paradoxes of Muslim identity in the subcontinental context.

An individualist like Jinnah, Azad's role in the history of the Muslims of India indicates what passes as "communalism" in South Asian historiography. Jinnah, the secularist and nationalist slipped a few notches when he began opposing the mixing of religion and politics by the Gandhian Congress in the early 1920s and fell from grace altogether when he stole the mantle of the Muslim community in the mid-1930s. By contrast, Azad is showered with accolades in Indian nationalist historiography for his steadfast opposition to the Muslim League's inexorable drift toward separatism and communalism.

Unlike Jinnah, who never affected any knowledge of Muslim history or philosophy, Islam was the vital component in Azad's identity and the main source of his intellectual and political orientation. In 1904, while still under the influence of Sayyid Ahmad Khan's reformist ideas, Azad made a reference to the Congress as a Hindu body.[56] A precocious young man of exceptional learning, Azad's early ideas were laced with the very Muslim exclusivity that was later to disqualify many of his less Islamically inclined co-religionists from the nationalist mainstream. In a poem published in *al-Hilal* at the time of the Kanpur massacre, Azad echoed Iqbal while expressing alarm at European machinations against Muslims:

> *With whose blood is Tripoli flooded? Of the Muslims*
> *Who, slain, lie quivering on the plains of Persia? The Muslims*
> *Whose blood flows in the Balkan Peninsula? The Muslims*
> *The land of Hindustan is athirst. It demands blood*
> *Whose? The Muslims*
> *At last it rained blood in Kanpur and the dust of Hindustan*
>   *is saturated with it*
> *Oh you Muslims: Where will you now reside?*[57]

Article after article in *al-Hilal* finds Azad preaching the ideal of Islamic brotherhood, declaring Muslim participation in politics a religious duty, and exhorting his co-religionists to organize themselves as a separate community under their own imam or amir. "There will be nothing left of us if we separate politics from religion," Azad wrote in his paper. More illuminating still was the categorical assertion that Muslims "need not follow the Hindus to determine their political policy." In fact, they "need not join any party" at all; they are the "ones to make the world join their party and follow their path."[58] Echoing Iqbal's despondency in the *Shikwa* and *Jawab-i-Shikwa*, Azad was crestfallen to realize that Muslims were "not united and organized as a community"; they had "no *quaid*" (leader) and amounted to "rabble scattered among the population of India"; they were living an "un-Islamic and irreligious life."[59] An exclusivism matched by an implicit sense of superiority was tempered only by Azad's consistently anti-colonial posture and support for the Congress.

With the exception of Azad and Iqbal, all the individuals mentioned so far hailed from provinces where Muslims were in a minority, U.P. in particular. Like Iqbal, Maulana Zafar Ali Khan was a product of the Punjab, a province known more for its parochialism and acquiescence to colonialism than for universalism and intrepid support for the nationalist cause. If Iqbal's

Islamic universalism and implicit humanitarianism remained suspect because of an exclusive concern with the ideal community of Islam and even led some of his more truculent critics to fault him for parochial excesses, Zafar Ali Khan's career belies most of the stereotypes of Punjabi Muslims. Brought up in a small rural hamlet of the Punjab, Karmabad, near Wazirabad, Zafar Ali Khan was intellectually at one with Iqbal, and politically in the same league as Mohamed Ali, with whom he had shared an education at Aligarh, and Azad.

Under his courageous editorship, *Zamindar* became the foremost Urdu daily in the Punjab, attaining a circulation of well over 20,000 during the Balkan wars. Though not as accomplished a poet as Iqbal, Zafar Ali Khan more than made up for it by putting the ideal of the self-affirming and dynamic individual into practice. His exhilarating public oratory and lively literary style were immensely popular among Punjabi Muslim youth. In contrast to Iqbal, Zafar Ali Khan managed to make himself understood to the unlettered in the Punjab and the Frontier Province, some of whom paid two pice to buy a copy of the *Zamindar* and one anna to have it read out to them.[60] Small wonder that the *Zamindar* came to be regarded as the "national organ of the Muslims" and its editor as a model for emulation.[61]

A firm believer in Hindu-Muslim unity and a supporter of the Congress, Zafar Ali Khan's primary goal was nevertheless worldwide Muslim unity. His vitriolic writings against the British raj and its intrigues against the Ottoman Empire kept him and his paper at sword points with the Punjab administration. *Zamindar*'s anticolonial stance resulted in the proscription of the paper on numerous occasions and the confinement, if not actual incarceration, of its editor even more frequently. Such moves were invariably countered by public campaigns to raise money for the revival of the newspaper. These were not restricted to the Punjab, but included a loyal readership in northern India.

Along with Mohamed Ali and Azad, Zafar Ali Khan used the journalistic medium to condemn Britain's lack of support for Ottoman Turkey at the time of the war in the Balkans. Together these three individuals did much to take pro-Turkish fervor among Indian Muslims to new heights. Zafar Ali Khan was in the vanguard of a campaign to collect donations for the Turkish cause. In June 1913, he personally delivered the donations to Sultan Muhammad in Constantinople, along with a selection of Iqbal's poetry and a solemn plea that in the interests of the Indian Muslims, who were the sultan's spiritual if not temporal subjects, Turkey should avoid getting trapped in a war with Britain.[62]

These thumbnail sketches of the ideological positions of key Muslim personalities who went on to play a leading part in Indian politics after World War I are intended here only to underscore the many possible variations in relations between the individual and the community. In enunciating a dynamic conception of the individual Muslim's relationship to the community of Islam, Iqbal drew upon normative ideals rather than existential realities. Infusing an abstract legal and political category of Muslims with a self-consciously Islamic spirit aimed at internal regeneration was something of an advance on the communitarian narratives appearing in the press. Yet the all-important balance between the individual and the community of Islam had ultimately to be fashioned in response to shifting contexts shaped by an interplay of factors not purely religious in nature. If the religious demarcator was sufficient to establish a Muslim's sense of distinction from non-Muslims, divergences along lines of class, region, language, and ideology militated against experiencing their communitarian identity in singular or monolithic terms. A religiously informed cultural identity might impel a Muslim to proclaim affiliation with the community of Islam as the single most important point of personal reference. However, Muslim self-identification could be restricted to India or expanded to include the Islamic world, depending on individual need or preference. Together with the myriad other dimensions in the life of an individual, the all-India and universal Islamic conceptions of the community left Muslims grappling uncertainly with alternative approaches to the idea of a common nationality.

The outbreak of World War I put Muslim ideas of nationality to a serious test. With Britain and Turkey in opposite camps, Islamic sentiments had to be weighed against the imperatives of subjecthood in colonial India. Forced to face the implications of their extra-territorial affiliations in the light of changed circumstances, Muslims reacted according to their place in the colonial system. Those with a stake in the collaborative networks of the raj tried justifying their loyalist stance by arguing that Britain, after all, was not directly waging war against Ottoman Turkey. Others, like Mohammad Ali Jinnah, took the opportunity to plump for Hindu-Muslim unity by engineering a working alliance, known as the Lucknow Pact, between the Congress and the Muslim League. The acceptance of separate electorates by the Congress in turn opened up the possibility of Muslims voluntarily joining mainstream Indian nationalism. In the aftermath of the war, the prospects of Muslim anti-colonialism making way for a united nationalist front seemed more promising than ever. Turkey's defeat and doubts about the future of the Ottoman *khilafat*, the ultimate symbol of Islamic temporal and spiritual sovereignty, found the Muslims of India standing at the threshold of a new definition of identity. By far the most dynamic moment in the history of colonial India, it saw the dialectic of inclusionary nationalism and exclusionary communitarianism molding individual Muslims in novel ways, prompting some of them to recast ideas of the community and the "nation" in both its restrictive and expansive dimensions.[63]

Notes

1. A focus on the city as the main example of Muslim affiliation with local habitats is in deference to the collective interest of the contributors to this volume. It does not imply that a variety of rural settings did not command an equal degree of emotive attachment for Muslim psyches.

2. K. C. Kanda, *Masterpieces of Urdu Ghazal: From 17th to 20th Century* (New Delhi: Sterling Publishers, 1994), p. 79. All translations are mine except those in quotation marks.

3. See Annemarie Schimmel, "Sacred Geography in Islam," in *Sacred Places and Profane Spaces: Essays in the Geographics of Judaism, Christianity, and Islam,* ed. Jamie Scott and Paul Simpson-Housley (New York: Greenwood Press, 1991).

4. Ralph Russell and Khurshidul Islam, eds., *Ghalib 1797–1869: Life and Letters* (Delhi: Oxford University Press, 1994), p. 29.

5. Kanda, *Masterpieces of Urdu Ghazal*, p. 8.

6. Muzaffar Abbas, *Urdu Main Qaumi Shairi* (Lahore: Maktabah-yi 'Aliyah, 1978) p. 52.

7. Ibid., p. 65.

8. Kanda, *Masterpieces of Urdu Ghazal*, p. 67.

9. C. A. Bayly, *Empire and Information: Intelligence Gathering and Social Communication in India, 1780–1870* (Cambridge: Cambridge University Press, 1996), p. 27.

10. Abbas, *Urdu Main Qaumi Shairi*, p. 134.

11. W. W. Hunter, *The Indian Musalmans*, new ed. (Delhi: Indological Book House, 1969), pp. 143–44.

12. *Aligarh Institute Gazette*, 1 December 1876, in *Selections from Vernacular Newspapers Published in Punjab, North Western Provinces, Awadh and the Central Provinces* (hereafter *Selections*, followed by IOL serial number) L/R/5/53, IOL, p. 706.

13. *Aligarh Institute Gazette*, 19 June 1877, in *Selections*, L/R/5/54, IOL, p. 424.

14. Altaf Hussain Hali, "Hubb-i-Watan," in *Jawahar-i-Hali*, comp. Iftikhar Ahmed Siddiqui (Lahore: Karavan Adab, 1989), p. 204.

15. Ibid., p. 205.

16. *Aligarh Institute Gazette*, 31 August 1878, in *Selections*, L/R/5/55, IOL, pp. 769–74.

17. Altaf Hussain Hali, *Musaddas-i-Hali* 1879 pt., (Lahore: Ferozesons, n.d.).

18. Hali, "Shikwah-i-Hind," in *Jawahar-i-Hali*, p. 323.

19. See ibid., pp. 314–30.

20. *Awadh Akhbar*, 20 December 1878, in *Selections*, L/R/5/55, IOL, p. 1049.

21. *Ahsan-ul-Akhbar*, Moradabad, 8 July 1880, in *Selections*, L/R/5/57, IOL, pp. 473–74.

22. *Aligarh Institute Gazette*, 10 July 1880, in ibid., pp.475–76.

23. *Mihiri Darkhshan*, 1 June 1879, in *Selections*, L/R/5/56, IOL, p. 443.

24. Speech at Patna on 27 January 1883, in *Writing and Speeches of Sir Sayyid Ahmad Khan*, ed. Shan Mohammad (Bombay: Nachiketa Publications, 1972), pp. 159–60.

25. Speech in Lucknow on 28 December 1887, in ibid., pp. 180–85.

26. Ibid., pp. 204, 209.

27. Ibid., pp. 180, 184, 210.

28. Speech at Gurdaspur on 27 January 1884, in ibid., pp. 266–67.

29. Peter Hardy, *The Muslims of British India* (Cambridge: Cambridge University Press, 1978), pp. 131–32.

30. Badruddin Tyabji to Sayyid Ahmad Khan, 18 February 1888, in *Political Profile of Sir Sayyid Ahmad Khan: A Documentary Record*, ed. Hafeez Malik (Islamabad: Institute of Islamic History, Culture and Civilization, 1982), p. 392.

31. Cited in Hardy, *Muslims of British India*, p. 131.

32. *Akhbar-i-Am*, Lahore, 15 January 1897, in *PNRR*, L/R/5?180, IOL, p. 52.

33. *Akhbar-i-Am*, Lahore, 7 December 1899, in *Punjab Native Newspaper Reports* (henceforth *PNNR*, followed by serial number), L/R/5/183, IOL, p. 724.

34. Barbara Metcalf, *Islamic Revival in British India: Deoband, 1860–1900* (Princeton: Princeton University Press, 1982), pp. 340–41.

35. Mehr Afroz Murad, *Intellectual Modernism of Shibli Nu'mani: An Exposition of His Religious and Political Ideas* (Lahore: Institute of Islamic Culture, 1976), p. 114.

36. *Sada-i-Hind*, Lahore, 12 November 1901, in *PNNR*, L/R/5/185, IOL, p. 730.

37. *Tribune*, Lahore, 26 November 1901, in ibid., p. 760.

38. *Tribune*, Lahore, 3 December 1901, in ibid., pp. 775–76.

39. *Watan*, Lahore, 15 March 1907, in *PNNR*, L/R/5/189, IOL, p. 75.

40. *Paisa Akhbar*, Lahore, 31 December 1906, in ibid., p. 7.

41. *Watan*, Lahore, 28 December 1906, in ibid., p. 9.

42. *Vakil*, Amritsar, 31 January 1907, in ibid., p. 43.

43. *Paisa Akhbar*, Lahore, 21 December 1909, in *PNNR*, L/R/5/190, p. 6.

44. The English translation of terms such as *qaum* and *millat*, which have connotations other than purely racial ones.

45. In *Bang-i-Dara*, or The Sound of the Caravan Bell, first published in 1923. There are many editions of Iqbal's collective works; my references are from *Kulliyat-i-Iqbal* (Karachi: Al Muslim Publishers,1994), p. 53.

46. *Baal-i-Jibreel* in *Kulliyat-i-Iqbal*, p. 19.

47. Ibid., p. 98.

48. Ibid., p. 132.

49. Muhammad Iqbal, *The Muslim Community: A Sociological Study*, ed. Muzaffar Abbas (Lahore: Maktab-i-Aliye, 1983), pp. 16–17.

50. Ibid., pp. 22–23.

51. Murad, *Intellectual Modernism of Shibli Nu'mani*, p. 106.

52. *Kulliyat-i-Shibli*, comp. Sayyid Sulayman Nadwi (Karachi, 1985) pp. 106–16, 119–21.

53. Mohamed Ali, "The Communal Patriot," in *Select Writings and Speeches of Maulana Mohamed Ali*, rev. ed., ed. Afzal Iqbal (Lahore: Islamic Book Foundation, 1987), pp. 75–77.

54. Mohamed Ali, "The Lingua Franca of India," first published in *The Comrade*, July 1912, in ibid., pp. 31–50.

55. Abdul Halim Sharar, *Urdu se Hinduon ke Ta'alluq* (The Relationship of Hindus with Urdu), lecture given at the Urdu Conference at Lucknow, 30 September 1916, VT 3890g, IOL. The Aryan race theory, more mythical than historical, was a significant component of the emerging discourse on Indian nationalism within which Sharar was seeking to locate India's Muslims.

56. See Ian Henderson Douglas, *Abul Kalam Azad: An Intellectual and Religious Biography*, ed. Gail Minault and Christian W. Troll (Delhi: Oxford University Press, 1988), p. 60.

57. N. B. Roy, "The Background of Iqbal's Poetry," in *The Sword and the Sceptre: A Collection of Writings on Iqbal, Dealing Mainly with his Life and Poetical Work*, ed. Riffat Hassan (Lahore: Iqbal Academy, 1977), p. 103.

58. Cited in Ali Ashraf, "Appraisal of Azad's Religio-Political Trajectory" in *Islam and Indian Nationalism: Reflections on Abul Kalam Azad*, ed. Mushirul Hasan (New Delhi: Manohar, 1992), p. 106.

59. Ibid., p. 108.

60. Ghulam Hussain Zulfiqar, *Maulana Zafar Ali Khan: Hiyat, Khidmat wa Asar* (Lahore: Sang-e-Meel Publications, 1994), p. 97.

61. *Secret Punjab Police Abstract of Intelligence*, Lahore, 21 February 1944, 36, no. 7, NCHCR, Islamabad, p. 116.

62. Zulfiqar, *Maulana Zafar Ali Khan*, pp. 108–9.

63. For an analysis of the different conceptions of sovereignty—divine, spiritual, and temporal—of Indian Muslims and the relationship between Indian nationalism and Islamic universalism in the aftermath of World War I, see chapter 5 of Ayesha Jalal, *Self and Sovereignty: Individual and Community in South Asian Islam since 1850* (London: Routledge; Delhi: Oxford University Press, 2000).

12 The Tangled Ends of an Empire and Its Sultan

Engin Deniz Akarlı

Port cities were the main beneficiaries of the rapid growth of maritime trade between Ottoman lands and the industrializing countries of Europe during the nineteenth century. By the turn of the twentieth century, the principal ports of foreign trade had become bustling economic, cultural, and political centers with larger and more cosmopolitan populations than ever. Istanbul led the way, as it had done for so long in the past, as a city conveniently located at the juncture of major sea and land routes in the eastern Mediterranean region and as the seat of an imperial government that ruled over far-flung territories.

Istanbul's population increased from about 375,000 in the 1830s–40s to 1,125,000 in 1912. Its composition, including a significant number of foreigners, reflected the rich ethnic and religious tapestry of the empire's population.[1] More monumental buildings were built in Istanbul for private, public, business, or religious uses during the nineteenth century than in any other comparable stretch of time in the city's past.[2] Its urban infrastructure saw significant improvements. New means of transportation and communications connected Istanbul to the provinces and to other countries more effectively. These developments made Istanbul a materially better place to live, as well as an economically and culturally livelier city.[3]

But the empire of which it was the capital disintegrated in the same period. At the end of World War I, in November 1918, the victorious European powers occupied Istanbul, contemplating its transformation into an international city. Instead, in October 1923, the Turkish nationalist forces liberated the city, if only to subordinate it to Ankara, the capital of a new state established in the heart of provincial Anatolia. Between the hammer of international designs and the anvil of a successful nationalist movement, Istanbul's sixteen-hundred-year history as an imperial city came to an end.

The nationalist movement was a reaction not only to Western European designs on the future of Anatolia, but, quite explicitly, also to the hegemony of Istanbul and other port cities. I will argue that in the late 1830s, the Ottoman leadership had opened the ports to Western European technologies, knowledge, and ideas, convinced of their promise for a brighter and beneficial future. Further development of Western European countries deepened and expanded the appreciation for their achievements, but there also began to emerge a feeling that the progress of certain countries happened at the expense of others. Unabashedly self-serving policies of the so-called Great Powers, especially in the last quarter of the nineteenth century, fanned the latter feeling. The increasingly arrogant, self-righteous, and racist categorizations of other cultures and peoples that became fashionable even in scholarly circles in Western Europe during the same period enhanced the frustration.

Istanbul and other Ottoman port cities were sites where the growing differences between natives and foreigners were most visible. Unlike the outright colonial cities of North Africa and India, the European and the native could not be totally segregated in Ottoman ports, and the local populations could not be totally marginalized. Instead, a semi-colonial situation emerged, which arguably allowed a broader space for mixing and interaction.[4] All the same, the original hopes for a shared sense of humanity, which the opening and expansion of port cities had kindled, gradually dimmed and seemingly evaporated in the flames of World War I. The Anatolian hinterland took over its ports. The following pages describe the broader context of this development, with an emphasis on the reign of Sultan Abdülhamid II (1876–1909) and his personal impressions of the developments taking place around him until his death in 1918.

Growing Up in a New Era (1842–1872)

Abdülhamid[5] was the second son of Sultan Abdülmecid, whose reign (1839–1861) witnessed the initiation of the Tanzimat reforms, intended to reorganize the Ottoman government, law, and society along lines inspired by Western European experiences. Closer economic and diplomatic ties with major European powers accompanied the reforms. The lifestyles of the elite also began to change under the influence of French and British ideas, tastes, fashions, and commodities. For about two decades, a generally optimistic outlook on life and the future of the empire prevailed in Istanbul and other major urban centers, and to a certain extent found its way even into the countryside. There was ground for hope. The exhausting civil war between Istanbul and Cairo and the long autocratic rule of Mahmud II (1808–39) were over; the empire's resources appeared abundant, and the new economic opportunities looked promising.[6]

Great Britain, unquestionably the leader of Europe and the world since the end of the Napoleonic Wars, maintained a friendly policy toward the Ottoman state. Other European powers acted in concert with Great Britain. Indeed, this was a generally peaceful and hopeful period for Europe, at least for its middle and upper classes. Liberal ideas and confidence in modern scientific and technological achievements inspired a sense of common destiny for humankind and the possibility of building heaven on earth. Borrowing and learning from one another, but especially the British, the most successful of all, appeared a normal course of action to follow in order to secure a place in the new order.[7]

Abdülhamid was born into this hopeful world.[8] His mother, Tîr-i Müjgan, died after a long illness when he was 11. One of his stepmothers, Parastu, who did not have children of her own, took Abdülhamid under her wing. She influenced him to acquire gentlemanly manners and to be careful with his money and words. Seeing little of his father, Abdülhamid grew up a lonely person in an exuberant palace. Like other princes, he was tutored in French, as well as more traditional subjects. He learned to play the piano and became a lifelong fan of Italian-style comic operas; he found classical Ottoman music "gloomy." He shunned the lively literature that developed during the Tanzimat period under European influence. He had a particular dislike for romantic novels, for he believed they inspired dreamy ideas that led to alienation and distress. Instead, he developed an interest in detective stories, travel and exploration accounts, and history. He also followed the major European newspapers carefully and became an eager student of European money markets and modern farming techniques. While still a prince, he developed a piece of land that his father had given him into a modern and profitable agricultural farm. He multiplied his profits by investing in European stocks. His banker friends were his teachers not only in monetary matters but also in the peculiarities and vicissitudes of European politics. He gained firsthand experience of the latter when he accompanied his uncle Sultan Abdülaziz (1861–76) on a royal tour of several European capitals and cities in 1867.

In his youth, Abdülhamid shared the hope as well as the advantages and opportunities offered by his era. Despite his attraction to European music and journalistic literature, European fashions and the cosmopolitan life of Istanbul's high society were of little interest to Abdülhamid. After a brief flighty period, he lived a conservative and self-consciously modest existence. He took long excursions in the vicinity of Istanbul and met people from different walks of life, but he preferred the company of his own family. He was fond of his daughters and devoted no less attention to their well-being and education than he did to that of his sons. Wood carving and inlaying were his favorite pastimes, and eventually he developed his skills in these crafts to a near professional level. He was also pious, with a keen interest in popular Sufism. This seems to have helped him build an inner strength guided by a folk wisdom of sorts. But his piety had political advantages, too, for during his sultanate, his contacts with Sufi orders served Abdülhamid as an effective means of communication with influential local leaders around the empire.

Abdülhamid, then, blended in his own way "the East" and "the West" to which he was exposed. He tried to do this without compromising his sense of princely dignity and personal integrity. The leading Ottoman statesmen and European diplomats were favorably impressed with his personality when he ascended the throne in 1876 at the mature age of 34.

The Crisis of the Tanzimat

The optimism that the Tanzimat policies first generated was gradually replaced by confusion, suspicion, and finally despair, as these policies led to unexpected developments and eventually to a profound economic and political crisis.[9] Commercial and legal privileges granted to the European powers, the open-door policy pursued in the Tanzimat era, ruptured the Ottoman social fabric. Trade and budget deficits soared. Heavy government borrowing at high interest rates at home and abroad delayed the inevitable financial crisis until 1875, when the treasury was forced to declare insolvency. Havoc erupted among European creditors, and the Russians seized the opportunity to advance their influence in the Balkans, threatening the Ottomans with war. Unrest mounted everywhere, fanning nationalist revolts among Christians in the Balkans and anti-Tanzimat movements among Muslims.

The government in Istanbul lost control. The Tanzimat leaders had streamlined the government but had failed to create an institutionalized structure of authority and policy making. Since the death of the last powerful Tanzimat minister Ali in 1871, senior statesmen had been engaged in a struggle to control the government. In May 1876, a group of ministers led by Midhat Paşa cooperated with the army to force the abdication of the reigning sultan Abdülaziz. His successor Murad V suffered a mental collapse and was deposed three months later. On August 31, Abdülhamid II succeeded him on the throne.

Meanwhile, a nationalist uprising in the Balkans turned into bloody ethnic and religious confrontations. The European powers joined forces to bring pressure on the Ottoman government to grant autonomy to the Christian population in those areas where they lived in large numbers. On 23 December 1876, Midhat responded by promulgating a constitution that assured basic civil liberties (including the equality of all subjects before the law) and provided for a bicameral parliament with an elected assembly and an appointed senate.

Insofar as it had been designed to forestall foreign intervention in internal affairs, the constitution was a failure. A disastrous war with Russia nearly brought the end of the Ottoman state in 1877–78. Large tracts of territory were lost not only to Russia and the Balkan states, but also to Great Britain and Austria-Hungary. Moreover, the Ottoman government agreed to pay a huge war indemnity to Russia and to the formation of an international agency to service the payment of the Ottoman public debt.

More directly, the constitution was intended as a solution to the authority crisis afflicting the Ottoman state. As such, it was the product of intensive discussions and reflected a consensus reached among the political elite (that is, the senior bureaucrats and bureaucrat-intellectuals). The constitution set certain limits on executive authority, but it left the sultan with great powers vis-à-vis both the cabinet and the parliament. It was on the basis of these constitutional prerogatives that Abdülhamid suspended the assembly a year later. Few influential figures objected to the sultan's decision. They had viewed the activities of the assembly with concern, partly because of the divisive nationalistic feelings aired at some of its meetings, but especially because of its members' enthusiastic (and often well justified) criticism of the ministers and provincial administrators.[10] This first experience with a parliament clearly contradicted Ottoman traditions of statecraft, which considered government the prerogative of a properly trained elite. Abdülhamid, who shared this perspective, appeared to the Ottoman statesmen a sensible sovereign who could provide the leadership necessary to deal with the grave problems facing the government. In this he did not disappoint his colleagues. In the early 1880s, the Ottoman government finally managed to bring its long crisis under reasonable control, gaining a new lease on life with Abdülhamid in charge.

It needs to be stressed that at this juncture the majority of the Ottoman political leadership supported Abdülhamid on the basis of a consensus that was reached through several years of quite broadly based intellectual and political debates,[11] power struggles, and experimentations with new models of government. Issues in dispute involved short-term crises awaiting immediate attention, as well as structural problems that called for a long-term plan of action for the survival of the Ottoman state in the modern world—the ultimate concern of the Ottoman political elite and intellectuals in general. The government's vulnerability to external pressure, the erosion of its internal authority and respectability and the deterioration of its finances loomed as the key structural issues. Abdülhamid commanded respect because he managed not only to produce practical solutions to immediate problems but also to put together a generally acceptable long-term agenda out of the ideas that circulated among political and intellectual circles and on the basis of advice he received from a wide variety of people.[12]

Eventually, however, confidence in Abdülhamid's leadership began to erode, partly because he was unable to fulfill some of his plans and partly because those he did fulfill created new dynamics and problems that undermined his style of government. We can observe this development by casting a glance at three major problem areas that preoccupied the Ottoman government: namely, its efforts to restore financial solvency, to enhance its prestige and authority among the populace, and to build an effective system of governance.

Fiscal and Economic Problems

Under Abdülhamid's leadership, the Ottomans sought to increase economic productivity and thus the government's tax base.[13] They believed they could achieve this if the government paid due attention first to the construction of modern transportation and communications networks and to other economic infrastructure investments, and second to the maintenance of law, order, and security in the land. Abdülhamid himself was convinced that people normally preferred to spend their lives trying to improve their livelihoods and enjoying the fruits of their labor and enterprise peacefully in the company of their families and friends. They would feel loyal to their government and shun political activism if the government provided the conditions necessary for a productive, secure, and peaceful life.

Whatever the plausibility of the sultan's views about the loyalty of his subjects, the Ottoman government was not in a strong position to implement unilaterally the remarkably detailed economic development plans and projects prepared during this period.[14] The state of Ottoman finances was a major problem. Around 30 percent of the entire government revenue went directly into the coffers of the foreign-controlled Public Debt Administration. An additional 40 percent was devoured by military expenditures deemed indispensable in an increasingly dangerous and belligerent world. A depression in world agricultural prices further strained Ottoman finances. In the face of a dearth of funds, the government felt forced to contract many of the important mines and planned projects to foreign concerns as monopolistic concessions. To a certain extent, the Ottoman government was able to use European vested interests to perpetuate its own policies, but the capitulatory commercial and legal privileges enjoyed by European powers, backed by threats of force, left the Ottoman government with little room to maneuver.

Despite these handicaps, considerable economic development was achieved during Abdülhamid II's reign, particularly after the 1890s. This development, combined with other factors, led to an outcome quite different than that desired by the sultan. Rising economic prospects in certain parts of the empire fanned the desire for autonomy from a government incapable of protecting local economic interests against foreign ones.[15] Everywhere, the desire to have a larger or fairer share of the resources led to the formation of new political alliances in opposition to the existing regime. Organized labor movements emerged in virtually all the major urban centers. In short, far from soothing political ambitions, economic development and new opportunities accelerated the politicization of the population.

Problems of Internal Integration and Islam

Another serious problem that the Ottoman government faced at the beginning of Abdülhamid II's reign was the alarming erosion of its authority.[16] Tanzimat reforms had aimed at creating an effective and efficient central government that also commanded the respect of the population through their equitable treatment before the law and incorporation into the administrative cadres. By the 1870s, however, the Ottoman state appeared to friend and foe alike closer to disintegration than ever. Turning the tide, restoring the prestige of the government, and then enhancing it to avoid a similar abyss became a major concern of Ottoman statesmen and intellectuals. They looked to distant days when Ottoman prestige had been at its height, studied successful governments of their times, and took stock of the Tanzimat policies in search of the most effective ways of dealing with the problem. The challenge they faced was to strengthen the social base of the government by rallying as much of the Ottoman population as possible around a common cause. Clearly, this task involved the generation of a modern body politic that was bound together not only by the coercive powers of the central government but also by a network of social alliances and a shared sense of identity.

Heterogeneity of the Ottoman population, the poor state of the economy and government finances, and vulnerability to external pressure rendered the political integration of the Ottoman Empire a gigantic task, if not an impossible one. These problems were recognized by the Ottoman leadership. Although the Ottoman state in the end proved unsalvageable, the solutions it sought have had important repercussions for people living in Ottoman lands.

After extensive debates, some failed experiments, and also by force of circumstances, a strategy took shape that involved an appeal to Islam in order to win the united support of the Muslim population while upholding the principle of legal equality in order to safeguard the loyalty of the non-Muslim minorities. Economic development, improvement of public services, and curtailment of foreign intervention in internal affairs were seen as equally essential for rallying the population around the Ottoman cause. Winning the support of Muslims without further alienating other subjects, however, was a goal that deserves independent treatment, because it was mostly around this point that Abdülhamid earned his image as a "reactionary" ruler.

The idea of appealing to Islam as a force of sociopolitical solidarity was by no means restricted to religiously or politically conservative elements. Indeed, it seems to have developed first among the so-called Young Ottomans who led the constitutionalist opposition against the Tanzimat ministers in the late 1860s and early 1870s.[17] Similarly, the constitutionalist Midhat clearly enjoyed the support of the seminary students when he vied for power in the mid-1870s.[18] Politicization of Islam as a means of salvaging the Ottoman state was on the rise. Ottoman isolation against Russia, the war and the consequent territorial losses to European powers, and the immigration of a large number of destitute Muslims of various ethnic backgrounds fleeing persecution in the Balkans and Russia all heightened religious sentiments and generalized the feeling that Tanzimat policies had failed the Muslim population while only fanning separatist tendencies among Christians.

Abdülhamid himself disliked the involvement of the seminary students in active politics, and believed it was not so much the Tanzimat objectives as it was their careless implementation that facilitated foreign intervention in Ottoman affairs and caused erosion of the respect for the sultanate. According to the sultan, had it not been for foreign intervention and Ottoman indiscretion that facilitated it, "[t]he hearts of all subjects might have been filled with love and loyalty toward their sublime sovereign through the diligent implementation of the laws and regulations that . . . [were] enacted after the promulgation of the Noble Rescript of the Rose Chamber [in 1839]."[19] Yet as things stood, "not only [did] the existing regulations concerning all branches of the government fall short of sustaining the interests and territorial integrity of the state, but they also fail[ed] to assure the true interests of the loyal subjects, and above all, of the distinguished religion of Islam, which is the reason of the strength and endurance of the state."[20]

Abdülhamid believed in the need to uphold the principle of the legal equality of all subjects that was established during the Tanzimat era, not only because he feared foreign intervention but because he sincerely considered an equitable system of justice essential for the respectability of government authority. He did not think, however, that this principle should prevent the Ottoman government from emphasizing Islam as a basis of social and political solidarity or from paying close attention to the moral and material needs of the empire's Muslim population. He believed the Muslims would "always be moved with [a feeling of] loyalty and reverence toward the office of the sultanate and the caliphate under the influence of their upbringing at home." They would desire the continuation of Ottoman rule and faithfully serve its causes, whereas the Christians would remain vulnerable to foreign manipulations and instigations.[21]

If Abdülhamid's views of his Christian subjects make his belief in an equitable system of justice sound hypocritical, he certainly did not think that the Western governments had a more objective attitude toward justice:

> The priority of the subjects who constitute a majority over the rest is an unavoidable necessity in any state. The Catholics, for example, are preponderant over the Protestants in countries where the former are in majority. . . . Likewise, the religion of the Sublime State of the Ottomans is the religion of Islam, and the Muslims are in majority among its subjects. Nevertheless, all subjects are treated most equally by the Sultanate. While this is a matter of fact . . . the Christian subjects are distinguished by the protection of foreign powers. . . . For example, if a Christian attacks a Muslim and wounds and even attempts to kill him, the foreign consuls interfere and want to prevent the trial of the Christian even if his aggression and cruelty are well-known facts. . . . The consuls pressure the central government for the immediate removal of the governors and other administrators who oppose their action.[22]

Abdülhamid had a point. We have to take into consideration the times in which he reigned. This was a period when the notion of justice even in its most secular or liberal forms was harnessed to militantly sectarian interest. New laws were imposed on natives at gunpoint not only in Islamic countries such as Egypt and Tunisia that had recently fallen under colonial rule, but around the world, from Latin America to China—all in the name of progressive justice. But the colonizer and the colonized—or for that matter, the "white" and the "colored"—were hardly equal before the law.[23] Nor was sensitivity to the role of religious feelings in political activity peculiar to Islam or the Ottoman Empire. It was on the upsurge everywhere.

In contrast to the basically liberal mood that had prevailed earlier in the century, religious fervor was becoming an increasingly conspicuous aspect of internal and international politics in the age of imperialism with rapid industrialization and its concomitant social problems. It is not a coincidence that the Dreyfus affair, the Zionist movement, and the Irish Question emerged in this period, just as the laicist French government made peace with the church and worked hand in glove with militant missionaries around the world. It is not a coincidence that a profoundly devout person like Gladstone rose to prominence in British politics. The arrogantly intolerant, even hate-mongering, views of Gladstone and others about "the Turks," which effectively meant "Muslims" in the Ottoman context at this point, left little room for dialogue.[24] It is in this broader historical context that we must understand the rather defensive Islamism of Abdülhamid II's generation.

From about the early 1880s, the Ottoman government began to pursue a threefold integration policy that emphasized Islam and was coordinated directly by the palace. First, it aimed at generating a consensus about the interpretation of Islamic political traditions in a way that was favorable to Ottoman interests. Toward this end, religious dignitaries from around the empire were invited to meetings in Istanbul and encouraged to prepare pamphlets for public use. Religious advisers close to the sultan were sent to the provinces regularly, partly as troubleshooters and partly as propagandists. Efforts were also made to bring the major Sufi orders closer together under the sultan's sponsorship and, hence, indirect control. Religious education in the rapidly expanding public school system was standardized, and many of the old-style primary religious schools were absorbed into the public school system under the control of the Ministry of Education.[25]

At another level, a deliberate effort was made to win the cooperation of the provincial Muslim notables.[26] According to Abdülhamid, the attempts to break the local influence of notables earlier in the century in an effort to strengthen the central government's authority had backfired. He considered the cooperation of the notables essential to restore the respectability of the Ottoman rule in the eyes of the common folk, to strengthen the latter's attachment to the government, and to keep them from "inexpedient behavior."[27] During his reign, influential notables from distant provinces were regular guests at the palace and maintained correspondence with the sultan. Everywhere, provincial notables became directly involved in the government, in local administration, as tax farmers and collectors, and as provisioners to government offices. Moreover, their children were provided attractive opportunities to enter the central government service. Finally, during Abdülhamid II's reign, special attention was paid to the predominantly Muslim provinces, which had been relatively neglected in the past.

Government investments were concentrated in these areas. The administrative and judicial branches of the government, as well as its law enforcement agencies, also expanded.

As already indicated, Abdülhamid and his advisors retained the principle of legal equality they had inherited from the Tanzimat period. They considered its effective implementation essential to maintain the loyalty of the non-Muslim population (which at that time constituted 55 percent of the population of Rumelia, 45 percent of the population in Istanbul, and 15 percent of the population of Anatolia and the Fertile Crescent). Indeed, the streamlining of the secular judicial system, the enhancement of its autonomy, its expansion deep into the provinces, and its equipment with a properly trained professional cadre are among the significant achievements of Abdülhamid II's reign.[28] Furthermore, non-Muslim communities continued to enjoy autonomy in their religious, cultural, and educational activities, as well as in their internal legal affairs. In those places where non-Muslims constituted only a small percentage of the population, and when non-Muslims belonged to small communities scattered around the empire, the guarantees offered by the government appear to have balanced the emphasis that it was putting on Islam and Muslims.[29] In places where Christians of the same ethnic background constituted a majority or a significantly large segment of the population, however, serious problems emerged. In these areas, particularly in eastern Anatolia where a militant Armenian nationalist movement developed, and in the hopelessly mixed Macedonia, Abdülhamid's provincial policy aggravated conflicts.

Abdülhamid II reigned in an age when ethnic and religious differences were commonly used for purposes of political mobilization. But if this mood of the age explains the Ottoman emphasis on Islam and Muslims, it also points to the problems that such an emphasis would entail in an ethnically heterogeneous environment. However sincerely the Ottoman government might try to balance its pro-Islamic policies by other means, those policies involved the choice of a political identity on grounds that by definition excluded parts of the population and so added yet another dimension to their grievances.

Abdülhamid II's policies ran into problems among the Muslims as well. These problems point to yet other complications that efforts to harness a religious tradition for specific political purposes may entail. At first, Abdülhamid's efforts to strengthen the social base of the government by paying closer attention to Muslims and to generate a sense of shared identity by emphasizing Islam enjoyed support, for he was responding to broadly shared concerns among the Muslim population. One can even conclude that his efforts bore some fruit. During his reign, the central government's respectability and visibility increased in many of the Asian provinces. Abdülhamid's policies also helped generate many new opportunities for the population. These and other developments, however, led to new social dynamics and power configurations. The sultan's reliance on notables, as well as other aspects of his policies, began to come under attack.

Politics is politics. It involves conflicting material and moral interests. Abdülhamid saw Islam as a resource of social solidarity that could be tapped to reconcile and control conflicting interest. But he could not monopolize Islam, try though he did. Others could resort to the same resource to contest the interpretations and methods adopted by the palace. A vehement and formidable Islamist opposition to Abdülhamid II's regime did exactly that, although for different reasons and without unanimity. Conflicting interpretations of Islam became a regular feature of the ongoing political struggles and debates in an increasingly politicized environment.[30] The Ottoman system of governance did not (and arguably could not) accommodate the growing political consciousness and the new social tensions emerging among the inhabitants of the Ottoman lands.

Friction and Discord within the Government

Abdülhamid II's reign saw an unprecedented expansion of government services and bureaucracy.[31] The government became involved in building and operating public land and waterways, railroads, telegraph, and other public works. General public education and public health services, credit institutions, and offices that supplied technical assistance to producers became widespread. All regular branches of the government, including the judiciary and the public security forces, also expanded. Many new professional schools were established and the old ones improved with the specific purpose of training a corps of technical government personnel (such as doctors, engineers, veterinarians, agricultural experts, teachers, officers, and the like), as well as better public administrators and jurists. In addition, official statistics and filing systems were improved, and elaborate regulations governing the recruitment, promotion, retirement, and dismissal of government personnel were enacted and applied. Except in the highest echelons, the administrative machinery became highly structured, marking a fundamental change over the situation at the beginning of Abdülhamid II's reign.

This new elaboration of bureaucratic structure penetrated deep into society and enhanced the visibility, control, and to a certain extent the respectability of the government. Equally important, it served as a mechanism to create a growing cadre of officials committed to the Ottoman cause. These positive developments were undermined, however, by major shortcomings. There were significant differences among the salaries of the highest ranking, intermediate, and lower bureaucrats, leading to considerable friction within the bureaucracy. Given the financial strain, payments were left in arrears quite frequently. This situation encouraged—even justified—bribery, especially among the petty officials whose salaries hardly sufficed to support a lifestyle in keeping with their social status. Bribery became a serious problem that impaired the government's image, as its frequency and variety intensified through the years.

Intermediate bureaucrats were relatively better off, although they, too, suffered from payment delays. The graduates of the newly established technical schools (including the young drill and staff officers) belonged to this group. It was among these technocrats that the most formidable internal opposition to Abdülhamid's regime took root. They were the ones who most bitterly felt the contradictions of the times.

At the technical schools, Western sciences and languages were taught alongside the values of Ottoman culture. Most of these schools were located in Istanbul or other major urban centers, the cosmopolitanism of which contrasted sharply with the provincial background of the majority of the students. With only a fragmented exposure to Westernized cultural tastes, lifestyles, and social expectations, most of the graduates were dispatched to serve in remote places, once more to confront the harsh realities of the empire. Each bureaucrat responded differently to these divergent influences, torn between feelings of rootlessness and reverence toward the past and ambivalent and romantic idealism toward the future. To whatever degree their attitudes converged, they reflected a general contempt for their contemporary conditions and the necessity for establishing a new sense of identity.

Other contradictions that embittered these young bureaucrats were related to the politicized nature of the upper reaches of the Ottoman officialdom. Each pasha was at once an administrative expert and a political figure, susceptible to the influence of different interest groups. Petitioning, persuasion, shared profits, and bribery were among the means available to influence a pasha's decision; the nature of the business at hand and the personality and current power of the pasha in question determined the means chosen. The intensity of contradictory foreign demands caused further frictions. Those officials who articulated the interests and views of different powers found themselves pitted against one another, as well as against those who articulated local interests. But I would like to put the emphasis here not so much on corruption as on the general sense of confusion about political objectives and procedures.

Senior officials from all branches of the government traditionally had been the elite of the Ottoman policy. They made their final decisions according to recognized procedures and traditions of advocacy that worked reasonably well for the much smaller cadres and the highly decentralized conditions of governance in the past. The attempts made since the beginnings of the nineteenth century to adapt political process to rapidly changing circumstances had failed to produce effective results. Despite the availability of many conscientious and capable pashas, the Ottomans found it difficult to act in concert unless under a shrewd arbitrator. Abdülhamid served as that arbitrator. He did not intend to alter the existing order of things radically. For one thing, he was outspokenly afraid of the pashas' proven ability to seat and unseat sultans; for another, Abdülhamid believed that it was "the royal fountain of favor" that produced "the best harvest on the field of sovereignty."[32] By distributing and withholding his favor and the more powerful positions within the government, he played the pashas against one another, thereby keeping their conflicting interests and views in check. He also subjected the resolutions of the cabinet submitted by the grand vizier to a thorough reexamination, particularly when they involved foreign interests. In this way, he sought personally to gain a comprehensive picture of events and ensure that he was in a position to counteract, or at least to delay, the demands that he deemed contrary to the interests of the state.

Abdülhamid's necessarily cumbersome maneuvers—and his concern for thoroughness—inevitably caused delays in the preparation of administrative decisions at a time when the increasing technical demands necessitated quick and unambiguous responses. Furthermore, Abdülhamid's favoritism in his relations with senior officials contrasted sharply with the objectified norms of administrative rationality emphasized for rank-and-file bureaucrats. The difference in criteria represented an effort to distinguish the political from the administrative. It ran counter, however, to the Ottoman tradition that viewed the incumbents of all governmental positions as politically privileged equals ruling over society. Accepted norms of differentiation were established along lines of the quality of one's education and seniority of service rather than family background. During Abdülhamid II's reign, however, sons of pashas were automatically accepted into the best schools and received leisurely commissions in the better parts of the empire (regardless of their real success at school); they were promoted faster than the more humble graduates of the same schools. The new bureaucrats (technocrats) considered themselves deprived of advancement opportunities.

This grievance and the cumbersome procedures at the helm of government reinforced the general sense of alienation among the young bureaucrats. They began to organize in opposition groups that seriously challenged the integrity and effectiveness of the entire administration and the armed forces.

The Finale

Many young Ottoman bureaucrats, officers, and intellectuals, bitter over the sultan's personal control of the key government positions and decisions, and demanding a better institutionalized and participatory political regime, joined the opposition led by the Union and Progress Committee. In 1908, sporadic mutinies among the army corps in Rumelia and Macedonia rapidly spread into a popular movement, as a medley of people with divergent political aspirations and interests made common cause with the Unionists. Thus, Muslim fundamentalists, Islamist reformists, and ardent nationalists from different ethnic groups, as well as the nascent modern labor organizations and conservative artisans and shopkeepers, joined in cheering for "liberty, fraternity, and equality." Abdülhamid realized the depth of the opposition and yielded to their demands. On 23 July 1908, he called for elections and agreed to limitations on his authority. Supporters of Union and Progress won the majority of seats in the parliament, but as the parliament and the cabinet became bogged down in a struggle over their respective rights, and as separatist movements in the Balkans intensified, the political situation remained tense. On 13 April 1909, a popular revolt broke out in Istanbul, led by religious groups and army units that had supported the 1908 revolution but now felt alienated from the Union and Progress Party. An army of loyal units and volunteers rushed from Salonika to crush this rebellion. Abdülhamid tried to persuade the mutineers to abandon their recalcitrance. All the same, he was accused of having instigated the rebellion and was dethroned on 27 April 1909.[33]

He spent the rest of his life under house arrest, first in Salonika, until its fall to Greece in November 1912, and then in Beylerbeyi, Istanbul, until his death. He had much time to watch the ships go in and out of Salonika Bay or through the Bosphorus, reminisce, and reflect on the news that reached him. The ex-sultan worried, as early as 1911, that the Ottoman state would be dragged into an imminent war between the British and German blocks. When war did in fact break out, he predicted its long duration, its victors, and its disastrous consequences for the Ottoman state and Muslims in general. But his sorrow was not confined to the Ottomans or the Muslims alone. From the beginning of the war, he mourned for the suffering that it would inflict on all human beings caught up in its destruction. In October 1916, he expressed full agreement with the socialists' call for immediate peace to bring an end to the human suffering caused by the war. When the news of the March 1917 revolution in Russia reached him, he was pleased. Not because it would help the Ottoman cause—he believed Russian withdrawal would lengthen the war but not prevent the ultimate victory of the British and their allies, because so long as the British ruled the oceans, they would continue to fight—but because at least the peoples of Russian lands would now be saved from the disasters of conflict, if only they could avoid a very likely civil war. Abdülhamid believed that since the late 1870s, the British had become increasingly determined to partition the Ottoman state and would do everything in their power to further weaken Islam. Nevertheless, when he learned about the indiscriminate German aerial bombardments of London, he deemed them "a dreadful act" and asked in bewilderment, "What is the crime of innocent civilians?! What can be obtained from killing them? What kind of a humanity is this? What kind of a civilization?" But his increasingly single-minded worry was the consequences of the war for Muslims. He wished his predictions about the effects of the war on Ottomans and Muslims were wrong and prayed for world peace. He died on 10 February 1918. A huge crowd congregated at his funeral procession, weeping for the last great sultan of Istanbul.

Epilogue

Shortly after Abdülhamid's death, the victorious powers began to occupy Istanbul and other major Ottoman ports. Their apparent determination to confine "the Terrible Turk" to a virtually landlocked narrow space in the Anatolian peninsula ignited a patriotic resistance movement. From its spontaneous and scattered beginnings, it grew into a well-coordinated democratic movement run by a national assembly of regional representatives that met in inland Ankara. An alliance of provincial notables and Ottoman civilian and military bureaucrats led the resistance, and the Muslim population of Anatolia at large, not only its Turkish-speaking component, provided the rank and file. Clearly, a sense of urgency had grasped these people. They feared, not unlike Abdülhamid II while under house arrest, that Christian Europe would continue to purge Muslims merely because they were Muslims. Muslims in other parts of the world saw in the Anatolian resistance movement a last-ditch effort to defend a part of Islam against European imperialism and provided moral and material support. In other words, a defensive sense of Islamic solidarity, rather than an articulate notion of Turkish nationalism, spurred the movement. All the same, the majority of the delegates in the national assembly maintained their patriotic focus. They aimed at the liberation and full independence of their collective constituency, which roughly corresponded to Turkey today. They nourished little sympathy for the Ottoman government in Istanbul.[34] Indeed, the national assembly adopted "Turkey" as the name of the lands over which it claimed sovereignty; it was a name given the Ottoman state by Europeans but hardly ever used by Ottomans themselves.

After four years of effective organization, a series of successful military campaigns, and careful diplomacy, the government in Ankara managed to win international recognition as the sole and fully sovereign representative of the people of Turkey. The Ottoman rule became extinct, along with its widely despised capitulatory treaties. As foreign troops evacuated Istanbul, the triumphant government of Ankara took charge of the city. Ankara's victory, however, came with a price to pay.

This was still an age dominated by masters of the oceans. No government could remain in continuous conflict with them, as Abdülhamid II had bitterly observed on several occasions. Ankara faced the same challenge, but a group of bureaucrats and officers who conducted Ankara's diplomatic relations were willing to make compromises on the basis of priorities quite different than those of Abdülhamid II's generation. Above all, they were ready to distance Turkey from Islam and other Muslim countries in return for British and French recognition of Ankara's bid for unfettered sovereignty over Turkey. They recognized that the British and French governments faced serious problems in maintaining the loyalty of the large number of Muslims under their rule. Many Muslims struggling against European rule looked up to the Anatolian movement and saw in it an effort to salvage the Ottoman caliphate, which had come to acquire a peculiar symbolic significance in Islamic countries over recent decades. It was this Islamic connection that some leaders in Ankara were ready to exchange for international recognition. They prevailed, arguably because otherwise a prolonged confrontation and even war with Britain and France would have been unavoidable.

Peace negotiations strengthened their position and helped them seize nearly exclusive leadership of the new regime. Shortly after the successful conclusion of the peace talks, the new leadership began to adopt a series of militantly secularist cultural reforms that aimed at turning all citizens of the republic into Europeanized "Turks," whether by persuasion or coercion, deliberately trying to separate them from their cultural roots. In the process, provincial notables found themselves relegated to a secondary position. Others who saw no reason to compromise their Islamic sentiments were likewise pushed aside, or they themselves stepped aside for patriotic concerns in order to avoid internal strife. Distancing Turkey from Islam and other Muslim countries involved distancing it from the democratic origins of its political regime as well.[35] In these two respects, the Anatolian movement turned against itself. Perhaps it could not be otherwise, given the hegemonic world view and the limitations of the age in which Ankara's victory occurred.

Pragmatic considerations were not the only motivation of the cultural reformists. They were in general positivist bureaucrats and intellectuals who shared contemporary Western views of Islam as a religion frozen in time and hence a detriment to rational progress. They sincerely believed that unless "the Turks" distanced themselves from their Islamic past, they were certain to fall back into the dark pit in which they had found themselves at the end of the Ottoman Empire or fall under the rule of their betters like most of the other Muslims in the world. Only a cultural transformation would ensure them of an honorable place among the civilized nations of the world. The reformers singled out Abdülhamid II as a signifier of the dark past and everything that a "Turk" should not be, just as he had been the epitome of "the Terrible Turk" whom Europeans wanted to throw bag and baggage back to the depths of Asia.

Clearly, these views mirrored the dominant discourses of contemporary Europe, which actually helped justify colonial hegemony over others as much as they did the growing power of the central governments and bureaucratic elites in an intensely nationalist age. The reformist leaders of Turkey were only nationalists, not colonialists. A colonial regime could not have pursued a similarly radical cultural policy, even if it sincerely wanted to. Rather, the colonial administrators of the high imperialist era of 1875–1945 condemned the natives both for not being like Europeans and for trying to be like them. The new leaders of Turkey, however, were absolutely serious about Europeanization, whether it involved building the country or rebuilding its people. They were determined to succeed where Abdülhamid II and his successors had failed. They wanted to halt the retreat of Ottoman Muslims into an ever narrower space, even if they had to compromise Islamic sentiments and reinvent a people according to the hegemonic norms that defined humanity at that juncture. It was a crippled sense of humanity, the humanity of those times, in a world deeply divided against itself, and the traumatic repercussions of an authoritarian cultural transformation were a heavy price to pay. But who can put a price on survival and Istanbul?

Notes

1. Donald Quataert, "The Age of Reforms, 1812–1914," in *An Economic and Social History of the Ottoman Empire, 1300–1914,* ed. H. İnalcık and D. Quataert (Cambridge: Cambridge University Press, 1994), p. 781. Compare with Stanford Shaw, "The Population of Istanbul in the Nineteenth Century," *International Journal of Middle East Studies* 10 (1979): 269–77. Also see Kemal Karpat, *Ottoman Population 1830–1914: Demographic and Social Characteristics* (Madison: University of Wisconsin Press, 1985), pp. 86–105.

2. See Pars Tuğlacı, *The Role of the Balian Family in Ottoman Architecture* (Istanbul: Yeni Çığır, 1993).

3. See İlhan Tekeli, "Kentsel Dönüşüm," *Tanzimat'tan Cumhuriyet'e Türkiye Ansiklopedisi* 4: 878–90; and Zeynep Çelik, *The Remaking of Istanbul* (Seattle: University of Washington Press, 1993) among numerous other sources.

4. Özdemir Kaptan (Arkan), *Beyoğlu* (Istanbul: İletişim, 1988); and Zeynep Rona, ed., *Osman Hamdi Bey ve Dönemi* (Istanbul: Yurt, 1993). Compare with Gwendolyn Wright, *The Politics of Design in French Urban Colonialism* (Chicago: University of Chicago Press, 1991); and Zeynep Çelik, *Urban Forms and Colonial Confrontations: Algiers under French Rule* (Berkeley: University of California Press, 1997).

5. Akarlı, "The Problems of External Pressures, Power Struggles, and Budgetary Deficits in Ottoman Politics under Abdülhamid II (1876–1909): Origins and Solutions," Ph.D. diss., Princeton University, 1976, pp. 10–23, 77–94; *Belge-*

lerle Tanzimat (Istanbul: Bosphorus University Press, 1978); "The Ottoman Government and Semi-Nomadic Tribes in Northern Jordan, 1846–1851" (in Arabic) in *Ottoman Documents on Jordan* (Amman: University of Jordan Press, 1989); "Provincial Power Magnates in Ottoman Bilad al-Sham and Egypt, 1740–1840," in *La vie sociale dans les provinces arabes à l'époque ottomane,* ed. by A. Temimi, vol. 3 (Zaghouan, Tunisia: CIEPO, 1988), pp. 41–56; and E.D. Akarlı, *The Long Peace: Ottoman Lebanon, 1861–1920* (Berkeley: University of California Press, 1993), passim.

6. This optimistic mood is evident not only in many contemporary accounts such as A. Ubicini's *Lettres sur la Turquie* (Paris: Chez Guillaumin, 1851) and D. Urquhart's *Turkey and Its Resources* (London: Saunders and Otley, 1833), but also in Ahmed Cevdet Paşa's critical recollections as in his *Tezakir* and *Maruzat.* See, for instance, the modern Turkish edition of the latter by Y. Halaçoğlu (Istanbul: Çağır, 1980), pp. 8–9.

7. This is the period discussed as the "Liberal Age" in Karl Polanyi, *The Great Transformation* (Boston: Beacon Press, 1957). Also see Hobsbawm, *The Age of Revolution, 1789–1848* (New York: Mentor, 1962); and *The Age of Capital, 1848–1875* (New York: Scribner, 1975).

8. The following brief account of Abdülhamid II's days as a prince is based on information one can obtain from two different kinds of sources: namely, recollections of the sultan himself and of people close to him, and publications hostile to him. Abdülhamid's recollections while he was under house arrest in Salonika and Beylerbeyi are related to us by his Unionist physician Atıf Hüseyin in 14 notebooks preserved in the Türk Tarih Kurumu Library, under manuscript number Y-255. Memoirs of Abdülhamid's daughters also provide useful information: Şadiye Osmanoğlu, *Hayatımın Acı ve Tatlı Günleri* (Istanbul: Bedir, 1966), and Ayşe Osmanoğlu, *Babam Abdülhamid* (Istanbul: Güven, 1960). Recollections of Abdülhamid published by Selek Publishing House, *Abdülhamid'in Hatıra Defteri* (Istanbul, 1960), includes information that seems to be authentic. Memoirs of Tahsin Paşa, Abdülhamid II's chief secretary, *Abdülhamid: Yıldız Hatıraları* (Istanbul: Muallim Ahmet Halit, 1931); and the anecdotes related by Joan Haslip in reference to Layard and Thomson, who knew Abdülhamid in his youth, are among other useful sources. Accounts hostile to Abdülhamid are numerous. Dorys' work mentioned above seems to have served as a key source for many others. Osman Nuri's *Abdülhamid-i Sani ve Devr-i Saltanatı,* 3 vols. (Istanbul, 1327), is a somewhat more balanced and useful account; it is obviously based on Paul Fesch, *Constantinople aux derniers jours d'Abdul-Hamid* (Paris: M. Rivière, 1907).

9. R. Davison, *Reform in the Ottoman Empire, 1856–1876* (Princeton: Princeton University Press, 1963), pp. 270–408, and Akarlı, "Problems," pp. 23–40, 94–104.

10. Hakkı Tarık Us, ed., *Meclis-i Meb'usan, 1293:1877, Zabıt Ceridesi,* 2 vols., (Istanbul: Vakit, 1940 and 1954); İlber Ortaylı, *İmparatorluğun En Uzun Yüzyılı* (Istanbul, 1983), pp. 116–17 and 192–93, and Us, "İlk Osmanlı Parlamentosu," in *Armağan: Kanun-u Esasi'nin 100. Yılı,* ed. Savcı et al. (Ankara: Milli Eğitim, 1978), pp. 169–82.

11. Şerif Mardin, *The Genesis of Young Ottoman Thought* (Princeton: Princeton University Press, 1962), and Mümtaz'er Türköne, *Siyasi İdeoloji Olarak İslam-cılığın Doğuşu* (Istanbul: İletişim, 1991).

12. Soon after he became the sultan, Abdülhamid issued a circular inviting suggestions from the leading statesmen on what should be done to improve the situation. Some of the responses to this circular are preserved among the *Yıldız Esas Evrakı* (henceforth, YEE) in the Başbakanlık archives. I refer to them in "Problems." In addition to these written reports, Abdülhamid sought the advice of others in individual or group meetings organized at the palace. Also see Stanford Shaw in *International Journal of Middle East Studies* 4 (1973): 359–65.

13. See Akarlı, "Economic Policy and Budgets in Ottoman Turkey, 1876–1909," *Middle Eastern Studies* 28/3 (July 1992): 443–476; and the relevant sections of Şevket Pamuk, *The Ottoman Empire and European Capitalism, 1820–1913* (Cambridge: Cambridge University Press, 1987), and of Donald Quataert, "The Age of Reforms," in *An Economic and Social History of the Ottoman Empire,* pp. 759–943.

14. For the plans prepared early under Abdülhamid II's reign, see *Belgelerle Türk Tarihi Dergisi,* vol. 4, nos. 19–22 (1969): 3–13, 11–18, 29–35, and 53–54, respectively, and *Belgeler,* vols., 5–8 (1968–71): 153–233.

15. See, for instance, the case of Mount Lebanon discussed in Akarlı, *The Long Peace.*

16. This section is based on my articles: "Abdülhamid II's Attempt to Integrate Arabs into the Ottoman System," in *Palestine in the Late Ottoman Period,* ed. D. Kushner (Leiden: E.J Brill, 1986), pp. 740–89; "Abdülhamid II's Islamic Policy," *Arab-Turkish Relations* (Ankara: Hacettepe University, 1979), pp. 44–60; "The Defense of the Libyan Provinces, 1882–1980," *Studies on Ottoman Diplomatic History* 5 (1991): 75–85; *Ottoman Documents on Jordan* (Amman: University of Jordan, 1989), and *The Long Peace.* Also see Cezmi Eraslan, *II. Abdülhamid ve İslam Birliği* (Istanbul: Ötüken, 1992) and other works mentioned in the following notes.

17. See note 11 above.

18. Davison, *Reform in the Ottoman Empire,* pp. 325–30.

19. YEE: 9/2006/72/4 (April 1894). Also see YEE: 9/2638/72/4 (ca. 1880), and YEE: I/156-XXV/156/3 (April 1895).

20. YEE: I/156-XXVI/156/3 (no date).

21. YEE: 9/2006/72/4 (ca. April 1894). Also see YEE: 8/1842/77/3 (June 1895), and YEE: 9/2610/72/4 (ca. 1904).

22. YEE: 11/1325/20/5 (October 1896).
23. Peter Fitzpatrick, "Law, Plurality and Underdevelopment," in *Legality, Ideology, and the State*, ed. D. Sugarman (London: Academic Press, 1983), pp. 159–81; Martha Mundy, "The Family, Inheritance, and Islam," in *Islamic Law: Social and Historical Contexts*, ed. Aziz al-Azmeh (London: Routledge, 1988), pp. 1–123; and Peter Gay, *The Cultivation of Hatred* (New York: Norton, 1993), pp. 68–95, esp. 84–95, among many other works.
24. See Owen Chadwick, *The Secularization of the European Mind in the Nineteenth Century* (Cambridge: Cambridge University Press, 1975), esp., pp. 229–66. For Gladstone and the Irish Question, see Ann P. Saab, *Reluctant Icon* (Cambridge: Harvard University Press, 1991); and Patrick Joyce, *Democratic Subjects: The Self and the Social in 19th-Century England* (Cambridge: Cambridge University Press, 1994), pp. 204–26. For the historical background of the Zionist movement, see Mitchell Cohen, *Zion and State* (New York, 1992). For changing relations between the French government and Catholic missions, see John P. Spagnolo, *France and Ottoman Lebanon, 1861–1914* (London: Ithaca Press, 1977), pp. 233–34 and passim, and Akarlı, *The Long Peace*, passim.
25. In addition to the works mentioned in note 16 above, see Butrus Abu-Manneh, "Sultan Abdulhamid II and Shaikh Abulhuda al-Sayyadi," *Middle Eastern Studies* 15 (1979): 131–53; Selim Deringil, *The Well-Protected Domains: Ideology and the Legitimation of Power in the Ottoman Empire, 1876–1909* (London: I.B. Tauris, 1998); Benjamin Fortna, "Islamic Morality in Late Ottoman 'Secular' Schools," *International Journal of Middle East Studies* 32 (2000): 369–93; Bayram Kodaman, *Abdülhamid Devri Eğitim Sistemi* (Istanbul, 1980), and Azmi Özcan, *Pan-Islamism: Indian Muslims, the Ottomans and Britain (1877–1924)* (Leiden: E. J. Brill, 1997).
26. On notables, see, in addition to the works mentioned in note 16 above, Butrus Abu-Manneh, "Sultan Abdulhamid II and the Sharifs of Mecca (1800–1900)," *Asian and African Studies* 9 (1979): 1–21; David D. Commins, *Islamic Reform: Politics and Social Change in Late Ottoman Syria* (New York: Oxford University Press, 1990), esp. pp. 104–15; Michel F. Le Gall, *In the Twilight of Ottoman Rule: Libya and Its African Hinterland, 1881–1911* (forthcoming); S. Tufan Buzpınar, "Abdülhamid II, Islam, and Arabs: The Cases of Syria and the Hijaz, 1878–1882," Ph.D. diss., University of Manchester, 1991; Eugene Rogan, *Frontiers of the State in the Late Ottoman Empire* (Cambridge: Cambridge University Press, 1999); and Gökhan Çetinsaya, "Ottoman Administration of Iraq, 1890–1908," Ph.D. diss., University of Manchester, 1994.
27. See YEE: I/165-XXXVIII/156/3 (Nov. 1902) and YEE: 9/2610/72/4 (ca. 1904).
28. This is the impression one gets from the scattered and often indirect information on the actual functioning of the legal system. Otherwise, the subject still awaits its historian. For brief reviews of legal developments, see Ülkü Azrak, "Tanzimattan sonra Resepsiyon," in *Tanzimat'tan Cumhuriyet'e Türkiye Ansik-*

lopedisi 3: 602–6; Shaw and Shaw, 246–49; the articles by Velidedeoğlu, Belgesay, and Taner in *Tanzimat* (Istanbul, 1940), pp. 139–232; Halil Cin, "Tanzimat Döneminde Osmanlı Hukuku ve Yargılama Usulleri" in *150. Yılında Tanzimat*, ed. Hakkı D. Yıldız (Ankara: Türk Tarih Kurumu, 1992), pp. 11–32, and Akarlı, *The Long Peace*, 132–46.

29. For brief assessments of the position of different ethnic and religious groups, see the articles by İlber Ortaylı, Stanford Shaw, and Cevdet Küçük in *Tanzimat'tan Cumhuriyet'e Türkiye Ansiklopedisi* 4: 994–1036, and Roderic Davison, "Nationalism as an Ottoman Response," in *Nationalism in a Non-National State*, ed. W. Haddad and W. Ochsenwald (Columbus: Ohio State University Press, 1977), pp. 25–55.

30. See İsmail Kara, *İslamcıların Siyasi Görüşleri* (Istanbul: İz, 1994), passim; Kara, ed., *Türkiye'de İslamcılık Düşüncesi: Metinler/Kişiler*, vol. 1 (Istanbul: Pınar, 1986); Commins, *Islamic Reform*, 49–144; and Şerif Mardin, *Religion and Social Change in Modern Turkey* (Albany: State University of New York Press, 1989), pp. 124–46.

31. Based on Akarlı, "Friction and Discord within the Ottoman Government under Abdulhamid II," *Boğaziçi University Journal—Humanities* 7 (1979): 3–26, and numerous memoirs of the young Ottoman bureaucrats of this period.

32. A. Vembéry, "Personal Recollections of Abdul Hamid II and His Court," in *The Nineteenth Century and After*, 66 (1909): 71. Also see Tahsin Paşa, pp. 42–44.

33. For these developments, see, for instance, Şükrü Hanioğlu, *The Young Turks in Opposition* (Oxford: Oxford University Press, 1995), pp. 167–199; Feroz Ahmad, *The Young Turks* (Oxford: Clarendon Press, 1969); and Sina Akşin, *31 Mart Olayı* (Istanbul: Sinan, 1972).

34. See, for instance, Hüseyin Kâzım Kadri, *Meşrutiyet'ten Cumhuriyet'e Hatıralarım*, ed. İsmail Kara (Istanbul: İletişm, 1991), among many other sources. Melih Karakullukçu's senior thesis, "Arnold Toynbee and the British Diplomatic Intelligence during the Great War: Expert and Ideology" (Brown University, History Department, Providence, 1997), casts a fresh light on dominant outlooks in Western Europe at this juncture.

35. Ahmet Demirel, *Birinci Meclis'te Muhalefet: İkinci Gurup* (Istanbul: İletişim, 1994). Also see Seyyid Bey, *Hilâfetin Mâhiyyet-i Şer'iyyesi* (Istanbul: TBMM Matbaası, 1924); and the memoirs of Hüseyin Kâzım Kadri, Rauf Orbay, Rıza Nur, Halide Edip Adıvar, and other alienated members of the first representative national assembly.

13 Racial Readings of Empire: Britain, France, and Colonial Modernity in the Mediterranean and Asia

Susan Bayly

The aim of this paper is to illuminate the tensions and complexities of *fin-de-siècle* colonialism by exploring two interrelated facets of intellectual life within the French and British empires. The focus of this twofold discussion is the often pessimistic and fearful understandings of modernity that emerge from popular imperialist tracts and race science journals, and from the writings of the many scholar-officials and academic researchers who saw themselves as key contributors to metropolitan Orientalist debates.

The two elements to be explored here are, first, those aspects of colonial thought which focused on concrete historical changes within the extra-European world, particularly those that both Europeans and non-Western commentators interpreted as collective "awakenings" of religious and national awareness. The second element is accounts of colonial life which emphasized modernity and change in intellectual practice. Here the emphasis will be on those who felt that the revolutionary innovations which they saw as taking place in the new physical and human sciences had profound importance for the understanding of colonial life.

This insistence on the explanatory power of science was a striking feature of *fin-de-siècle* Orientalism: it went hand in hand with a widely shared view that in this age of both alarming and exhilarating modernity, the human mind itself was undergoing profound and irreversible changes. These transformations were often conceived in highly negative terms, with first the expectation and then the actual experience of the First World War giving rise to bleak speculations about the fragility of Western civilization and the innumerable dangers—often conceptualized as emanating from the Asian and Islamic "East"—which were supposedly threatening European power and nationhood.

This was not, then, a picture of modernity and dynamism as existing solely among the so-called advanced races of the Western world. Indeed, at the turn of the century, both French and British Orientalists regularly described the mental faculties of a surprisingly wide range of peoples as moving into a new evolutionary plane through their encounters with the forces of global modernity. Almost everywhere, said these commentators, there were "stirrings" and "awakenings" among the all-important groups of educated non-Europeans who were referred to within the French empire as "évolués."[1]

These regional intelligentsias were widely thought of as being especially large and active in both British India and the French-ruled Mediterranean, and to a lesser extent in Indochina. They were the groups to whom Orientalists regularly looked when they speculated about human awareness in both East and West being transformed by everything from aviation and the cinema to the appeal of such innovatory mental perspectives as pan-Islamism and Bolshevism. Much importance was also attached to the various forms of revolutionary nationalism which had recently taken root in Turkey and China and were also known to be gaining adherents in many colonial societies.

My argument, therefore, is that the most important influence on those who participated in Orientalist debates from the 1890s to the 1920s was a perception of the extra-European world as an arena of momentous change and dynamism. Those who thought in these terms included many important early nationalists, religious reformers, and cultural revivalists from both French- and British-ruled colonial societies. Indeed, by the early twentieth century, it was often these key contributors to indigenous political and cultural life for whom the idea of the newly galvanized and modernizing "Orient" was particularly potent and inspiring, especially where it could be translated into a message of impending doom for Western colonial power.

This chapter's focus is the two great "Oriental" environments that were subject to French and British colonial rule: the Islamic Mediterranean and the "Indic" East. This will involve an exploration of similarities as well as contrasts in writings and debates on the transformations which important fin-de-siècle commentators saw as overtaking both the North African and Near Eastern littoral—most notably in French-ruled Algeria, Morocco, and

Syria, as well as in the British and French colonies and client kingdoms of Indochina and India.

The aim here is to overcome the limitations of old-style "area studies" scholarship, as well as the tendency to treat the French and British imperial systems in isolation from one another. Both approaches tend to overlook the interconnections of culture and ideology which created cross-cutting channels of communication among British, French and other continental Orientalists. Even more important at the turn of the century were the globe-trotting Asian and Mediterranean pilgrims, traders, and *literati* who were encountering a remarkable melting-pot culture of debate and polemic in their travels to such far-flung centers as Yokohama, Johannesburg, and Cairo. These links and contacts brought together Islamic modernists, Indian and Sinhala Aryan revivalists, and a host of other apostles of nationhood and cultural regeneration from virtually every East and West Asian colonial society. There is much to be learned by taking note of these encounters; among those discussed below is the *Revue du Monde Musulman*'s remarkable account of an exchange between a traveling Muslim reformer and a Shinto official attempting to defend his conception of modern Japanese nationhood.

This is not to deny the value of detailed regional studies in understanding both Orientalist writings and the shaping of intellectual life within the individual societies of the colonial world. Nevertheless, there is much to be gained from recognizing that both Western and non-European intellectuals had extremely wide horizons by the end of the nineteenth century, and this was strongly reflected in their theories of race and culture. Thus a wide range of white and non-white colonial commentators had come to think of the world as a continuum of great interconnecting ethno-cultural territories, each marked by a distinctive heritage of race and polity, and each posing its own particular challenges to "modern" men. In the East, both Anglophone and francophone writers attached great importance to the idea that there was a rich common heritage linking the peoples and polities of "Aryan" India with those areas of Southeast Asia (modern-day Laos, Cambodia, and Vietnam) which had come to be referred to as Indochina, or even "*Inde transgangétique.*"[2]

Within the major French Orientalist institutions, above all the École Française d'Extrême Orient (founded 1898), a long line of late nineteenth- and early twentieth-century archaeologists, ethnographers, lexicographers, and cultural geographers pursued this notion of France as both interpreter and critical contributor to the history of civilization in Indochina. Their writings portrayed this region as Asia's great cultural crossroads, a meeting point of the two superior civilizations of the East: the Chinese and the Indian/Hindustani/Sanskritic. At the same time, Indochina was also widely seen as the home of important pre-Aryan aboriginal cultures which had surviving offshoots amongst the so-called tribals of both India's and Indochina's highland regions.[3]

Furthermore, French commentators made much of the special form that France's civilizing mission (*la mission civilisatrice*) had taken in Indochina, where scholars and administrators claimed to have both revived and galvanized this composite high tradition, restoring its monumental architecture, regenerating its traditional monarchies, and endowing the world with untold spiritual riches through the scholarly output of its officially sponsored epigraphers and textual specialists. It was even claimed that the scope of this civilizing mission extended to the heart of so-called Aryan Asia, the Indian subcontinent.

Marginal as they were economically and strategically, the French possessions in Pondichery and Chandernagor were proudly hailed as "*territoire français*" in late-nineteenth- and early twentieth-century imperialist tracts. Like Beirut and Cairo, these enclaves, with their presses, schools, and francophone learned societies were prized in Orientalist circles as bastions of French influence and intellectual power. They were especially important as vantage points from which French scholars could match or even outdo the achievements of Britons (and Germans) in the amassing of expertise on both Aryan and non-Aryan peoples. This in turn was an area of scholarship which aroused increasing interest and concern after the turn of the century as the apocalyptic writings of race theorists and eugenicists pointed ever more emphatically to the degenerative dangers that were supposedly threatening "Aryan" peoples in the West, and at the same time, to the stirrings of activated faith and national awareness that these thinkers saw as transforming the Indic branches of the "Aryan" race.[4]

As for the other regional focus of this paper, the Mediterranean basin, this too was a part of the world that was evoking deeply alarmist ethnogeographical theorizing. Here Orientalist commentators had a rich field for observation and analysis. Much that was being said about the racial composition and cultural essences of contested colonial terrain in India and Indochina was being proposed in very similar terms for the religions and polities of the Mediterranean. For this area too there was a notion of interacting ethno-cultural territories, with French Orientalists giving particular emphasis to their role as bringers of scientific and spiritual insight to the two broad regions which they termed the Levant (modern-day Syria, Lebanon, and the biblical Holy Land) and the Maghreb (Algeria, Morocco, and Tunisia). In these cases, however, debates about the supposedly innate fanaticism of Islam or the allegedly uncivilized and anarchic proclivities of Semitic or Arab "racial types" acquired extra urgency from the growing strategic sensitivity of the entire area.[5]

Furthermore, these regions of the Mediterranean littoral were much closer to the heartland of the so-called Aryan West, and were often represented as lost zones of classical high culture and Christian civilization which were being restored to greatness by the achievements of modern imperial rule. In Algeria, colonial lobbyists claimed that the presence of the fast-growing white settler population was reimplanting Latin Christian civilization in a land which had supposedly been reduced to barbarism by the Semite nomad intruders who had despoiled the advanced agrarian and urban environments of North Africa at the time of the Arab conquests.[6]

Here, too, Western Orientalists claimed to have discovered distant kin who could be reclaimed as allies and clients of the white ruling race. In this case, these supposed racial cousins were the speakers of Berber languages, much glorified in colonial polemic as people of superior racial stock, and even as the descendants of red-haired, fair-skinned, Christianized European Vandal tribes which had supposedly survived in North Africa as a race of "hardy," "vigorous," and "civilized" mountaineers who had bravely resisted the incursion of the rootless and predatory Arab "hordes."[7]

From the turn of the century, much was done to inject new scientific rigor into these theories, especially by environmental theorists like Dr. J. P. Bounhiol of Algiers. Citing new developments in crystallography and particle physics, Bounhiol claimed in 1919 that the differences between "inferior" and "superior" races were determined by the mechanisms of human blood chemistry. The respiratory systems of tropical plains-dwellers had supposedly been required to adapt to oxygen-deficient low-altitude habitats in ways that made them mentally and physically weaker than highlanders.[8]

Once again, there were complex interactions between Western and indigenous contributions to these debates. It should be borne in mind here that from the late nineteenth century, there was an extraordinarily high level of movement into France by North Africans, especially Muslims from Kabylia and the other so-called Berber heartlands. This flow of migrants grew remarkably during the First World War: 173,000 Algerians served in the French army between 1914 and 1918, and another 119,000 Algerian civilians were transported to the metropole to replace French workers who had been called up into the military. By 1918, as much as a third of the male population of Algeria was employed in metropolitan France.[9]

It is hardly surprising, then, that there was such remarkable breadth and vigor in intellectual exchanges between French and North African thinkers, both before and after the Great War. As Salem Chaker has shown, the most notable *fin-de-siècle* contributors to the Arab-Berber debate were Algerian Muslims who attained posts as licensed government schoolmasters (*instituteurs*). From the turn of the century, such figures as the schoolmaster-folklorist and lexicographer Amar (or Said) Boulifa became promoters of Berber literary and cultural revival, enlisting the aid of village bards and savants in their drive to collect Berber poems, proverbs, and folktales, and publishing their findings in the form of dictionaries, grammars, ethnographies, and poetry collections.[10]

There are striking parallels here with the development of Hindi cultural and linguistic revival in India, and particularly in the assertively independent role taken by native intellectuals in these campaigns. In the case of the Berber "awakening" movement of the 1890s and 1900s, Algerian Muslims like Boulifa and the Tuareg lexicographer Cid Kaoui were particularly insistent on the claim that their Berber identity was rooted in language rather than race. They insisted that the Berber tongue could be shown to have especially pure linguistic variants—by which they meant "uncontaminated" by Arabic—in remote areas of Morocco, and among the Tuareg peoples of the western Sudan (modern-day Mali and Chad). And, having made their remarkable enthnographic forays into these distant places, well beyond the frontiers of Algeria, they constructed their own ethno-geography of Berber North Africa, adapting Western archaeological and epigraphical techniques to recover and adapt the archaic pre-Arabic Berber script for modern use. On this basis, they proclaimed that as Berbers they possessed a written language and were thus demonstrably not "primitives," but heirs to a civilized and literate high culture.[11]

The eastern Mediterranean too became an arena for racial and ethno-cultural speculations of this kind. For French commentators the emphasis here was on pan-Islamism and Turkish nationalism, the key question being the extent to which Turkish self-strengthening within the Ottoman Empire represented a decisive break toward the modern by the supposedly lethargic or "fanatical" Muslim inhabitants of these turbulent lands, and whether this in turn would pose a particularly dangerous Eastern challenge to the Western world. And here again, there were powerful indigenous voices in these debates, with notable contributions from *fin-de-siècle* anti-Ottoman polemicists like Halil Ganem and Nadra Moutran, who predicted the imminent fall of the "gangrenous" Ottomon Empire, and looked to such people as the "virile" Christian Maronites and adherents of the "humanitarian" Ba'hai sect as bringers of modernity and regeneration to the oppressed Levant.[12]

Eugenics and Race Theory

Both the British and French versions of these theories contained an underlying core of evolutionist racial doctrine that requires particular emphasis here. At the turn of the century, ethnology, the now discredited science of race, had become an even more pervasive contributor to Orientalist analysis than had been the case in the 1860s and 1870s, when ethnological ideas had played a central role in shaping key models and stereotypes throughout the non-European world.

Evolutionist teachings had left a particularly strong imprint on European understandings of both caste and ethno-religious or communal differences in India. They were central, too, to the interpretation of the demographic catastrophes being experienced by both Pacific islanders and Amerindian tribes. Yet the concerns of both British and continental ethnology were very far from being confined to the colonial world. Indeed, the teachings of race theorists were invoked with particular vehemence in debates about the European balance of power and the fears aroused by such far-reaching national catastrophes as France's defeat by Germany in 1870.[13]

Abhorrent as their methods and teachings are to us today, it is important to understand the enormous influence of race theory both within and beyond Western intellectual circles, and enduring long after the colonial era. Around the turn of the century, the discipline greatly enhanced its prestige and credibility through the claims of its practitioners to have perfected their methodologies through the use of new scientific techniques. This is a striking feature of contributions to the metropolitan race-theory journals, especially those dealing with such key evolutionist issues as native population decline in the Pacific and North America, and the possibility of so-called physiological acclimatization by whites in the tropics.

Those writing on such topics in the major ethnology publications, including the *Journal of the Ethnological Society of London* and the *Bulletins de la Société d'Anthropologie de Paris*, drew extensively on the work of practitioners in a host of allied disciplines, most notably linguistics, genetics, and archaeology, and even the ultra-modern and highly controversial field of psychoanalytic theory.[14]

The teachings of ethnologists were, of course, a critical element in European colonial thinking and policy making. Both France and Britain were major centers of research and debate on racial topics: everywhere from India to Algeria, Indochina and Tahiti, the colonial subject peoples of both powers were subjected to relentless ethnological scrutiny by scholar-officials and other self-proclaimed experts in the techniques of bodily and cranial measurement (anthropometry), by which the proponents of race science believed that they could determine the racial identity of any given human population.

This in turn made it possible to judge which peoples were advanced or inferior in ethnological terms. According to the race theorists, civilization was the unique endowment of those at the highest levels of evolutionary development; even among the so-called higher races only some were predisposed by their racial heritage to attain the two supreme evolutionary attainments of humankind. These were, respectively, the emergence of purified or rational forms of monotheist faith, and the realization of nationhood—the two often being seen as mutually reinforcing and interpenetrating. It was the emphasis on nationhood as a supreme expression of both reason and spirituality that made the teachings of race science so persuasive to new intelligentsias throughout the colonial world. It is therefore wrong to see race science as an exclusively Western or European discipline. Evolutionist racial principles were ardently embraced by nationalists and cultural revivalists from virtually every part of the extra-European world.[15]

Central to the thinking of race scientists was an insistence on the historic role of the so-called Aryan race as bringer of high culture and civilization to the world, annihilating or marginalizing those who were supposedly inferior in racial terms. For ethnologists, all human history was an epic of ceaseless struggle between "advancing" and "down-going" races; every human institution—including all forms of religious faith and all types of political organization—was an expression of the radically different endowments of "race spirit" and "race genius" with which each ethnologically identifiable racial group was endowed.

Hitherto, of course, it had been the supposedly dynamic and creative Aryans who had reached the two supreme evolutionary attainments: nationhood and monotheist religion. Yet it was also central to ethnological analysis that all races—including the hardy, world-conquering, fair-skinned Aryans—were subject to the same implacable forces of evolution which decreed that degeneration and decline were inevitable, and that the loss of racial energy or racial vigor might one day overtake even Aryan civilization.

From the turn of the century, the rise of eugenics as a potent new offshoot of race science added a further dimension to these anxieties. The supporters of such fast-growing organizations as Britain's Eugenic Education Society and National Council for the Promotion of Race Regeneration, and France's *Alliance Nationale pour l'Accroissement de la Population* (National Alliance for Population Growth) wrote in apocalyptic terms about the disasters which must soon befall those nations that did not take urgent steps to promote their national strength through the protection of their collective racial stock. Eugenic themes were very prominent in both metropolitan and colonial debates about whether those who were defined as members of the Anglo-Saxon or French Gallo-Celtic races were losing their vigor and virility, and might soon be supplanted in the global "struggle for mastery" by other dangerously "restless" and "advancing," peoples.[16]

Much cited here were the threats posed by other Europeans, especially Germanic Teutons. But at the turn of the century there was also much alarm at what many ethnologists regarded as signs of advancement and racial awakening among "fresh," dynamic, and "virile" peoples to the East: this included the populations of Eastern Europe and West Asia who were defined in racial terms as Slavs and Turks and, above all, the Aryan peoples of Indic Asia.[17]

In France, eugenics and race theory were strongly marked by the application of new statistical methodologies which appeared to confirm long-held fears that the country had an alarmingly low birth rate compared to all its European rivals. Crucial here was the 1911 publication of the demographer Jacques Bertillon's key eugenicist tract, *La dépopulation de la France*.

Bertillon was a principal contributor to the enduring French eugenicist cult of the *famille nombreuse*. His argument was that France was being fatally enfeebled by its people's low fertility; other nations, especially Germany, were showing themselves to be far more vigorous in promoting those qualities of virility and selfless solidarity which were indispensable to the survival of both families and nations. Bertillon was thus deeply disparaging about what he called the "colonization" of France by large numbers of Italians and other immigrants. With their teeming fecundity, he wrote, these "Français artificiels" were an alien and even dangerous presence in such cities as Marseilles, where their values and way of life were not and never could become "francisé" (frenchified).[18]

British eugenicists were often equally apocalyptic, especially in the wake of the First World War, when polemicists like James Marchant, author of *Birth-Rate and Empire*, warned bleakly that Western civilization was on trial, and that all the signs of degeneration and catastrophe that had portended the collapse of the great classical civilizations were visible in his own time, including "the break-up of family life, the deterioration of the moral and physical stamina of the people."[19] Marchant therefore called on Britons to turn their energies to the task of "race renewal"—by which he meant seeding the empire with strong British "stock," and the prevention of what eugenicists constantly pointed to as the supposedly excessive rate of breeding among those defined as the "weak" and the "feeble-minded."[20]

All this is a chilling anticipation of the extreme racial ideologies of the 1930s. Yet at the turn of the century, this cry of nationhood in danger was much heard. It was articulated with particular force by the motley array of ultra-nationalists and anti-Semitic extremists who came to the fore in French public life at the time of successive metropolitan crises of empire from the late 1880s to the outbreak of the First World War. Most of these radical nationalists were strikingly unlike their counterparts in Britain in identifying defenders of the republican imperialist tradition—Jules Ferry and Léon Gambetta particularly—with the pernicious forces of "modernity and cosmopolitanism" which in their view were endangering France and all Christian civilization.[21]

Ethnological and eugenicist arguments were prominent, too, at the time of the two great pre-war imperial dramas in the Mediterranean—the 1905 Morocco crisis and the 1911 Franco-German Agadir confrontation—when once again it was "German barbarism" that was held up as a great menace from which France must protect the civilized world.[22] In all these cases, racial arguments were invoked by defenders of the army and the church, and by proponents of "revanche" and "national revival" in preparation for the expected war with Germany. References to race were especially prominent in these polemicists' calls for the purging from national life of those supposedly alien and ethnologically degenerate forces that were held to be infiltrating French institutions and undermining the nation's economic and moral health.

As will be seen below, these evolutionist and eugenic concerns had ramifications in virtually every debate about the culture of French-ruled Oriental societies in both North Africa and the Levant. Their importance was most notable in the debate about the peopling of France's most valuable colonial possession, Algeria, with white settlers who were predominantly of non-French origin. They were also central to controversies about which of the native racial "stocks" of both the Maghreb and Indochina might be molded into suitable clients and military recruits without becoming a danger to French authority and power. Even more importantly, there were enthusiastic responses to race science from virtually all the Western-educated intelligentsias of the "Orient" and the Mediterranean littoral, including those of China and Japan and the colonial societies of Islamic and Indic Asia. Japan in particular had keen proponents of the view that strong nationhood could be built only on the foundations of eugenically sound family life.[23]

In everything from the teachings of the Arya Samaj to the prophesies of national and even specifically Aryan regeneration in Persia and Turkey, we meet Muslims, Hindus, and even Japanese and Sinhala Buddhist thinkers deploying the themes of scientific race theory. These include the ethnologists' insistence on the irresistible expansion of advancing races at the expense of weak, degenerate, or "savage" peoples. Claims of expansiveness were central to assertions that true nationhood was within the grasp of those peoples hitherto defined by Western ethnologists as backward in evolutionary terms, and therefore lacking the ability to attain national awakening.

Much favored, too, were assertions about the inextinguishable animosities and repulsions that supposedly divided race from race, and a strong emphasis on the importance of eugenic awareness in matters concerning the modernization of one's traditional society and culture. Notable examples here are the many *fin-de-siècle* Indian nationalists and cultural revivalists who warned of the dangers of "mongrelization" if Indians heeded the calls of Hindu social reformers for the promotion of intercaste marriage. And in both French- and British-ruled colonial societies, educated Muslims were keenly aware of the disparaging eugenicist arguments which were advanced from many modernist quarters in attacks on the "backward" Islamic institution of polygamous marriage.[24]

It is important to note too that the period from the 1890s to the 1920s saw rapid growth in the key institutions and arenas of Western Orientalist scholarship. Like Britain and Germany, France was an extraordinarily prolific producer of writings and statistical surveys on both tradition and modernity in the non-European world. Those who made their mark in French Orientalist circles came from a strikingly wide range of institutional backgrounds, including the metropolitan and colonial *lycées*, universities, museums and medical foundations, and a host of other establishments, including specialized scientific bureaus, often with close ties to the military.[25]

Particularly important in this respect were the large state-sponsored archaeological and ethnographic missions, especially the Mission Archéologique d'Indochine (with headquarters in Hanoi, and affiliated offshoot institutions throughout South and Southeast Asia). This foundation was reconstituted in 1898 as the École Française d'Extrême-Orient (EFEO) and given a wide brief as a sponsor of research expeditions and publications, including the *EFEO Bulletin*.[26]

Among the major metropolitan institutions which were either established or massively expanded in this period were the École des Langues Orientales and the Musée Guimet, which had been founded in 1879 as a museum of "living religions." By 1900, the Guimet had acquired a magnificent collection of Asian art and manuscripts, though retaining its original purpose as a sponsor of research into the spiritual and devotional systems of the great Eastern civilizations.[27] Equally renowned was the Mission Scientifique au Maroc, under whose auspices was published the remarkable *Revue du Monde Musulman* (hereafter *RMM*). The mission's director, Alfred Le Chatelier (also founding editor of the *RMM*) was appointed to a new chair of Muslim "sociologie et sociographie" at France's premier metropolitan academic institution, the Collège de France, in 1903.[28]

Like Le Chatelier himself, the Morocco Mission's prolific research teams were strongly influenced by the new sociological paradigms of Emile Durkheim and his followers. For the ethnographers and ethno-geographers of the Morocco Mission, the expansion of French power into Morocco was a momentous opportunity for the advancement of Durkheimian social science.[29] The physical sciences contributed crucial new models and paradigms for those seeking insight into the cultures of colonial peoples; once again many researchers saw this as especially important in recently occupied lands which they represented as new frontiers for the expansion of scientific knowledge.

The Christian missions were another key source of Orientalist expertise. This was the case in Indochina, where studies of the so-called "Moi" or Montagnard "tribals" were dominated well into the twentieth century by a combination of military and Roman Catholic missionary ethnographers.[30] The Orientalist expertise achieved by French missionary fathers in both the

Maghreb and the eastern Mediterranean was even more notable. The key case here is that of the remarkable Cardinal Lavigerie, hailed as a hero of the French civilizing mission for his humanitarian achievements as founder of the famous White Fathers missionary order, and also for his efforts as an excavator of Algerian archaeological sites dating from the age of St. Augustine. At the turn of the century this mapping of the ancient sites of North African Christianity was a central element in the claims of the Maghreb's white settlers to be the agents of an Iberian-Latin racial revival on the southern Mediterranean littoral.[31]

There was also a massive proliferation of writings produced by France's vigorous and polemical colonialist lobby, the *parti colonial*. These lobbyists' most important outlets to the learned world were the regional geographical societies that were founded from the 1870s onwards in provincial towns with strong colonial links, including Marseilles and Lyons, and also in the major colonial centers, especially Algiers and Hanoi. The geographical societies pursued a broad range of ethnological and Orientalist themes in their widely publicized conferences and lecture series, and in such journals as the *Bulletin de la Société de géographie d'Alger et de l'Afrique du nord* and the *Bulletin de la Société de géographie de Marseille*.[32]

Religion and Race in the Dynamic "Orient"

A remarkable feature of *fin-de-siècle* racial thinking in both Britain and France was the conceptualization of "Indic," as well as Muslim, faith as being collectively gripped by stirrings of political and spiritual energy. This thinking was often expressed in alarmist and hostile terms, yet it would be wrong to disregard the diversity which characterized these accounts of change and dynamism in "Oriental" religious life. The phenomenon of pan-Islamism evoked many of the most surprising expressions of recognition and even enthusiasm at the prospect of modern awakening both within and beyond the colonial world.

From the 1890s to the time of the First World War, a multitude of Western commentators studied the writings of Muslim religious modernists and political commentators throughout both "Indic" Asia and the Islamic Mediterranean. It was above all the activities of these Muslim educators, journalists, publishers, and literati that led influential Orientalists to express a belief in the spread of shared modern values and aspirations which they saw as building cultural bridges from one end of the Muslim world to the other. Indeed this very phrase, the Muslim world or *monde musulman*, came into general use at this time in precisely this sense of a dawning Muslim consciousness which was forward-looking, liberal, and eager to replace traditional modes of life with those of an activated and rationally informed sense of Islamic identity.

These notions were especially strong in the prolific writings of the Muslim and European scholars and literati who contributed to that all-important organ of liberal opinion on *fin-de-siècle* Islam, the *RMM*. Even its title proclaimed this journal's positive views about the growth of worldwide Muslim consciousness. As Edmund Burke III has shown, the force of pan-Islamism and the associated upheavals that were attending the rise of the Young Turks and their nationalist and cultural revivalist counterparts in India, Persia, and Central Asia were the underlying preoccupations of virtually everything published in the *RMM*.[33] Its language was strongly ethnological, yet when it proclaimed that its purpose was "to make Islam known as it is actually evolving," its editors' intentions were very different from those who used race theory to differentiate between the supposedly static and backward East and the dynamic, progressive, individualist West.

From its foundation in 1906 until well after the First World War, the *RMM* had an enthusiastic following among both French and British Orientalists. Its commentators shared a conviction that in the new political and cultural movements which they believed they were seeing everywhere from West Asia to the Indonesian archipelago, they were witnessing a "springtime of the Muslim peoples."[34]

This idea of Muslims reaching a crossroads, with pan-Islamism being both a danger and a moment of opportunity for both the East and the Christian West, had much in common with Orientalist comment on the awakening of "Aryan" race energies in the Indian subcontinent. Most influential on this topic were the British commentators who read portentous racial meanings into the rise of late nineteenth- and early twentieth-century Hindu and Buddhist revivalist organizations, especially the Arya Samaj, the Ramakrishna Mission movement, and the worldwide Buddhist resurgence movement led by Anagarika Dharmapala.[35]

In the 1920s, the emergence of Indochina's remarkable Cao Dai religion evoked strikingly similar responses. Fascination with the ethnological implications of Cao Dai was especially marked among French observers for whom this syncretistic faith's exaltation of Confucius, Sun Yat-Sen, and Victor

Hugo as prophets of modernity and spiritual enlightenment seemed either a potential subversion of colonial power, or a means by which Oriental wisdom and French science could fuse and strengthen one another, and in so doing uplift and invigorate the decadent West. In this respect there is a striking parallel with Theosophy, which, like Cao Dai, had fervent Western adherents and a sizable following among anti-colonial cultural nationalists in India and Ceylon.[36]

In all these cases, those who were optimistic about the advance of reason and progress in the Orient saw both the Mediterranean and the Indic East as being energized and invigorated by the emergence of dynamic new intelligentsias. It was these groups of progressive thinkers whom the *RMM* had in mind when it used the term "liberal classes" (*les classes libérales*). Included in this category were the French empire's so-called *évolués*, but there was also much enthusiasm for the spread of progressive thought and values in many other Muslim lands among teachers, journalists, literati, and professional men, as well as many Western-educated officials and trading people.

In their writings on the Muslim world, the *RMM*'s contributors attached particular importance to such people's participation in the public arena. Those writing for the journal regularly conveyed that it was above all as readers and contributors to newspapers that educated Muslims were playing this key role as guarantors of social and political progress for their fellow believers. It was the liberal Muslim's receptiveness to modernity that would hold at bay the pernicious forces of tradition, especially the dangerous enthusiasms that anti-Muslim polemicists denounced as the Islamic predisposition toward "fanaticism." The achievements of educated women were a particular focus in the *RMM*'s coverage of progressive evolution in Muslim lands.

All this was obviously very far from the Islamophobic stereotypes which were still appearing in colonialist journals and race-theory writings. Indeed, from just before the First World War until well into the 1920s, there was a particularly virulent spate of publications on Islam. The most striking of these were by French Orientalists who made much of their credentials as men of the modern sciences, especially psychology and psychoanalysis. André Servier's 1913 polemic, *La Psychologie du musulman* (published in English in 1924, with an introduction by the theorist of white "rebarbarization" in North Africa, Louis Bertrand), offers a potent distillation of these views. Conspicuous in Servier's text is a parade of fashionable brain science jargon in support of his claims about the irrationality and sterility of the "Muslim mind." His chapter headings sum up the repellant outcome of his "scientific" approach:

- Islam, by its immutable dogmas, has paralyzed the brain and killed all initiative;
- The Bedouin–Fatalism–endurance–insensibility, Semitic anarchy–egoism–sensuality;
- Arab decadence in Persia, Mesopotamia, and Egypt . . . Political nullity—absence of creative genius—absence of discipline—bad administration—no national unity . . . servile position of women;
- The Musulman community is theocratic- religious law, inflexible and immutable.[37]

Even outside the Muslim world, many French and British commentators were deeply suspicious of the *évolué*, or "native gentleman." These included the polemicists who denounced the subversive activities of assertive intelligentsias in India, Indochina, and the Maghreb, insisting that few, if any, inhabitants of these regions could ever be truly remade into reliable clients or collaborators, and that the emergence of true nationhood among them was at best a distant prospect. For both Asia and the Muslim Mediterranean, some theorists of race and culture insisted that the making of the *évolué* was a particularly slow and painful process; those who were being entrusted with the benefits of French education and potential rights of French citizenship had to be carefully watched for signs of inferior racial predispositions.

Of particular concern to Indochina specialists were supposedly scientific indications that individualism was alien to the Asian mind, and that this was the critical race failing which was overriding the Vietnamese intelligentsia's capacity to evolve toward authentic French cultural and political allegiance. Charles Robequain thus warned his readers not to be taken in by the *évolué*'s education and modern garb: "[Beneath] his collar and soft hat, the son of Indo-China keeps the character and deep-seated tastes of his race." Having returned from his studies in France, the educated native will tend to fall into "a kind of intellectual nonchalance and insurmountable apathy, no longer able to learn or to perfect himself." "Hence," says Robequain "[for] a long time to come, new tendencies will have to compromise with the traditions and hidden forces characteristic of the race, and French and native influences will have to merge."[38]

All this throws into even sharper relief the decidedly un-Islamophobic sentiments of the *Revue du Monde Musulman*. In the eyes of the *RMM*'s contributors, the Muslim and Indic East were bubbling with new and progressive intellectual and social energies because of the growing influence of intelligentsias (*les classes libérales*) in virtually every Muslim land from the Maghreb and Egypt to Persia, the Russian-ruled Caucasus, Malaya, India, and China.[39] The *lettrés* who were given particular prominence in *RMM* essays and press summaries included the supporters of liberal constitutionalism in Persia, the Balkans, and the Arab and Turkish-dominated regions of the Ottoman Empire, together with a wide range of religious reformers, including those schooled in reformed versions of the Islamic curriculum.

Journalists and editors were especially important for the *RMM*'s view of progress and evolution in the Muslim world. Every number of the journal included a detailed set of press reports, including announcements of the founding of new "native" newspapers and reviews, and lengthy digests of their contents. This coverage of Turkish, Urdu, Arabic, Caucasian, and Persian newspaper writings consistently conveyed to the *RMM*'s readership an impression of intellectually dynamic Muslim editors and writers (as well as many local Christians and Jews) who expected their readers to be keen followers of modernist religious and philosophical debate and to share their enthusiasm for news of scientific and technical innovation.

One typical *RMM* newspaper summary covers a two-month period in 1909 in which Egyptian newspapers were said to have noted the announcements of important new sightings made by Western astronomers, and to have hailed the achievements of the American explorers Peary and Cook, who had recently claimed to have reached the North Pole. The same survey also refers to an account of a debate in the Beirut press on the topic of Darwinian evolution involving the controversial Muslim journalist and religious modernist Rashid Rida. There is also coverage of another Levant journal which had published both a learned disquisition on the philosopher Averroes's concept of monism and an item extolling the newly invented phonograph as an instrument of social progress.[40]

The influence of radical new political ideologies was also made much of in the *RMM*'s newspaper extracts. In 1907, it noted the appearance of three Arabic journals published in Tunis. Two were said to be intended for Muslim readers, including a weekly edited by Mr. Essadok bin Ibrahim, whose aims were described as defending the interests of native workers and "ameliorating the economic and social condition of the Arab proletariat"; the third, published by a Tunisian Jew, was quoted as demanding "more light and justice" for the editor's North African co-religionists.[41]

An especially notable feature of the RMM was its publication of items which were strongly critical of French colonial policy, especially where these were seen to be inimical to the growth of liberal intelligentsias. Thus in 1907, the journal carried an essay by the German Orientalist Martin Hartmann, which noted that although France was putting a modest amount of resources into "native" education in Tunisia and Algeria—though largely at primary level—it was regrettable that the Maghreb was not developing an independent Muslim press on the same scale as British India's. This, Hartmann implied, was a sign that India's British authorities were significantly more far-sighted than the French in their dealings with potential Muslim collaborators.[42]

Even so, in 1911, the RMM's press survey noted the launch of a French language newspaper, Le Rachidi, which it said was being published in the Algerian town of Djidjelli. According to the RMM, Le Rachidi had a French managing director and "un Arabe" as chief editor, one Monsieur Nassih. Unsurprisingly, given the authoritarianism of Algeria's colonial regime, the journal's stance was Francophile and paternalist: its motto was "Par la France pour les Indigènes," and it described its aims as the achievement of rapprochement between European and native "elements."[43] Nevertheless, in this volatile and often violent society, with its fiercely Islamophobic tradition of white settler dominance, it was daring for the publication even to hint at these interracial tensions, expressing the hope that its coverage of matters of generalized local interest might lessen the animosities and mistrust existing between the locality's whites and Muslims.

This was in effect a declaration of belief in the power of liberal institutions to promote progressive social forces, and even to foster the growth of nationhood, however apparently unpropitious the terrain. The implication then was that as readers of the same locally based modern newspaper, Europeans and educated Muslims would acquire bonds of "imagined community" within a shared public sphere. Indeed, having learned from the experience of being Djidjelli or Algiers newspaper readers, they might even join hands one day with their European and Muslim counterparts in Algiers's other towns and cities, thus achieving a final evolutionary move toward shared national awareness. Similar sentiments and expectations inform a great deal of the RMM's coverage of Muslim newspapers.

All this, of course, is close to what Benedict Anderson describes in his account of the role of the *fin-de-siècle* and early twentieth-century urban press in the Philippines in giving rise to a new experience of collective modernity, and ultimately to a sense of shared Filipino nationhood.[44] What is striking in the Algerian case, however, is that there is so much more ambiguity about the shared awareness that the *Rachidi's* Muslim and European readers might be attaining. Overt anti-colonialism would have been impossible to express in this setting; yet it is possible that the *RMM's* coverage may have been signaling the beginnings of a sense of shared Algerian national identity.

The implications of this are complex and problematic. Until well into the twentieth century it was Algeria's white settlers, rather than Muslims (*indigènes*), who identified themselves as "*Algériens.*" The term *Algérien* was strongly associated with the claims which were being made by a whole host of Islamophobic white supremacists about the forging of a new white Algerian race.[45] Algeria's vast nineteenth-century influx of Italian, Maltese, Spanish, and Corsican white settlers was hailed for its endowments of "fresh" and "virile" race energies. By hybridizing them with *pieds noirs* of metropolitan French origin, French race theorists said that *colons* were creating a wholly new racial composite which would reinvigorate or "rebarbarize" the declining racial stock of metropolitan France, and ultimately the whole of Europe. At the turn of the century, Algeria's towns and cities had given rise to a host of publications and literary circles whose members were eager to demonstrate the vigor and creative energies of this white Algerian race.[46]

In sharp contrast to all this, the *Rachidi* newspaper seems to be signaling exactly the opposite of this vision of an Algerian imagined community which excluded the Muslim *indigène*. The key points of reference in the *Rachidi's* formulations are Frenchness and French nationhood. Its imagined readers were to look beyond Algeria to the "greater France" of *metropole*, plus assimilated colonial societies. They were to aspire to a universalizing ideal of French culture which embraced native *évolués*, as well as those of metropolitan French origin, without regard to race. The most daring feature of this newspaper's writings was the fact that it felt able to raise the most controversial issue concerning the *indigènes* of pre–First World War Algeria, this being the debate about conscription and citizenship for Algerian Muslims. This measure was bitterly opposed by the white *colon* lobbies, and it was therefore very notable that Nassih bravely stated his support for universal male conscription for Muslims, on the condition, he said, that those called up received fair compensation, meaning legal rights equivalent to those of white French citizens.

The suggestion that British officials were more enlightened than the French in their treatment of Muslim intelligentsias appears very regularly in the *RMM*. This, of course, was a highly provocative notion, given the long tradition of claims about the unique sophistication of French insights into the religions and cultures of Oriental peoples. Yet the *RMM* had much to say about the relatively benign forms of pan-Islamism which its contributors found in British India; the implication here was that a much more dangerous stirring of Islamic consciousness would take root in French-ruled territories unless France made more constructive overtures to its colonies' "modern men."

To illustrate this claim, the *RMM* offered an account of comments reportedly made in 1907 by two Indian Muslims at a lecture on pan-Islamism delivered to a London audience by *The Times'* editor, Valentine Chirol, a prolific pre-war commentator on Indian affairs. The two Muslims are identified as "Major Syed Hassan" and "Ameer Ali"; the latter is probably Amir Ali, an early supporter of the Muslim League who had settled in London after his retirement as leader of the Patna Bar.[47] The French translation of the two Muslims' remarks is notable for its use of phrasing with powerful significance for Francophone readers.

Both commentators are credited with a use of language that faithfully reproduces French republican phraseology. According to the translator's rendering, these are Muslims whose pan-Islamic sentiments are informed by humane and progressive principles. The report has them speaking in terms of the rights of man—of liberty, equality, and a hatred of religious zealotry and bigotry. Pan-Islamism in this form is to be seen as a wholly positive force. Thus the rather surprising view taken here is that under enlightened British colonial rule, pan-Islamists have reached a plane of evolutionary awareness which is directly parallel to that of humanity's most advanced form of consciousness: the French republican ideal.[48]

Linking the Mediterranean and the Modernizing East

The "modern" perspectives of the *RMM* gave particular prominence to those bearers of new religious and cultural messages who were making intellectual and personal contacts with one another far beyond the confines of narrow geographical or linguistic units. Hostile observers too proclaimed insistently that faiths once derided as inert and stagnant—not only Islam, but also Hinduism, Buddhism, and Confucianism—were apparently all in the grip of great spiritual renewals and transformations. Much scholarly and polemical energy was focused on the Hindu revivalist Swami Vivekananda, on the Sinhala Buddhist polemicist Anagarika Dharmapala, and on the many other great *fin-de-siècle* prophets of global awakening whose pronouncements were interpreted both as claims of uplifting world mission and as dangerous calls to arms.

What many British and continental Orientalists found especially remarkable at this time was the fact that such a multitude of these newly energized and assertive people from the Mediterranean and Indic East were finding ways to speak and interact independently, rather than relying on narrow lines of contact and communication within a single colonial homeland. One striking manifestation of this was the quickness of regional newspapers to respond to events in distant regions, including those ruled by other foreign powers. The *RMM* reported extensively on Indian Muslim newspapers' attacks on the French. In 1911, Indian editors expressed fierce indignation at the prospect of the French annexation of Morocco; there was also an outcry over the Italian occupation of Tripolitania (Libya), with calls for boycotts of Italian goods and other militant action to show that Indian Muslims understood that these moves constituted a threat of annihilation to the "whole of Islam."[49]

Even more striking is the apocalyptic language quoted in *RMM* extracts from the Egyptian press at the time of the so-called Tlemcen *hijra* of 1911. This much publicized mass migration of as many as 2,000 Muslims to Ottoman-ruled Syria from the Algerian spiritual center of Tlemcen evoked vigorous anti-French comments in Egypt's Arabic-language newspapers, with much sympathy being expressed for these Muslims who were said to have pronounced Algeria a land of ruin and impiety which had been rendered unfit for habitation through the despoliations of French rule.[50] Elsewhere, too, there were denunciations of European actions in both Egypt and the Maghreb, and accusations that by their actions as colonial rulers the European powers had already ensured after a single decade that the new age of the Christian calendar would be "a century of murder and blood."[51]

What this coverage makes especially apparent is that these assertive modern Muslims and other Asians were being galvanized by models of science, progress, and nationhood which were far from being exclusively Western or

European in origin. It is above all Japan that appears in these accounts as the great new source of inspiration for both "Indic" and Mediterranean followers of modernity. This comes across especially strongly in *RMM* contributions from Muslim writers.

Among the most notable of the essayists who wrote for the *RMM* was F. Farjenel, whose article, "Le Japan et l'Islam," appeared in 1907.[52] Farjenel's account paints an elegiac picture of worldwide Muslim reactions to the outcome of the 1904 Russo-Japanese war, pointing to Turkish, Urdu, Persian, and Arabic newspaper coverage of Japan's annihilation of the Russian imperial fleet, and describing this sensational event as having aroused throughout Asia, Africa, and every "Muslim land," a collective thrill of awakening (*un frisson de réveil*).[53]

For Muslims above all, Farjenel says, this sense of shared exultation in the intellectual and military prowess displayed by a "people of the yellow race" had aroused a potent vision of interactions and shared cultural inspiration. On the other hand, he says, newspapers in India were reporting that young men of both Muslim and Hindu faith were flocking to Japan to acquire the new technical and military skills which were the special glory of its progressive national policies. This vision of Japan as a domain of forward-looking education was of particular importance for Farjenel, who cited it in support of his controversial position as a proponent of radical curricular reforms in the Islamic teaching syllabus at al-Azhar.

Yet this flow of modern influences was emphatically not seen as a one-way process. On the contrary, Farjenel reports on Egyptian press comments about the prospect of eager modernists from Japan turning for intellectual and cultural inspiration to the Muslim world. Soon, say these Cairo newspapers, delegations of Japanese pupils would be studying at al-Azhar. Ultimately, he maintains, as they discovered its power as a faith of reason and science, the Japanese people would convert *en masse* to Islam.

This was, of course, a period when a remarkably diverse array of Asian cultural revivalists and religious nationalists were touring the world in attempts to build broad international links and contacts for their movements of Buddhist, Hindu, or Muslim resurgence. Swami Vivekananda and Angarika Dharmapala were among the most prominent of these. Visits to Japan were a particularly important feature of these travelers' itineraries, especially at the time of the Tokyo International Congress of Religions, in 1900.

The writer and educational reformer Hajji Muhammad Ali was among the notable Muslim modernists who included Japan on his itinerary. The *RMM* took particular note of his writings about the voyages which he undertook, beginning in 1891, when he left his birthplace in Caucasian Georgia to become a student of Arabic and the Islamic sciences in the *madrasas* of Constantinople, Cairo, and the Hijaz. In his later journeys in 1895, 1900, and 1903, he reported on visits to native-born and expatriate Muslims living as far afield as India, the Yemen, Zanzibar, Mozambique, and South Africa, with subsequent trips to visit Muslims living in Malaya, Burma, Hong Kong, Indochina, and even Manchuria.

With his proficiency in Urdu, Turkish, Arabic, and Georgian, and some knowledge at least of English, Mandarin, Japanese, and Malay, the Hajji was clearly an embodiment of that spirit of modernity that the *RMM* saw as characterizing the dynamic "liberal classes" of the Muslim world. Its report conveys that wherever he went, the Hajji was treated as a man of distinction and a source of insight into worldwide Muslim affairs.[54]

Yet visiting Japan in 1900, the Hajji encountered difficulties which show how problematic it could be for proponents of resurgent faith and nationhood in different lands to achieve a common understanding of modernity. The *RMM*'s account suggests that he had regarded Japan as a progressive but also largely secular society, tolerant in its willingness to allow the building of mosques in the international trading enclave at Yokohama, but lacking in commitment to its own faiths, and therefore ripe for conversion to Islam. But when he sought permission from what the *RMM* calls Japan's *"directeur de cultes"* to seek out potential Japanese converts and teach them the precepts of the faith, he received an emphatic refusal.

The rejection reportedly came in the form of a letter conveying that Islam, even in the self-consciously modernist form championed by Hajji Muhammad Ali, was not modern enough for the Japanese. According to the *RMM*, the point at issue was the legal safeguarding of marriage, which had come to be so widely regarded around the world as a crucial test of modernity and national achievement. Thus, speaking on behalf of the official Shinto priestly hierarchy, itself a department of state from the time of the modernizing Meiji Restoration of 1868, the government's spokesman Mr. Shiba rejected the Hajji's application on the grounds of Islam's known backwardness in this area. The Qur'an, says his letter, gave divine sanction to polygamy; Hajji Muhammad was therefore seeking to spread religious teachings that contravened Japanese law and morality.[55]

onclusion

This chapter has had a number of aims. First it has sought to establish that to appreciate the complexities of *fin-de-siècle* modernity, it is important to look for interpenetrations and contacts that transcend narrow geographical limits. There was thus an attempt to show how much osmosis there was between the French and British colonial systems at the level of both thought and action, even in times of ultra-nationalist tension and rivalry. It also argued that the two broad regions which were explored, the Mediterranean littoral and "Indic" Asia, were powerfully linked, both at the level of the Western Orientalist debate and in the interactions of their globe-trotting indigenous thinkers and writers.

The second point was that despite the constraints which they faced under authoritarian colonial regimes, non-European thinkers made extraordinarily vigorous contributions to the Orientalist debate. To a considerable extent, this reflects the powerful rivalries which existed between the major colonial powers, with writers from both the Mediterranean and the Indic East frequently finding ways to play one colonial power off against another through press comments and contributions to learned journals.

Thirdly, it is notable that Western writings on the "Orient" were often far more nuanced and sophisticated than is often supposed. Learned commentaries on Islam were not all one-dimensionally hostile and ignorant in their account of Muslim faith and culture. Indic Asia too was often, if not invariably, treated with respect and even awe in Orientalist accounts, with particular emphasis on "stirrings" of nationhood and prophetic religious modernity in the further reaches of the "Aryan" East.

A further point is that in both positive and negative accounts of these two great extra-European environments, evolutionist race theories were remarkably influential and enduring. This continued to be the case as Orientalist debates became increasingly dominated by "scientific" concepts of modernity. Indeed, it is clear that at the turn of the century and beyond, an extraordinarily wide range of intellectual battles were framed in racial terms. In the arena of colonial debate, racial perspectives defined positions ranging from the ultra-conservative to the most daringly liberal and progressive.

Finally, it is important to stress that this continued insistence on the power of race in the concerns of modern peoples and nations was not simply a system of thought conceived by Europeans to create demeaning stereotypes of the Indic or Muslim "other." On the contrary, although race theory obviously did do much to advance colonial interests in both the French and British empires, the application of evolutionist ideas to colonial environments was merely one element of a much larger and more complex intellectual enterprise. Indeed, at the turn of the century, the most dynamic developments in racial thinking were taking place on two very different fronts. Within Europe, they were central to debate about the impending decline of Western civilization and nationhood; among non-Europeans, they were a potent basis on which new concepts of both Islamic and "Indic" faith and nationhood were being built.

Notes

1. Both citizenship and exemption from the *indigenat* penal codes could be granted to *évolués*, i.e., non-whites who were deemed to have been "civilized" by French schooling and/or soldiering. There was restricted "native" representation on Algeria's turbulent white settler-controlled city councils and on its higher budgetary body, the Délégation Financière. See Robert Aldrich, *Greater France: A History of French Overseas Expansion* (Basingstoke: Macmillan, 1996), pp. 212–22; Raymond Betts, *Assimilation and Association in French Colonial Theory, 1890–1914* (New York 1961); David Prochaska, *Making Algeria French: Colonialism in Bône 1870–1920* (Cambridge: Cambridge University Press, 1990); Charles-Robert Ageron, *Modern Algeria. A History from 1830 to the Present*, 2nd ed. (London: Hurst, 1990).

2. This Indic continuum also embraced the Dutch-ruled Indonesian archipelago (or Insulinde). On Indochinese linguistic and cultural studies, see George Coedes, "Études indochinoises," *Bulletin de la Société des Études Indochinoises* 26, no. 4 (1951): 437–62; Georges Taboulet, "De quelques travaux historiques récents sur l'Indochine française," *Revue d'histoire des colonies* 36, no. 126 (1949): 154–91.

3. These formulations owed much to the cultural geographers Pierre Gourou and Charles Robequain, and hence to Vidal de la Blache's theories of culture and environment. See Pierre Gourou, *Les pays tropicaux. Principes d'une géographie humaine et économique*, 2nd ed. (Paris, 1948); and Charles Robequain, *L'évolution économique de l'Indochine française* (Paris, 1939). On Braudel's debt to Vidal de la Blache, see Peter Burke, *The French Historical Revolution: The Annales School* (London: Polity Press 1986), p. 37; on *fin-de-siècle* social science and the popularization of ethno-geographical theories of nationhood, see Gerard Noiriel, *The French Melting Pot: Immigration, Citizenship and National*

Identity (London, 1996); and Herman Lebovics, *True France: The Wars Over Cultural Identity 1900–1945* (Ithaca: Cornell University Press, 1992).

4. Even Pacific islanders were drawn into these debates. See A.J. Ballantyne, "Comparative Ethnologies: India and New Zealand in the Nineteenth Century," Ph.D. diss., University of Cambridge, 1999.

5. In North Africa, ethno-geographical debate focused on the claims of Orientalists who had constructed a picture of the Maghreb as a terrain of long-running confrontation between opposing Berber and Arab "racial elements." See Alfred Bel, "Caractère et développement de l'Islam en Berberie," in *Histoire et historiens de l'Algérie*, vol 4, ed. Stephane Gsell (Paris: Librairie Felix Alcan, 1931), pp. 177–206; and Patricia Lorcin, *Imperial Identities: Stereotyping and Race in Colonial Algeria* (London: I.B. Tauris, 1995). The notions of scientific modernity that came to dominate this debate will be discussed below.

6. Jacques Zeiller, "L'histoire ancienne de l'Afrique chrétienne," in *Histoire et historiens de l'Algérie*, 4: 111–37.

7. On attempts to identify ethnological ties between the Berbers and such peoples as the Vandals, Basques, and Phoenicians, and the ancestors of Egypt's Coptic Christians, see Jules-René Anselin "Rapport sur Bougie," *Bulletins de la Société d'anthropologie de Paris* 1860): 155–68; M. Michel, "Sur la parenté des Egyptians, des Berbers et des Basques," *Bulletins de la Société d'anthropologie de Paris* 4 (1863): 365–67; Dr. Bertholon, "Note sur l'identité des Basques et des Phéniciens," *Bulletins de la Société d'Anthropologie de Paris* 7, no. 4 (1896): 663–71; Michael Brett and Elizabeth Fentress, *The Berbers* (Oxford: Blackwell, 1996), p. 165.

8. See J. P. Bounhiol, *Bulletin de la Société de Géographie d'Alger* 25 (1920): 156–71; Lorcin, *Imperial Identities*.

9. Ageron, *Modern Algeria*, p. 78.

10. Salem Chaker, "L'affirmation identitaire berbère à partir des 1900," *Revue de l'Occident Musulman* 44 (1987): 13–33.

11. Ibid.

12. Nadra Moutran, *La Syrie de demain*, 2nd ed. (Paris: Plon-Nourrit, 1916); on Ganem (Ghanim), see Albert Hourani, *Arabic Thought in the Liberal Age 1798–1939* (Oxford: Oxford University Press, 1962), pp. 264–65.

13. For ethnologists' views on population decline in the Pacific and North Africa, see H. Gros, "Les populations de la Polynésie française en 1891. Étude ethnique," *Bulletins de la société d'anthropologie de Paris* 7, no. 4 (1896): 144–97; and Arsène Dumont, "Note sur la demographie des Musulmans en Algérie," *Bulletins de la Société d'anthropologie de Paris* 8, no. 4 (1897): 702–17; compare Ballantyne, "Comparative Ethnologies" and S. Bayly, "Caste and 'Race' in the Colonial Ethnography of India," in *The Concept of Race in South Asia*, ed. Peter Robb (Delhi: Oxford University Press, 1995), pp. 93–137.

14. Joseph Desparmet's attempt to contribute to the study of North African maraboutism (Islamic mysticism) by collecting data on dreams and the unconscious is discussed in S. Bayly, "French Colonialism and the Political Anthropology of Crisis," unpublished paper presented to the Department of Social Anthropology, University of Cambridge, January 1999. (Especially notable is Desparmet's account of the subversive political content of Algerians' dreams and prophecies during the First World War. See Joseph Desparmet, "Ethnographie traditionelle de la Mettidja: l'enfance [1]," *Bulletin de la Société de Géographie d'Alger* 25 (1920): 123–55. On the use made of new discoveries in archaeology in *fin-de-siècle* ethnological debate see Arsène Dumont, "Ethnographie tunisienne," *Bulletins de la Société d'Anthropologie de Paris* 7, no. 4 (1896): 393–95.

15. See, e.g., Frank Dikötter ed., *The Construction of Racial Identities in China and Japan* (London: Hurst, 1997).

16. See S. Bayly, "Caste and Race"; and Elazar Barkan, *The Retreat of Scientific Racism: Changing Concepts of Race in Britain and the United States between the World Wars* (Cambridge: Cambridge University Press, 1992).

17. Charles Morris, *The Aryan Race: Its Origins and Achievements* (London, 1888); see C. Bayly in this volume on similar debates about the Egyptian Copts.

18. Jacques Bertillon, *La dépopulation de la France. Ses conséquences — ses causes. Mésures à prendre pour la combattre* (Paris: Librairie Felix Alcan, 1911).

19. James Marchant, *Birth-Rate and Empire* (London, 1917), p. 12. The key colonial policy-maker Albert Sarraut bemoaned the "renaissance of Asia" as against the postwar "decline of the West" (quoted in Christopher Andrew and A. S. Kanya-Forstner, *France Overseas: The Great War and the Climax of French Imperial Expansion* [London: Thames and Hudson, 1981], p. 242).

20. Marchant belonged to a pressure group calling for control of the commercial cinema; like many eugenicists he saw modern consumer culture as a menace to "racial health."

21. On anti-republican extremism, see Robert Tombs, *France 1814–1914* (London: Addison Wesley Longman, 1996), 435–54.

22. James J. Cooke, *New French Imperialism, 1880–1910: The Third Republic and Colonial Expansion* (Newton Aboot: David & Charles, 1973), pp. 107–74.

23. Dikötter, *The Construction of Racial Identities.*

24. On French ethnologists' concerns about so-called "race mixing" between highland *Montagnard* peoples and lowland Khmers and "Annamites," see J. Charles-Roux, ed., *Exposition universelle de 1900. Les colonies françaises. Colonies et pays de protectorats: Indochine* (Paris, 1900), p. 190; compare S. Bayly, "Hindu Modernizers and the 'Public' Arena: Indigenous Critiques of Caste in Colonial India," in *Swami Vivekananda and the Modernization of Hinduism* (Delhi: Oxford University Press, 1998), pp. 93–137.

25. M. Bell, R. Butlin, and M. Heffernan, eds., *Geography and Imperialism, 1820–1920* (Manchester: Manchester University Press, 1995).

26. Britain's counterpart of the EFEO was the School of Oriental and African Studies (founded 1916). One of the more colorful scholar-adventurers attached to the EFEO was the Sinologist Paul Pelliot (1878–1945), whose exploits as a soldier, diplomat and/or spy are described in René Grousset, "Figures d'Orientalistes," *Bulletin de la Société des Études Indochinoises* 26, no. 4 (1951): 413–26.

27. In 1905, in the sober setting of the Guimet's library, an audience of statesmen and savants witnessed a *"danse brahmanique"* (Brahmanical dance) performed as a tribute to the museum's Orientalist ideals by the famous entertainer, spy, and courtesan Mata Hari. See Keiko Omoto, "Émile Guimet et le musée des religions," *Beaux Arts* special number: *Musée Guimet: Musée National des arts Asiatiques* (1993): 9–12.

28. Edmund Burke III, "The Sociology of Islam: The French Tradition," in *Islamic Studies: A Tradition and Its Problems*, ed. M. Kerr (Malibu: Undena Publications, 1980), pp. 73–88.

29. See Burke, "The Sociology of Islam," and Edmund Burke III, "The First Crisis of Orientalism," in *Connaissances du Maghreb. Sciences sociales et colonisation*, ed. Jean-Claude Vatin et al. (Paris: CNRS, 1984), pp. 213–26.

30. Oscar Salemink, "Mois and Maquis: The Invention and Appropriation of Vietnam's Montagnards," in *Essays on the Contextualization of Ethnographic Knowledge*, ed. G. Stocking. History of Anthropology, vol. 7 (Madison, Wisc.: University of Wisconsin Press, 1991).

31. Tombs, *France 1814–1914*, p. 456; Lorcin, *Imperial Identities*; Dr. Laupts, "Populations d'Algérie," *Bulletin de la Société d'anthropologie de Paris* (1898): 388–408; Dr. Bertholon, "La France dans l'Afrique du nord: coloniser ou assimiler?" and "Populations d'Algérie," *Bulletins de la Société d'Anthropologie de Paris* (1897): 509–36.

32. Also the *Bulletin du comité de l'Afrique française*. See Andrew and Kanya-Forstner, *France Overseas*; Stuart Persell, *The French Colonial Lobby, 1889–1938* (Stanford 1983); Heffernan, in *Geography and Imperialism*; Pierre Brocheux and Daniel Hemery, *Indochine: La colonisation ambigüe 1856–1954* (Paris: CNRS, 1995), pp. 38–39.

33. See Burke, "The First 'Crisis' of Orientalism."

34. Ibid., 225.

35. See, e.g., Morris, *Aryan Race*; The Earl of Ronaldshay, *The Heart of Aryavarta: A Study in the Psychology of Indian Unrest* (London, 1925).

36. Spiritualism, which sought rapprochement between "Oriental" wisdom and Western rationality, had wide appeal in both Britain and France. Like most of his cabinet, the radical politician Emile Combes, whose government weathered the 1905 Morocco crisis and implemented a controversial anti-clerical program in 1902–4, was both a Freemason and a keen spiritualist. See Tombs, *France: 1814–1914*, pp. 469–70; on Cao Dai, see Jayne Werner, *Peasant Politics and*

Religious Sectarianism: Peasant and Priest in the Cao Dai in Vietnam (New Haven: Yale University Press, 1981); Gabriel Gobron, *History and Philosophy of Caodaism* (Saigon: Le-Van-Tan Printing House, 1950).

37. André Servier, *Islam and the Psychology of the Muslman*, trans. A. S. Moss-Blundell (London: Chapman & Hall, 1924).
38. Robequain, *L'évolution economique*, p. 13.
39. *RMM* 1 (1907): 114.
40. *RMM* 9, no. 3 (1909): 325–26, 336–37.
41. *RMM* 7 May 1907, p. 243.
42. *RMM* 1, no. 3 (1907): 453–57.
43. *RMM* (1911); André Nouschi, *La naissance du nationalisme Algérien* (Paris: Les editions de minuit, 1962), p. 23. Like other prominent Algerians, including Freemasons and members of the nationalist Young Algeria movement, this journal's editor was placed under police surveillance at the outbreak of the First World War. Report of Police Commissaire for Constantine, 22 October 1914, Carton 9H 16: GGA, "*Affaires indigènes*," folder 9H17, Archives d'Outre-Mer, Aix-en-Provence, France.
44. Benedict Anderson, *Imagined Communities: Reflections on the Origin and Spread of Nationalism*, 4th ed. (London: Verso, 1987).
45. See Lorcin, *Imperial Identities*.
46. On the works of white Algerian settler-*literati* including Robert Randau, Raoul Genella and Annette Godin, see Charles Tailliart, *L'Algérie dans la littérature française*, vol. 2 (Paris, 1925); Prochaska, *Making Algeria French*; Lorcin, *Imperial Identities*.
47. See C.A. Bayly, *Origins of Nationality in South Asia* (Delhi: Oxford University Press, 1998), p. 114.
48. *RMM* 2 (1907): 60–62; compare *RMM* 9, no 3:11 (1909): 500.
49. *RMM* (1911): 551–52.
50. *RMM* 7–8 (1911): 374.
51. *RMM* 8 (1911): 551–2.
52. *RMM* 1, no.1 (1907): 101–14.
53. Ibid., p. 101.
54. *RMM* 3, no. 1:9 (1907): 120–27.
55. Ibid., pp. 127–28.

14 Alexandria: A Mediterranean Cosmopolitan Center of Cultural Production

Robin Ostle

Between the 1890s and the 1920s, the Arab provinces of the eastern and southern Mediterranean regions went through some of the more dramatic phases in their recent history. The protracted decline of the Ottoman Empire, arguably the most successful political system in Islamic history, had entered its terminal stage, accelerated by World War I. European domination over the Maghreb countries and Egypt reached its high point; new nation states emerged in the eastern Mediterranean region, albeit in highly circumscribed and incomplete forms of independence.

The port cities of the eastern and southern Mediterranean, from Beirut to Algiers, were vital centers of cultural, economic, and political activity and the main points of access for the European powers to the Arab Mediterranean countries.[1] They were at the same time the principal windows onto the Mediterranean for some sectors of these Arab societies. They were also, crucially, the principal havens for cosmopolitan Mediterranean populations, societies that coexisted with the indigenous inhabitants and their local notables: a variety of Jewish communities, Armenians, Greeks, Italians, French, Maltese, Spanish, and significant numbers of the Syro-Lebanese diaspora. In cultural terms, both symbiosis and conflict marked these cosmopolitan centers and their hinterlands as national identities of the Arab Mediterranean states were articulated over the course of the twentieth century. Port cities by their nature are always different from their hinterlands, and this difference is felt by the inhabitants and emphasized in their cultural statements. It is a sense of difference that transcends the common regional differences present in every country.

The city of Alexandria and the role it has played—and continues to play—in the cultural history of modern Egypt is a case in point. As the British imperial order tightened its grip over Egypt, Alexandria was able to develop a significant degree of autonomy for its Mediterranean population. In 1907, there were 14 non-Muslim communities whose respective consulates provided a range of legal and social privileges[2] that allowed these notables effectively to regulate the life of the city. The indigenous Muslim notable families were in no sense excluded from the system. The scions of the prominent Muslim families went to the same schools as their Mediterranean counterparts, and they belonged to the same social circles and would usually converse in French, the lingua franca of Alexandria since the late nineteenth century. From 1890 to 1940, Alexandria had a typically cosmopolitan Mediterranean society, other versions of which existed in Beirut, Tripoli, Tunis, and Algiers. In the upper reaches of this society, prominent Egyptians—Muslim, Coptic, and Jewish—rubbed shoulders with their Greek, Italian, and Armenian counterparts. Although each group ultimately had its own national loyalty, this was often less important than the common cultural experience that they shared.

This paper introduces three artists—a painter, Muhammad Nagi, and two poets, Khalil Mutran and 'Abd al-Rahman Shukri—to illustrate how certain creative individuals reacted to the dilemma of cosmopolitan culture and national identity during the period in question. If one considers how the dominant strands of Egypt's new national identity were perceived between 1910 and 1940, especially by the new intellectual elites who had been educated in mainly non-Azhari institutions, it is clear that this vision is informed by strong Mediterranean influences. The historical legacies of the pharaohs, the Greeks, and the Romans are at least as prominent as that of their Muslim counterparts, as the national iconography produced by Muhammad Nagi and other pioneers of modern Egyptian painting and sculpture make clear. The same is true of literature: for example, pharaonic motifs abound in the neoclassical poetry of Ahmad Shawqi (1868–1932), in the novels and plays of Tawfiq al-Hakim (1898–1987) before 1940, and even in the very earliest novels of Naguib Mahfouz (b. 1911). But this Mediterranean cosmopolitan vision of the new nation state was not without its strains and contradictions: the vast majority of the Egyptian population lived in the countryside and their lives were conditioned by very different cultural and economic imperatives. In a significant number of Nagi's paintings and drawings, one can see him trying to come to terms with these contradictions. At a very different level in Alexandrian society, the poet 'Abd al-Rahman Shukri struggled to contain the psychological stress caused by his desire for the emotional and metaphysical liberation he was ultimately unable to achieve.

Khalil Mutran illustrates the significant role played by the numerous Syrians and Lebanese who came in increasing numbers to Egypt during the last three decades of the nineteenth century and who were pivotal in modern Arab culture in journalism, literature, and politics. The paper by Elisabeth Kendall in this volume highlights the central position of Alexandria between 1870 and 1900 in this context, home as it was to a significant Syrian community who were deeply involved in the myriad entrepreneurial activities in and around the port city. Not the least important of these activities was the increasing involvement of private individuals and their capital in the founding of new journals and newspapers. That the population of Alexandria had become so cosmopolitan in Mediterranean terms can be demonstrated by the fact that Egypt became acquainted with the motion picture at the same time as Europe did. A group of Levantine individuals established the Egyptian cinema that, along with its counterpart in India, was to become one of the great film industries outside Europe and North America.

Muhammad Nagi (1888–1956)

Muhammad Nagi was typical of the cosmopolitan high society of Alexandria in the first half of the twentieth century. He was a representative and representer of the good life of Alexandria's *grand bourgeoisie,* and was fully integrated into the Levantine society that so aroused the suspicions of Lord Cromer.[3] In the eyes of the colonial administrator, people like Nagi and his peers tended to blur the all-important distinctions of identity, raising questions in the colonial mind as to whether they were "semi-European" or "semi-Egyptian."

Nagi's early life as a privileged member of the Turko-Egyptian elite of pashas and beys in Egypt's second city included attending the Swiss school and acquaintance with Ungaretti, the founder of the Hermetic movement, and the Futurist Marinetti. His intellectual formation followed the pattern among the new elites, including higher education in a European institution. Nagi studied law at the University of Lyons from 1906 to 1910, and then, until 1914, indulged his true passion by studying painting at the Fine Arts Academy in Florence.[4] His earliest works are patently impressionist in style and inspiration, reflecting his great admiration for and acquaintance with

Claude Monet. He gradually evolved toward a much more expressionist use of color, especially in his many vibrant representations of life in rural Egypt. Nagi was a typical example of the modern Egyptian Mediterranean man and his background of privilege and wealth was of considerable assistance in creating this profile.[5] His cultural and artistic formation had much in common with that of many of the writers, artists, and intellectuals who were prominent in Egypt from independence until the revolution of 1952. The writers Muhammad Husayn Haykal (1888–1956), Taha Husayn (1889–1973), Ahmad Zaki Abu Shadi (1892–1955), Tawfiq al-Hakim (1898–1987), and 'Ali Mahmud Taha (1902–1949), the sculptor Mahmud Mukhtar (1891–1934), and the painter Mahmud Sa'id (1897–1964) are only some of the more obvious names one can offer in this context.

In common with most of them, Nagi was deeply involved in the national enthusiasms that gripped Egypt between the revolution of 1919 and the proclamation of the constitutional monarchy in 1923, and through his painting he contributed much to the new national iconography of the period. His mural in the hall of the National Assembly was completed in 1922 and bears the same title as Mukhtar's famous statue, "The Renaissance of Egypt."[6] The pharaonic motifs shared by this mural and Mukhtar's statue were dominant in the art and literature of the early years of Egyptian independence: the theme of resurrection symbolized for the new nation state the revival of the power and the glory once enjoyed by pharaonic Egypt.

By far the most Mediterranean version of national iconography produced by Nagi was his enormous mural, *The School of Alexandria*. He began preliminary work on it at around the same time as Taha Husayn published *Mustaqbal al-Thaqafa fi Misr* (The Future of Culture in Egypt, 1938), a book that stressed Egypt's debt to Mediterranean culture.[7] This painting was to occupy at least ten years of Nagi's life; he produced numerous preliminary sketches and some preliminary studies in oil for it (fig. 14.1). Today the finished mural, measuring approximately 8 meters by 3, hangs in the main meeting hall of the governorate of Alexandria.[8] It is a monumental celebration of the rich amalgam of religious and cultural traditions to which modern Egypt is heir; it is also an obvious reference on Nagi's part to Raphael's *School of Athens*, which decorates the Stanza della Segnatura in the Vatican.

In the *School of Alexandria*, the background is dominated by a statue of Alexander the Great; the central foreground is occupied by the figure of St. Catherine of Alexandria. On one side, Archimedes is shown handing on the heritage of Greek civilization to Ibn Rushd. The figures surrounding this

FIGURE 14.1 Muhammad Nagi. Preliminary study in oil (date unknown) for "School of Alexandria." *Private Collection, Oxford.*

central group are a carefully chosen mixture of Egyptian and European artists, writers, and intellectuals whose identities vary in the preliminary studies. In the completed mural, both Ungaretti and the modern Greek Alexandrian poet Cavafy are among the Europeans depicted; the Islamic reformer Muhammad 'Abduh, the sculptor Mahmud Mukhtar, the liberal intellectual Lutfi al-Sayyid, and the scholar Taha Husayn appear among the Egyptians.

The architectural details are also a mixture of the ancient and the contemporary: the top right corner shows Ptolemy's Pharos, and the line of the horizon is formed by the waterfront of the eastern port. The mural as a whole is the ultimate statement in art of the essentially Mediterranean nature of Egyptian civilization as seen by Nagi, the modern Alexandrian. It is obvious that this Mediterranean sense of cosmopolitan identity was one that could scarcely be shared by the vast majority of Egypt's population, whose culture was Islamic and who lived as peasants in the rural hinterlands of an urban center such as Alexandria. This was the dilemma that writers, artists, and intellectuals faced between 1910 and 1950: although the historical legacies of the Egyptians, the Greeks, the Romans, and the Muslims inspired a new generation of Egyptian nationalists, the present that they had to confront was one of poverty and ignorance in a society ill-equipped to meet the aspirations of the new nation state. A significant number of the major works of literature that appeared between 1910 and 1950 revolve, directly or indirectly, around the dilemma of the educated urban sophisticate struggling to come to terms with fellow countrymen with whom he has little or nothing in common, apart from the fact that they inhabit the same territorial space. In this context one can mention Haykal's novel, *Zaynab*; Mahmud Tahir Lashin's short story, *Hadith al-Qarya* (Village Story); Tawfiq al-Hakim's novel, *Yawmiyyat Na'ib fi'l-Aryaf* (Diary of a Country Lawyer), or his play, *Ughniyat al-mawt* (Song of Death); and Yahya Haqqi's novella *Qindil Umm Hashim* (The Saint's Lamp). This is only the beginning of a possible list.[9]

Nagi's family house in Alexandria overlooked the Mahmudiyya Canal, one of the major links between the port of Alexandria and the northwest delta as far as the town of al-Mahmudiyya on the Rosetta branch of the Nile. The canal passed through the village of Abu Hummus, where the Nagi family owned property and that was the site from which Nagi made most of his observations of the Egyptian countryside. In the days of Nagi's youth the Mahmudiyya Canal was a constant spectacle of boats, people, and produce that went to and fro between the Mediterranean port city and the rural hinterland of the delta, but it was from the village of Abu Hummus itself that Nagi was to derive his own contributions to the dominant dilemma of cosmopolitan culture and national identity.

Nagi's canvas, *The Family in the Village* (fig. 14.2), is dated 1937, the same year in which Tawfiq al-Hakim published his novel *Yawmiyyat Na'ib fi'l-Aryaf* (Diary of a Country Lawyer). Both works comment on the cultural antitheses between literature and art. The Westernized elegance of the father of the artist and his sister on the right side of the canvas contrasts incongruously with the naked peasant child, the farm animals and birds, the mud-brick dwellings and the surrounding villagers. The common features between this painting and key literary works such as Lashin's *Hadith al-Qarya* (Village Story) are striking.

If one examines the representation of the Egyptian countryside in literature between 1910 and 1950, one finds a constant process of alternation between pastoral and satire, between celebrating the countryside as the cradle of the virtuous community and the haven of traditional national val-

FIGURE 14.2 Mohammad Nagy "The Family in the Village" (1937). *Private Collection, Oxford.*

ues, and confronting it as the principal source of the problems that faced the new nation state: poverty, disease, and lack of modern education. Although Haykal's novel *Zaynab* is in no sense devoid of social criticism, the pastoral element is particularly strong, as it is in much of the nature poetry of Ahmad Zaki Abu Shadi and other of his colleagues in the *Apollo* group who formed the core of the Romantic movement in Egypt.[10] By contrast, in *Yawmiyyat Na'ib fi'l-Aryaf* (Diary of a Country Lawyer) the social criticism is fierce, albeit mitigated by humor.

It is possible to trace a similar alternation in the paintings and drawings of Muhammad Nagi, on the one hand, and in the literature, on the other. In view of his social background and education, it is hardly surprising that much of his work should represent an essentially urban fascination with the vibrant colors and the undoubted natural beauties of rural Egypt. Works such as *Girl with Bean Flower* (1942), *The Basket Maker* (date uncertain), or *The Fisherman* (1945[?]) (fig. 14.3) are relatively untroubled visions of rural Egypt. These pictures reflect something of an air of rural charm and contentment; they do not suggest extreme poverty, social degradation, or representations of the disinherited of the earth. They convey a sense of dig-

FIGURE 14.3 Muhammad Nagy "The Fisherman" (1945?). *Private Collection, Oxford.*

nified and honorable labor with no negative or critical undertones to disturb a time-honored social order.

It is rare for Nagi to disturb this relatively harmonious vision of life in an Egyptian village. In *Women Making Bread* (1929 or 1934[?]) (fig. 14.4), the use of vibrant color is typical of many of his rural scenes, but here it does not detract from the sense of unending toil and drudgery that was the lot of most of the inhabitants of Abu Hummus. The women all squat in various lowly postures, very much at the same level as the accompanying animals. The woman in the left foreground cradles a sleeping child and stares out of the canvas with an expression that is both resigned and reproachful. The large rough feet and tattooed hands of the woman on the right are manifestly made for a life of labor in which leisure has no place.

Nagi produced hundreds of drawings in pencil, crayon, or pastel; many of these were essentially details that he subsequently incorporated into his larger, more finished works. Often he produced preliminary oil versions of

FIGURE 14.4 Muhammad Nagy "Women Making Bread" (1929, or 1934?). *Private Collection, Oxford.*

some of his large murals, *School of Alexandria* being a case in point. But it is above all through his numerous drawings that one can follow Nagi's obsession with representations of rural Egypt. Through these spontaneous drawings, the urban sophisticate in spite of himself comes much closer to the unvarnished hardship of the world as it might have been felt by the peasants who are the subjects of so many of these drawings.

These few examples of the work of Muhammad Nagi will suffice to illustrate the dilemma of visions of the countryside as an essential theme of national authenticity, and as a hidden world of poverty and deprivation that he and others viewed as outside observers. The Mediterranean cosmopolitanism to which Nagi belonged has now almost disappeared from Alexandria. Since World War II, the population has continued to expand, but the cultural effects are dramatically different from those that created the cosmopolitanism of the late nineteenth and early twentieth centuries. By 1975, the population of Alexandria had reached 2.5 million. Since 1950, most of the non-Arab elements of the population have almost entirely disappeared. The city is hemmed in by *bidonvilles*. Abu Hummus has come to Alexandria. The city familiar to Muhammad Nagi, Mahmud Sa'id, Constantine Cavafy, and Lawrence Durrell now belongs to history.

Khalil Mutran (1872–1949)

Mutran, a member of the Syro-Lebanese community, had a vital impact on the development of Arab culture in the eastern Mediterranean during the early years of this century. He was born in Ba'albek of a Lebanese Catholic family and educated at the Roman Catholic Patriarchal College in Beirut, where he studied French and Arabic literature.[11] As a student, he was involved in the anti-Ottoman political activity that was prevalent among progressive young Arab intellectuals of the time. After a reported attempt on his life by Ottoman agents, his family became concerned for his safety, so he left for Paris, where he spent two hectic years immersed in literature and opposing the rule of Sultan Abdülhamid. Mutran might well have followed other members of his family to join the Syro-Lebanese community in Latin America. Instead, he left Paris in 1892 for Alexandria. Egypt remained his adopted country until his death in 1949.

Through his contacts in the Lebanese community of Alexandria, Mutran obtained a job on the editorial staff of *al-Ahram*, where he worked until the paper transferred its base to Cairo in 1899. The fact that *al-Ahram* was first published in Alexandria indicates the important role the city played in the development of the Egyptian press. Mutran was actually offered the post of editor-in-chief, but he preferred to launch his own journalistic initiatives. After he left *al-Ahram* in 1900, he started his own fortnightly review, *al-Majalla al-Misriyya*, and in 1902 he launched a new daily, *al-Jawai'b al-Misriyya*. The review lasted for three years and the daily for five, but neither was a great financial success. He then became involved in business and speculation and is said to have amassed a significant fortune before he lost it in 1912 in a disastrous deal that left him all but bankrupt. He bounced back to be appointed secretary to the khedival agricultural society, where he earned great respect as an agriculturalist and an economist. He was also closely involved in the initial planning of the Bank Misr, and he served with energy and distinction as director of the Egyptian National Theater Company.

Although Mutran was prominent in a number of areas in Egyptian public life, his lasting contribution was to modern Arabic poetry. To him belongs the credit for making the first significant moves away from the neoclassical mode.[12] The combination of his early political *engagement* and taste for literary innovation seemed to make him the complete romantic previously unknown in Arabic literature. His first published volume of verse, the *Diwan al-Khalil* (Cairo, 1908), contains a number of poems of a powerful subjective lyricism, a concern for social justice, and criticism of political tyranny. If one looks in the literary sections of *al-Majalla al-Misriyya*, one realizes how important the periodical press was for the more progressive developments in modern Arabic literature, and of the role that Mutran himself played. In the issue dated 15 October 1901, he reviewed a number of poems by the Italian Futurist writer and ideologue, Filippo Tommaso Marinetti, suggesting that aspects of Marinetti's compositions could benefit Arabic poetic style. Marinetti wrote these particular poems in French, and they appeared in Paris in *La Revue Blanche* in July 1901. To be thinking in comparative terms of Arabic poetry and the European *avant-garde* so early in the twentieth century was revolutionary. Although Marinetti (1876–1944) was an Alexandrian by birth and early education and was amongst Muhammad Nagi's acquaintances, there is no evidence of any direct contact between him and Mutran. The impression that emerges from the pages of *al-Majalla al-Misriyya* is of a restless intellectual who constantly moved towards new ideas in many fields, of which literature was particularly important.

When one puts Mutran's general radical enthusiasms alongside his experiments with meter and rhyme and his introduction of dramatic narrative poetry into Arabic, a mold-breaking literary career of striking importance seems to be emerging. But the great enigma of Mutran's life is that his subsequent poetic career did not build on the considerable achievements of his first *Diwan*: three further volumes of verse were produced after the 1908 collection; these were published together with the initial volume in 1948. What they make clear is that Mutran in effect reverted to being a respectable member of the Egyptian neoclassical establishment, and the friend and contemporary of the Egyptian pillars of this literary style, Ahmad Shawqi and Hafez Ibrahim. There is a constant and unresolved tension throughout his work: for every poem of powerful personal introspection such as "al-Masa'" ('Evening'), written in Alexandria in 1902, there are many other pieces of traditional elegy and eulogy. There are also poems for all manner of social and political occasions, very much in the neoclassical style, particularly in the later stages of his career.

Although it is fair to say that Mutran did not fulfill all the aspirations as a poet that he himself expressed as a young man, the innovations he indicated through his work were much appreciated by later generations of poets both inside and outside Egypt. Ahmad Zaki Abu Shadi, another prominent Alexandrian, and the group of poets who congregated around the *Apollo* magazine in the 1930s and who looked upon Mutran as something of a mentor, are a case in point.[13] The early years of his career held promise in this combination of political commitment and adventurous cosmopolitan cultural endeavor. This was something that he could not sustain. Of all the literary arts, poetry was the area in which change was the slowest to appear, at least until 1948. Mutran was a cosmopolitan Mediterranean Arab who was willingly and comfortably absorbed by the dominant culture of the Egyptian hinterland.

'Abd al-Rahman Shukri (1886–1958)

'Abd al-Rahman Shukri provides an interesting contrast to the *grand bourgeois* Muhammad Nagi and the Lebanese immigrant and one-time entrepreneur Khalil Mutran. His father was an employee of the maritime traffic department in the port of Alexandria at the time of the 'Urabi Revolution (1881–82), and was dismissed and imprisoned for his political activities on behalf of the revolutionaries.[14] After his release, he found employment in Port Said where the young 'Abd al-Rahman was born in 1886, but he remained in contact with the revolutionaries. One of Shukri's childhood memories were of visits to his father's house in Port Said by 'Abd Allah al-Nadīm, the journalist, orator, and political activist of the 'Urabi Revolution who spent years as a fugitive from the British. After primary school in Port Said, Shukri continued his education at the Ra's al-Tin Secondary School in Alexandria. After the baccalaureate, he enrolled in the Cairo school of law, but was expelled because of his political activities on behalf of Mustafa Kamil's Nationalist Party. He ultimately graduated from the Cairo teachers' training college, after which he spent three years (1909–12) at Sheffield University College in England studying English and literature. On his return to Egypt in 1912, he was appointed a teacher of English language and history in the same Ra's al-Tin secondary school in which he had been a pupil.

Unlike his two colleagues and contemporaries, the writers and journalists Ibrahim 'Abd al-Qadir al-Mazini (1890–1949) and 'Abbas Mahmud al-'Aqqad (1889–1964), Shukri was not prominent in public life; he spent most of his professional career in relative obscurity as a teacher and then head-master of Ra's al-Tin secondary school, an institution that lacked the prestige of the Abbasiyya secondary school that was to provide the site for some of the faculties of the new University of Alexandria.

Shukri was at the height of his creative powers between the years 1909 and 1919. His first volume of verse appeared in 1909 before his departure for England, and the second volume in 1913, just after his return. The third, fourth, fifth, and sixth sections of his collected works all appeared between the years 1915 and 1918. The prefaces that he wrote to these books are in some ways even more important than the poetry they introduce, because they reveal the great breadth of his knowledge of literature and criticism of eighteenth- and nineteenth-century England, ideas he felt were relevant to the culture and society of the new Egyptian nation.

Two little-known prose works published by Shukri in Alexandria in 1916, his autobiographical *Kitab al-I'tiraf* (Book of Confessions) and *Kitab al-Thamarat* (Book of Fruits), are accounts of the problems facing a sensitive young Egyptian at a time of great political instability and social flux.[14] The author is prone to grandiose dreams, but suffers from a chronic inability to realize them. He is full of excitement about the future, but given to pessimism because of the long years of tyranny his country has endured. He is a constant victim of doubt and bewilderment, caught between the old and the new, and does not know how to plan his future development. Shukri was a vigorous advocate of the primacy of the imagination, inspired as he was by the English romantics and the criticism and essays of William Hazlitt, but the fevered wanderings of this imagination far beyond the bounds of his own indigenous cultural conventions are profoundly disturbing, as well as exhilarating. The *Confessions* describe his development from childhood super-stitions to total denial of religious belief, before eventually rediscovering his faith:[16]

In my childhood I was very superstitious, seeking the company of old women to hear stories about the supernatural to the extent that their stories filled every corner of my mind which became a huge world teeming with magic and demons. . . . Later I went through a phase of religiosity during which I became immersed in books of devotion which described the characteristics of wickedness as well as God's horrible punishment. . . . I subsequently turned to reading books of poetry and literature, so I became aware of the beauty of the world and my terrors which had been inspired by religion grew less. I then passed through the stage of doubt and quest. . . . I denied the existence of God with the same fanaticism as that with which others asserted their faith in Him. Yet my denial alarmed me without satisfying my mind, for it never explained to me what I am, why I exist, and whither I shall be going. . . . I used to roam the streets of the city at night (for night seemed to accord with my feelings of despair and sorrow), look-ing at the stars, asking them about life and death, God and man, this world and the next. But the stars merely looked back at me as if in pity and in sadness . . . and life then felt heavier than a nightmare or a horrifying dream. . . . Eventually I regained my faith, having learnt that the universe has a huge spirit with its own life and personality and that this spirit inspires its will to the various individual spirits and that the Fates are its subalterns.

What we have here is an example of the psychological dislocation brought about through the changes that accompany transitions away from the dom-inant conventional idioms of taste and expression. One area of cultural ten-sion that Shukri was unable to resolve in his poetry (and most probably in his personal life) was the problem of sexuality. This is the most tortured and ambivalent part of his work. He has a typical romantic obsession with the dual nature of love as an amalgam of spiritual yearning and physical lust, and this obsession stalks his work along with an increasing misogyny. Critics have remarked on the poet's fixation with death and physical decay, particu-larly in his poems on beautiful women.[17]

There is no doubt in Shukri's own mind that his painful dilemmas were shared by the majority of educated Egyptian youth of his generation. This young Alexandrian was a significant pioneer in the expression of emotional and metaphysical liberation through literature, in spite of all the manic-depressive reactions that he himself experienced as a result. Later generations of Arab Romantic poets were able more easily to abandon themselves to Shukri's blend of the imagination and the passions, but even for them to translate these from literature into life was usually problematical.

These three Alexandrians active between 1890 and 1940 all made significant contributions to modern Egyptian, and indeed modern Arabic, culture. The fact that they were all inhabitants of a port city is relevant to the contributions they made. Muhammad Nagi, the *grand bourgeois*, insisted on both the cosmopolitan and Mediterranean nature of Egyptian culture, although his own works demonstrate some of the contradictions inherent in this approach. It is a view of the national culture that was particularly popular in the years 1910–40, and in spite of all the attacks and pressures to which such a view is subjected today, there are those who still uphold the validity of this broadminded and essentially cosmopolitan approach. Khalil Mutran's early career, which took him from Beirut to Paris to Alexandria, seemed to indicate a future of restless innovation in literature and in life; instead, he adapted comfortably to the dominant neoclassical culture of the upper echelons of Egyptian society. This was a case of the hinterland absorbing the young Lebanese radical. Although it is not easy to fit 'Abd al-Rahman Shukri into a social category, "lower middle class" is probably the nearest one can achieve. In his case it is perhaps understandable that the cultural cosmopolitanism that he sought to adopt for his own poetry and his own existence was achieved at a personal cost that led some to question his mental stability. He was an early example of the alienated individual who has a love-hate relationship with his own culture and that of Western Europe.

One of the terms in Arabic for "seaport" is *thaghr*: it also means the part of a country from which an enemy invasion is feared, or a hostile frontier, or a boundary between the countries of the Muslims and the unbelievers. In this sense the port cities of the eastern and southern Mediterranean in the late nineteenth century were genuine *thughur*. Alexandria was one of the most complete examples of such a "cultural borderland," to adapt Anzaldúa's term.[18] It was a space of energetic symbiosis and confrontation, and it continues today to play a similarly provocative role in modern Egyptian culture.

Notes

1. This material on port cities, and Alexandria in particular, is taken from the article by Robert Ilbert, "De Beyrouth à Alger: La Fin d'un ordre urbain," *Vingtième Siècle* 32 (1991): 15–24.
2. Ibid., p. 19.
3. Ibid., p. 20.
4. For these and other biographical details on Nagi, see Badr al-Din Abu Ghazi, 3 *Jīl min al-ruwwād* (Cairo: al-Hay'at al-Misriyaa al-'Amma lil-kitab, 1975), pp. 131–41. See also Effat Naghi, Christine Roussillon, et al., eds, *Mohamed Naghi*, Les Cahiers de Chabramant (Cairo, n.d.), pp. 51–59.
5. See R. C. Ostle, "Modern Egyptian Renaissance Man," *Bulletin of the School of Oriental and African Studies (BSOAS)* 57, no. 1 (1994): 188. See also Ostle, "The Dilemma of Cosmopolitan Culture and National Identity: The Case of Muhammad Nagi, 1888–1956," *Asiatische Studien/Etudes Asiatiques* 50, no. 2 (1996): 399–410.
6. Hamed Said, *Contemporary Art in Egypt* (Cairo: Ministry of Culture, 1964), pp. 116–20.
7. A. H. Hourani, *Arabic Thought in the Liberal Age* (Oxford: Oxford University Press, 1962), pp. 327–38.
8. R. C. Ostle, "Muhammad Nagi (1888–1956)," in *Alexandrie en Egypte/ Alexandria in Egypt* Mediterraneennes/Mediterraneans 8–9 (Autumn 1996): 168–73.
9. For a fuller discussion of the representation of the countryside in literary texts, see R. C. Ostle, "The City in Modern Arabic Literature," *Bulletin of the School of Oriental and African Studies* 49, 1 (1986): 193–202.
10. M. M. Badawi, *A Critical Introduction to Modern Arabic Poetry* (Cambridge: Cambridge University Press, 1975), pp. 116–29.
11. For the biographical details on Mutran, see ibid., pp. 68–70.
12. R. C. Ostle: "The Romantic Poets," in *The Cambridge History of Arabic Literature: Modern Arabic Literature*, ed. M. M. Badawi (Cambridge: Cambridge University Press, 1992), pp. 84–88.
13. Ibid., pp. 110–31.
14. For details of Shukri's life, see the preface to his complete works by the editor Niqula Yusuf, *Dīwān 'Abd al-Raḥmān Shukrī* (Alexandria, 1960), pp. 2–15.
15. *Kitāb al-i'tirāf* (*Book of Confessions*) and *Kitāb al-thamarāt* (*Book of Fruits*) (Alexandria: Jurjī Gharzūzī Printing Press, n.d.).
16. The quotation is taken from M. M. Badawi, *A Critical Introduction to Modern Arabic Poetry* (Cambridge, 1975), p. 93.
17. Ibid., p. 101.
18. Gloria Anzaldúa, *Borderlands/ La Frontera: The New Mestiza* (San Francisco, 1987).

15 Between Politics and Literature: Journals in Alexandria and Istanbul at the End of the Nineteenth Century

Elisabeth Kendall

Unlike Europe, where the book had nearly two centuries to take root before the journal emerged, in the Ottoman Empire, the journal quickly became the main reading matter for intellectuals. Many Ottoman books were in fact simply collections of articles that had already been published in journals. The journal, which enjoyed both currency and less rigorous censorship, had by the end of the nineteenth century become an important forum for political, social, and cultural ideas, able to act as both a mirror and an instigator of change.

As the Egyptian and Turkish journal could only flourish after the printing press had been introduced from abroad, it was natural that Alexandria and Istanbul by their very nature as port cities should play a key role in their early development. Both cities enjoyed a lively and dynamic culture, thanks in part to the various foreign elements active in them. The fusion of journalism and a vital cultural scene in Alexandria and Istanbul encouraged a truly new departure in the development of literature and the arts in Egypt and in Turkey. Over time, Cairo and, to a lesser extent, Ankara, beginning in the early 1920s, also became centers for the production of cultural journals. However, Alexandria and Istanbul never lost their importance in propelling cultural momentum through the journalistic medium.

The foreign influence in literary journalism was substantial. It came most obviously through the foreign journals published in the region, but also through Turkish and Arabic journals published in Europe, translation and adaptation of foreign literary works, and the Turkish and Arab writers who spent time in Europe and brought Western culture back with them.

The first journals in both Egypt and Turkey were foreign initiatives in the ports of Alexandria and Istanbul in the 1790s. In Istanbul, the French set up a press in their embassy in 1795, but after Napoleon's invasion of Egypt in 1798, it was closed and French journalistic activity moved from Istanbul to Alexandria. In Egypt, the French published *al-Tanbīh*, the first newspaper in Arabic, which appeared in Alexandria at the turn of the nineteenth century, over a decade before the official Egyptian organ, *Jurnāl al-Khidīw*, was founded in Cairo. Although Italian was in fact the dominant foreign language under Muhammad 'Ali, giving rise to journals such as *Il Progresso* in Alexandria in 1858–59, French journals came to dominate, peaking in the years following the British occupation in 1882. Egypt's first journal dedicated to cultural matters was again French; called *Miscellanea Aegyptica*, it was launched in Alexandria by the Association littéraire d'Egypte in 1843. Other early French journals in Alexandria with a cultural content were the short-lived *L'Echo des Pyramides* (1827), which emphasized the importance of education, and *Le Phare d'Alexandrie* (1842), notable for its steady stimulation of Alexandrian culture over many years by virtue of its long life, rather than for any specific cultural emphasis or contribution.

As capital of the Ottoman Empire, Istanbul had a particularly fertile foreign-language press. Of the 47 journals to appear there in 1876, only 13 were in Turkish; the others were mainly Greek, Armenian, and French.[1] Italian journals were blocked by the Austrian post. As in Alexandria, French journals were probably the greatest influence in the evolution of a native press. For instance, the influence of French journals in İzmir in the 1820s persuaded Mahmud II that journals could exercise power, and then led him to send for the Frenchman Alexandre Blacque to launch *Le Moniteur Ottoman* in Istanbul in 1931. By the 1860s, Istanbul began to rival İzmir as a center of French journalism in Turkey. Of particular cultural significance were *Le Phare du Bosphore* (1870), whose editor Kiriakopoulos moved it to Egypt when it closed in 1890, and *Stamboul* (1875), which had the greatest cultural impact under the editorship of a French literature teacher, Regis Delbeuf.

Turkey's first non-official journal in Turkish, *Ceride-i Havadis*, was founded by an Englishman in Istanbul in 1840. This and its supplement, *Ruzname Ceride-i Havadis*, provided both model and training ground for writers like Ahmet Midhat, Şair Ali, Münif Paşa, and Ebüzziya Tevfik. It introduced readers to Western literary and nonliterary writing through translation. It was in the supplement that one of the first Turkish translations of European literature, an abridged version of Victor Hugo's *Les Misérables*, was serialized in 1862. *Ceride-i Havadis* was also instrumental in helping adapt the Ottoman Turkish language to modern terminology and the more succinct expression favored by European journals at the time.

The fact that Turks were exposed to foreign ideas and journalistic language earlier than Arabs influenced the modernization of Arabic. The Arabic of the official journals published bilingually in the Ottoman Arab provinces was sometimes only intelligible if one could compare it with the Turkish.[2] Egypt's official organ, *al-Waqā'i' al-Miṣriyya*, was also published bilingually; the Arabic was translated from the Turkish until 1842 when Rifa'a Rafi' al-Tahtawi reversed the procedure. By then there was even some direct interchange between Turkey and Egypt in the field of journalism. Littérateurs like Ibrahim al-Muwaylihi, Faris al-Shidyaq, Mehmet Murat, Jamal al-Din al-Afghani, Salim 'Abbas al-Shalafun, Lewis al-Sabunji, and Salim al-Hamawi, who was the initiator of independent journalism in Alexandria, were engaged in culturally significant journalistic activity in both Istanbul and either Cairo or Alexandria.

Alexandria's role in the development of Egyptian journalism was naturally not as dominant as Istanbul's in the development of Turkish journalism, because the latter enjoyed the status of capital as well as port city. Egypt's first indigenous Arabic journals appeared in Cairo. Both Egypt and Turkey recognized the potential power of the journalistic medium at the same time, when Muhammad 'Ali first published *al-Waqā'i' al-Miṣriyya* (*Jurnāl al-Khidīw* in its early rudimentary form) in Cairo in 1828 and Sultan Mahmud II unveiled *Takvim-i Vekayi* in Istanbul in 1831. Although both these official organs, beginning about 1840, sometimes included literary subjects alongside the official, moral, and technical, it was really independent journals that raised matters of literary and cultural interest.

The first private indigenous journals were founded about the same time in both Egypt and Turkey, with the emergence of a reading public, albeit an extremely limited one; the establishment of telegraphic connections, a postal service, and Reuter's news agencies made the rise of an independent press possible in the 1860s. The spark to ignite these possibilities came from growing political awareness and an emerging national consciousness in both Egypt and Turkey.

Such private initiatives appeared first in Istanbul, inspired in part by the flurry of journalistic and political activity resulting from the Crimean War in the 1850s. Young Western-looking intellectuals like İbrahim Şinasi, Agah Efendi,[3] Ali Suavi, Namik Kemal, Ziya Pasha and Ahmed Vefik Pasha led the initiative. İbrahim Şinasi, in particular, played a pivotal role in the cultural development of the waning Ottoman Empire. He collaborated with Agah Efendi to launch the first private independent journal, *Tercüman-i Ahval* (1860–67), before leaving to start *Tasvir-i Efkâr* in 1861. Important writers whom these journals helped to bring to maturity were Mustafa Refik, Mehmet Şerif, Ziya Pasha, whose patriotic poems have become proverbial, and Ahmet Vefik Pasha, who set up a theater in Bursa, translated works by Molière, Shakespeare, and Schiller, and became minister for education.

Şinasi's first editorial in *Tercüman-i Ahval* signaled an important departure for Turkish journalism, for it stated clearly that simply furnishing the reader with news was not enough. The new journal stressed the importance of education and debate, and the right of readers to express their opinions.[4] It was in the pages of *Tercüman-i Ahval* that the first press debates were sparked with the British-owned *Ceride-i Havadis*, and that a literary work, Şinasi's verse comedy *Şair Evlenmesi*, was first serialized. Şinasi published a good deal of poetry in *Tercüman-i Ahval* and *Tasvir-i Efkâr*, both French poetry that he translated, and his own verse, which was remarkable more for its content than its form. His real impact lay in his powerful prose articles, in which he made a considerable breakthrough in simplification of the language in order to project his ideas beyond the usual limited literary circles. From the outset he recognized the importance of writing "on a level which the general public will easily be able to understand,"[5] and he reaffirmed this commitment to serving the public in his opening editorial to *Tasvir-i Efkâr*.[6] Through his liberal politics and his propagation of Western ideals like freedom, justice, equality, and constitutional government, Şinasi paved the way for the foundation of a secret society known as the Young Ottomans, in which early protest journalists gathered. Şinasi's significance and influence lay in his fusion of literary and political activity, a potent combination for the newly independent journal in Turkey. The ideals he propagated through his journals became the themes of the didactic realist novels of the late nineteenth century.

Others of these early Turkish journalists also combined political and literary skill. Agah Efendi, for example, who had launched *Tercüman-i Ahval* and whose involvement with the Young Ottomans forced him into exile twice, was also a member of the Gedik-Paşa theater literary committee. He collaborated with prominent men of letters such as Recaizade Ekrem, Ebüz-ziya Tevfik, Ahmet Midhat, and Namik Kemal in the translation and adaptation of plays. Namik Kemal played an even more significant role in the development of cultural journalism. It was he who took over the editorship of *Tasvir-i Efkâr* when Şinasi was forced into exile in 1865, and shared Şinasi's fierce belief in liberty and patriotism. At the same time, he was a talented poet and dramatist and a firm believer in the power of the press to advance the nation and provoke debate in intellectual circles. His series "The Problem of the East" resulted in his exile to Europe, leaving the journal in the hands of Recaizade Mahmut Ekrem, another leading literary figure. When Kemal returned to Istanbul, he became a writer for *İbret*, formerly a satirical journal, but turned more cultural and political when taken over by Ahmet Midhat in 1872. When Kemal's fiery articles resulted in suspension, he used the time to write his patriotic play, *Vatan Yahut Silistre*. *İbret* was finally closed down by the authorities for printing an article about this play in 1873. Despite its short life, *İbret* had great influence among a significant elite, especially the Young Ottomans. Its other main contributors were Ebüz-ziya Tevfik, Reşat Bey, and Nuri Bey.

Other private journals followed the model set by *Tercüman-i Ahval* and *Tasvir-i Efkâr* to fuel the Young Ottoman debate. Notable among them were Münif Paşa's *Mecmua-i Fünün*, which introduced Turks to various Western ideas on philosophy and science; the journals of Filib Efendi, which included *Muhbir* (1866–67), edited by the Islamic reformer Ali Suavi; *Mecmua-i Maarif* (1867); *Tarakki* (1868); *Vakit* (1875); Ali Efendi's *Basiret* (1869–78), in which Ahmet Midhat publicized his radical proposal for a written form of the vernacular language; and Ahmet Midhat's *Devir, Bedir,* and *Dağarcik,* all launched and closed in 1872 for the radical educational and political reforms they advocated. Because the Ottoman authorities were more tolerant toward the foreign press in Istanbul, some of Turkey's earliest journalists were able to publish their articles in local French periodicals, and then in Turkish journals as "translations."

These later journals did not generally achieve the same heady mix of literature and politics attained by Şinasi and Namik Kemal in Tercüman-i Ahval and *Tasvir-i Efkâr*. A decade later, Mehmet Murat's *Mizan* (1886–90) included literary articles alongside the more numerous political ones, but Murat tended not to integrate a political element directly into original literary works as Şinasi had done. He promulgated a comprehensive reform program and boldly criticized the system of rule, but he also wrote a long series of articles on contemporary Turkish literature in 1888–89, in which he discussed significant Turkish works influenced by European literature. These reviews marked significant progress in Turkish literary criticism, for in addition to the usual discussion of plot, they also discussed form, content, style, and characterization, and considered the aesthetic unity of the work as a whole. When *Mizan* was forced to close in 1890, Murat wrote his novel *Turfanda mi yoksa Turfa mi?* that carried his reformist ideas. *Mizan* was briefly relaunched from Cairo in 1896–97.

In Egypt, the first privately run Arabic journals emerged in Cairo, starting with ʿAbd Allah Abu al-Suʿud's semi-independent *Wādī al-Nīl* in 1867, soon followed by Ibrahim al-Muwaylihi and ʿUthman al-Jalal's *Nuzhat al-Afkār* in 1869, the first completely independent, if short-lived, privately published journal. The introduction of independent Arabic journals in Alexandria soon followed, thanks mainly to an influx of Syrian emigrés looking for greater freedom and opportunities in Egypt.[8] Publishing was a good business opportunity for a small entrepreneur; it required little investment and could be run by a couple of people. In 1873, the Syrians Salim and ʿAbdu al-Hamawi published the first private Alexandrian Arabic journals, the weekly political and literary *al-Kawkab al-Sharqī* and the daily commercial and literary *Shuʿā al-Kawkab*. Khedive Ismaʿil soon ordered their closing, so little is known about their contents, but it seems likely that Salim al-Hamawi published some of his poetry that, in later years at least, was critical of Ismaʿil.[9] Hamza Fath Allah, who went on to become editor of the Alexandrian journals *al-Burhān* (1882) and al-Iʿtidāl (1882), gained experience by writing for al-Hamawi's early journals. A well-known philologist, Hamza Fath Allah, also wrote poetry famous for its convoluted syntax and difficult vocabulary. Alexandria was not to have a journal that wielded true influence through a successful marriage of political and literary subjects expressed in a simple language until the 1880s, nearly two decades later than in Istanbul.

Jamal al-Din al-Afghani's presence in Egypt in the 1870s played a key role in the development of the early independent press. He helped inspire protest movements demanding greater independence from Turkey and Europe and a stronger Egyptian identity. Protests increased in the late 1870s after the establishment of European financial control suggested imminent European domination. It was natural that writers should have felt a greater sense of urgency to reach the public at this time of increasing nationalist fervor, and that an independent press should develop to express it. Jamal al-Din al-Afghani then moved from Cairo to Alexandria, considering a port city to be better for receiving news.[10] Meanwhile, the same Salim al-Hamawi who had launched the first independent Alexandrian Arabic journals turned his hand in 1878 to purely political journalism with the publication of *al-Iskandariyya*.

As in Istanbul, where protest journalists were associated with the secret Young Ottoman society, so in Alexandria the clandestine Young Egypt society supported journals and even launched its own *Misr al-Fatā*, published in French and Arabic, in 1879. The weekly *Misr* (est. Cairo 1877), edited by the Syrians Adib Ishaq and Salim al-Naqqash, moved to Alexandria in 1879. Alongside it was launched *al-Tijāra*. Both Ishaq and al-Naqqash had come to Egypt with the intention of focusing on the theater; however, politics ruled the day and after the failure of al-Naqqash's theater, they concentrated their efforts on political activity. *Misr* and *al-Tijāra*, despite their brief existence, stirred up Alexandrian intellectuals, as Jurji Zaydan testifies. Zaydan, novelist, journalist, and founder of *al-Hilāl*, the second-longest-running cultural journal in Egyptian history, acknowledged *Misr and al-Tijāra* as pillars in the evolution of Egyptian journalism, carrying the level of intellectual debate forward through their use of an unprecedented direct language.[11] When these two journals were closed down, *al-Mahrūsa* and *al-'Asr al-Jadīd* were launched in 1880 to replace them. Although nominally edited by Salim al-Naqqash, *al-'Asr al-Jadīd* was actually edited by 'Abd Allah al-Nadim, and after him the Syrian man of letters Salim 'Abbas al-Shalafun. Another Syrian, Fadl Allah al-Khuri, became editor of *al-Mahrūsa* until it moved to Cairo, but the 'Urabi revolt in 1882 forced them also to suspend publication.

The most significant of the men of letters gathered around Adib Ishaq in Alexandria was 'Abd Allah al-Nadim, a contributor to *Misr*, *al-Tijāra*, *al-Mahrūsa*, and *al-'Asr al-Jadīd*. Like Şinasi in Istanbul, al-Nadim's importance lay in his ability to combine political and literary activity. He was a skilled orator and poet, so the journalistic medium allowed him to play a leading role in agitation that led to the 'Urabi revolt. Al-Nadim went on to establish *al-Tankīt wa-l-Tabkīt*, his own weekly journal in Alexandria, in 1881. Like Şinasi, al-Nadim recognized the importance of using simple language to spread his ideas beyond a limited intellectual elite. He wrote many of his fictional sketches and episodes in the vernacular. Their popularity became apparent when he declared his intention to discontinue the practice: his fans inundated his journal with letters begging him to continue. The success of his journal lay in its prose, written in "a style which the educated will not despise and the ignorant will not need to have explained."[12]

Nadim's fictional work in his journals was highly didactic, as was typical of the time; moral teaching was a major justification for literature. He also introduced modern European concepts such as irony, allegory, and several levels of meaning into his fiction. Like Ahmet Midhat and Recaizade Mahmut Ekrem in the Istanbul journals of the 1860s and 1870s, al-Nadim criticized the blind imitation of Western habits, and he found a new way of satirizing them through use of transliterated foreign words in his sketches. His episodes were often constructed around middle-class characters and scenes. Although it is probably an exaggeration to consider these rudimentary fictional episodes as the first examples of the modern Egyptian short story, they were significant in capturing the spirit and concerns that preoccupied Arabic narrative discourse for many years.

Yet again political events predominated at the expense of literary continuity. Al-Nadim's didactic fictional episodes were allocated less and less space as the national question became more urgent. In 1881, after only nine issues, al-Nadim renamed his journal al-Ṭā'if and moved it from Alexandria to Cairo to become the official organ of the 'Urabi revolt; in the new version he used only classical Arabic. Nevertheless, al-Nadim's didactic episodes established a firm link between journalism and short fictional forms. Their popularity continued in al-Nadim's Cairo journal al-Ustādh (1892–93) and others, such as Muhammad al-Muwaylihi, would use these forms as the basis of future development. Even recently, al-Nadim's rebellious journals have proved inspirational for others attempting to revitalize Egyptian culture and society. At the end of the 1970s, for example, Ahmad Rayyan, in his vanguard journal al-Nadāha, praised al-Nadim's journalism as a motivating and revolutionary force, a model of positive and influential interaction with the Egyptian public;[13] the poet and political agitator Muhammad Ibrahim Mabruk named his journal, published in Alexandria in 1980, al-Nadim.

That protest journals dominated the cultural scene in Istanbul and Alexandria at this early stage rather than more specialized literary journals is not surprising. Although Istanbul in the 1860s and 1870s had its literary journals, it was not yet time for such specialized initiatives to take root. Rising national awareness absorbed too much energy and talent among young Ottomans, as was the case in Egypt a decade later.

Very little is now known about these early endeavors in Istanbul. *Mecmua-i İber-u İntibah*, Turkey's first specialized literary journal, was published by a group of enthusiastic literary-minded young men and ran only eight issues in 1862–64; *Mecmua-i İbretnüma* was published by the *Cemiyet-i Kitabet* and ran to only 16 issues in 1865–66; *Ravzat-ül Maarif* was a literary and scientific journal that ran only six issues in 1870–71; Agop Baronyan's *Tiyatro*, launched in 1874, was the first Turkish journal devoted to the theater; and Ebüzziya Tevfik's *Muharrir* ran only eight issues in 1876–78. The problem was that the reading public was still extremely limited. With the onslaught of so many new concepts and ideas, readers were hungry for knowledge on a variety of subjects, and limited disposable income would naturally favor purchase of the more eclectic journals. In Istanbul, stamp duty introduced in 1875 probably also helped to eliminate more marginal journals.

By the late 1880s, after the infiltration of many new concepts and ideas from Europe, Turkish and Egyptian society had reached a high enough level of cultural sophistication for more specialized cultural journals to succeed without the need to couple them with a nationalist or political agenda to spark the readers' interest. Many of those journalists who favored a strong political content shifted their activity to Europe. At the end of the 1860s, Turkish literati like Namik Kemal, Ziya Paşa, and Ali Suavi published *Hürriyet*, *Muhbir*, and *Ulûm* in London and Paris; just over a decade later, Egypt's politically motivated writers were making the same shift. Adib Ishaq and al-Afghani, for example, left Alexandria to publish *Miṣr al-Qāhira* and *al-Urwā al-Wuthqā* in Paris. In the late 1870s, Abdülhamid II's abandonment of the constitution also encouraged the Turkish intelligentsia to shift their journalistic activity to Europe, where they turned out journals like *Hayal* in Paris and London and *Istikbal* in Geneva.

Between 1890 and 1908, politically motivated journalists in Turkey shifted their activity in earnest to Europe; in Egypt, they began to move to Cairo at the expense of Alexandria. Adib Ishaq's *Miṣr* in 1881, al-Nadim's *al-Ṭā'if* in 1882, Muhammad Farid and Hamza Fath Allah's *al-Burhān* in 1884, and *al-Maḥrūsa* in 1887 all moved from Alexandria to Cairo; even Salim al-Hamawi, the father of independent Alexandrian journalism, relocated to Cairo in 1886 to launch *al-Falāḥ*; when al-Nadim restarted his journalistic activities in the 1890s, he chose Cairo rather than Alexandria to publish more of his fictional sketches and political poetry in *al-Ustādh*. Even *al-Ahrām* finally shifted to Cairo in 1899. Although Bishara Taqla had intended to continue an Alexandrian edition of *al-Ahrām*,[14] it was soon incorporated into the main Cairo edition. By the beginning of the twentieth century, only 28 percent of Egypt's Arabic journals were being published in Alexandria, as opposed to 65 percent in Cairo.[15] Turkey's center of journalism remained (and still remains) Istanbul.

The increasing concentration of Egypt's political press in Cairo, where the British were installed, meant that once Alexandrian journalistic activity regained its momentum in the late 1880s it was more culturally oriented. One of the most prolific writers in Alexandrian journalism at this time was Najib Gharghur. In 1887, he launched a weekly satirical journal *al-Babaghā'*, modeled on the Bolognese *Il Paparillo*, but it ran for only five issues. He then became editor of Salim al-Khuri Bishara's literary journal *al-Manāra* (1888), which also represented Italian cultural influences in Alexandria, as its illustrations were drawn by a famous Bolognese artist. This, too, was short-lived, and Gharghur went on to found *al-Ḥaqīqa* with Faraj Mazrahi the same year. It covered a broad range of subjects, including literary material. Several famous Egyptian and Syrian writers contributed to it. Gharghur left to edit *al-Ittiḥād al-Miṣrī*, also in Alexandria in 1889, and *al-Ḥaqīqa* passed to the Lebanese Jurj Marza but did not last long. Marza then joined another Syrian, Antun Nawfal, in editing *al-Surūr*, a general cultural journal founded in Alexandria by Niqula 'Abd al-Masih in 1892. This lasted an entire decade, owing largely to the innocuous and eclectic nature of its content. *Al-Ahrām*, Egypt's longest running newspaper, founded by the Taqla brothers in 1876 after their arrival from Lebanon, also had a cultural impact during its Alexandria period. Salim Taqla had been active in the theater in Beirut, and *al-Ahrām* played an important role in encouraging early interest in the theater, with its regular theater news and reviews. Nevertheless, unlike European journals in Alexandria at the time, Arabic journals still tended to approach the theater as something newsworthy but not of specifically literary interest.

Of greater literary significance despite their much shorter life spans were *al-Rāwī* and *Ḥadīqat al-Adab*, both founded in Alexandria in 1888. In addition to stories and poems, Khalil Ziniyya's monthly *al-Rāwī* contained social studies, intellectual thought and opinion, and humorous anecdotes, but it was closed down by Riyad Paşa in 1890 after Ziniyya introduced political commentary. Among its contributors were well-known men of letters such as Najib Gharghur and Najib al-Haddad. After it closed down, the Syrian Ibrahim al-Yaziji, who was to play a significant role in Egyptian journalism in the early twentieth century, advised Ziniyya not to relaunch it. Al-Yaziji recognized the need for smaller, cheaper, more specialized journals to stir up literary debate.[16]

Ḥadīqat al-Adab was Egypt's most specialized literary journal to date. It was yet another initiative of Najib Gharghur, who intended it as an outlet for his own fictional work and Arabized versions of famous European works. Despite its popularity it was forced to close (in 1889?) because it had no license. Gharghur then concentrated his efforts over the following two decades on editing Rufa'il Mashaqa's general cultural journal, al-Ittihad al-Misri (1881), as well as launching more general cultural journals: al-Ibtisam together with Rufa'il Mashaqa in 1894, al-'Ām al-Jadīd and Abū al-Nuwās in 1895, and al-Āmāl in 1899, all still in Alexandria.

Alexandrian cultural journalism gained momentum in the 1890s with 19 new general cultural journals in Arabic and several in French, as opposed to only three in the 1880s, and 39 newspapers as opposed to 12 in the 1880s.[17] Of note were al-Fatāh (1892), the first women's journal in Egypt, founded by Hind Nawfal, a Syrian woman whose family was very active in Alexandrian journalism at this time. The literacy rate of women in Alexandria was twice that of Cairo.[18] Another cultural journal soon sprang up to cater to the needs of women: Anīs al-Jalīs (1898) was founded by Alexandra de Avierino, who contributed much to the Alexandrian cultural scene by holding literary salons and printing literary works, including poetry collections by Najib al-Haddad and Lewis al-Sabunji. Najib al-Haddad and his brother Amin, both of them poets, were among those to contribute to de Avierino's journal. The brothers themselves founded Lisān al-'Arab in Alexandria in 1894. Noted for its pure language, it was used as both a political vehicle for criticizing the Ottoman Sultan and a literary vehicle for publishing the Haddads' poetry. It ceased publication when Najib al-Haddad died in 1899. It never matched the fiery fusion of the political and literary achieved by al-Nadim.

Like Alexandria, Istanbul in the 1880s also saw the development of a purer cultural journalism, as political protest journals shifted to European capitals under the more rigorous censorship of Abdülhamid II. Among those journals of cultural significance were Tevfik Ebüzziya's Mecmua-i Ebüzziya (1880–87, 1894–1912) and Ahmet Midhat's Tercüman-i Hakikat (1878). The latter played an especially important role in the development of education and in the formation of a broader reading public. It covered a wide range of subjects in easily comprehensible language, and Midhat's own translations and adaptations did much to popularize literature. It demonstrated a changing perception of literature, shifting the emphasis from form to content. Beşir Fuat wrote that he was more interested in ideas than style,[19] and he criticized writers for favoring expression over truth.[20] The journal provided a platform for writers like Hüseyin Rahmi Gürpinar, Halide Edipe Adıvar, Ahmet Rasim, who went on to produce more than 100 literary works and translations, and Ahmet İhsan Tokgöz, who later sparked a whole new literary movement through his journal *Servet-i Fünûn*.

Mahmut Celalettin and Samipaşazade Baki's weekly *Hazine-i Evrâk* also had its impact in the early 1880s, despite its short life (1882–83). Like *Tercüman-i Hakikat*, it tempered its language to appeal to a broader public. It included numerous translations and managed to gather both experienced and new young Turkish writers of the Tanzimat period into a single forum. Namik Kemal, Recaizade Mahmut Ekrem, Münif Paşa, and Abdülhak Hamid were among its contributors. Its initiative was continued in *Gayret*, another short-lived but significant cultural journal published by Menemenlizade Tahir in 1886–87. It included many of the same contributors as *Hazine-i Evrak* and emphasized the importance of debate by printing numerous readers' letters.

By the 1890s, literary journalism in Istanbul was established enough for Ahmad İhsan Tokgöz to launch *Servet-i Fünûn* with more long-term success. Tokgöz had previously published the pamphlets *Şafak* in 1886 and *Umran* in 1889, both of them short-lived, but important in stirring up literary circles in preparation for *Servet-i Fünûn*. Unlike *Hazine-i Evrâk and Tercüman-i Hakikat*, *Servet-i Fünûn* did not attempt to employ a simple and popular style of language, but its interest in literary matters was apparent from the very first issue. The opening issue began a serialization of Nabizade Nazim's novel *Seyyie-i Tesamüh*; the second issue began to publish a series of articles on literary analysis by the same writer. Among the pieces that appeared in this journal's first five years were seminal works like Ahmet Rasim's *Leyal-i Izdirap* and *Meşakkat-i Hayat*, Recaizade Ekrem's *Araba Sevdasi*, and Halit Ziya's *Canbaz*. The importance of *Servet-i Fünûn* peaked in the years 1896–1901, when it became the organ of *Edebiyat-i Cedide* (the new literature), which dealt with various new literary tendencies rather than a common aesthetics. The poet Tevfik Fikret assumed an important editorial position, and new writers like Cenab Şahabettin, Hüseyin Cahit, Ali Ekrem, and Ahmet Reşit were introduced in its pages. Readers became familiar with numerous Western writers and thinkers, including Flaubert, Balzac, Sainte-Beuve, Heriot, and Ruskin, among others. Of particular importance was a series of articles on aesthetics by Hüseyin Cahit and a series called "Life and Books" by Ahmet Şuayip, which presented many modern ideas and concepts of literature and the arts.

The significance of *Servet-i Fünûn* was that it managed to incorporate independent experimental literary endeavors within its broader framework and inject new blood into literary life by regularly publishing unknown young writers and poets. In years to come, various innovative groups such as *Fecr-i Ati* (1910), *Şairler Derneği* (1919), and *Yedi Meşale* (1928) were able to reach a much broader readership by publishing their manifestos and literary works in *Servet-i Fünûn*. Thus it was able to nurture innovation while continuing to feed the mainstream, ensuring its survival at the same time as directing future literary and cultural development. It managed to rise above the political struggles between the old regime and new elites that had closed down so many other literary journals in the last quarter of the nineteenth century. The impact it made on the cultural scene is shown by readers' letters published in its thousandth issue.[21]

Thus a market for specialized cultural journals was cultivated in Istanbul and Alexandria. However, it was the early political protest journals in Istanbul in the 1860s and Alexandria in the 1870s and 1880s that initiated Egyptian and Turkish literary journalism, for men like Şinasi and al-Nadim engaged a readership by sparking public feeling through their patriotism and political agendas. Although the literacy rate was still very low in both Istanbul and Alexandria, those who were literate had a sense of cultural and political responsibility, aware of themselves as members of the educated elite. This was exemplified in men like İbrahim Şinasi, Ahmet Midhat, and 'Abd Allah al-Nadim, who attempted to simplify the Turkish and Arabic languages in order to propagate their ideas among a broader public. Given Turkey and Egypt's strong oral tradition and café culture, it is likely that their work also reached beyond the educated elite.

The ties between journalism and literature are evidenced by many names that were as important to the history of literature as they were to the history of the press: Namik Kemal, İbrahim Şinasi, Ebüzziya Tevfik, and Ziya Paşa in Istanbul; Salim al-Naqqash, 'Abd Allah al-Nadim, and Najib Gharghur in Alexandria; and Ya'qub Sanu', Jurji Zaydan, and Ibrahim al-Yaziji in Cairo. This link remains strong even today, both in terms of reflecting the contemporary literary scene and directing that of the future. For although it has become the norm in both Egypt and Turkey for writers and poets to earn their living writing for mainstream journals, at the same time the journal's cheapness and immediacy compared to the book made it the ideal vehicle for *avant-garde* literary groups. The port cities of Alexandria and especially Istanbul continue to be particularly fertile in this type of innovation, in which the journal's fusion of literature and politics, first undertaken by Şinasi and al-Nadim, is most apparent. It is this potent combination that enables such journals to have an impact on the cultural scene out of all proportion to their often brief lives.

Notes

1. Ahmet Emin Yalman, "Notes on the Development of the Turkish Press," in *Cumhuriyet Basin Tarihi, 1923–73*, ed. Fuat Süreyya Oral (Ankara, 1974), p. iv.
2. Ami Ayalon, *The Press in the Arab Middle East* (New York, 1995), pp. 184–85.
3. It was in fact Agah Efendi who had organized the Turkish postal system.
4. Opening editorial in *Tercüman-i Ahval*, 21 October 1860.
5. Ibid.
6. Opening editorial in *Tasvir-i Efkar*, 27 June 1862.
7. *Basiret*, 23 May 1871.
8. Syrian emigrés were also instrumental in the development of Egyptian journalism before World War I, and in fact owned about 20 percent of Egypt's newspapers and journals before World War I. Thomas Philipp, *Syrians in Egypt* (Stuttgart, 1985), p. 98, cited in Beth Baron, *Women's Awakening in Egypt* (New Haven, 1994), p. 16.
9. Filib di Tarrazi, *Tārīkh al-Ṣiḥāfah al-'Arabiyyah* (Beirut, 1913–33), 3: 39.
10. Muhammad Rashid Rida, *Tārīkh al-Ustādh al-Imām al-Shaykh Muhammad 'Abdu*, (Cairo, 1906), 1: 45.
11. Jurji Zaydan, *Tarājim Mashāhir al-Sharq* (Cairo, 1911), part 2, p. 77.
12. *Al-Tankīt wa-l-Tabkīt*, 6 June 1881.
13. Ahmad Rayyan, "'Abd Allah al-Nadim wa-l-Tankīt wa-l-Tabkīt," *al-Nadāha* no. 2 (1979?): 9–11.
14. *Al-Ahrām*, 31 Oct. 1899.
15. Calculated from the list in Ahmad Maghazi, *al-Ṣiḥāfah al-Fanniyyah fī Miṣr* (Cairo, 1978), p. 182.
16. Ibrahim al-Yaziji, letter to Khalil Ziniyya. Cited in di Tarrazi, *Tārīkh al-Ṣiḥāfah*, 3: 93.
17. Calculated from lists in Filib di Tarrazi, o.c., vol. 4.
18. Robert Ilbert, *Alexandrie 1830–1930* (Cairo, 1996), 1:363.
19. *Tercüman-i Hakikat*, 7 Jan. 1887.
20. *Tercüman-i Hakikat*, 2 Feb. 1888.
21. *Servet-i Fünûn*, July 1910.

16 Printing and Urban Islam in the Mediterranean World, 1890–1920

Juan R. I. Cole

Islamic reformism, in both its liberal and conservative forms, grew up with the printing and telegraphic revolutions in the Muslim world.[1] That early reformist figures such as the Muslim nationalist Sayyid Jamal al-Din Asadabadi "al-Afghani," the liberal reformist Muhammad 'Abduh, and the far more conservative Rashid Rida published in and were associated with newspapers has long been recognized, but the full implications of their involvement in the print medium for Mediterranean urban Muslim culture have not yet been explored. The importance of cities here should be obvious. Rural illiteracy was exponentially higher than urban. The rural world was not entirely detached from the technologies of literacy, but was largely a consumer rather than a producer of printing. Newspaper articles read aloud often reached villagers. In terms of Muslim practice, the rural areas were far more likely to be the sites of shrine-based Sufi worship than were cities, and peasants lived in a religious world of miracles, daily dependence on what they thought of as the divinely directed forces of nature for their livelihood, and pleas for intercession that resonated with their relationship to their landlords. In contrast, cities, as the primary entrepot for the nineteenth- and early twentieth-century information economy of telegraphy, publishing, modernist ideas, and the importation of printed materials, were in a sense all "information ports."

In view of Marshall McLuhan's famous dictum that the medium is the message, can we identify any ways in which print itself had an impact on the content of Muslim reformism in the late nineteenth and early twentieth century?[2] Did journalistic technologies, including the wire services, affect print's diffusion and organization? What do the rates and techniques of literacy in the period 1890–1920 tell us about the nature of the movement? How is printing implicated in the rise of a new sort of public sphere, in new conceptions of the "nation," and even in a new sort of conception of the author?[3] The most prominent and thoughtful of the European historians concentrating on these sorts of issues, Elizabeth Eisenstein, has indefatigably explored the impact of printing on the Renaissance, the Reformation, and the Enlightenment.[4] Her approach has been unfairly criticized for being overly deterministic and monocausal (in fact she is a careful scholar, attentive to nuance), but that she has illuminated an important and neglected element in modernity is widely accepted. Ironically, students of the frontiers of the Muslim world have been among the first to think seriously about the meaning of the advent of print for Islam, and little has so far been written about this subject in regard to Arab Islam.[5]

The Eisenstein approach to printing as an agent of change might on the surface be thought open to the charge that ruptures and discontinuities are emphasized at the expense of a sense of the continuities in history. Christopher Bayly has recently addressed this problem for South Asia, arguing that a premodern communication ecumene prevailed in the subcontinent, consisting of specialists in written documentation of various sorts (Brahmins, Muslim clergy, court reporters, and scribes) as well as oral networks of gossip that operated across gender lines.[6] In Bayly's view, the British empire did not so much displace this Indian network of communication as gradually penetrate and coopt it. This argument from local knowledge and continuity is a powerful one, and forms a useful corrective to the frequently encountered conviction that the British entirely re-created India. But it does not necessarily contradict the Eisenstein approach. She notes that in the Renaissance, for instance, printing initially was used to publish books on magic and other subjects of great popular interest. That is, printing can be employed, ironically enough, to perpetuate pre-print modes of thinking and forms of knowledge. Still, she insists on a number of features of print that do have cognitive consequences, including the exactitude it makes possible with regard to diagrams (enabling scientific and engineering knowledge to spread in a way that hand-copied manuscripts simply did not), the ability to index a text, which now has fixed page numbers, and the simple accessibility of the text inexpensively to large numbers of readers. Not everything changes with the coming of print, but some ways of thinking and operating do change. My concentration on Islam here acknowledges that the preexisting ecumene of knowledge in the southern Mediterranean was not so much displaced as put to new uses, a point that meshes with Bayly's work.

The urban information networks of the southern Mediterranean, previously sustained by diplomatic pouch, merchant private post, trading diasporas, travelers, Sufi orders, mosque sermons, sailors, and gossip, were powerfully amplified in the period after about 1850. Relatively new technologies of information and transportation burgeoned, including printing and the private press, telegraphy, and regularized state-run mail delivery. There were also the increasing dominance of the steamship on sea, the expansion of railroads on land, and significant increases in urban literacy. After 1890, one sees many new uses of these transportation and communication technologies, as in the way the telegraph and the expatriate press were mobilized in Iran during the revolt against the tobacco monopoly in 1891–92, and in the 1905–11 and 1908–9 revolutions in Tehran and Istanbul. Alexandria, Beirut, İzmir (Smyrna), and Istanbul, along with hinterland information ports such as Cairo, Damascus, Tabriz, and Tehran, were gathered into a web of information and intelligence that was not so much new as now enormously more lush and rapid. At the same time, they were becoming a regional subunit in a global information ecumene in which European dominance was often challenged by the ways in which peoples of the global south appropriated the new technologies for their own purposes.

I will survey the impact of printing on Islamic reform movements in the urban centers of the Muslim world, with a special focus on Egypt. Private printing sometimes began in seaports, as in Alexandria, the original home in the 1870s of the famous *al-Ahram* newspaper as well as other important organs, such as *al-Tijarah* (Commerce), spurred by the foreign news more readily available there. But as telegraph lines and rails were laid to the capitals, the printing presses tended to move closer to the halls of power, assured that the foreign and economic news would in any case come over the wire.

I conducted a keyword search in the online bibliographic database, OCLC Worldcat (with 40 million entries). When I looked under "place of publication," it immediately became clear that there was far more book printing in capitals than seaports in the period 1890–1920. In those decades, 1,405 books now held by Western academic libraries were published in Cairo, but a mere 72 in Alexandria (in Arabic, Hebrew, and Greek—I had to limit the languages because of the large number of Alexandrias in the world). There were 2,865 titles published in Istanbul in all languages, but only 111 from the major port city of İzmir. Iran had no major port (Bushire was a small place), but Tabriz filled the role of overland port, the entrepôt linking Iran and its Asian hinterland to the Ottoman Empire and points west. Western libraries have 326 books published in those three decades in Tehran, but only 47 published in Tabriz. Beirut formed the major exception to this rule. The catalog showed 718 titles published there in these years, but only 141 from the provincial capital of Damascus. Still, Ottoman Syria had a number of administrative centers, and Beirut certainly played the role of a geographical "central place" in this regard.

The numbers in each case are no doubt unreliable and low, because Western libraries collected haphazardly from those years. But there is no particular reason to think that the ratio between capital cities and port cities was skewed (note that Istanbul stood out in being both). The situation was quite different with regard to periodicals, especially those of minority communities such as Greeks, Armenians, Italians, French, and British, who typically published many newspapers in the cosmopolitan ports such as Alexandria and İzmir, and whose press tended to be oriented toward secular, bourgeois concerns, in contrast to the more Islamic tinge of some periodicals issuing from Cairo and Istanbul.

The Chinese invented and combined the basic elements of printing (paper, ink, and relief surfaces) in the opening centuries of the common era, and in the period circa 1000–1310 they developed moveable-type printing, first using clay pieces and then wooden blocks. The invention spread in East Asia as far as Korea, where in the fifteenth century bronze metal moveable type was employed for the first time. Europe learned paper-making ultimately from China, in the twelfth century, and it is possible, though not established, that knowledge of other elements of the technology migrated west along the Silk Road. Indigenous printing techniques were known in Fatimid and Mamluk Egypt, but their uses were limited to purposes such as decorating fabrics and playing cards, and for unknown reasons the expertise was lost.[7] In any case, moveable-type printing was developed for Roman letters in western Europe 1430–50, thereafter spreading rapidly throughout what is now Germany, Holland, France, England, Spain, and Italy, becoming well entrenched by 1500.

Gutenberg-style printing did not become widespread in the Middle East at this time, though why this should have been remains mysterious. Jews exiled from Spain who took refuge in Istanbul established presses, and the technology was certainly known, at least superficially, to Middle Easterners. Scholars have often blamed the resistance to the adoption of printing in Muslim realms on the influence of the powerful corps of scribes, whose livelihoods were threatened by the press, and on cultural attitudes among rulers and learned men exalting the Arabic script as too sacred to be desecrated through mechanization. Robinson has emphasized the orality of the transmission of religious and other knowledge in the Muslim world, to which print posed a challenge.[8] Knowledge was not to be gained through private reading but through master-disciple dissemination. I agree that these attitudes are important, but they were not perhaps so universal as Robinson and others suggest. Although Egyptian scholars in the Ottoman period insisted on the oral, master-disciple model of learning, they criticized their Turkish and Kurdish colleagues who studied the rational sciences for neglecting the transmitted, religious sciences, acidly remarking that their technique was "a book in the hand and not in the heart."[9] The great late-medieval scholar al-Suyuti was criticized for writing books on subjects for which he had had no teacher, but telling as the criticism is about attitudes, so also is al-Suyuti's behavior significant.[10] The insistence on person-to-person oral transmission seems to have been strongest in Islamic sciences such as hadith studies, but not nearly as rigid in, say, philosophy and the sciences, where books were often read independently.

I would not wish entirely to discount more material factors. Private printing also did not flourish in eastern Europe or Russia until the mid-eighteenth century, nor in most of Afro-Asia, much of it not Muslim. (The exceptions were China, Japan, and Korea, which published thousands of books using their indigenous versions of the technology.)[11] Rudi Lindner points to the paucity in the Middle East of specialized metallurgical and other knowledge for working the metals used to make moveable type and to construct the necessary machines, the low rag content in Middle Eastern paper of the time, and likewise the unavailability of the rare materials needed for ink and knowledge of how to process them. He also notes the social-control issues, insofar as the Ottoman state was well aware of the subversive potential of print culture.[12] Other factors, such as the apparently low rate of literacy in the early modern period and the smallness of any middle class with disposable income for buying printed materials, should also be taken into account. Social structure as a whole may have overdetermined the resistance to print. The quasi-feudal systems dominating the areas of Eurasia outside western Europe typically were oriented toward the agrarian economy of the military appanages rather than toward urban activities; they frequently overtaxed their artisans, denied cities autonomy, and attempted to control speech and culture more closely than was common in, for example, England or Holland. The onset of mercantile capitalism in western Europe along with the subsequent establishment of the great seagoing empires may have been important for the spread of printing, given the need they generated for fast dissemination of accurate knowledge about trading conditions and prices, and this sort of capitalism involved social and economic developments also not paralleled in eastern Europe or the Middle East at that time.

In Iran and South Asia, adoption of the printing press was further impeded by preference for the cursive *nasta'liq* script, which is difficult to reproduce with metal type. The invention of lithography by Aloys Senefelder in 1796 allowed calligraphers to continue produce their work in *nasta'liq* and so greatly aided adoption of printing. In lithography, the design is executed with a greasy crayon on a stone or limestone slab; then the stone is dampened with water, which the grease repels. Printing ink adheres to the grease but not the damp stone, allowing the design to be printed. Muslim calligraphers wielded the greasy crayon to produce books and newspapers in the nineteenth century with an alacrity not apparent in the earlier experiments with moveable-type printing. Lithography, and in more recent times photo-offset printing, allowed Urdu newspapers in Pakistan and India to be hand-written right into the 1980s, when calligraphers finally began to be displaced by computer-generated fonts and texts.

The preference in the Arab world for the straight, hard-edged naskh style of calligraphy, which is more easily reproduced by printing presses, made lithography less central there, but did not make the Arabs more precocious printers. The only place in the eighteenth-century Muslim world where moveable-type Arabic-font printing was pursued energetically by private printers was in Istanbul, where the famous Mütaferrika Press was active for decades. Although some Arabic printing was carried out, especially by Syrian Christians, its amount and circulation were extremely limited. The first big Arabic-language publication program was the governmentally backed one of Mehmet 'Ali Paşa in Egypt, from the 1820s.[13] The books printed at the official Bulaq press included Ottoman, Persian, and Arabic texts, mainly classical works or translations from European languages. The print runs were small, in the range of 500 copies, and they were mainly distributed by the state to government employees, students in the new civil schools, and military cadets and officers. Occasionally private presses printed

Arabic works—with increasing frequency from the 1850s—but not until the mid-1870s did private Arabic-language printing become a big business in Egypt. Egyptian literacy may have risen from around 1 or 2 percent of the population in 1800 to around 7 percent in 1900 (during the same century, the population more than doubled); this relatively vast change was connected to the new educational programs of the Egyptian reform bureaucracy and made easier through print technology for the inexpensive and exact reproduction of textbooks, dictionaries, geographies, grammars, and other materials.[14]

Manuscripts were not only expensive and time-consuming to produce, but the need to avoid scribal transmission errors gave rise to practices that encouraged only the elite to read. Fancy rhythmic prose and the use of parallelisms allowed authors to fight back against the corruption of their texts by copyists, because rhyming limited the ways in which an unvoweled Arabic word could be read, as did the use of repetition. In consequence, however, authors were forced frequently to employ obscure synonyms, the meanings of which would not be known to the less educated reader. The need for rhyming prose was even reflected in Arabic lexicography, where many medieval dictionaries were arranged by the last letter of the word.

The drawbacks of parallelism and obscure vocabulary were of little importance when writers were producing work for a wealthy patron and a limited circle, but such a procedure was inadequate to the demand for printed information that grew up in the last third of the nineteenth century. Printing freed authors from the necessity of semantically double-loading their texts, because hundreds of copies could be made, error-free, from a single plate. The decline of a preference for rhyme in favor of straightforward prose, and the rise of a taste for simplicity and avoidance of little-known words all coincide with the burgeoning of print culture. With the proliferation from the mid-1870s of private newspapers dependent on newsstand sales and subscriptions, journalists in particular gained an incentive to write clearly, because their ability to sell copy increasingly depended on it. Journalists were, moreover, greatly influenced by the Arabic translations of news off the European wire services, such as Reuters, transmitted by telegraph. Because telegraph companies charged by the word, telegraphy encouraged succinctness, and the wire news reports reflected this. Thus, it was not only print culture that freed and impelled writers to adopt a new, more terse and clear style, but also the new technology of telegraphy (invented in 1844 and widespread in Egypt from the 1860s). In 1872, Egyptian government telegraph lines carried 238,521 Arabic-language messages.[15]

Thousands of members of the governmental class were made literate by Egyptian government publishing and education programs and were acculturated to reading the official newspaper and printed books, which allowed more and more adventurous, personal reading, dissociated from the memorization techniques that dominated the al-Azhar seminary's pedagogy. Robinson sees this new independence of readers from the tutelage of the ulama as a key result of printing, with pivotal implications for cognitive style.[16] The Bulaq printing program set the stage for the rise of urban Muslim reformism by beginning the creation of a reading public that included both high officials and people of the middling sort, who were willing to venture into the world of new and of neoclassical ideas promulgated by the printed book. The proliferation of newspapers in Egypt and Syria in the 1870s and 1880s went even further in widening the impact of print, because these were read aloud in coffeehouses and households and villages—though the Islamist authors were for the most part urban notables. I have estimated Egyptian newspaper readership in the early 1880s at around 75,000 nationwide, not counting the coffeehouse audiences. As readership in 1860 was nil, this change is remarkable even in a population of 8 million, and it is connected to the graduation of 10,000 or so civil-school students in the Isma'il period plus the proliferation of Qur'an schools. Newspapers continued to proliferate and their readership to grow in British Egypt, and the challenges to absolute monarchy in Iran from 1905 and in the Ottoman Empire from 1908 allowed an enormous expansion of the press in the East.

Muslim Reformism and the Print Context

The Salafiyyah (hearkening back to the pious forebears) movement was, despite the differing emphases of its major founders, generally characterized by some salient themes. These included the need to recover a direct contact with classical Islamic texts, rather than relying on late glosses and superglosses; reform of Arabic language and education in view of its centrality as the language of scripture; a criticism of traditionally trained ulama as hidebound prisoners of a non-empirical scholasticism; an attack on Sufi orders and leaders as decadent (though this element of Islamic reformism was more pronounced in the Arab world than in the Ottoman Empire, Central Asia, or India) and on many folk practices as departures from pristine Islam; a rebuttal of Christian European assaults on Islam; and a polemic against Muslim rulers who collaborated with European colonialism.

Although this program cannot by any means be accounted for solely or even primarily by the impact of printing, the new medium did affect Muslim reformist thought. Even colonially dominated Muslim realms, such as French Algeria and British India, became sites for the publication of Islamic texts, including the Qur'an. Alarmed at this development, the Ottoman sultan went so far in the late nineteenth century as to ban the printed and lithographed Qur'ans of Leipzig and Bombay from importation into his realms, probably fearing that colonial authorities would use the fact that they were mass-producing these texts for the edification of believers to help justify their colonization of Muslims.[17] European missionaries printed and distributed large numbers of Arabic Bibles in the nineteenth-century Middle East, as well as evangelical apologies for Christianity and attacks on Islam such as that of the nineteenth-century pietist, Carl Gottlieb Pfander. The Protestant message of *sola scriptura*, of "only scripture" as a spiritual authority, became known through translations into Arabic of works on European history and religion. In response to the Christian European onslaught, Muslims produced apologies for Islam, such as that of Rahmat Allah, which were widely printed and read. The argument between the evangelist Pfander and the Muslim learned man Rahmat Allah became more than a mere oral debate in mid-nineteenth-century North India largely because of the printing press.[18] The earlier print debate has its later analogue in 'Abduh's reply to French administrator and polemicist Gabriel Hanotaux.[19]

The proliferation of relatively inexpensive lithographed copies of the Qur'an allowed the circulation of the sacred text much more widely among the non-elite, whose previous exposure to scripture was largely oral, involving memorizing or listening to those who had memorized. The first Qur'an lithographs preserved in the British Library were made at Kazan in Russia, in 1817 and 1832, at Calcutta in 1831, and in Iran at Shiraz (1830) and Tabriz (1842). The Qur'an was regularly lithographed in Bombay, Lucknow, and Delhi beginning around 1850. There are Istanbul lithographs of the Muslim sacred scripture from 1881, 1884, 1888, and 1890, coinciding with the height of Sultan Abdülhamid II's pan-Islamic campaign. There do not appear to be stand-alone lithographed Qur'ans coming out of Cairo before about 1890, but the Ottoman and Indian editions no doubt circulated in Egypt, and Bulaq printed the text with commentaries, such as that of the Mu'tazilite al-Zamakhshari (1864) and that attributed to the Sufi Ibn al-'Arabi (1867). Later on, in 1890–1920, it became increasingly common for a penny press to print particular suras of the Qur'an or commentaries on them, often in the non-Arab East with interlinear translation into local languages, making such materials available to an ever widening audience for both study and ritual purposes. A wholly unscientific tabulation of Qur'ans, suras, and commentaries published in the Muslim world in the years 1890–1920 according to the OCLC Worldcat electronic list for U.S. libraries, along with evidence for the first part of the 1890s from the British Library, shows 79 items that have place and date of publication (these include reprintings of earlier editions). This is surely only a fraction of those actually published.

What is clear is that capital cities were major centers for the printing of the Qur'anic text in the years 1890–1920. Over 40 percent of my sample was printed in Cairo in British Egypt, even though that city had seen little of this sort of publishing under the khedives (only one Qur'an came from cosmopolitan Alexandria in these years, and only three from Beirut, in my sample). Some 17 percent were published in Istanbul (a port as well as a capital), but primarily before the 1908 Second Constitutional Revolution, when Sultan Abdülhamid II was pushing Qur'an printing and distribution as part of his pan-Islamic policy. About 7 percent of the printed Qur'anic text in my sample was published in Delhi, but I believe this figure to be extremely skewed toward the low end, insofar as U.S. repositories did not collect Indian publications in the early twentieth century and many of my Indian citations come from the 1890s in the British Library listing of printed books. Moreover, Lahore and a number of other cities in British India were important publishing centers. Although Tehran and Tabriz lithographs accounted for 8 percent of the sample, and although even in far-flung Shanghai in 1920 someone brought out a book of selections from the Qur'an in Arabic and Chinese, the indications are that, especially after Abdülhamid's dethronement, the primary centers for publishing the Qur'an in 1890–1920 were cities, especially capitals, of the British empire with substantial Muslim populations. Although the British colonialists practiced censorship of printed materials, they had no fear of the Qur'an itself or of conservative ulama who might feel that printing the Qur'an was sacrilegious. Ironically, reformers like 'Abduh and Rida were actually enabled to promulgate a more textually based Islam to ordinary folk under the shadow of the Union Jack. Although the printing was largely done in internal capitals, port cities remained important as sites for the importation from abroad of such printed Qur'ans and Islamic reformist literature as the journal *al-Manar* (read in Shiraz and Jakarta).

As for what exactly was published in the way of Qur'an commentaries, these tended to be the straightforward Baydawi, the medieval rationalist al-Zamakhshari, the scripturalist Ibn Taymiyyah, and the modernist 'Abduh, along with other classical and very early works, though of course the commentaries of Sufi mystics such as Qashani (ascribed to Ibn 'Arabi), Mirghani, and al-Ghazali also appeared.

The text of the Qur'an itself was becoming increasingly available to ordinary folk, with the inexpensive printings of individual suras (including, in the East, those with interlinear translations) being especially important. And the ordinary folk were increasingly literate, though more in the Arab world and Anatolia than in British India.

The printed Qur'an could be indexed (and many concordances were printed in this period), verses could be looked up for exact citation and study, and a chronological approach to the surah could be attempted with far greater ease than when parts of the book were available only in one's memory. A different way of thinking about the Qur'an emerged. This ability to peruse the Qur'an at any time allowed a more scripturalist approach to Islam to gain plausibility, especially for the sort of urban notables who, all over Africa and Asia, read the reformist Muslim periodicals. The middling sort and certainly the newly literate members of the lower middle class in the cities could not have afforded illuminated manuscript Qur'ans. The Muslim reformism of Sayyid Jamal al-Din and Muhammad 'Abduh was hardly fundamentalist, but their deprecation of later accretions did have a scripturalist bias. Printing, like the early reformist movement itself, contained the potential to promote both humanist rationalism among intellectuals and scripturalist fundamentalism among the less educated.[20]

Printing and lithography therefore raised many questions about Islamic textuality. In addition to allowing the inexpensive circulation of the Qur'an, they also permitted the less costly promulgation of a host of other classical religious texts. One reason the Salafis could afford to dismiss the late glosses of the Azharites, produced by scribes relatively inexpensively as textbooks, is that the classical knowledge was no longer so inaccessible. Multi-volume works such as early Qur'an commentaries or Ibn Khaldun's *Muqaddimah* were extremely expensive in manuscript form, and found only in the libraries of the rich. The Bulaq press editions of the nineteenth-century khedival government allowed mere scholars to buy such works, and the new institution of the public library made them available even to the relatively poor.

Not only did less well-off authors now have access to more books, but they could hope to become professional writers themselves. 'Abd Allah al-Nadīm, son of an Alexandria artisan, parlayed his linguistic gifts into a career as a journalist in the late 1870s, and his anti-imperialism and Muslim nativism were influenced by that of Sayyid Jamal al-Din and Muhammad 'Abduh. In a previous generation it is unlikely that Nadim could have been more than an indigent poet of the popular classes, a purveyor of the *zajal*. As it was, his newspaper *Tankit wa Tabkit* (It Is to Laugh, It Is to Cry) had a circulation in the thousands and his later *al-Ta'if* became the chief ideological organ of the 'Urabists. His satirical but more subdued *al-Ustadh* was published in Alexandria in the 1890s.[21]

Sayyid Jamal al-Din's career as a public Muslim intellectual in Egypt and, later, in Paris and Istanbul, was in some large degree made possible by print culture from the 1870s. A Shi'ite Iranian who had studied in the shrine city of Najaf but did not stay long enough to garner genuine theological credentials (*ijazahs*) from the mujtahids there, he had no particular standing to claim Islamic leadership as a learned man or *'alim*. In the Ottoman Empire and Egypt he dissimulated his Iranian Shi'ite background, and the fixity of print allowed him to fabricate an identity as a Sunni Afghan that lasted into the mid twentieth century, through the influence of al-Manar Press, until Nikki Keddie penetrated beyond it.[22] Sayyid Jamal al-Din was lionized from 1876 on by the anti-imperialist Lebanese journalists Adib Ishaq and Salim Naqqash, and by Egyptian Muslims who had newly taken up journalism, such as Muhammad 'Abduh and Muhammad Shamsi. Newspapers such as *Miṣr* and *Mir'at al-'Asr* (Cairo) and *Tijarah* (Alexandria) made his reputation, reported on his speeches and activities, and regularly praised him.[23]

The emergence of a new sort of authoriality that created Sayyid Jamal al-Din as a public, Muslim intellectual was in some large part made possible by the print culture of private journalism. He used printing in his anti-British *al-'Urwa al-Wuthqa* newspaper, in the publication in India (by lithograph) of his attack on Sir Sayyid Ahmad Khan as a Westernized materialist, and in his later pan-Islamic activities. In the period 1880–1908, pan-Islamism was among the major urban ideologies spread along printing networks in the greater Mediterranean and its Afro-Asian hinterland, with the great capital-port of Istanbul as its center.[24] As Foucault has suggested, an author's name is not a simple referent, as are other proper names. The author's name, such as "Sayyid Jamal al-Din," involves a complex set of cultural references, evoking key cultural artifacts at the same time as it functions as an individual description.[25] For Muslim reformers, "Sayyid Jamal al-Din" became a giant, and merely invoking his name was often sufficient to authorize new cultural practices. Clearly, key features of the print revolution in the nineteenth-century Muslim world contributed to aspects of this new authoriality, allowing him to comment and be heard on contemporary issues such as the third Anglo-Afghan war while it was being fought, or the British occupation of Egypt, or the tobacco revolt in Iran. In 1800, a thinker of his sort would have been known only by face-to-face encounters or by laboriously copied-out manuscripts with limited circulation.

Sayyid Jamal al-Din's attack on the scholasticism of nineteenth-century Muslim philosophy and his appeal for a philosophic and scientific spirit of inquiry reflected the ideals of some Enlightenment and nineteenth-century European intellectuals that had been largely unknown in the Middle East before the print-driven translation movement of the 1830s and after. By the 1870s, Egyptian physicians were reporting their original scientific discoveries in tropical medicine to educational journals such as *Rawdat al-Madaris*. Although an earlier generation of intellectuals such as Hasan al-'Attar occasionally also conducted experiments and contradicted classical authorities such as Avicenna, they did not publish their methods or results and so these remained purely personal achievements.[26] It was not only new knowledge and experimentation that underpinned the changed attitude among secularly trained thinkers, but the ability to disseminate discoveries widely and with exactitude through print.

The journalists who supported Sayyid Jamal al-Din's line, such as Salim al-Naqqash and 'Abd Allah al-Nadīm, were able to become more than simple writers, emerging as owners and publishers of their own newspapers, in short, as entrepreneurs in an economy in transition from late Ottoman prebendalism to capitalism. By taking nativist, anti-imperial stances during Egypt's debt crisis, they clearly aimed at increasing their sales among the disgruntled public. A charismatic figure like Sayyid Jamal al-Din, who made news by speaking in public, also potentially helped sales, so that it may have repaid these print capitalists to help create his legend.[27] If it is hard to think of a figure like him in earlier eras of Islamic history, an intellectual but not a fully trained member of the ulama, a publicist but not a poet, a journalist and activist, it is perhaps because he was a fish in the water of print culture, who would earlier have had no medium in which to swim.

Neoclassicism and Muslim Nationalism

The wider accessibility of classical Arabic texts made an impact on canons of Arabic literary taste and on Islamic thought in the second half of the nineteenth century. During the period of Ottoman domination of the Arab world (1516–1917), the language of administration, of court chronicles and panegyrics, and of much literature tended to be Ottoman Turkish. Arabic was used for shari'a (Islamic-law) court records, and an Arabic chronicle tradition survived in desultory fashion in Egypt and Syria, but only in the mid eighteenth century, with the weakening of Istanbul and the rise of Mamluk successor-states, does one see a thoroughgoing revival of the Arabic chronicle. Even its proponents such as al-Jabarti were capable of many solecisms and grammatical irregularities. I can attest that nineteenth-century Egyptian archival documents in Arabic sometimes employ rather colloquial grammar. The printing of classical Arabic texts required editors to seek grammatical standardization, and reading them allowed laypersons to encounter nonscriptural prose that predated the Ottoman-period decline of standardization in the written language.

The Bulaq Press printed, in addition to many classical grammars, such works as the pre-Islamic poetry of the *Mu'allaqat*, and presses in Iran and India put out relatively inexpensive editions of the *Nahj al-Balaghah* (Path of Eloquence) attributed to 'Ali ibn Abi Talib, which was characterized by a chaste and direct Arabic style and probably actually derives from tenth-century Baghdad. Muhammad 'Abduh's devotion to Arabic language reform must be seen at least partially in this context (he edited the *Nahj al-Balaghah*, for instance).

The now more widely available classical texts carried not only stylistic canons but also ideas. Sayyid Jamal al-Din, an Iranian Shi'ite who inclined to the Shaykhi school, propounded a theology that contained strong doses of Mu'tazilism, an early rationalist school whose central tenets had largely been absorbed into the theology of Twelver Shi'ites and that were especially emphasized by Sheikh Ahmad al-Ahsa'i (d. 1826).[28] The unknowability of God, the createdness of the Qur'an, the requirement that God and his creation be good and just and rational, were all premises shared by Shi'ites like al-Afghani and the early Mu'tazilites. With the printing revolution, many early accounts of Mu'tazili ideas circulated as well. The Bulaq Press brought out a two-volume edition of al-Zamakhshari's Mu'tazilite Qur'an commen-

tary in 1864, and it was regularly reprinted in several urban centers thereafter. Muhammad 'Abduh's neo-Mu'tazilism, his rationalism and humanis-
tic assertion of the Qur'an's createdness, then, had roots not only in the
influence of Sayyid Jamal al-Din, but also in classical texts made more widely
available to him and his audience by print technology. 'Abduh could already
consult many more books more easily than his father or grandfather could
have, and so could discern conflicts and discrepancies among classical
schools more readily, and pick and choose those principles that suited him.[29]
When Shaykh 'Illish challenged him on his Mu'tazilite ideas, 'Abduh replied that, having thrown off the whole idea of blind obedience to a school,
he had no intention of boxing himself into a narrow neo-Mu'tazilism, either.
Throwing off blind obedience, greater religious individualism, and more
detailed knowledge of theological options all were in part made possible by
the printing revolution. Muslim reformers often sought a return to original
sources and a standardization and rationalization of areas such as Islamic
law. Again, the technology of print greatly aided the attainment of this goal.
Manuscripts of multi-volume works in the areas of Islamic oral sayings (hadith), law (fiqh), jurisprudence, and even the decrees of the ruler (qanun-
name) seldom had title pages or indexes, lacked standardized page numbers,
and were difficult to compare. The expense of manuscripts prevented many
scholars from seeing a great number in their lifetime. Printing technology
allowed Rifa'ah al-Tahtawi to suggest the collection of khedival decrees to
serve as the basis of Egyptian law. The Ottoman project of the Mecelle,
involving the standardization of Islamic law, was made feasible in large part
because of the tools provided by print.

Print culture allowed some Muslim reformist debates to have wider repercussions than they otherwise would have had. Beth Baron has demonstrated that the women's press in late-nineteenth-century Egypt formed an
important context for the debate on women's liberation, to which 'Abduh,
Qasim Amin, Rashid Rida, and Malak Hifni Nasif contributed in the opening years of the twentieth century.[30] Had such women's writings, or Amin's
Tahrir al-Mar'ah (The Liberation of Women) remained manuscripts, hand-
copied on a one-by-one basis, their impact would have been considerably
diluted. As it was, women's journals and speeches, along with the works of
men such as Amin, were printed in hundreds of copies and provoked debate
in a whole Mediterranean network of newspapers and journals.[31] Gender
segregation had earlier limited women's participation in public events and
debates. As Habermas says, printing and journalism created a public sphere

and a public opinion.[32] It was a sphere in which women like Malak Hifni Nasif could openly join in the Muslim-reformist debates on women and religion in the teens of the twentieth century, a sort of intervention women would have found much more difficult in the days of manuscript culture.

Because Arabic was the lingua franca of Muslim intellectuals, the first wave of printing created a wider, contemporary community of discourse. Egyptian periodicals were read in Ottoman Istanbul and Anatolia, as well as Iran and South Asia. Ottoman Turkish was also widely known and Istanbul periodicals had their (now often forgotten) influence in Cairo, Damascus, Tabriz, and Bukhara. These print and readership networks formed an important context for the pan-Islamic movement with which Sayyid Jamal al-Din in particular was associated, as well as for the more Arab-centered projects of Muslim reformism associated with 'Abduh and Rida later on. As Benedict Anderson has argued, print capitalism allows the growth of an imagined community bounded by territory and language, which can be imbued with a mythical naturalness.[33] Sayyid Jamal al-Din sought a sort of Muslim nationalism, yet the conditions for its achievement were also in part undermined by transborder effects of printing and education. Egyptian literacy rose to 7 percent by the end of the nineteenth century, but very few of those readers could read Ottoman Turkish. Printing may have contributed to the possibility of envisaging pan-Islam, but it at the same time helped undermine it by encouraging language-specific communities of discourse. The Iranian intellectual Aqa Khan Kirmani, associated with a pan-Islamic group in the port of Istanbul in the early 1890s, wrote diatribes against the decadence of Arabs and Islam, and in praise of Persian and old Persian religion. Particularistic, linguistic nationalism was also powerfully enabled by printing. It could be argued that printing in the Ottoman Empire prepared the way for and enabled secularism, and that Ataturk cleverly used language and script reform to undermine any budding Turkish Islamism (as opposed to Kurdish and Turkish provincial traditionalism), which then did not emerge in a big way until much later in the twentieth century. Printing as a medium could be put to many potential uses. Islamic reformism was a major such use, but only one of many.

Printing could lend support to colonial officers and hangers-on among the French and British and to trading and service diasporas such as the Greeks, Armenians, Jews, and Maronites, typically based in the Mediterranean seaports. In the period 1890–1920, it also laid the basis for the emergence of a new field of the imagination on which nationalist ideas could be

inscribed by some groups, whether the Young Turks, the Iranian Constitu-
tionalists, or the Egyptian regionalists around Ahmad Lutfi al-Sayyid, Sa'd
Zaghlul, and the Wafd party, supported by the newspaper al-Jaridah. But it
would be wrong to ignore the ways in which the pre-existing information
ecumene of Muslim learning, writing, and speaking was continued, amplified, and often reconfigured by printing as well.

The rise of a new sort of public sphere that Habermas sees as having in
part developed out of the burgeoning of an uncensored press in eighteenth-
century Britain has its counterpart, ironically enough, in British Egypt,
where the press continued to be under political pressure but was much freer
to address Islam and Islamic reform than it had been under the khedives.
The pan-Islamicist imagining of a Muslim nation both confirms and subverts
Benedict Anderson's notion of print capitalism driving a new conception of
national relatedness. He coded religion as "universal" and tied to dynastic
rule as a medieval phenomenon subverted and displaced by the territorial,
largely secular nation-state. In fact, pan-Islam proved more imaginary than
imagined as a practical project of state-building, and its bankruptcy was
complete by 1924, when the Ottoman caliphate was abolished by the secularist nationalist Atatürk. Yet Islam and Muslim reform did reemerge as
central to Middle Eastern state-building projects later in the twentieth century in ways that suggest that the Andersonian antimony between medieval
religion and modern nationalism is too lacking in nuance. Printing and its
use by Muslim reformers do create new forms of authoriality in the period
1890–1920, helping account for the reputations of Sayyid Jamal al-Din,
Muhammad 'Abduh, and Rashid Rida. "Sayyid Jamal al-Din" remains not
a delineated individual, but rather a generic Muslim reformer, bland and
detached from specifics, with a Sunni overtone. This death of the individual
and his subsumption by the reformist "author" allows for the ways in which
his very name helped subsequent reformers legitimate modernist or fundamentalist projects, and the voluminous printed remains of the generic reformist "author" outweigh the manuscript evidence for his specificity and
particularity. Thus, Keddie's restoration of Sayyid Jamal al-Din the individual to history is resisted most fiercely precisely by those in the Arab world
who have the most invested in him as the bland "author" of Muslim modernism as a discursive practice.

Several important features of Muslim reformist thought can be shown to
resonate with and to have been affected by the primary vehicle of its diffusion, the printing press. The rise of printing encouraged greater public lit-

eracy and coincided with increased numbers of children being schooled, creating an audience for new ideas that had been minuscule earlier in the century. The emphasis on a return to original sources and the recovery of Mu'tazilism and other classical Muslim ideas were made easier through the printing in the nineteenth century of large numbers of Arabic texts, many of them from the classical period. The concern with language reform clearly ties in with the rise of privately owned, for-profit newspapers driven by the need for clear and concise, widely understandable copy. Sayyid Jamal al-Din, Muhammad 'Abduh, and Rashid Rida were all journalists at some time in their lives, and some of their supporters were as well.

The imperatives and nature of print journalism had a great impact on debates over constitutionalism and the woman question, as framed by re-formers of both sexes. Printed books, newspapers, and telegraphy also al-lowed news of the entire Muslim world to reach readers quickly, and so encouraged pan-Islamic emphases. These media made the threat of Euro-pean colonialism more vivid, as with the expatriate Persian press campaign against a tobacco monopoly granted by the Iranian state to a British carpet-bagger in 1891–92, or the pan-Islamic support for the beleaguered Ottoman caliphate during and just after World War I. Clearly, the Muslim reformers had other motives in pressing these concerns, including the actual problems of a peripheral bourgeoisie, of Muslim culture, and of European encroach-ment. Indeed, this reformism must be situated in the urban middle and upper-middle classes, and its opposition to both traditional ulama and pop-ular folk Islamic practices has much to do with its class and geographical location. But printing was more than simply a new medium in which to debate these issues. It helped shape the perception, language, and articula-tion of the problems themselves.

Notes

1. Anwar Jindi, *Tarikh al-sihafah al-Islamiyah* (Cairo: Dar al-Ansar, 1983); Sami 'Abd al-'Aziz, *al-Sihafah al-Islamiyah fi Misr fi al-qarn al-tasi' 'ashar* (al-Mansurah: Dar al-Wafa' lil-Tiba'ah wa-al-Nashr wa-al-Tawzi', 1992).
2. Marshall McLuhan, *The Gutenberg Galaxy: The Making of Typographic Man* (Toronto: University of Toronto Press, 1962).
3. For these issues, to be explored below, see Jürgen Habermas, *The Structural Transformation of the Public Sphere: An Inquiry into a Category of Bourgeois Society*, translated by Thomas Burger with the assistance of Frederick Lawrence

(Cambridge: MIT Press, 1989); Benedict Anderson, *Imagined Communities: Reflections on the Origin and Spread of Nationalism* (New York: Verso, 1991), and the essay, "What is an Author?" in Michel Foucault, *Language, Counter-memory, Practice: Selected Essays and Interviews*, ed., with an intro., by Donald F. Bouchard; translated from the French by Donald F. Bouchard and Sherry Simon (Ithaca: Cornell University Press, 1977), pp. 113–38.

4. Elizabeth L. Eisenstein, *The Printing Press As an Agent of Change* (Cambridge: Cambridge University Press, 1979). See also Lucien Febvre, *The Coming of the Book: The Impact of Printing 1450–1800* (Atlantic Highlands, N.J.: Humanities Press, 1976).

5. Adeeb Khalid, "Printing, Publishing, and Reform in Tsarist Central Asia," *International Journal of Middle East Studies* 26 (May 1994): 187–200; and Francis Robinson, "Technology and Religious Change: Islam and the Impact of Print," *Modern Asian Studies* 27, no. 1 (1993): 229–51; and for the contemporary period, see David B. Edwards, "Summoning Muslims: Print, Politics, and Religious Ideology in Afghanistan," *Journal of Asian Studies* 52 (August 1993): 609–28.

6. Christopher Bayly, *Empire and Information: Intelligence Gathering and Social Communication in India, 1780–1870*. Cambridge Studies in Indian History and Society (Cambridge: Cambridge University Press, 1996).

7. Richard W. Bulliet, "Medieval Arabic Tarsh: A Forgotten Chapter in the History of Printing," *Journal of the American Oriental Society* 107 (July–Sept. 1987): 427–38; Bulliet, "Printing in the Medieval Islamic Underworld," *Columbia Library Columns* 36 (May 1987): 13–20.

8. Robinson, "Technology and Religious Change."

9. Ibrahim Salamah, *L'Enseignement islamique en Égypte* (Cairo: Bulaq Press, 1938), pp. 88–89.

10. E. M. Sartain, *Jalal al-Din al-Suyuti* (Cambridge: Cambridge University Press, 1975), pp. 122–23.

11. Peter F. Kornicki, *The Book in Japan: A Cultural History from the Beginnings to the Nineteenth Century* (Leiden: E. J. Brill, 1998).

12. Rudi Lindner, "Icons among Iconoclasts in the Renaissance," in *The Iconic Page in Manuscript, Print and Digital Culture*, ed. George Bornstein and Theresa Tinkle (Ann Arbor: University of Michigan Press, 1998), pp. 89–107.

13. Abu al-Futuh Ahmad Ridwan, *Tarikh Matba'at Bulaq* (Cairo: al-Matba'ah al-Amiriyyah, 1953); Khalil Sabat, *Tarikh al-Tiba'ah fi al-Sharq al-'Arabi* (Cairo: Dar al-Ma'arif, 1966).

14. See chapter 5, "The Long Revolution in Egypt," in Juan R. I. Cole, *Colonialism and Revolution in the Middle East: Social and Cultural Origins of Egypt's 'Urabi Movement* (Princeton: Princeton University Press, 1993), pp. 110–132;

Ami Ayalon, "Political Journalism and Its Audience in Egypt, 1875–1914," *Culture and History* 1 (1997): 100–20;

15. Cole, *Colonialism and Revolution*, p. 112.

16. Robinson, "Technology and Religious Change," pp. 244–45.

17. Selim Deringil, "The Invention of Tradition As Public Image in the Late Ottoman Empire, 1808 to 1908," *Comparative Studies in Society and History* 35 (January 1993): 3–29; Deringil, "Legitimacy Structures in the Ottoman State: The Reign of Abdülhamid II (1876–1909)," *International Journal of Middle East Studies* 23 (August 1991): 345–59.

18. Avril Powell, *Muslims and Missionaries in Pre-Mutiny India* (London: Curzon, 1993).

19. See Muhammad 'Abduh, *al-A'mal al-Kamilah li al-Imam Muhammad 'Abduh*, ed. Muhammad 'Amarah, 6 vols. (Beirut: Arab Institute for Studies and Publishing, 1972), 3: 201–40; Mirza Abu'l-Fadl Gulpaygani, *Miracles and Metaphors*, tr. Juan R. I. Cole (Los Angeles: Kalimat Press, 1982), pp. 88–96; and Abu Bakr 'Abd al-Raziq, *al-Shaykhan al-Afghani wa-Muhammad 'Abduh yaruddan 'alá Iftira'at al-Mustashriqin 'ala al-Islam wa-al-Muslimin* (Cairo: Maktabat Misr, 1992).

20. Cf. Eisenstein, *Printing Press*, pp. 366–67.

21. 'Abd al-Mun'im Ibrahim al-Disuqi Jumay'i, *Abd Allah al-Nadim* (Cairo: Matba'at al-Jablawi, 1980); Cole, *Colonialism and Revolution*, see index under Nadim.

22. Nikki R. Keddie, *Sayyid Jamal al-Din al-Afghani': A Political Biography* (Berkeley: University of California Press, 1972); Rudi Matthee, "Jamal al-Din al-Afghani and the Egyptian National Debate," *International Journal of Middle East Studies* 21 (May 1989): 151–69.

23. Cole, *Colonialism and Revolution*, pp. 135–51; Juan R. I. Cole, "New Perspectives on Sayyid Jamal al-Din al-Afghani in Egypt," in Rudi Matthee and Beth Baron, eds., *Iran and Beyond: Essays in Middle Eastern History in Honor of Nikki R. Keddi*, (Costa Mesa, Calif: Mazda Publishers, 2000), pp. 13–34.

24. Jacob Landau, *The Politics of Pan-Islam*, rev. ed. (Oxford: Oxford University Press, 1994).

25. Foucault, "What Is an Author?"

26. Peter Gran, *Islamic Roots of Capitalism: Egypt, 1760–1840* (Austin: University of Texas Press, 1979).

27. Cole, *Colonialism and Revolution*, pp. 126–63.

28. For Sheikh Ahmad al-Ahsa'i, see Juan R. I. Cole, "The World as Text: Cosmologies of Shaykh Ahmad al-Ahsa'i," *Studia Islamica* 80 (1994): 145–63.

29. Cf. Eisenstein, *Printing Press*, p. 74.

30. Beth Baron, *The Women's Awakening in Egypt: Culture, Society, and the Press*

(New Haven: Yale University Press, 1994); and see the essays by Booth, Abu-Lughod, and Shakry in Lila Abu-Lughod, *Remaking Women: Feminism and Modernity in the Middle East* (Princeton: Princeton University Press, 1998).

31. Juan R. I. Cole, "Feminism, Class and Islam in Turn-of-the-Century Egypt." *International Journal of Middle East Studies* 13 (1981): 387–407.

32. Habermas, *Structural Transformation of the Public Sphere.*

33. Anderson, *Imagined Communities.*

17 Space and Time on the Indian Ocean Rim: Theory and History

Sugata Bose

"[T]here comes a moment," Bernard Bailyn writes in his review essay on "The Idea of Atlantic History,"

> when historians, wherever they may be located and whatever their personal backgrounds, blink their eyes and suddenly see within a mass of scattered information a new configuration that has a general meaning never grasped before, an emergent pattern that has some kind of enhanced explanatory power. That happened somewhere along the line in the past three decades, to bring the idea of Atlantic history into focus. Those glowing moments of illumination, suffusing at different times and in different ways the thought of many historians working on many problems, are where the real excitement lies.[1]

A very similar claim can be made about the idea of Indian Ocean history as it has evolved in the minds of many historians on several continents, but, if we believe Bailyn about the inspiration behind Atlantic history, there is one major difference. "The concept of Atlantic history," he tells us, "did not develop in imitation of Braudel's concept of Mediterranean history," "the impulse" behind which was "not so much intellectual as 'poetic.'" "Nobody I know," Bailyn asserts, "is or has been poetically enraptured by the Atlantic world."[2] I have a sneaking suspicion that some scholars of the Atlantic world might wish to contest Bailyn on this particular point. But so far as the Indian

Ocean rim is concerned, there is no question that its history is enmeshed with its poetry, as will be clear even from my engagement with problems as prosaic as spatial and temporal boundaries.

An Inter-Regional Arena

The twentieth century was barely three years old when Curzon, the British viceroy of India, led a flag-waving naval flotilla out of Karachi harbor into the western Indian Ocean. The relative positions of the ships were so admirably maintained that "the lights of the squadron as seen by the night . . . presented an apparently stationary pageant."[3] Addressing the sheikhs of Trucial Oman in a darbar room on board the *Argonaut*, "fitted up and decked with gold-worked carpets and handsome embroideries," on 21 November 1903, Curzon explained why Great Britain sought dominance in the region:

The history of your States and of your families, and the present condition of the Gulf, are the answer. . . . We found strife and we have created order. . . . The great Empire of India, which it is our duty to defend, lies almost at your gates. . . . We are not now going to throw away this century of costly and triumphant enterprise; we shall not wipe out the most unselfish page in history. The peace of these waters must still be maintained; your independence will continue to be upheld; and the influence of the British Government must remain supreme.[4]

In Curzon's imperious public rhetoric, the sovereign independence of the Gulf sheikhdoms and the supreme influence of the British sovereign had been neatly placed on two sides of the same coin. On 18 and 19 November, the viceroy met the sultan of Muscat, whose "demeanour," he had been pleased to report privately to His Majesty's Government, was "that of a loyal feudatory of the British Crown rather than of an independent sovereign."[5] Curzon similarly reported the visit on 28 and 29 November to Kuwait, which had been made a British protectorate in 1899, to have been "regarded by the ruler as finally . . . setting the seal upon the protection and overlordship of the British Power."[6] The "success and completeness of the Viceroy's tour," J. G. Lorimer tells us, "were to some extent marred" by a diplomatic incident at Bushehr, where the Iranian authorities refused to be reduced to the status of the Sultan of Muscat. Unable to get his way on the definition of sovereignty and the corresponding protocol, Curzon abandoned plans of disembarking at the Iranian port. A little more than a decade later, tens of thousands of Indian troops in Britain's colonial army were hurled into the Mesopotamian campaign of World War I, and, despite a 1915 debacle at Kut-Amara, helped eventually to carve out the mandated territory of Iraq.

India had clearly been the economic prize during Britain's "century of costly and triumphant enterprise" in the Indian Ocean. Although important economic connections linked the entire region, the imperial interest in the Red Sea and the Gulf from 1800 until nearly 1930 had been primarily strategic. When the global crisis of the 1930s Depression took the bottom out of the pearl economy, Kuwait, for example, was reported by the British to be in the grip of "suffering and acute want," which "showed itself in the form of gangs of beggars, who . . . roam[ed] the town."[7] On the eve of World War II, Alan Villiers found Kuwait city "to be composed of some eight thousand houses and . . . perhaps 70,000 or 80,000 people. Its roads were unmade (except for a brief mile or so running to the Sheikh's town palace, at the eastern end): its narrow streets a windy, sanded maze, threading in and out among the low walled houses and the roofed bazaars." But, he noted, "half the sheikhdom swam upon a vast underground lake of oil,"[8] and Kuwait's ruler had already signed an oil concession to an Anglo-American conglomerate. As the twentieth century entered its last decade, it was not altogether surprising that the United States would not be of a mind to throw away its "century of costly and triumphant enterprise."

Oceans tend to have a certain timeless quality, and it is best to remind ourselves at the outset of the political and economic changes that have occurred in the nineteenth and twentieth centuries, of which the redefinition of state sovereignty in the nineteenth century and the discovery of oil in the twentieth century are two of the more salient. As I was beginning my research on the Indian Ocean a few years ago, I was invited by some artistically oriented graduate students at Yale "to sketch the history of the region in swift, introductory strokes . . . [and] paint its intellectual history as it has developed over the past few decades"[9] — a daunting task. I had attempted to fulfil my charge by dividing the vast canvas into three overlapping parts. For the purposes of this essay, I have preserved that broad design, but the brush-strokes dipped in the sources of many archives have made the picture rather more complex. First, I will take up the issue of spatial boundaries that might help us theorize and historicize the Indian Ocean as an inter-regional arena of political, economic, and cultural interaction. Second, I will turn to the issue of temporal thresholds that need to be addressed to define a meaningful scheme of periodization for Indian Ocean history. Third, I will explore some thematic issues that may help lend coherence to a field of study that demands an ability to engage in fairly large-scale comparisons. In doing so, I hope to convey some of the feel and flavor of my own work while placing my arguments in the larger historiographical context.

Spatial Boundaries

As will already have been noticed, I have chosen to characterize the Indian Ocean as an "inter-regional arena" rather than as a "system," a term preferred by several other scholars. An inter-regional arena lies somewhere between the generalities of a "world system" and the specificities of particular regions. Regional entities known today as the Middle East, South Asia, and Southeast Asia underpinning the rubric of area studies in the Western academy are relatively recent constructions that arbitrarily project certain legacies of colonial power onto the domain of knowledge in the post-colonial era. The "worlds" of the Indian Ocean and, for that matter, the Mediterranean have ingrained in them a much greater depth of economic and cultural meaning. Tied together by webs of economic and cultural relationships, they nevertheless had flexible internal and external boundaries. These "worlds," where port cities formed the nodal points of exchange and interaction, have been so far best theorized, described, and analyzed by historians of the pre-modern and early modern periods. They have not generally formed the canvas on which scholars have written histories of the modern era. If the Mediterranean world was seen to be swamped by a world capitalist system with a global reach, the organic unity of the Indian Ocean rim was widely assumed to have been ruptured with the establishment of European political and economic domination by the latter half of the eighteenth century.

The Portuguese presence in the Indian Ocean in the sixteenth century and the Dutch role in the seventeenth century have formed the subject matter of some interesting revisionist work,[10] but insightful work on the Indian Ocean as an inter-regional arena and level of analysis in the period after 1750, and especially after 1830, is still in its early stages. Colonial frontiers came to obstruct the study of comparisons and links across regions and left as a lasting legacy a general narrowing of scholarly focus within the framework of area studies. Macro models such as the world-systems perspective,[11] although transcending these limitations, tend to view an omnipotent West as the main locus of historical initiative and are too diffuse to take adequate account of the rich and complex, inter-regional arenas of economic, political, and cultural relationships. Micro approaches such as subaltern studies have done much to recover the subjecthood of marginal actors, but have been overall a little too engrossed in discourses of the local community and the nation to engage in broader comparisons.[12] One way to disturb the essentialized views of India or Islam that had been colonialism's legacy to area studies is to unravel the internal fragments; the other is to render permeable and then creatively trespass across rather rigidly drawn external boundaries. It is to the latter effort that a reconceptualization of the Indian Ocean as an inter-regional arena can lend some much needed momentum.

In attempting to introduce the issue of spatial boundaries with a few swift brushstrokes, I realize I have already scattered some paint on the area of the canvas I had set apart for temporal thresholds. It is hard to deal with one to the exclusion of the other, but it may be worthwhile to pause and concentrate for a moment on the ways in which historians have approached the problems of spatial limits and elements of unity of the Indian Ocean region. As K. N. Chaudhuri has shown, "space is a more fundamental, rational and *a priori* dimension for social action than time-order and succession" and takes primacy in historical understanding.[13]

Although the ocean referred to in old Arab navigational treatises as *al-bahr al-Hindi* has long been perceived as having some kind of unity, there can be no single answer to the question of its geographical extent. The spatial boundaries of the Indian Ocean varied according to the nature of cultural, economic, and political interactions under consideration and certainly altered over time. M. N. Pearson concludes his discussion on this point by saying that "like the currents and the winds" the ocean "really knew no frontiers,"[14] and scholars had to proceed with certain rule-of-thumb sketches of its limits. For the 1500–1800 period, he seems to suggest outer boundaries drawn by the east African coast up to the Red Sea and going east all the way along the Asian coast through the Arabian Sea and the Bay of Bengal to the Straits of Malacca. It can be argued that in the early nineteenth century southern Africa and western Australia were drawn more emphatically into the orbit of the human history of the Indian Ocean.

More important for any project aimed at unraveling the symbiotic activities of people on land and at sea is a discussion of the principles of unity and disunity that have been seen to have undergirded the Indian Ocean as an inter-regional arena of economy and culture. Scholars recognize at the broadest level that the "essential unity of the Indian Ocean 'world' " until the eighteenth century was "determined by the rhythms of long-distance maritime trade." In addition to this dimension of economic unity, there were "*certain* cultural commonalities" that set the peoples of the Indian Ocean world "apart from the peoples of contiguous 'worlds' such as the Mediterranean and East Asia."[15] Different historians of the Indian Ocean have addressed the problem of unity and commonalities in a variety of ways. K. N. Chaudhuri has made the most deliberate attempt to have his history from the rise of Islam to 1750 be informed by a "rigorous theory of the concept of unity and disunity, continuity and discontinuity, ruptures and thresholds."[16] The unity of economic and social life in the Indian Ocean realm takes on "analytical cohesion," according to Chaudhuri, "not from the observable unity of a spatial construct but from the dynamics of structural relations."[17] These relations can only be defined and analyzed through a series of mental processes. Complicating a Braudelian intuitive approach to long-term structures that remained invariant over time with a Foucaultian reexamination of human cognitive logic and Cantorian set theory, Chaudhuri presents a sharper analysis of boundaries, ruptures, and thresholds in Indian Ocean history than Braudel was able to offer in his work on the Mediterranean. Chaudhuri deploys as three key analytical instruments the concepts of topology, order, and metamorphosis in his engaging exploration of the historical interaction between units of space and society.[18]

Yet it remains an open question whether the recourse to mathematics in fixing the inner and outer limit of a set fares much better than a historian's intuitive presumptions in resolving the problem of the spatial limits of an inter-regional arena of human interaction. In Chaudhuri's scheme, the Indian Ocean blends imperceptibly into Asia, comprised of four distinct but comparable "civilisations"—Islamic, Sanskritic Indian, Chinese, and Southeast Asian. If Braudel's gaze from the south of France failed to acknowledge the historical actors on the southern and eastern shores of the Mediterranean, the limitations of Chaudhuri's perspective become apparent in the marginalization of Africa. 'The exclusion of East Africa from our civilizational identities," he writes, "needs a special word of explanation. In spite of its close connection with the Islamic world, the indigenous African communities appear to have been structured by a historical logic separate and independent from the rest of the Indian Ocean."[19] This special word on Africa seems to fall short of an explanation.

Other historians less ambitious about contributing to grand theory have offered alternative typologies of unity amidst diversity in the Indian Ocean region. James de Vere Allen advances an argument about three layers of unity: racial, influenced by patterns of migration; cultural, emanating out of India; and religious, shaped primarily by the spread of Islam.[20] M. N. Pearson sees "considerable unity in matters of monsoons, ports, ships and sailors." Another unifying factor can be noticed in "the widespread distribution of certain products from particular areas." For example, from the sixteenth to the eighteenth century, the great majority of the inhabitants across the Indian Ocean wore Indian cottons that came from one of three major production centers in Gujarat, Coromandel, and Bengal.[21] Among several other elements of commonality, if not unity, Pearson lists, one of the more important ones was supplied by religious activities, especially the Muslim hajj, which was crucial to the working of a large and complex cultural and trade network in the pre-modern and early-modern period.

Did the Indian Ocean rim continue to be a coherently definable inter-regional arena after the imposition of European economic and political domination by the latter half of the eighteenth and the first half of the nineteenth century? If so, what principles of unity might have sustained this level of economy and culture in an age when it had become part of and in many ways subservient to a global set of interconnections? Most historians of the Indian Ocean have simply not addressed this issue, preferring to assume the end of the unity of the Indian Ocean system or arena, as I would prefer to call it, around the middle to late eighteenth century. However, C. J. Baker and I found in our histories of agrarian regions in colonial India that migrant capital and labor played a crucial role in forging a system of inter-regional specialization and interdependence across the Bay of Bengal involving the old settled agrarian zones, newly developed rice frontiers, and the plantations and mines sector between 1850 and 1930.[22] Recently, Rajat Kanta Ray has suggested in a very substantial and thoughtful essay that "the imposition of the hegemony of Western capital and the disruption of the older Indian Ocean economy constitutes a process much more complex than is to be comprehended in terms of a unidimensional history of the expansion of 'the capitalist world economy.'" In fact, he argues that the Indian and Chinese chain of trade and finance stretching from Zanzibar to Singapore formed "a distinct international system that never lost its identity in the larger dominant world system of the West."[23] Ray interprets the "colonial expansion of the international capitalist economy of Europe and the rise of the new pan-Asian economic formation dubbed the bazaar"[24] as related historical processes of the modern era.

I would add that there were strands other than the ties of intermediary capital that sustained the Indian Ocean rim as an inter-regional arena of economy and culture. My own research on the period from about 1800 to 1950 suggests that pre-existing inter-regional networks were utilized, molded, reordered, and rendered subservient by Western capital and the more powerful colonial states, but never torn apart until these came under severe strain during the 1930s. Almost throughout the age of European colonialism, the Indian Ocean rim was characterized by specialized flows of capital and labor, skills and services, ideas and culture. Not to be mistaken as continuity between the pre-colonial and colonial eras, this calls for a reinterpretation of the nature of the European colonial and para-colonial enterprise of domination, as well as a subtler understanding of the unities and distinctive features of the cultures and idioms of anti-colonial resistance. As I study the fortunes and fears of migrant Indian merchants, moneylenders, soldiers, and laborers, I am more convinced than ever of the imperative of blending imaginatively the dimensions of economy, politics, and culture in a reconceptualization of the Indian Ocean as an inter-regional arena in the nineteenth and twentieth centuries. But if theory is not to be disconnected from history and space from time, I need at this stage to turn to that part of the canvas where temporal thresholds can be sketched in and juxtaposed with the sweeping lines of spatial limits.

Temporal Thresholds

The Indian Ocean has been traversed by a number of distinguished historians of the *longue durée*. Whether they have taken on a whole millennium or just a couple of centuries, most have chosen to concentrate on the premodern and early modern periods. What emerges from these studies of long- and medium-term movements in trade and culture in the Indian Ocean until the eighteenth century is a picture of a well-integrated inter-regional arena of economic and cultural interaction and exchange. Particularly important connections of material life, politico-military organization, economic institutions, and social-religious ideology were forged across the Ocean during the millennium that stretched from the eighth to the eighteenth century. The modification of these links in the late eighteenth and early nineteenth century has been shown by C. A. Bayly to have critically influenced the nature of the colonial transition in South and Southeast Asia and European ascendancy in the Middle East.[25] Economists and political scientists have also written about the direct links of the political economy of the recent decades since the oil boom of 1973. The study of linkages and the comparative context is just beginning to receive the attention it deserves in historical research spanning the period from circa 1830 to 1970. It is this apparent hiatus between the early colonial and contemporary periods that claims my research interest and which my discussion of the matter of temporal thresholds will primarily engage.

I should like to preface my comments on the Indian Ocean inter-regional arena during the transition to colonialism in the late eighteenth and early nineteenth century with a few remarks about the periodization of its earlier history. It is the ancient if not the eternal quality of the ocean that has appealed not just to historians but to poets and philosophers. Although coastal trading links between India and Mesopotamia go back nearly five millennia, it was the cracking of the code of the *mausim* or monsoon probably in the seventh century B.C. that, as Kenneth McPherson puts it, "dramatically extended the range of human movement across the Ocean, making possible increased direct contact between the Middle East, South Asia and Southeast Asia."[26] The thriving agrarian and urban economies of the Achaemenid and Mauryan empires provided the basis for the exchanges between the Middle East and South Asia, which predated the crafting of close links between South and Southeast Asia. By the beginning of the Christian era there was a perceptible shift in the balance from the earlier emphasis on luxuries to staple goods in the commodity composition of the Indian Ocean trade. At key centers throughout this realm sprang up important expatriate communities of South Asian merchants, who appear to have been more direct agents of cultural diffusion in Southeast Asia than in the Middle East. The old Indian Ocean arena managed to cast a spell on the imaginative mind of a leading twentieth-century Bengali poet, Jibanananda Das. In his famous poem *Banalata Sen*, he evoked its atmosphere:

A thousand years have I been roaming the world's pathways,
From Ceylon to Malaya in darkness of night across oceans

Much have I traveled; in the gray universe of Bimbisara, Ashoka,
Yes, I was there; deeper in the darkness in Vidarbha metropolis,
A weary soul, I, life's waves all around foaming at the crest,
A moment or two of peace she gave me, Natore's Banalata Sen.

Her hair, darker than the darkest Vidisha night,
Her face, Sravasti's carved ivory; on the distant sea
As a lost sailor of a rudderless ship
Sees on a sudden the line of an island's green
Have I seen her in the darkness; she has asked "where have you been,
  so long?"
Raising her eyes like a bird's nest, Natore's Banalata Sen.

At day's end, like the sound of dewdrops
Evening descends; the seagull wipes the sun's scent from its wings;
When all the colors of the world have faded the Manuscript prepares
For stories then in colors of fireflies, glowing,
All the birds come home—all the rivers—life's transactions end;
There remains only darkness, and to sit face to face with Banalata Sen.

Or, in another less well-known epigrammatic poem he let his imagination
fly in a westerly direction:

A thousand years just play like fireflies in the darkness
Pyramids all around, the stench of the dead,
Moonlight on the sand, palm shadows scattered
Broken pillars, as if: Assyria stands dead, pale.
The smell of mummies in our bodies, life's transactions have all ended.
"Do you remember?" she asked, and I gasped, "Banalata Sen."[27]

South Asian mariners and merchants played the key integrative role in
the economy and culture of the Indian Ocean during the first millennium
of the Christian era. After the third century, their ties were closer to Southeast Asia than to the Middle East, as Arabs and Persians began to play a
more active role in the western Indian Ocean during the decline of the
Roman Empire. The Chinese mercantile presence in Southeast Asia began
to take the form of a serious rivalry to South Asians, but also provided another
strong link in the Indian Ocean chain, from the tenth century. In the elev-

enth century, Arabs and Persians, as well as a few South Asians, began to draw the Somali and Swahili coast of East Africa more firmly into the Indian Ocean network. The rapid spread of Islam across the Indian Ocean between the thirteenth and fifteenth centuries wove a new pattern of economic and cultural unity throughout this vast inter-regional arena. By the fifteenth century, Arab and Indian merchants, mostly Muslim but some Hindu and Jain as well, were in the vanguard of maritime economic activity from the Mozambique coast in the west to the Moluccas in the east. At the same time, Sufi preachers fanning out from the port cities into the agricultural hinterlands were creating a common world of religious-cultural ambience and sensibility. It is the period from the fourteenth to the sixteenth century that Ashin Das Gupta identifies as marking the peak of indigenous maritime activity in the Indian Ocean region.[28]

Some recent scholarship on the Indian Ocean in the sixteenth and seventeenth centuries teaches us that the early European forays did not fundamentally alter or undermine the principles of economic and social integration in the region.[29] Blair B. Kling and M. N. Pearson characterize it as "an age of partnership" between Europeans and Asians; Sanjay Subrahmanyam, in his work on southern India in the sixteenth and seventeenth century, dubs it "an age of contained conflict." Anthony Reid's work on Southeast Asia in this period disabuses us of any simplistic notions of economic and societal decline.[30] Overall, in the words of Ashin Das Gupta, "after the first violent overture," the Portuguese in the sixteenth century "settled within the structure and were, in a way, swallowed by it." The English and the Dutch in the seventeenth century also worked to a certain extent "within the indigenous structure and except the few pockets in Indonesia claimed by the Dutch, they were everywhere one more strand in the weave of the ocean's trade."[31]

Indian Ocean historians, so adept at defying the constraints of arbitrary spatial boundaries imposed by conventional area studies, have been by and large remarkably diffident about crossing the great temporal divide of the eighteenth century. But that has not prevented many of them from making confident assertions about the decisive end of a millennium in Indian Ocean history. A few examples will suffice. André Wink in his introduction to *al-Hind* distinguishes "five successive stages" in what he calls a "millennium of Islamic expansion." His scheme locates the fifth stage in the eighteenth century, when "finally, India's core position is subordinated to metropolitan British control and the integrative network of Indian Ocean relations is destroyed."[32] Chaudhuri, in his classic *Asia before Europe,* writes of 1750 as marking the end of "a life-cycle of human civilisation."[33] In Das Gupta's view, the "most important change" that occurred in the eighteenth century was "the growing importance of the European factor in the Indian Ocean and the eventual sundering of the organic unity of trade and shipping towards the close of the period."[34] For McPherson, too, "by the eighteenth century the boundaries of th[e Indian Ocean] world were crumbling as it was overwhelmed, physically and economically, by European merchants and soldiers."[35] Something dramatic certainly happened in the eighteenth century. Yet, paradoxically, the abandonment by most historians of the Indian Ocean as an inter-regional arena of analysis on the assumption that its organic unity had been sundered has made it especially difficult to ferret out the key elements of change during the transition to colonialism. This in turn has hampered the development of a historical method that would unsettle the discredited, yet entrenched, notions of a West versus rest and other accompanying dichotomies. The historiographical challenge in this regard is to keep in play an Indian Ocean inter-regional arena of economic and cultural interaction as an analytical unit while avoiding the pitfalls of assuming any uncomplicated and unsustainable thesis about continuity.

One insightful essay published in 1990 that does problematize the question of "colonial insertion" into the political economy of India and, by extension, of the Indian Ocean, is Bayly and Subrahmanyam's on portfolio capitalists. They define the portfolio capitalist, an ubiquitous figure on the Indian scene since 1500, as "an entrepreneur who farmed revenue, engaged in local agricultural trade, commanded military resources (war animals, arms and human labour), as well as on more than the odd occasion had a flutter in the Great Game of Indian Ocean commerce."[36] The beginnings of the process of erosion of one significant item in the portfolio—independent seaborne commerce—are shown to lie in tough competition from European private trade at the turn of the eighteenth century. One of the ultimate beneficiaries of the process was a university on the east coast of the United States, Mr. Elihu Yale having been prominent among the rising private traders of that moment on the Coromandel coast. The "nabobs" were different from the typical Asian portfolio capitalist in two ways: they were linked to the East India Company and eventually to the colonial state and they dramatically altered the scale of British remittances out of India. By around 1820, Bayly and Subrahmanyam tell us, the company's state had taken a series of measures to cut the cord between commerce and political power, which had contributed to the undoing of the indigenous states and had the potential to threaten the colonialists once they had acquired state power. They suggest in conclusion that the building of networks and portfolios by Indian expatriates in Southeast Asia and the Middle East later in the nineteenth century borrowed "much more from the 'Chinese model' of overseas intermediation than from South Asian portfolio capitalism."[37] I would argue that although there were certain analogies between the Chinese and Indian patterns of inter-regional links across the Indian Ocean in this period, the Indian variant also bore some of the unmistakable marks of colonial difference. The spatial boundaries and temporal thresholds shaping the Indian Ocean's modern and postmodern history might be lent some further perspective and depth by painting in a set of important, related themes that will clarify the elements of comparison, continuity, and change.

Connections and Comparisons

A comparative examination of three broad themes is indispensable to imparting a measure of coherence to our understanding of the colonial and post-colonial periods in Indian Ocean history. First, the role of colonialism in restructuring states and redefining ideologies of sovereignty is of critical importance. Several scholars have by now exposed the violence embedded in state-making processes in early modern Europe, and Geoffrey Parker, among others, has noted the export of violence abroad by European "warrior nomads who differed little from the Mongols or the Mughals."[38] By the late eighteenth and early nineteenth century, however, the character of state violence engaged in by the British colonial state was qualitatively different from the warfare of the age of Mughal ascendancy and hegemony. The "centralized state which was created in the colonial period was an entirely new political innovation in the Indian Ocean region."[39] Its key novel feature in India was one of the largest European-style standing armies in the world, which came into being during the Revolutionary and Napoleonic wars. In the early nineteenth century, the soldiers of this colonial army crossed the *kalapani* (dark waters) to fight in Ceylon, Java, and the Red Sea area. Later in the nineteenth century and during the first half of the twentieth century, Britain's Indian army was deployed even more widely in imperial operations in Africa, the Middle East, Southeast Asia, and China. From the early nineteenth century onwards, the state penetrated society much more deeply than it had before and reshaped several institutions in law, landed rights, religion, and some customs. It was at this time that wandering peoples on land were either settled and sedentarized or branded "criminal tribes" and their counterparts at sea termed "pirates." Piracy may have been an old profession, but it was now infused with a new meaning. Curzon claimed in 1903 that "a hundred years ago . . . almost every man was a marauder or a pirate."[40]

The change in the meaning of sovereignty was fraught with even greater consequences. Pre-colonial states and polities generally possessed a shared and layered concept of sovereignty that had helped create certain autonomous spaces for the inhabitants of port cities. Surat and Aden, for instance, had been part of the great land-based Mughal and Ottoman empires, "yet they had autonomy enough not to be unduly harassed by their inland masters."[41] The notion of indivisible and unitary sovereignty imported under colonial conditions from Europe represented a major break from ideas of good governance and legitimacy that had been widespread in the Ottoman, Safavid, and Mughal domains and their regional successor states. What was more, the British juxtaposed to their own monolithic sovereignty a particularly spurious version of sovereignty invested in the persons of re-invented "traditional" rulers in post–1857 India (Kashmir being a good example)[42] and extended it to coastal polities in the Arabian Sea, the Persian Gulf, and the Bay of Bengal around the turn of the century. This sovereignty accorded to some of the sheikhdoms was, as Curzon let slip in 1903, no more than the other side of the coin on which the supremacy of British power was clearly engraved. The Indian Ocean realm then experienced a sea-change in the concept of sovereignty in the age of high imperialism, which has lingered on as colonialism's most poisonous legacy in the post-colonial era.

The second theme deserving close investigation is the relationship of Asian intermediary capital and migrant labor with the broader structures of colonial and para-colonial capitalism. Historians of India have been pointing out the brief congruence of interests of indigenous merchants and bankers with the East India Company that facilitated the transition to colonialism.[43] Yet it is also becoming clear that once the company had state power within its grasp, it generally clobbered indigenous merchant capitalists in most Indian regions. In other words, there was a significant decline in the position of most intermediate groups on whose collaboration colonial rule had initially rested. Bayly, to whom a continuity thesis is often simplistically attributed, states in his joint article with Subrahmanyam that the British had made "considerable strides by 1830 towards wiping the middle ground clean" of portfolio capitalists.[44] The timing of the erosion of these figures actually varied with the progress of colonial conquest. The Jagat Seths, whose large purse had aided the conquest of Bengal in 1757, were forced during the brief revival of the nawabi under Mir Kasim in the early 1760s to pay up what was owed to the British and then move bag and baggage from their mansion in Murshidabad to live in virtual detention in Monghyr. Several Hindu and Parsi financiers of cotton production and trade who helped finance the British takeover of Gujarat in 1803 had reasons to regret their alliance by the 1810s. The Hotchand family, which bankrolled the British possession of Sind in 1842, paid for their sins by rapidly losing out in the area of shipping and seaborne trade, but survived as landlords and bureaucrats.

What needs to be recognized, however, is that it was precisely in certain sectors of seaborne commerce, the item that was supposed to have dropped out of the portfolio of Indian men of capital in the eighteenth century, that some found opportunities for profit in the nineteenth century. The rise of the Omani empire stretching from Muscat to Zanzibar in the early nineteenth century gave certain Gujarati communities the opening they needed to create a lucrative niche in the inter-regional arena of Indian Ocean revenue-farming and trade. Later in the century, Indian traders and financiers followed the British imperial flag to engage in what was perhaps dependent seaborne commerce but that nevertheless enabled them to carve out sectors or pockets of local dominance in Southeast Asia, East Africa, and the Middle East. Indian intermediary capital and migrant labor were of critical importance in the rice frontiers of Burma, Thailand, and Vietnam, the rubber plantations of Malaya, the sugar plantations of Natal and Mauritius, initially the slave trade and later the cloves economy in Zanzibar, the ivory trade and the coconut and cashew economy in Mozambique, the pearl economy of the Gulf and the Red Sea, the coffee economy of Yemen, and the bazaars of southern Iran. In addition to their role as financiers, Indians were selling agents for British, Indian, and finally Japanese manufactured products, including textiles. Rajat Ray argues that their long historical experience in "handling money" enabled Indian, Chinese, and Baghdadi Jewish specialist communities to adjust to the age of European colonial capitalism and dominate the bazaar economy of the Indian Ocean.[45] Although the argument has general plausibility, a couple of caveats are in order. The Bhatias and Memons from Kutch who rose to prominence in East Africa and the Middle East and the Chettiars from Tamilnad who came to the fore in Southeast Asia were new dominant groups and not the same, old banking communities from an earlier age. Second, one needs to be careful not to write out of history the dogged resistance of sailing communities in the Arab and Malay regions, while acknowledging the dominance that European shipping came to exercise in the waters of the Indian Ocean. An overemphasis on the relevance or irrelevance of earlier skills in the age of the communications revolution of the later nineteenth century runs the risk of falling into a technological determinism, when historical outcomes were actually being influenced by a more complex interplay of domination, collaboration, and resistance among economic and political actors. With the solitary exception of the Sassoons, none of the Asian intermediary capitalists was able to break into the arena of high finance in the colonial era. The entire intermediary structure was also vulnerable to the possibility of coming unhinged as a result of crises at the higher echelons of the capitalist architecture and the foundation of agrarian production below, as was revealed in dramatic fashion during the 1930s Depression.

The so-called Indian and Chinese models of inter-regional links were different in the ways in which the flows of capital were related to the flows of labor. In the case of the Chinese in Southeast Asia, the movement of labor seems to have been tied in a dependent relationship to the movement of intermediary capital. In the Indian instance the two flows were not only quite separate but the colonial state played an important part in regulating the movement of indentured labor across the Indian Ocean and also farther afield to the Caribbean and Fiji. Although Chinese capital and labor in Malaya look integrally connected, the Kling laborers and Chettiar capitalists were distinct immigrant groups.[46] The Indian migrations of the colonial era also contained a significant component of professional and service people, the most famous among them being Gandhi in his South African period. The relationship of these migrants with local peasants and laborers often came to be fraught with deep tensions and constitutes one of the more important subplots in the story of anti-colonial and post-colonial nationalisms in Southeast Asia and Africa. Cosmopolitanism in composition in the port cities and their hinterlands no longer translated easily into cosmopolitanism of attitude in the colonial era. The early decades of this century saw a quickening of the pace of anti-colonial nationalisms at these sites, but also an accentuation of related sectarian and communitarian conflicts. The latter cannot be explained without addressing the question of inter-regional flows of capital and labor that exhibited superficial signs of continuity but underwent qualitative transformation in the colonial era.

The third theme we cannot afford to ignore is the role of Islam in particular and religiously informed universalism in general as an overarching unity and in its varied regional and cultural settings. Pre-modern and early modern historians of the Indian Ocean have shown that Islam had signified both integration and cosmopolitanism in that wide realm. We need to reconceptualize the experiences of Muslim encounters with European colonialism, long objectified by a weighty Orientalist tradition that has come under serious challenge but has not yet been laid to rest. A comparative approach by Indian Ocean historians to the strengths and weaknesses, bonds and fissures, of Islam as an ideology of anti-colonial resistance in the nineteenth and twentieth centuries may well be a worthwhile exercise. What went through the minds of Indian Muslim soldiers as they fought under the British imperial flag during World War I and served in an army of occupation in parts of the Middle East? In the same period, how did leading Indian Muslim thinkers invoke Islam to justify their conscientious objection to the war? Why did so many Indians become deeply concerned with the fate of the sultan-caliph towards the war's end? The Khilafat movement of 1919 was, after all, the first mass nationalist movement of all-India proportions.[47] Islam had been one key element in the unity of the Indian Ocean in earlier age; what was its role in the age of high imperialism and its continuing aftermath?

Those Indian soldiers fortunate enough to serve in areas of the Middle East where the shells were not exploding around them could still exult in the glories of common cultural symbols. As Lance Dafadar Mahomed Khan of the 15th Lancers wrote from Shiraz to Dafadar Mahomed Khan of the 18th Lancers stationed in France on 16 December 1917: "I was very lucky; when marching from Isfahan to Shiraz I saw Rustam's picture and that of King Darius on a mountainside. I also saw Jamshed's shrine and that of Tamas and many other interesting relics 2500 years old. I also saw the throne of Solomon and the fort of Bairam. I was fortunate enough to see more holy places when I got to Shiraz, the shrines of Sheikh Sadi the poet, of Hafiz and of Shah Chiragh and relics of many others of our holy men."[48] In May 1920, a picture of the Shatt-al-Arab adorned the frontispiece of the magazine *Muslim Bharat*. Inside was printed Kazi Nazrul Islam's celebrated poem which opened with the stirring lines:

Shatt-al-Arab, Shatt-al-Arab, poot juge juge tomar teer.
Shahider lohu, dileerer khun, dhelechhe jekhane Arab beer.[49]

(Shatt al-Arab, Shatt al-Arab, sacred are your ancient shores.
The blood of martyrs and the brave have been shed here by Arab
    heroes.)

The last lines mourned the shared pain of the loss of independence of
India and the Middle East. Havildar Quarter-Master Nazrul had briefly enlisted in the army. He never traveled west of Karachi, but his literary imagination knew no bounds. He spent his Karachi days perfecting his Persian
and trying his hand at translating the Rubaiyats of Hafiz. In October 1921,
Nazrul's great literary ballad "Kamal Pasha" appeared. By way of novels and
poems set in the gardens of Iran and the battlefields of Mesopotamia, Turkey,
and Central Asia, Nazrul eventually became acknowledged as the revolutionary poet-laureate of India.

The twentieth century on the Indian Ocean rim has witnessed oppression
and liberation, terrible destruction, and remarkable creativity. For all the
conflicts between rival empires, nation-states, sects and communities, there
were also voices emanating from cultures of that region for whom the ocean
was a symbol of universal humanity—its unfathomable depths matched by
its leap into horizonless infinity. As Rabindranath Tagore put it in a wistful
mood on seeing the ocean's reflection as the *Harana Maru* sailed from
Colombo to Marseilles in October 1924:

Lift, O lift, O sky, your still, blue curtain,
        I will look among the stars for the jewel from
The garland of the fleeting moment. I will seek
            From where, in autumn, comes for an instant
The twilight gleam, from where, along with rain,
            descends upon the earth the evening jasmine, and
From where the storm receives its diadem of lightning
            With a sudden flare.[50]

During this voyage he wrote the early poems of *Purabi* (Of the East), as
well as a prose diary called *Pashchim Jatrir Diary* (Diary of a Westbound
Traveler).[51]

In July 1924, the poet traveled east from Madras in the French ship
Amboise. His only motive in making this journey in response to an invitation
from archaeologists in Java was "to collect source materials there for the
history of India and to establish a permanent arrangement for research in

this field."[52] His Bengali followers quickly established a Greater India Society in Calcutta on the eve of his voyage to Java. But first came a stopover in the Malay Peninsula that afforded an opportunity not only for a rapturous welcome by Indian and Ceylon Tamils as well as Gujarati Khojas and Banias, but also a conversation with the Chinese literati. In Penang he wrote a foreword for Lim Boon Keng's English translation of *The Li-Siao: An Elegy on Encountering Sorrows*, by the ancient Chinese poet Chu-yuan. Tagore was less enthused by Indian military conquests in Southeast Asia than by the processes of cultural interaction facilitated by Hindu Brahmanas and Buddhist Shramanas. On board the ship *Plancius* in the Straits of Malacca, Tagore wrote his poem "Srivijayalakshmi," celebrating the renewal of a bond after a thousand-year separation.[53] The Srivijaya empire had patronized the Buddhist university at Nalanda and enjoyed friendly ties with the Pala kingdom of Bengal; both had suffered military defeat at the hands of the Cholas of south India in the 1020s.

Malaya and Java, Tagore lamented in his *Java Jatrir Patra* (Letters of a Traveler to Java),[54] were great Muslim societies under European colonial subjugation. It was his desire to see Muslim countries with Muslim sovereigns that led him to board a Dutch airplane to travel to Iran and Iraq in April 1932.[55] Not only was Tagore too old and infirm by this time to stand a long journey by sea, but a new mode of transportation was already beginning to revolutionize travel in the Indian Ocean arena. Tagore was as welcome in Bushire as Curzon had not been. He saw all the sights of Iran that Lance Dafadar Mahomed Khan had seen in 1916. The Iranians had imbibed enough of modern European race theory to welcome Tagore as "fellow Indo-Aryan," but Tagore's main identity was as a poet and an honorary Sufi, and the highlight of his visit was the encounter with Sadi and Hafiz in Shiraz. Tagore had made Hafiz's acquaintance as a boy through his father's translations from the Persian. Overwhelmed by the effusive welcoming address, he pointed out that the only weight on his side of the scale was that he was present in Iran in person. Hafiz had received an invitation from the ruler of Bengal, but his ship had been forced to turn back. At Hafiz's graveside, the custodian of the cemetery brought out a large square volume of Hafiz's *diwan* and asked Tagore to open it with a wish and his eyes shut. "Will the tavern's door be flung open," Tagore read when he opened his eyes, "and with it the tangled knots of life unfasten? Even if vain religious bigots keep it shut, have faith, that by God's will, the door will open." Tagore had no doubt that he and Hafiz were long-lost friends who had together filled many cups of wine.[56] In his essay *Parashye* (In Persia), Tagore wrote: "Each country of Asia will solve its own historical problems according to its strength, nature and need, but the lamp that they will each carry on their path to progress will converge to illuminate the common ray of knowledge . . . it is only when the light of the spirit glows that the bond of humanity becomes true."[57]

In neighboring Iraq, Tagore fulfilled a childhood fancy by visiting a Bedouin tent. He was just reflecting on how different his life nurtured by the rivers of Bengal was from the struggle for existence in the desert, when the Bedouin chief startled him with the language of universal humanity. "Our Prophet has taught us," the chief said, "that he is a true Muslim from whom no fellow human-being fears any harm."[58] From his hotel room in Baghdad, Tagore could see the wooden bridge over the Tigris built by General Maude, which the 28th Punjabis, 53rd Sikhs, 67th Punjabis, and the 2nd and 4th Gurkhas had crossed in March 1917.[59] At a civic reception in his honor— once the flow of Arabic poetry had ebbed—Tagore spoke about Hindu-Muslim conflict in India and invited his hosts to resend their message with its universalist ideal once more across the Arabian Sea. He expressed this sentiment even better in a poem-painting signed "Baghdad May 24 1932":

> *The night has ended.*
>   *Put out the light of the lamp*
>   *of thine own narrow corner*
>   *smudged with smoke.*
>   *The great morning which is for all*
>   *appears in the East.*
>   *Let its light reveal us*
>   *to each other*
>   *who walk on*
>   *the same*
>   *path of pilgrimage.*[60]

Notes

1. Bernard Bailyn, "The Idea of Atlantic History," Working Paper No. 96001, International Seminar on the History of the Atlantic World, 1500–1800, Harvard University, p. 22.

2. Ibid., p. 2.

3. J.G. Lorimer, *Gazetteer of the Persian Gulf, Oman and Central Arabia*, vol. 1, *Historical*, p. 2627.

4. Ibid., pp. 2638–2639.

5. Ibid., p. 2636.

6. Ibid., p. 2648.

7. *Persian Gulf Administration Report 1931* (India Office Library), p. 7.

8. Alan Villiers, *The Indian Ocean* (London, 1952), pp. 87, 92.

9. This was for the opening paper at the conference on "Trade and Agrarian Change in the Indian Ocean," 3–4 December, 1995, Yale University.

10. See, for example, M. N. Pearson, *The Portuguese in India* (Cambridge, 1987); Om Prakash, *The Dutch East India Company and the Economy of Bengal, 1630–1720* (Delhi, 1988); and Sanjay Subrahmanyam, *Improvising Empire: Portuguese Trade and Settlement in the Bay of Bengal 1500–1700* (Delhi, 1990).

11. The best-known exponent of this approach is Immanuel Wallerstein, *The Modern World System* (New York, 1974). See also his "The Incorporation of the Indian Subcontinent into the Capitalist World-Economy," in Satish Chandra ed., *The Indian Ocean: Explorations in History, Commerce and Politics* (Delhi, 1987), pp. 222–53.

12. For a notable exception written with great literary flair, see Amitav Ghosh, "The Slave of MS. H. 6," in *Subaltern Studies*, 7 (Delhi, 1992): 159–220.

13. K. N. Chaudhuri, *Asia before Europe: Economy and Civilisation of the Indian Ocean from the Rise of Islam to 1750* (Cambridge, 1990), p. 112. For an insightful discussion of the interaction of space and time in the mental domain and the distinctive characteristics of "perceived" space and time, see chapter 5 on "The Structure of Space and Society."

14. Ashin Das Gupta and M. N. Pearson eds., *India and the Indian Ocean, 1500–1800* (Calcutta, 1987), p. 11.

15. Kenneth McPherson, *The Indian Ocean: A History of People and the Sea* (Delhi, 1993), pp. 3–4.

16. Chaudhuri, *Asia before Europe*, p. 9.

17. Ibid., p. 23.

18. Ibid., ch. 5.

19. Ibid., p. 36.

20. James de Vere Allen, "A Proposal for Indian Ocean Studies," in *Historical Relations across the Indian Ocean*, report and papers of a meeting organized by Unesco, 15–19 July 1974 (Paris, 1980), pp. 137–51.

21. Das Gupta and Pearson, *India and the Indian Ocean*, p. 17.

22. C. J. Baker, "Economic Reorganization and the Slump in South and Southeast Asia," in *Comparative Studies in Society and History*, 23, 3 (July, 1981); *An Indian Rural Economy: The Tamilnad Countryside, 1880–1955* (Delhi, 1984);

Sugata Bose, *Agrarian Bengal: Economy, Social Structure and Politics, 1919–1947* (Cambridge, 1986); *The New Cambridge History of India: Peasant Labour and Colonial Capital* (Cambridge, 1993).

23. Rajat Kanta Ray, "Asian Capital in the Age of European Expansion: The Rise of the Bazaar, 1800–1914," *Modern Asian Studies* 29, 3 (1995): 553–54.

24. Ibid., p. 554. Ray views the bazaar nexus occupying the intermediate tier of a three-tiered system with European capital at the top and the world of peasants, peddlers, and pawnbrokers below as providing the critical link across the Indian Ocean during the long nineteenth century. The concept of the bazaar here is quite removed from the narrow and ahistorical notion of it as atomistic person-to-person transactions popularized by Clifford Geertz. The bazaar refers to wholesale commerce above the level of local markets and even more importantly to "the indigenous money market which finances, through promissory notes, bills of exchange (suftajas, hundis, etc.) and other negotiable instruments, the wholesale and forward trade over the longer distances."

25. C. A. Bayly, "Beating the Boundaries: South Asian History, c. 1700–1850," in Sugata Bose, ed., *South Asia and World Capitalism* (Delhi, 1990); C. A. Bayly, *Imperial Meridian: The British Empire and the World 1780–1830* (London, 1989), ch. 2.

26. McPherson, *Indian Ocean*, p. 44.

27. *Jibanananda Daser Sreshtha Kabita* (The Best Poems of Jibanananda Das) (Calcutta, 1974), pp. 51–52, 65 (my translation).

28. Ashin Das Gupta, *Malabar in Asian Trade, 1740–1800* (Cambridge, 1967), p. 7.

29. However, Bayly has very recently advanced the provocative and persuasive argument that the early European forays were rather more disruptive of Asian economic and political arrangements than has been recognized by historians of the Indian Ocean. See his "A presenca portuguesa no Oceano Indico e a emegencia do 'Estado Moderno,' 1498–1978," *Oceanos* 34 (June 1998).

30. See Blair B. Kling and M. N. Pearson, eds., *The Age of Partnership: Europeans in Asia before Dominion* (Honolulu, 1979); Sanjay Subrahmanyam, *The Political Economy of Commerce: Southern India, 1500–1650* (Cambridge, 1990); and Anthony Reid, *Southeast Asia in the Age of Commerce, 1450–1680* (New Haven, 1988).

31. Das Gupta and Pearson, *India and the Indian Ocean*, pp. 28, 39.

32. André Wink, *Al-Hind: the Making of the Indo-Islamic World*, vol. 1, *Early Medieval India and the Expansion of Islam Seventh to Eleventh Centuries* (Delhi, 1990), p. 3. See also André Wink, "Al-Hind: India and Indonesia in the Islamic World-Economy, c. 700–1800," in *The Ancien Regime in India and Indonesia*, special issue, *Itinerario* 1 (1988): 33–72.

33. K. N. Chaudhuri, *Trade and Civilisation in the Indian Ocean: An Economic*

History from the Rise of Islam to 1750 (Cambridge, 1985), p. 211 and *passim*.

34. Das Gupta and Pearson, *India and the Indian Ocean*, p. 39.

35. McPherson, *Indian Ocean*, p. 4; see also pp. 8, 198–200.

36. Sanjay Subrahmanyam and C.A. Bayly, "Portfolio Capitalists and the Political Economy of Early Modern India" in Sanjay Subrahmanyam, ed., *Merchants, Markets and the State in Early Modern India* (Delhi, 1990), p. 259.

37. Ibid., p. 264.

38. Geoffrey Parker, *The Military Revolution: Military Innovation and the Rise of the West, 1500–1880* (Cambridge, 1988), p. 115.

39. McPherson, *Indian Ocean*, p. 243.

40. Lorimer, *Gazetteer of the Persian Gulf*, vol. 1, *Historical*, p. 2638.

41. Das Gupta and Pearson, *India and the Indian Ocean*, p. 13.

42. Mridu Rai, "The Problem of Legitimacy in Kashmir: Religion and Rights, 1846–1947," Ph.D. diss., Columbia University, 1999.

43. See C. A. Bayly, *Indian Society and the Making of the British Empire* (Cambridge, 1990).

44. Subrahmanyam and Bayly, "Portfolio Capitalists," p. 264.

45. See Ray, "Asian Capital."

46. Ibid., p. 522.

47. For some answers to these questions, see Ayesha Jalal, *Self and Sovereignty: Individual and Community in South Asian Islam since 1850* (London, 2000), ch. 5.

48. L/MIL/5/827, India Office Records and Library, London.

49. *Nazrul Rachanabali*, vol. 1 (Dhaka, 1993), p. 34.

50. From *The East in Its Feminine Gender: Poems and Songs of Rabindranath Tagore*, trans. Charu C. Chowdhuri and ed. Krishna Bose and Sugata Bose, forthcoming.

51. See ibid. and Rabindranath Tagore, *The Diary of a Westward Voyage*, trans. Indu Dutt (Westport, Conn., 1975).

52. Rabindranath Tagore to Ramananda Chattopadhyay, 28 May, 1927, cited in Prabhat Kumar Mukhopadhyay, *Rabindrajibani*, vol. 3, 3rd ed. (Calcutta, 1991), p. 312.

53. Ibid., pp. 314–23.

54. See, Rabindranath Tagore, *Javajatrir Patra*, in *Rabindra Rachanabali*, vol. 19, pp. 452–526.

55. He also wanted one of the Muslim sovereigns to endow the chair in Persian Studies at his university in Shantiniketan. Reza Shah Pahlavi obliged.

56. Rabindranath Tagore, *Parashye*, in *Rabindra Rachanabali*, vol. 22 (Calcutta, 1957), pp. 457–61.

57. Ibid., pp. 515–16.

58. Ibid., pp. 499–502.

59. On the Indian troops' entry into Baghdad, see "The War Diaries of the Mesopotamian Campaign," L/MIL/17/5/3789 (India Office Records, British Library).

60. Tagore, *Parashye*, pp. 495–96; Rabindranath Tagore, *Sphulinga*, in *Rabindra Rachanabali*, vol. 27 (Calcutta, 1965), p. 3.

Index

Abadan, 86

'Abbas Mahmud al-'Aqqad, 326

'Abd al-Ghafur, 39

'Abd al-Rahman 'Awf, 152

'Abd al-Rahman Shukri, 314–15; cosmopolitanism, 326; early life, 325–27; and Namik Kemal, 326; poetry, 326–28; and religion, 326; sexuality, 327

'Abd al-Rahman Sumaqiyya, 152, 153

'Abd Allah Abu al-Su'ud, 335

'Abd Allah al-Nadim: didacticism, 337; and 'Urabi revolt, 325, 337; as journalist, 355, 356; use of vernacular, 336–37. *See also* 'Urabi revolt.

'Abdu al-Hamawi, 335

Abduh, Muhammad: 10, 183; and Arabic, 359; and al-Azhar, 161; and W.S. Blunt, 162, 344; and Mu'tazilism, 358; and Qur'an, 354

Abdul-Hadis, 105

Abdul Halim Sharar, 252–54

Abdülaziz, 264, 265

Abdülhak Hamid, 341

Abdülhamid, 153, 262; and İzmir, 211; as "reactionary" ruler, 269; and "Shi'i threat," 117; as arbitrator, 275–76; and censorship, 340; childhood, 262; and Christians, 270; conservatism, 147; and constitution, 338; counter-coup, 147; dethroned, 277; and discord in government, 274; expansion of government, 273–74; favoritism, 275–76; final years, 277; fiscal moves, 267–68; and Hijaz Railway, 140; hobbies, 264; inclinations, 263–64; and Islam, 269–70; and Khilafa, 119; on legal equality, 269, 272; and Muslim notables, 271–72; and non-Muslim communities, 272; opposition to, 276; ousted, 147; and pashas, 275–76; problems with policies, 272–73; and Qur'an, 353, 354; and seminary students, 269; and Shi'i, 125; student years, 263–64; and Sunni proselytizing, 117–18; suspends Assembly, 265; assumes throne, 114, 265; and Tanzimat, 269; and technocrats, 274; views of, 266